Design and Maintenance of Accounting Manuals

Fourth Edition

Update Service

BECOME A SUBSCRIBER!

Did you purchase this product from a bookstore?

If you did, it's important for you to become a subscriber. John Wiley & Sons, Inc. may publish, on a periodic basis, supplements and new editions to reflect the latest changes in the subject matter that you ***need to know*** in order to stay competitive in this ever-changing industry. By contacting the Wiley office nearest you, you'll receive any current update at no additional charge. In addition, you'll receive future updates and revised or related volumes on a 30-day examination review.

If you purchased this product directly from John Wiley & Sons, Inc., we have already recorded your subscription for this update service.

To become a subscriber, please call **1-800-225-5945** or send your name, company name (if applicable), address, and the title of the product to:

mailing address: **Supplement Department**
John Wiley & Sons, Inc.
One Wiley Drive
Somerset, NJ 08875

e-mail: **subscriber@wiley.com**
fax: **1-732-302-2300**
online: **www.wiley.com**

For customers outside the United States, please contact the Wiley office nearest you:

Professional & Reference Division
John Wiley & Sons Canada, Ltd.
22 Worcester Road
Rexdale, Ontario M9W 1L1
CANADA
(416) 675-3580
Phone: 1-800-567-4797
Fax: 1-800-565-6802
canada@jwiley.com

John Wiley & Sons, Ltd.
Baffins Lane
Chichester
West Sussex, PO19 1UD
ENGLAND
Phone: (44) 1243 779777
Fax: (44) 1243 770638
cs-books@wiley.com.uk

Jacaranda Wiley Ltd.
PRT Division
P.O. Box 174
North Ryde, NSW 2113
AUSTRALIA
Phone: (02) 805-1100
Fax: (02) 805-1597
headoffice@jacwiley.com.au

John Wiley & Sons (SEA) Pte. Ltd.
37 Jalan Pemimpin
Block B # 05-04
Union Industrial Building
SINGAPORE 2057
Phone: (65) 258-1157
Fax: (65) 463-4604
enquiry@wiley.com.sg

Design and Maintenance of Accounting Manuals

Fourth Edition

A Blueprint for Running an Effective and Efficient Department

Steven M. Bragg
Harry L. Brown

JOHN WILEY & SONS, INC.

This book is printed on acid-free paper. ♾

Published by John Wiley & Sons, Inc., Hoboken, New Jersey

Published simultaneously in Canada.

Library of Congress Cataloging-in-Publication Data:

ISBN 0-471-41559-6

Printed in the United States of America
10 9 8 7 6 5 4 3 2 1

In memory of Wheaton, who always wanted to
write an accounting book and sail around the world
(not necessarily in that order).

Contents

Preface

Lack of adequate documentation is one of the largest pitfalls facing any accounting system. One of four excuses is usually given: (1) nobody reads it, (2) the hands-on approach in which each person teaches another is a better method, (3) written policies and procedures are too confining, and (4) nobody has the time to write documentation. In a constantly changing accounting world, none of these excuses can stand very long.

Throughout this book about designing and maintaining good, acceptable, and readable accounting documentation, our message is that you should write as well as you speak—clearly, simply, and understandably. As the old saying goes, there are two rules for good documentation. Rule 1 is "Write to be understood by a reader you may never meet face to face." Rule 2 is "Follow Rule 1."

If an accounting staff and company executives are to be fully informed, this flood of material must be read and, when necessary, related to the accounting operations at your company. The dissemination of information on this scale cannot be handled orally or with periodic meetings and brief memos to the staff involved. Thus, there is a need for clear, consistent documentation to describe the accounting system being used, the principles involved, the policies that management wishes enforced, and the procedures describing what is to be done and how it is to be performed on a daily basis.

This book covers the development, implementation, and maintenance of nine different accounting manuals. Two of these are almost mandatory: the *general accounting manual* that describes account coding schemes and how to code accounting transactions, and the *policy/procedure statement* system that provides full information to anyone needing to know a company's accounting policies and the procedures to maintain them.

The other seven manuals are optional, but as you read about them you will find that they supplement and complement the primary accounting documentation; they are the lubricant of the accounting system, and as such are useful for increasing the efficiency of operations. If none of the following manuals are developed, certain portions of each will appear in the basic manuals but in less depth. They are:

- *Period-end manual*. This describes the actions, reports, and schedules to be completed in sufficient detail to assure that the period-end closing is accurate, consistent, usable, and timely.
- *Budgeting manual*. This describes the specific steps to be followed to create the annual budget, as well as task responsibilities by position.
- *Property accounting manual*. This shows the forms that should be filled in and stored to maintain a proper database of all corporate fixed assets, describing when items were purchased or constructed, where they are located, and how they were disposed of.
- *Forms manual*. This describes every form in detail—its use, limitations, and completion.

- *User manual*. This provides information to non-accountant employees who are involved in initiating or adding to an accounting document. This manual provides a list of employees by function, a condensed chart of accounts, and instructions for completing specific forms that are later used by the accounting department, such as the employee expense report.
- *Information technology manual*. This is a condensation of portions of the technical computer processing instructions that accountants must handle, and can extend to basic operating procedures for the information technology staff.
- *Human resources manual*. This contains a list of all policies related to human resources activities, as well as specific procedures required to perform operations within the human resources department.

This book gives the reader a wide variety of real-life examples for constructing all of the manuals just noted, as well as pertinent advice on how to write clearly, construct easy-to-use manuals, and issue both paper-based and electronic manuals. It should be the one-stop solution for anyone constructing accounting manuals.

June, 2002
Centennial, Colorado

Acknowledgments

My background in procedures development stems entirely from a number of years in the consulting division of Ernst & Young, which employed many of the finest writers in the United States, including Janice "Red Pen" Roehl. Jan, you emptied a few red pens correcting my habits, and I appreciate the help.

About the Authors

Steven Bragg, CPA, CMA, CIA, CPM, CPIM, has been the Chief Financial Officer or Controller of four companies, as well as a consulting manager at Ernst & Young and auditor at Deloitte & Touche. He received a master's degree in finance from Bentley College, an MBA from Babson College, and a Bachelor's degree in economics from the University of Maine. He has been the two-time president of the 10,000-member Colorado Mountain Club. Mr. Bragg resides in Centennial, Colorado. He has written or co-authored the following books:

Accounting and Finance for Your Small Business (Wiley)

Accounting Best Practices (Wiley)

Accounting Reference Desktop (Wiley)

Advanced Accounting Systems

Business Ratios and Formulas (Wiley)

The Controller's Function (Wiley)

Controllership (Wiley)

Cost Accounting (Wiley)

Financial Analysis (Wiley)

Government Accounting Best Practices (Wiley)

Just-in-Time Accounting (Wiley)

Managing Explosive Corporate Growth (Wiley)

Outsourcing (Wiley)

Sales and Operations for Your Small Business (Wiley)

Harry L. Brown is the former Director of Financial Affairs and an instructor in the School of Professional Accountancy at the University of Southern Mississippi.

Chapter 1

ACCOUNTING MANUALS

1.1 INTRODUCTION

Ask a dozen accountants to name the major method of communicating in their accounting operations and they will probably describe the accounting manual. However, you will get 12 answers about what the manual is, varying from a simple listing of account names and numbers to an academic treatise of the philosophy and practice of accounting as used in that particular environment.

In its simplest form, the accounting manual documents the meaning of sets of descriptive numbers used in an organized manner to record, summarize, and report information. It may contain descriptions of one or more of the systems and procedures that explain the basic accounting structure of the enterprise.

However, the manual can be much more than numbers and definitions. It may contain organization charts to show responsibility and lines of authority, policy, formulas, clerical procedures, special industry terminology, data processing rules and procedures, forms descriptions and uses, and so on. It is the general map through which one can learn to travel through a company's operations.

Every business enterprise has an accounting system, from the self-employed person operating a small business out of his or her home to charitable, not-for-profit organizations, educational institutions, governmental agencies, industrial and service companies, and so on. The system may be completely undocumented, possibly just a checkbook and a list of receipts, or it may be an elaborate, difficult-to-maintain, small library of books and manuals used by large national and international companies.

An accounting manual has three basic purposes: to answer questions, to instruct accounting personnel, and to provide consistent reporting of business transactions. As a printed document, it must be useful and, more importantly, *used*. Therefore, it should be *formal*—not in the sense of being rigid and unyielding, but in the sense of being complete and consistent.

It should be available to all who need it or think they need it. Certainly, the accounting staff needs the manual. Also, line supervisors, managers, and others who submit accounting data should have the manual available to them.

It should always be *current*, a condition requiring a method of publishing changes, additions, and deletions very quickly (see the discussion of electronic methods of distribution in Chapter 4). Finally, the manual should be *easy to use* as a tool to answer questions of consistency, accuracy, and clarity of presentation.

A word of warning: Unless the contents of a manual are to be used exclusively by accountants in the accounting operation, the accountants must turn *their* terminology into *our* terminology—that is, terminology that can be understood by non-accountant users of the manual. Avoid accounting jargon at all times.

For reference purposes, *accounting manual*, as used in this book, includes all the modules described in this chapter. The reader has the choice of developing selected modules and combining them into one accounting manual or maintaining each one as a separate manual. The modules are:

- General accounting manual
- Accounting procedures
- Year-end manual
- Budgeting manual
- Property accounting manual
- Forms manual
- User manual
- Information technology manual
- Human resources manual

Each of these modules is briefly described in the following sections, and more fully described in the indicated chapters.

1.2 GENERAL ACCOUNTING MANUAL

The general accounting manual includes a general description of the overall accounting system, the chart of accounts, account descriptions, activities calendars for the accounting staffing, accounting policies, and descriptions of the key process cycles. Parts of the general accounting manual are usually included in the user manual to provide account coding information to other departments, such as purchasing and receiving, so that they can code transaction documents or otherwise provide accounting information. The general accounting manual is covered in Chapter 2.

The chart of accounts is the basic underlying account code structure that is used to record information in the general ledger. To create the chart, one prepares a list of every account number and name, which should include every asset, liability, ownership, income, and expense item. Then a one or two sentence definition is written for each line item in the chart of accounts. The list of definitions developed here will be the primary reference of permitted actions—and, more importantly, those that are not permitted—in each account being used. If divisions or departments are included in the corporate structure, then the account code structure can be stretched into a longer format to accommodate codes that can be traced to specific operating entities within the organization.

Job descriptions are extremely useful for determining which employee positions are responsible for which tasks, as well as to form a basis for periodic job reviews. These descriptions are most easily compiled by interviewing the staff members to see what they already do; on an ongoing basis, the descriptions can be adjusted to shift work among personnel to achieve increased levels of efficiency.

An activities calendar should be constructed not only for the entire department but also for each person within it. An activity calendar should itemize exactly which tasks should be completed on each day of the month. It forms the basis for task assignments within the accounting department, and is an excellent visual tool for managing the department's function. The calendar will be in a constant state of flux, as work tasks are constantly shifted among different staff members or moved to different time slots to create a balanced work flow for the department as a whole.

A more complete manual would contain a section on accounting principles and general procedures. For example, the company might indicate that it follows a published industry account numbering and format procedure, or that it operates in accordance with control guidelines laid down by the American Institute of Certified Public Accountants (AICPA).

Finally, the manual may contain flowcharts of the principal process cycles used by the company (such as the purchasing and order fulfillment cycles) as well as related procedures. The documentation of these key underlying activities gives the reader a broad conceptual overview of how the key accounting activities work, and how documents flow from function to function in order to complete tasks.

1.3 ACCOUNTING PROCEDURES

The accounting procedures used must be clearly stated in a consistent format. To aid in the construction of such a manual, Chapter 3 itemizes a number of key writing, style, and mechanics guidelines. It also describes how to create an understandable flowchart that can accompany a procedure, including the most common direction of flow and types of graphics to use. The chapter also notes how to calculate and interpret readability statistics for a procedure. In addition to these general guidelines, the chapter describes how to lay out a simple procedure format and accompanying header, which are used in all subsequent chapters whenever example procedures are shown. Next, we cover the key work steps needed to construct a procedures manual, itemizing the process flow required to ensure that the information contained within a procedure is accurate. Finally, there is an itemization of suggested procedures that can be used. This list is by no means complete, because accounting systems will vary widely by industry, and even between companies within the same industry; nonetheless, it provides a core set of procedures that can be expanded upon to create a complete set of company-specific procedures.

With the basic procedure construction information in hand, one can then proceed to the creation of actual accounting procedures. Chapter 5 assists in this process by presenting a long list of actual procedures. They are summarized into the following categories for easy reference:

- Acquisitions
- Billing
- Budgeting
- Credit
- Financial statement preparation
- Fixed asset transactions
- Funds management
- Internal auditing
- Payroll
- Purchasing

The majority of the procedures were taken from the procedures manuals of several real companies that use different software packages and operate in different industries. Consequently, some of the most detailed information listed in the procedures will only be applicable to very specific situations, and must be modified to meet the reader's needs. Other procedures, such as those applying to acquisitions and budgeting, are more broad-based and can be applied to one's existing systems with comparatively little modification.

1.4 YEAR-END MANUAL

The year-end manual is probably better described as a year-end assignments list. It defines all of the tasks that must be accomplished at the end of a company's fiscal year to close the books and prepare the required accounting statements, schedules, and narrative for the annual report.

Once prepared, the year-end manual is updated annually for any changes in the fiscal year-end closing procedures. Such changes come about by a change in management, a change in auditors, or an expansion or contraction of year-end procedures caused by a change in accounting systems. The revised year-end manual is usually issued one or two months before the fiscal year-end to every employee assigned to complete one or more closing tasks. The manual is sometimes assembled in cooperation with the outside auditors, and working papers or schedules required by them are included as tasks. The year-end and period-end manuals are discussed in Chapter 6, which covers specific closing activities, the soft close, and closing procedures that are tailored to specific accounting positions.

1.5 BUDGETING MANUAL

Most organizations of any size spend a considerable amount of time creating budgets for at least the upcoming year, and perhaps for multiple years. If so, they have found that this is a complex and highly iterative process that impacts virtually every part of a company. In Chapter 7, we present the system of interlocking budgets and describe how they are structured so that one can see how information is first assembled for the sales budget. This information then cascades down into a series of "cost of goods sold" budgets that determine targeted inventory levels, purchasing volumes, production targets, and requirements for facilities as well as direct labor. After these steps are completed, budgets for supporting functions—such as general, administrative, and marketing—are added to the set of budgeting documents. The chapter contains a complete example of these interlocking budgets, as well as a discussion of flex budgeting, under which the supporting budgets all automatically change if revenue levels vary from the initial budgeted level. There is also coverage of the budgeting process and how budgets can be used as an integral part of corporate control systems.

1.6 PROPERTY ACCOUNTING MANUAL

The typical organization only tracks its fixed assets through some bare-bones entries in a depreciation calculation that itemizes the general type of asset, when it was purchased, what it cost, and the amount of its monthly depreciation. However, there are many other details that should be tracked, such as the presence of warranties that can be used in the event of a product failure, the location of each asset, and contact information about suppliers. A truly comprehensive set of information about each fixed asset is recorded in the property accounting manual, which is described in Chapter 8.

The chapter describes how to accumulate costs for projects that are being developed in-house with a project cost report. It also describes how to collect and organize information about land projects, which require the accumulation of special information such as legal descriptions, zoning classifications, and assessed value. There are additional discussions and different forms to cover land improvement projects, building projects, and the purchase of factory equipment, office equipment, vehicles, leasehold improvements, and leases. The chapter concludes with a complete example of a property accounting manual, showing the indexing, procedures, cost sheets, and instructions for the completion of each form.

1.7 FORMS MANUAL

Forms are the vehicles that carry information and approvals throughout the accounting map. They record the authorization and the purpose of a transaction and what actions are accomplished, such as buying, selling, making, biding, moving, adding, deleting, changing, and so forth. Forms are the foundation of computerized data processing activities. Developing and maintaining a forms manual need not be difficult or burdensome.

Chapter 9 provides a form survey worksheet to identify needed forms, presents a number of basic rules for creating forms, and then shows how to create form descriptions and compile them into a formal forms manual.

1.8 USER MANUAL

The user manual is most useful in companies where non-accountants initiate or prepare original accounting forms or documents that provide accounting information to the general accounting operation. Examples of such transactions are the hiring or termination of an employee or the submission of an expense report for reimbursement. Other examples of user manual procedures are petty cash reports, receiving reports, shipping documents, branch sales and activity, requests for special supplier payments such as subscriptions, dues, contractual services performed locally, and so on.

This manual can be general in nature or may contain specific abstracts from the general manual, forms manual, and policy/procedure statements. Usually it contains abstracts from other manuals, so it can be easy to prepare. It is designed for mass distribution to departments or individuals who use or prepare accounting documents, initiate account transaction coding, have some knowledge of the accounting process, or receive summary accounting reports. It can also be used as a training tool for non-accounting supervisors, secretaries, and others who are involved in adding or checking data on accounting input documents.

Instructions for creating a user manual, as well as a complete example of such a manual, are shown in Chapter 10.

1.9 INFORMATION TECHNOLOGY MANUAL

This manual has limited distribution, principally to the accounting and information technology staff members who are responsible for submitting forms and data to computer operations for data entry, processing, storage, and retrieval of the data for accounting use, as well as those responsible for ongoing computer system maintenance and development. This manual is unique in that it contains both forms descriptions and procedures. It may also contain details of file record contents and codes used, descriptions of output reports, and the data and calculations used to report each item on an output information report. The information technology manual is addressed in Chapter 11.

Chapter 11 provides a comprehensive set of policies related to systems development, which are:

- Project charter standards
- Work plan standards
- Project team roles and responsibilities
- Risk management standards
- Project status reporting standards
- Issue management standards
- Project completion debriefing standards

The policies can be easily adapted to one's needs with minimal modification. The chapter also contains a series of procedures covering a variety of tasks in the areas of computer system maintenance, the setup of new employees with computers, and the primary tasks involved in the development of new computer systems.

In addition to the fundamental components of the information technology manual, the chapter also covers the use of system survey reports to conduct an inventory of computer systems, as well as a computer reports questionnaire to see if long-standing reports can be reduced or eliminated from use. The chapter also covers the key elements of documentation for database tables and output reports. It finishes with a discussion of the key elements that should be included in a disaster recovery manual, which may be a separate manual or contained within the main information technology manual.

1.10 HUMAN RESOURCES MANUAL

As was the case for the information technology function, the human resources function is frequently under the supervision of the controller of chief financial officer, especially in smaller firms. Consequently, Chapter 12 is included so that one can see a comprehensive list of 28 human resources policies and 11 procedures that can be used to process the variety of transactions related to the payment of employees. Examples of policies included in the chapter are termination, grievance, sexual harassment, and jury duty. The employee pay procedures include the processing of changes to employee pay, cafeteria plan deductions, garnishments, and terminations.

1.11 ISO 9000 QUALITY STANDARDS

With the growth of international trade, particularly in raw materials and parts, customers are demanding assurances that distant suppliers are producing quality products. In an effort to provide that assurance, the International Standards Organization (ISO) issued the ISO 9000 quality standards. Acquiring certification is a lengthy process, but has proven to be necessary for those companies wishing to operate on a global basis.

During the ISO certification process, companies have learned the risk of having poor documentation and documentation practices. Many have therefore had to make significant changes in documentation to achieve certification.

ISO 9000 highlights the importance of comprehensive and well-written manuals for the production of quality products. The same is true for accounting. The quality of the output of the accounting system also depends on sound documentation practices. Accountants and particularly auditors have taken a leadership role here. The AICPA has issued the *Statement of Auditing Standard 55*. The *Consideration of Internal Structure in the Financial Statement Audit and Internal Control—Integrated Framework* is published by the Committee of Sponsoring Organizations (COSO) of the Treadway Commission. Both acknowledge the importance of documentation in the internal control structure.

There are several ISO standards. ISO 9000-1, *Quality Management and Quality Assurance Standards—Guidelines for Selection and Use* provides an overview of ISO 9000. ISO standards 9001, 9002, and 9003 provide quality assurance standards for manufacturers as well as service organizations.

All ISO 9000 standards require quality system documentation. ISO 9000 Quality System Standard 4.2.2, "Quality System Documentation," states that "all the quality system elements, requirements, and provisions should be clearly documented in a systematic and orderly manner." This very general statement was given more detail in ISO 9004 Standard 17.2, "Quality Documentation," which stated the following:

> The system should require that sufficient documentation be available to follow the achievement of the required product quality and the effective operation of the quality management system. Appropriate sub-contractor documentation should be included. All documentation should be legible, dated (including revision dates), clean, readily identifiable and maintained in an orderly manner. Data may be hard copy or stored in a computer.
>
> In addition the quality management system should provide a method for removing and/or disposing of documentation used in the manufacture of products when that documentation has become out of date. The following are examples of types of documents requiring control: drawings; specifications; blueprints; inspection instructions; test procedures; work instructions; operation sheets; quality manual; operational procedures; quality assurance procedures.

The standard explains that the quality manual can be one document supported by several tiers of other documents, each becoming progressively more detailed. For example, there may be an overall system manual and one or more specific procedural manuals. Together, these documents define the complete quality system. This standard is expounded upon in a handbook published by the ISO, *Documentation and Information*, and ISO 10013, *Guidelines for Developing Quality Manuals*.

The ISO 9004-2, "Guidelines for Services," describes the standard documentation system. Standard 5.4.3.1 states that the appropriate quality system documentation includes:

> (a) Quality manual: This should provide a description of the quality system as a permanent reference. It should contain the quality policy; the quality objectives; the structure of the organization, including responsibilities; a description of the quality system, including all elements and provisions that form part of it; the

> quality practices of the organization; the structure and distribution of the quality system documentation . . .

This standard is followed by Standard 5.4.3.2, "Documentation Control." This standard requires that documentation be legible, dated, clear, and readily identifiable, and that it carry authorization status. Methods should be established to control the issuance, distribution, and revision of documents. The methods should ensure that documents are "approved by authorized personnel; released and made available in the areas where information is needed; understood and acceptable to users; reviewed for necessary revision; removed when obsolete."

The ISO standards cited here require firms to maintain a "quality manual." Companies are not required to maintain an accounting manual, but we certainly recommend that every firm have one. Also, a firm's auditors expect an accounting manual, because adequate documentation is described by Statement of Auditing Standard (SAS) 55 as one of the primary control procedures and thus is an integral part of the control structure.

Again, the ISO standards suggest that the quality manual be one document, supported by several tiers of other documents, each becoming progressively more detailed. The ISO gives the example of an overall system manual and one or more specific procedural manuals, which together define the complete quality system. This book describes a system in which a company's accounting manual is composed of multiple modules that include the general accounting manual, accounting procedures, year-end or period-end manual, budgeting manual, property accounting manual, forms manual, user manual, information technology manual, and human resources manual. This is just one possible design, but is quite similar to that recommended by the ISO for the quality manual.

ISO 9000 requires that the quality manual contain the quality policy as well as the quality objectives. Most accounting manuals explain a firm's accounting policies, but many accounting manuals fail to provide a statement of the objectives of the accounting system. This would be a positive addition to the manual. Such a provision might include a mission statement for the accounting department, a vision statement, and some specific strategies that the department has adopted to reach the vision.

This section illustrated that ISO 9000 standards call for the documentation of quality systems, which includes a quality manual. With this knowledge in hand, accountants can offer their expertise in documentation to their firm's quality control function. Accountants in firms that are undergoing ISO 9000 certification can also learn from the quality control function, as recommendations for changes in the quality documentation may have an impact on company-wide procedures, especially in purchasing. For further information on ISO 9000 and the ISO in general, see the ISO site on the World Wide Web at www.iso.ch.

1.12 IN THE BEGINNING

To begin improving the current accounting system documentation, one should determine the strengths and weaknesses of the current documentation. To do this, questionnaires should be sent to the controller, the professional accountants on the staff, the clerical personnel in accounting, and the managers of departments related to accounting but not part of the accounting department. These departments generally are purchasing, shipping, receiving, finance, and human resources, as well as any other department that furnishes information to accounting.

Exhibit 1.1 is a questionnaire for determining the current status and use of an accounting manual. One form should be used for each separate manual. Enter the general name of the manual, the date that the form must be returned to the person designated to summarize the data, and the department or name of that person (who may also be a consultant). The employee receiving the questionnaire completes the form as follows:

- If the designated manual is not used at all by the recipient, it should be left blank and returned. If used, the frequency of use should be checked.
- A section should address some of the common problems with documentation. These questions are answered "yes" or "no," along with an example to illustrate any "no" answers.
- The recipients answer each use with "yes" or "no" and enter a final overall rating of the manual being surveyed.

Exhibit 1.2 is the Summary of Current Accounting Description, which is compiled by the person designated to do so. This person should be knowledgeable about the current documentation and may be the principal writer. The reviewer completes this form as follows:

- Enter the formal name of the manual, the person responsible for maintaining its contents and distribution lists, and a brief description of the manual being surveyed.
- Enter the normal distribution of the manual in general terms, such as accounting personnel or designated departments.
- Describe the general format of the manual, such as numbered sections, indexing, and general layout. Also describe how the manual is available via electronic media or some other method.
- Describe how the manual is updated. Is it edited and changed periodically, such as each year, or are only new items distributed as needed?
- Describe any other possible sources of documentation, such as file folders of examples of transactions or forms, or textbooks.
- Describe anything the reviewer thinks may be a major weakness. (The principal weaknesses are listed in the questionnaire.)
- Summarize individual questionnaires for the groups shown. There should be some weighting of each user group. Also, the yes-no answers to question two of the individual questionnaires should be summarized to determine whether there are definite patterns of weakness.
- Enter an opinion about whether improved documentation is needed, with explanations of what principal weaknesses were discovered.

MANUAL: General Accounting Manual

Name of Reviewer ____________________ Title ________________ Dept.______________

I. __ Check here if your position does not require use of this accounting manual. Then stop your work on this questionnaire and return it to the address below.

How often does your position require you to use this accounting manual? Check the appropriate frequency.

____ Daily
____ Several times per week
____ One or two times per week
____ Several times per month
____ One or two times per month
____ Several times per year
____ One or two times per year

II. For this manual, did you find any of the following? Give a specific example of any item marked "No" on the other side of this form.

1. Manual was not readily available.	____ Yes	____ No
2. Information needed was missing.	____ Yes	____ No
3. Information was not clearly written.	____ Yes	____ No
4. Contained terms and jargon I did not know.	____ Yes	____ No
5. Information was difficult to locate.	____ Yes	____ No
6. Information was not current.	____ Yes	____ No
7. Other problems	____ Yes	____ No

III. Rate how useful the manual is for each of its uses. (Use a 10-point scale, where a 1 is not at all useful and a 10 is tremendously useful.)

Use	Rating
a. Training new personnel	____
b. Ensuring uniformity and consistency of reports	____
c. Evaluating controls	____
d. Communicating new policies, procedures, and information	____
e. Overall rating	____
f. Other uses (please list):	____

Return completed form by __________ (date) to ________________________ Controller's Office

Exhibit 1.1. Current Accounting Documentation Questionnaire

1. Manual ______________________ Person Responsible ______________________

   Brief description of the contents of the manual:

2. What is the distribution of the manual (who has manuals)?

3. Describe the format of the manual. Are they distributed in printed form or part of an electronic document system? If they are distributed on electronic media, describe the system used.

4. If the manual is updated, how often? How is the update accomplished?

5. Are there other sources of documentation of the accounting function/system besides the manual described above?

6. Is there anything in this documentation that you feel is a major weakness? If yes, describe.

7. SUMMARY OF QUESTIONNAIRES: How was the accounting documentation rated on a 10-point scale, where 1 is not at all useful and 10 is tremendously useful?
   ____ Controller.
   ____ Average of all accounting professional staff.
   ____ Average of managers of departments related to accounting.
   ____ Average of all accounting department clerical staff.

8. Does it appear that there is a need for more documentation? Explain.

Exhibit 1.2. Summary of Current Accounting Documentation

Once the survey is completed and discussed with appropriate personnel such as the chief financial officer, controller, and treasurer, the task to develop new documentation can begin.

1.13 PROCEDURES TO WRITE AND CHANGE PROCEDURES

Though many people want to sit down at a computer and immediately start writing procedures, this usually leads to a set of documents with poor formatting and inconsistent writing. When such documents are issued, readers find them difficult to read, so many ignore them, thereby voiding the purpose of the procedures.

A better way to approach procedure writing is to first create procedures that describe not only how to create a new procedure, but also how to update an existing one. These two tasks are documented in the sample procedures shown in Exhibits 1.3 and 1.4.

Policy/Procedure Statement	Retrieval No.:	PROC-01
Brasto Publishing	Page:	1 of 1
	Issue Date:	10/28/0X
Subject: How to Write a Procedure	Supersedes:	N/A

1. **PURPOSE AND SCOPE**
This procedure is used by any employees who require some assistance in determining the methodology for creating a new procedure.

2. **RESPONSIBILITIES**
WRITER Staff Writer

3. **PROCEDURES**

3.1 WRITER **Access Procedure Template**

Go to the Word subdirectory and access the template file for a procedure. Fill in the blanks on the form and give it to the controller to be entered into the corporate procedures database. The blanks on the form include the following areas:

1. *Purpose and Scope*. List the reason for the procedure and specify who is expected to use it.
2. *Definitions*. Describe any words used in the procedure that readers may not be familiar with.
3. *Responsibilities*. List the employee positions that are responsible for completing various steps in the procedure.
4. *Procedures*. List all the steps in the procedure. The level of detail should be sufficient for a user to complete the described steps without having to ask for additional assistance.
5. *References*. Note any related procedures or documents that the user should refer user should refer to that will help in understanding this procedure.
6. *Records*. Note where the documents (if any) resulting from this procedure are to be stored, as well as where documents needed for it are located.
7. *Governing Policies*. List the policies that set boundaries for activities described in this procedure.

3.2 WRITER **Review Document**

Issue the preliminary procedure document back to all employees who are involved with the activities described within it, and ask them to review its content. Be sure to specify a due date.

3.3 WRITER **Enter Adjustments**

Once the revised procedure document is returned, enter all adjustments into the database, print the final version, and release it to all personnel who are listed on the approved distribution list. Put a hard copy of the new procedure in the master procedures manual.

Exhibit 1.3. How to Write a Procedure Statement

Policy/Procedure Statement Brasto Publishing **Subject: How to Change an Existing Procedure**	Retrieval No.: Page: Issue Date: Supersedes:	PROC-02 1 of 1 10/28/0X N/A

1. **PURPOSE AND SCOPE**
This procedure is used to facilitate an orderly change in an existing procedure.

2. **RESPONSIBILITIES**

USER	Procedure User
WRITER	Staff Writer

3. **PROCEDURES**

3.1 USER **Copy the Procedure**
Fill out the procedure change notice and make any changes to the procedure. Alternatively, obtain a hard copy of the existing procedure and mark any changes directly onto it in red ink.

3.2 USER **Turn in the Request Form**
Turn in the request form to the procedure writer. Keep a copy for your records in case the original is mislaid.

3.3 WRITER **Input Data Changes**
Enter the requested changes to the procedure. Give the rough draft to the user who requested the change and ask that it be proofed for errors. When the procedure is returned, make any additional changes and print out the final version.

3.4 WRITER **Distribute the Procedure**
Release the procedure to all employees who are on the distribution list for this procedure. File a copy of the revised procedure in the master procedures manual.

Exhibit 1.4. How to Change an Existing Procedure Statement

Chapter 2

GENERAL ACCOUNTING MANUAL

2.1 INTRODUCTION

The general accounting manual is intended for the use of the accounting staff, both at the headquarters location and at any outlying locations that may have somewhat less broad-based accounting functionality. It may also be requested by internal and external auditors, who use it as input to their decisions to test the level of control on various types of company transactions. In rare cases, it may also be used as evidence in legal disputes, such as when a company must prove its level of controls if accused under the Foreign Corrupt Practices Act.

The manual is most efficiently produced if it is printed in a single standard format, rather than being subdivided for people or locations having limited accounting responsibilities. However, in situations where the number of documented transactions is excessively large, it may make sense to separate the documents into orderly groupings for specific recipients so that a limited number of standard manuals can be issued, rather than a complete set.

There are a variety of documents that may be included in the general accounting manual. The decision to include or exclude a document should, to some degree, be based on the number of times that documents are needed. For example, if an assistant controller is constantly being pestered with questions about what account codes to use for various transactions, then it makes sense to include a set of standard journal entries in the manual. However, if information is constantly being revised, then it should be distributed separately, rather than being contained within the manual. For example, a company phone list should be updated separately, as employee departures and new hires will call for ongoing updates. Another reason for including information in the manual is that it is part of a new employee's training. For example, a transaction that describes the basic entry of accounts payable invoices into the computer system is useful to a new hire, even though this may become second nature within a week and will never be used again. This type of document needs to be included simply as a reference for those employees whose skill levels are still ramping up.

The contents of the general accounting manual usually include the chart of accounts, because this is a useful reference tool for making general ledger entries. It should also include accounting term definitions; these may be standard terms found in any accounting text, but should also include terms noted in a company's accounting software package so that new users of the system will understand the meaning of particular data entry fields. The manual should also include job descriptions for all accounting positions so that each person knows his or her responsibilities. There should also be an activities calendar for each position, which is an extremely useful way to keep the accounting staff informed of their duties on particular days of the month. Another useful addition is a complete set of corporate policies that apply to the accounting department. This information is usually supplemented by an overview of all key process cycles and their supporting procedures, which typically form the bulk of the manual. These documents give users crucial information about what transactions are allowed, how they fit into the greater scheme of linked procedures throughout the company, and how each procedure must be completed. The following sections describe the contents of each section of the general accounting manual.

2.2 CHART OF ACCOUNTS[1]

This section covers the types of account numbering formats that can be used to construct a chart of accounts, and also lists sample charts of accounts that use each of the formats. All of the charts of accounts shown follow the same general sequence of account coding, which itemizes the accounts in the balance sheet first, and the income statement second. That sequence is as follows:

- Current assets
- Fixed assets
- Other assets
- Current liabilities
- Long-term liabilities
- Equity accounts
- Revenue
- Cost of goods sold
- Selling, general, and administrative expenses
- Income taxes
- Extraordinary items

[1] Much of this section is from *Accounting Reference Desktop*, Steven Bragg, copyright ©2002 John Wiley & Sons. This material is used by permission of John Wiley & Sons, Inc.

(a) Three-Digit Account Code Structure

A three-digit account code structure allows one to create a numerical sequence of accounts that contains up to 1,000 potential accounts. It is useful for small businesses that have no predefined departments or divisions that must be broken out separately. A sample chart of accounts using this format is shown below:

Account Number	Description
010	Cash
020	Petty cash
030	Accounts receivable
040	Reserve for bad debts
050	Marketable securities
060	Raw materials inventory
070	Work-in-process inventory
080	Finished goods inventory
090	Reserve for obsolete inventory
100	Fixed assets—Computer equipment
110	Fixed assets—Computer software
120	Fixed assets—Furniture and fixtures
130	Fixed assets—Leasehold improvements
140	Fixed assets—Machinery
150	Accumulated depreciation—Computer equipment
160	Accumulated depreciation—Computer software
170	Accumulated depreciation—Furniture and fixtures
180	Accumulated depreciation—Leasehold improvements
190	Accumulated depreciation—Machinery
200	Other assets
300	Accounts payable
310	Accrued payroll liability
320	Accrued vacation liability
330	Accrued expenses liability—Other
340	Unremitted sales taxes
350	Unremitted pension payments
360	Short-term notes payable
370	Other short-term liabilities
400	Long-term notes payable

500	Capital stock
510	Retained earnings
600	Revenue
700	Cost of goods sold—Materials
710	Cost of goods sold—Direct labor
720	Cost of goods sold—Manufacturing supplies
730	Cost of goods sold—Applied overhead
800	Bank charges
805	Benefits
810	Depreciation
815	Insurance
825	Office supplies
830	Salaries and wages
835	Telephones
840	Training
845	Travel and entertainment
850	Utilities
855	Other expenses
860	Interest expense
900	Extraordinary items

Notice how each clearly definable block of accounts begins with a different set of account numbers. For example, current liabilities begin with "300," revenues begin with "600," and cost of goods sold items begin with "700." This not only makes it easier to navigate through the chart of accounts, but is also mandated by many computerized accounting software packages.

(b) Five-Digit Account Code Structure

A five-digit account code structure is designed for those organizations with clearly defined departments, each of which is tracked with a separate income statement. This format uses the same account codes for the balance sheet accounts that we just saw for three-digit account codes, but replicates at least the operating expenses for each department (and sometimes for the revenue accounts, too). An example of this format is as follows, using the engineering and sales departments to illustrate the duplication of accounts:

Account Number	Department	Description
00-010	xxx	Cash
00-020	xxx	Petty cash
00-030	xxx	Accounts receivable

00-040	xxx	Reserve for bad debts
00-050	xxx	Marketable securities
00-060	xxx	Raw materials inventory
00-070	xxx	Work-in-process inventory
00-080	xxx	Finished goods inventory
00-090	xxx	Reserve for obsolete inventory
00-100	xxx	Fixed assets—Computer equipment
00-110	xxx	Fixed assets—Computer software
00-120	xxx	Fixed assets—Furniture and fixtures
00-130	xxx	Fixed assets—Leasehold improvements
00-140	xxx	Fixed assets—Machinery
00-150	xxx	Accumulated depreciation—Computer equipment
00-160	xxx	Accumulated depreciation—Computer software
00-170	xxx	Accumulated depreciation—Furniture and fixtures
00-180	xxx	Accumulated depreciation—Leasehold improvements
00-190	xxx	Accumulated depreciation—Machinery
00-200	xxx	Other assets
00-300	xxx	Accounts payable
00-310	xxx	Accrued payroll liability
00-320	xxx	Accrued vacation liability
00-330	xxx	Accrued expenses liability—Other
00-340	xxx	Unremitted sales taxes
00-350	xxx	Unremitted pension payments
00-360	xxx	Short-term notes payable
00-370	xxx	Other short-term liabilities
00-400	xxx	Long-term notes payable
00-500	xxx	Capital stock
00-510	xxx	Retained earnings
00-600	xxx	Revenue
00-700	xxx	Cost of goods sold—Materials
00-710	xxx	Cost of goods sold—Direct labor
00-720	xxx	Cost of goods sold—Manufacturing supplies
00-730	xxx	Cost of goods sold—Applied overhead
10-800	Engineering	Bank charges

10-805	Engineering	Benefits
10-810	Engineering	Depreciation
10-815	Engineering	Insurance
10-825	Engineering	Office supplies
10-830	Engineering	Salaries and wages
10-835	Engineering	Telephones
10-840	Engineering	Training
10-845	Engineering	Travel and entertainment
10-850	Engineering	Utilities
10-855	Engineering	Other expenses
10-860	Engineering	Interest expense
20-800	Sales	Bank charges
20-805	Sales	Benefits
20-810	Sales	Depreciation
20-815	Sales	Insurance
20-825	Sales	Office supplies
20-830	Sales	Salaries and wages
20-835	Sales	Telephones
20-840	Sales	Training
20-845	Sales	Travel and entertainment
20-850	Sales	Utilities
20-855	Sales	Other expenses
20-860	Sales	Interest expense
00-900	xxx	Extraordinary items

In this example, all expense accounts are replicated for every department. This does not mean, however, that all accounts must be *used* for every department. For example, it is most unlikely that bank charges will be ascribed to either the engineering or sales departments. Accordingly, those accounts that are not to be used can be rendered inactive in the accounting system so that they never appear in the general ledger.

(c) Seven-Digit Account Code Structure

A seven-digit account code structure is used by those companies that not only have multiple departments, but also multiple divisions or locations, for each of which the management team wants to record separate accounting information. This requires the same coding structure used for the five-digit system, except that two digits are placed in front of the code to signify a different company division. These new digits also apply to balance sheet accounts, because most organizations will want to track assets and liabilities by division. The following chart of accounts, which identifies accounts for divisions in Atlanta and Seattle, continues to use the engineering and sales departments as an example of how the seven-digit account code structure is compiled.

Account No.	Division	Department	Description
10-00-010	Atlanta	xxx	Cash
10-00-020	Atlanta	xxx	Petty cash
10-00-030	Atlanta	xxx	Accounts receivable
10-00-040	Atlanta	xxx	Reserve for bad debts
10-00-050	Atlanta	xxx	Marketable securities
10-00-060	Atlanta	xxx	Raw materials inventory
10-00-070	Atlanta	xxx	Work-in-process inventory
10-00-080	Atlanta	xxx	Finished goods inventory
10-00-090	Atlanta	xxx	Reserve for obsolete inventory
10-00-100	Atlanta	xxx	Fixed assets—Computer equipment
10-00-110	Atlanta	xxx	Fixed assets—Computer software
10-00-120	Atlanta	xxx	Fixed assets—Furniture and fixtures
10-00-130	Atlanta	xxx	Fixed assets—Leasehold improvements
10-00-140	Atlanta	xxx	Fixed assets—Machinery
10-00-150	Atlanta	xxx	Accumulated depreciation—Computer equipment
10-00-160	Atlanta	xxx	Accumulated depreciation—Computer software
10-00-170	Atlanta	xxx	Accumulated depreciation—Furniture and fixtures
10-00-180	Atlanta	xxx	Accumulated depreciation—Leasehold improvements
10-00-190	Atlanta	xxx	Accumulated depreciation—Machinery
10-00-200	Atlanta	xxx	Other assets
10-00-300	Atlanta	xxx	Accounts payable
10-00-310	Atlanta	xxx	Accrued payroll liability
10-00-320	Atlanta	xxx	Accrued vacation liability
10-00-330	Atlanta	xxx	Accrued expenses liability—Other
10-00-340	Atlanta	xxx	Unremitted sales taxes
10-00-350	Atlanta	xxx	Unremitted pension payments

10-00-360	Atlanta	xxx	Short-term notes payable
10-00-370	Atlanta	xxx	Other short-term liabilities
10-00-400	Atlanta	xxx	Long-term notes payable
10-00-500	Atlanta	xxx	Capital stock
10-00-510	Atlanta	xxx	Retained earnings
10-00-600	Atlanta	xxx	Revenue
10-00-700	Atlanta	xxx	Cost of goods sold—Materials
10-00-710	Atlanta	xxx	Cost of goods sold—Direct labor
10-00-720	Atlanta	xxx	Cost of goods sold—Manufacturing supplies
10-00-730	Atlanta	xxx	Cost of goods sold—Applied overhead
10-10-800	Atlanta	Engineering	Bank charges
10-10-805	Atlanta	Engineering	Benefits
10-10-810	Atlanta	Engineering	Depreciation
10-10-815	Atlanta	Engineering	Insurance
10-10-825	Atlanta	Engineering	Office supplies
10-10-830	Atlanta	Engineering	Salaries and wages
10-10-835	Atlanta	Engineering	Telephones
10-10-840	Atlanta	Engineering	Training
10-10-845	Atlanta	Engineering	Travel and entertainment
10-10-850	Atlanta	Engineering	Utilities
10-10-855	Atlanta	Engineering	Other expenses
10-10-860	Atlanta	Engineering	Interest expense
10-20-800	Atlanta	Sales	Bank charges
10-20-805	Atlanta	Sales	Benefits
10-20-810	Atlanta	Sales	Depreciation
10-20-815	Atlanta	Sales	Insurance
10-20-825	Atlanta	Sales	Office supplies
10-20-830	Atlanta	Sales	Salaries and wages
10-20-835	Atlanta	Sales	Telephones
10-20-840	Atlanta	Sales	Training
10-20-845	Atlanta	Sales	Travel and entertainment
10-20-850	Atlanta	Sales	Utilities
10-20-855	Atlanta	Sales	Other expenses
10-20-860	Atlanta	Sales	Interest expense

10-00-900	Atlanta	xxx	Extraordinary items
20-00-010	Seattle	xxx	Cash
20-00-020	Seattle	xxx	Petty cash
20-00-030	Seattle	xxx	Accounts receivable
20-00-040	Seattle	xxx	Reserve for bad debts
20-00-050	Seattle	xxx	Marketable securities
20-00-060	Seattle	xxx	Raw materials inventory
20-00-070	Seattle	xxx	Work-in-process inventory
20-00-080	Seattle	xxx	Finished goods inventory
20-00-090	Seattle	xxx	Reserve for obsolete inventory
20-00-100	Seattle	xxx	Fixed assets—Computer equipment
20-00-110	Seattle	xxx	Fixed assets—Computer software
20-00-120	Seattle	xxx	Fixed assets—Furniture and fixtures
20-00-130	Seattle	xxx	Fixed assets—Leasehold improvements
20-00-140	Seattle	xxx	Fixed assets—Machinery
20-00-150	Seattle	xxx	Accumulated depreciation—Computer equipment
20-00-160	Seattle	xxx	Accumulated depreciation—Computer software
20-00-170	Seattle	xxx	Accumulated depreciation—Furniture and fixtures
20-00-180	Seattle	xxx	Accumulated depreciation—Leasehold improvements
20-00-190	Seattle	xxx	Accumulated depreciation—Machinery
20-00-200	Seattle	xxx	Other assets
20-00-300	Seattle	xxx	Accounts payable
20-00-310	Seattle	xxx	Accrued payroll liability
20-00-320	Seattle	xxx	Accrued vacation liability
20-00-330	Seattle	xxx	Accrued expenses liability—Other
20-00-340	Seattle	xxx	Unremitted sales taxes
20-00-350	Seattle	xxx	Unremitted pension payments
20-00-360	Seattle	xxx	Short-term notes payable
20-00-370	Seattle	xxx	Other short-term liabilities
20-00-400	Seattle	xxx	Long-term notes payable
20-00-500	Seattle	xxx	Capital stock
20-00-510	Seattle	xxx	Retained earnings
20-00-600	Seattle	xxx	Revenue
20-00-700	Seattle	xxx	Cost of goods sold—Materials

20-00-710	Seattle	xxx	Cost of goods sold—Direct labor
20-00-720	Seattle	xxx	Cost of goods sold—Manufacturing supplies
20-00-730	Seattle	xxx	Cost of goods sold—Applied overhead
20-10-800	Seattle	Engineering	Engineering—Bank charges
20-10-805	Seattle	Engineering	Engineering—Benefits
20-10-810	Seattle	Engineering	Engineering—Depreciation
20-10-815	Seattle	Engineering	Engineering—Insurance
20-10-825	Seattle	Engineering	Engineering—Office supplies
20-10-830	Seattle	Engineering	Engineering—Salaries and wages
20-10-835	Seattle	Engineering	Engineering—Telephones
20-10-840	Seattle	Engineering	Engineering—Training
20-10-845	Seattle	Engineering	Engineering—Travel and entertainment
20-10-850	Seattle	Engineering	Engineering—Utilities
20-10-855	Seattle	Engineering	Engineering—Other expenses
20-10-860	Seattle	Engineering	Engineering—Interest expense
20-20-800	Seattle	Sales	Sales—Bank charges
20-20-805	Seattle	Sales	Sales—Benefits
20-20-810	Seattle	Sales	Sales—Depreciation
20-20-815	Seattle	Sales	Sales—Insurance
20-20-825	Seattle	Sales	Sales—Office supplies
20-20-830	Seattle	Sales	Sales—Salaries and wages
20-20-835	Seattle	Sales	Sales—Telephones
20-20-840	Seattle	Sales	Sales—Training
20-20-845	Seattle	Sales	Sales—Travel and entertainment
20-20-850	Seattle	Sales	Sales—Utilities
20-20-855	Seattle	Sales	Sales—Other expenses
20-20-860	Seattle	Sales	Sales—Interest expense
20-00-900	Seattle	xxx	Extraordinary items

2.3 ACCOUNTING TERM DEFINITIONS

Though it is not necessary to include an entire dictionary of accounting terms in the general accounting manual, it is useful to include those that are commonly used within the company's transactions, as well as those that appear in its accounting software. Of particular importance are those terms that are unique to the industry within which the company operates. For example, the oil and gas, software, and movie industries have special terminology that cannot be learned through regular accounting classes.

Definitions should be concise and meaningful. One or two sentences of definition are usually sufficient. Because the definitions are references sources, they should be developed for quick and easy look-up. For example, the definition for "fixed asset" may be listed under "A," using the header "Asset, fixed." If a user goes to the "F" section of the definitions, there should be a referral statement, such as "Fixed asset, *see* Asset, fixed." This standard indexing method should make it as easy as possible to find a specific definition. An example of a series of accounting term definitions is as follows:[2]

Backflushing. A method for recognizing incurred costs from the production process that records transactions at the point when production is completed, rather than when materials are released from the warehouse area.

Batch cost. A cost that is incurred when a group of products or services are produced, and which cannot be identified to specific products or services within each group.

Benchmarking. The process of comparing a company's processes and outputs to those of other organizations to determine the "best of class," which a company can then emulate internally to improve its profitability, efficiency, or competitive position.

Bill of materials. A listing of the quantities of all parts and subassemblies that comprise a product. It frequently includes additional information, such as the standard scrap rate to be expected when using each component. It is of great value for a number of applications, such as backflushing and product costing.

Book inventory. The amount of money invested in inventory, as per a company's accounting records. It is comprised of the beginning inventory balance, plus the cost of any receipts, less the cost of sold or scrapped inventory. It may be significantly different from the actual on-hand inventory, if the two are not periodically reconciled.

Book value. An asset's original cost, less any depreciation that has been subsequently incurred.

By-product, *see* Joint production.

A different approach to the inclusion of accounting term definitions in the manual is to define every account listed in the chart of accounts. By doing so, any accounting personnel who are responsible for entering transactions into either the general ledger or its supporting journals will have a better idea of which accounts should be used. This can save a great deal of time later on, when incorrectly applied transactions must be researched and corrected. The following sample definitions are used for the three-digit sample chart of accounts that was described earlier in this chapter.

[2] Definitions are from *Cost Accounting: A Comprehensive Guide,* Steven Bragg copyright ©2001 John Wiley & Sons. This material is used by permission of John Wiley & Sons, Inc.

Account Number	Name	Definition
010	Cash	Money deposited at the bank. If there are restrictions on deposited cash, then it is accounted for as a long-term asset.
020	Petty cash	Money retained in the petty cash box.
030	Accounts receivable	Money due from customers for services received or products shipped, but not yet received. If there are amounts due from officers or employees, these moneys are listed under "other accounts receivable."
040	Reserve for bad debts	A reserve fund that is held as a contingency against the nonpayment of outstanding accounts receivable. This account should always have a credit balance.
050	Marketable securities	Cash that is invested in easily traded equity or debt securities. The cost of acquiring these securities is included in the account.
060	Raw materials inventory	The amount of materials kept on hand for eventual inclusion in finished goods. All freight costs associated with the acquisition of raw materials are included in this account.
070	Work-in-process inventory	The cost of partially completed units of production. Costs stored in this account include raw materials, and any raw materials or overhead used to date.
080	Finished goods inventory	The cost of completed products that have not yet been shipped to customers. Costs stored in this account include all raw materials, direct labor, and overhead used during the production process.
090	Reserve for obsolete inventory	A reserve fund that is held as a contingency against the eventual write-off of any types of inventory that no longer have a resale value.
100	Fixed assets—Computer equipment	Purchased computer equipment exceeding the corporate capitalization limit that has an expected life of greater than one year.
110	Fixed assets—Computer software	Purchased computer software exceeding the corporate capitalization limit that has an expected life of greater than one year.
120	Fixed assets—Furniture and fixtures	Purchased furniture exceeding the corporate capitalization limit that has an expected life of greater than one year.
130	Fixed assets—Leasehold improvements	Improvements made by the company to its leased properties, exceeding the corporate capitalization limit, that has an expected life of greater than one year.
140	Fixed assets—Machinery	Purchased production equipment exceeding the corporate capitalization limit that has an expected life of greater than one year.
150	Accumulated depreciation—Computer equipment	The total of all depreciation charged against the computer equipment fixed asset account, net of disposed assets. This account has a credit balance.
160	Accumulated depreciation—Computer software	The total of all depreciation charged against the computer software fixed asset account, net of disposed assets. This account has a credit balance.

170	Accumulated depreciation—Furniture and fixtures	The total of all depreciation charged against the furniture and fixtures fixed asset account, net of disposed assets. This account has a credit balance.
180	Accumulated depreciation—Leasehold improvements	The total of all depreciation charged against the leasehold improvement fixed asset account, net of disposed assets. This account has a credit balance.
190	Accumulated depreciation—Machinery	The total of all depreciation charged against the machinery fixed asset account, net of disposed assets. This account has a credit balance.
200	Other assets	An account in which minor asset items are stored that do not fit into any other asset account categories.
300	Accounts payable	Both billed and accrued commitments to pay suppliers for services rendered or products shipped to the company.
310	Accrued payroll liability	An obligation to pay wages to employees, but which has not yet been paid.
320	Accrued vacation liability	An obligation to pay for earned vacation time to employees, but which has not yet been paid.
330	Accrued expenses liability—Other	An account in which minor accrued expenses are stored, or those accrued expenses are stored, that do not occur on a recurring basis.
340	Unremitted sales taxes	Sales taxes to government entities that are a company obligation to make as a result of selling products or services into the geographic areas governed by those entities, but which have not yet been made.
350	Unremitted pension payments	Pensions payments that are an obligation of the company to make into the employee pension fund, but which have not yet been made.
360	Short-term notes payable	Debt obligations that are due for payment in less than one year.
370	Other short-term liabilities	An account in which minor liability items are stored that do not fit into any other liability account categories.
400	Long-term notes payable	Debt obligations that are due for payment in more than one year.
500	Capital stock	The amount of funds received from investors in exchange for the issuance of common or preferred stock.
510	Retained earnings	Total corporate earnings since the creation of the company, less dividends and any prior period adjustments.
600	Revenue	The sale of products or services, or receipts from investments, such as interest, royalties, or dividends.
700	Cost of goods sold—Materials	The direct cost of materials associated with the sale of a tangible product. This includes all materials listed on a product's bill of materials, plus all scrap incurred during production, less the resale value of any by-products.
710	Cost of goods sold—Direct labor	The labor expense required to produce a product or service, which is limited to assembly labor.
720	Cost of goods sold—Manufacturing supplies	The cost of supplies consumed when a product is manufactured. This includes all incidental machinery maintenance supplies and packaging materials.

730	Cost of goods sold—Applied overhead	The cost of manufacturing, excluding materials, direct labor, and supplies. Includes depreciation on manufacturing equipment and facilities, as well as factory administration, indirect labor, maintenance, production employees' benefits, quality control and inspection, production facility rent, repair expenses, rework labor, and spoilage.
800	Bank charges	The expense associated with credit card fees, bank service charges, and the cost of printing checks.
805	Benefits	The expense associated with medical insurance, dental insurance, long-term and short-term disability insurance, and health club reimbursement fees. All employee payroll deductions to co-pay benefits should be credited against this account.
810	Depreciation	The expense associated with the periodic reduction of the value of fixed assets, in accordance with a standard value-reduction methodology.
815	Insurance	The expense associated with key-man life insurance, business insurance, and workers' compensation insurance.
825	Office supplies	The expense associated with miscellaneous tangible office purchases, such as paper products, printer cartridges, and diskettes.
830	Salaries and wages	The expense associated with employee pay, which includes salaries, wages, severance payments, signing bonuses, and accrued wages.
835	Telephones	The expense associated with "800" phone service, incoming phone lines, and cell phones. The cost of phone equipment is charged either to office supplies or to fixed assets, depending upon the dollar-value purchased.
840	Training	The expense associated with outsourced training suppliers, tests, and purchased training materials. It does not include travel costs associated with employee travel to training classes, nor the salary cost of inhouse training personnel.
845	Travel and entertainment	The expense associated with the travel of either employees or reimbursed contractors. Includes air fare, lodging, parking, and meals.
850	Utilities	The expense associated with water, heat, waste removal, and electricity fees charged by utilities.
855	Other expenses	Includes all incidental expenses under $500 that do not readily fall into any other category. Consult with the assistant controller before making entries into this account.
860	Interest expense	The expense associated with the interest cost of revolving debt, interest on late payments to suppliers, and outstanding company bonds. Also includes accrued interest on unpaid interest expenses.
900	Extraordinary items	Any expense that is both unusual and infrequent, such as a gain on a troubled debt restructuring or the loss of foreign assets due to governmental expropriation. No entries to this account are allowed without the controller's approval.

Other definitions for accounts that are commonly used by the accounting staff include:

Travel and Subsistence

- *Meals and lodging.* Includes meals and lodging costs (hotel, motel, etc.) in accordance with company policy for reimbursement. Per diem allowances for meals and lodging are included here.
- *Travel in private vehicle.* Includes travel in employee-owned vehicles at the currently approved mileage reimbursement rate.
- *Travel in rented vehicle.* Includes daily car rental fees from outside providers.
- *Travel in public carrier.* Includes air, bus, and train travel.
- *Travel in motor pool vehicles.* Includes charges for the use of company-owned vehicles at the approved rates. Costs of air travel for the company-owned airplane are included here.
- *Other travel costs.* Includes such incidental expenses as tips, telephone calls, taxis, tolls, and parking while on a company-authorized trip. Tips on meals are included in meal costs.
- *Conference and registration fees.* Includes registration fees for seminars, workshops, conferences, and similar meetings. Tuition for schools and workshops is included here. If meals and lodging fees included in registration fees cannot be separated, then they are included here.

Communications

- *Postage.* Includes postage charges for mailing, as well as service and rental fees for postage machines, and periodic service fees charged by online postage providers.
- *Express postage.* Includes all freight costs for express delivery services, including pickup fees.
- *Cell phones.* Includes the basic monthly fees, as well as roaming charges, for all issued cell phones.
- *Telephone local service.* Includes the basic monthly charges for all phones.
- *Telephone long distance.* Includes the charges for all long distance services, including the WATS line, line rentals, and telegraph charges.
- *Telephone installation and maintenance.* Includes all charges for the installation of phones and subsequent maintenance of the phone system.

Marketing

- *Advertising.* Includes the cost of classified advertising for employee hiring, as well as required advertising for published purchasing bids.
- *Publicity and public information.* Includes the cost of radio, television, and live shows promoting the company, as well as related layout and copy costs.

Rents

- *Rental of buildings and floor space*. Includes payments to others for buildings, rooms for events, and floor space in buildings for special events. Rental of housing facilities and meeting rooms is included here.
- *Rental of computer equipment*. Includes the rental or lease cost of computer software and equipment, such as payments on operating leases.
- *Other rentals*. Includes any rental that cannot be recorded in other rental accounts.

Repairs and Maintenance

- *Repairs, streets and parking*. Includes repairs and other maintenance on roads, streets, drives, and parking lots.
- *Repairs, building and grounds*. Includes wages and material costs of repairing, cleaning, and maintaining buildings and grounds. Outside contractor costs for this purpose are recorded here.
- *Repairs, office equipment*. Includes the costs of repairing and maintaining office equipment such as furniture, copiers, and facsimile machines. It does not include maintenance on the phone system.
- *Maintenance contracts, equipment*. Includes the annual contract costs for maintenance contracts on office equipment.
- *Repairing and servicing other equipment*. Includes the costs of repairing and servicing machinery, engineering equipment, laboratory equipment, shop equipment, and other equipment not classified in the preceding repair accounts.

Fees, Professional

- *Engineering fees*. Includes out-of-pocket fees for professional engineering services.
- *Auditing fees*. Includes the costs of auditing fees to outside independent auditors. Other incidental costs of the audit, such as supplies, telephone, postage and printing charges related to the audit, are included here.
- *Medical fees*. Includes direct payments to others for medical services, including preemployment physicals and lab tests.
- *Legal fees*. Includes all fees paid to attorneys, appraisers, notaries, and witnesses, in addition to court costs and legal document recording fees.
- *Laboratory and testing fees*. Includes outside laboratory fees and fees paid to outside agencies for testing services other than medical services.
- *Consultant expense reimbursements*. Includes travel costs paid to consultants and other nonemployees.

Other Contractual Services

- *Insurance and fidelity bonds*. Includes the cost of all casualty and liability insurance and fidelity bond coverages.
- *Dues*. Includes approved dues for company memberships in professional organizations.
- *Subscriptions*. Includes the cost of subscriptions to newspapers, magazines, and periodicals.
- *Computer software acquisitions*. Includes the initial cost of acquiring operating or systems software packages. Included is the purchase price, related freight, and software manuals.
- *Computer software maintenance*. Includes the annual maintenance fees to maintain purchased software systems.

Maintenance Supplies

- *Land improvement supplies*. Includes asphalt, cement, joint fillers, curbing, and so forth used in repairing or replacing roads, sidewalks, and parking lots on company property.
- *Building construction supplies*. Includes lumber, caulking, steel, fabricated metal parts, flooring, ceiling tiles, plaster, lime, and other materials used in repairing or renovating buildings.
- *Paints and preservatives*. Includes interior and exterior paints, wood preservatives, and road striping materials used for remodeling or maintenance.
- *Hardware, plumbing, and electrical supplies*. Includes all hardware, plumbing parts and accessories, and electrical wire or parts, including lights used in maintaining or renovating buildings.
- *Custodial supplies and cleaning agents*. Includes all custodial supplies of an expendable nature, such as cloths, brooms, cleaning compounds, mops, or pails.

Office Supplies

- *Printing, binding, and padding*. Includes the cost of printing, binding, and padding paid to outside contractors.
- *Duplication and reproduction*. Includes the paper, toner, and other supplies used in the company copy machines.
- *Office supplies*. Includes all office supplies and materials, such as pens, paper, pencils, staples, paper clips, and so forth.

Equipment Supplies

- *Fuels*. Includes vehicle fuels (gasoline, diesel fuel, propane) purchased for motor pool vehicles or airplanes.
- *Lubricating oils and greases*. Includes lubricating oils and greases used for all vehicles and machinery.

- *Tires and tubes*. Includes the purchase of tires and tubes for all vehicles in the company motor pool.
- *Repair and replacement parts*. Includes the purchase of vehicle and machinery repair and replacement parts and supplies.
- *Shop supplies*. Includes the cost of shop supplies, such as shop rags, windshield cleaner, glues and cements, brushes, degreasers, solvents, and so forth, used in equipment repair and maintenance operations.
- *Small tools*. Includes small tools used in manufacturing operations that are below the corporate capitalization limit.

2.4 JOB DESCRIPTIONS

A key management task is determining who is responsible for each task. Otherwise there is no way to control the flow of activities or know who should be contacted about fixing problems. The typical departmental structure typically includes one or more assistant controllers reporting to the controller, each of whom is responsible for a selected set of functional areas, such as accounts payable and accounts receivable, or cost accounting and the general ledger. Below these personnel are a number of accountants and clerks. Within these reporting relationships, it is necessary to define the exact job description of each position, which should be included in the general accounting manual. The format used for each job description should identify a position by title, rather than by the name of the person currently holding the job, so that the manual does not have to be changed every time a person switches positions. Here are examples of job descriptions that should be included:

Controller[3]

Reports to: Chief Financial Officer

Responsibilities	**Timing**
Accounting	
Assist in the annual audit as required	Annual
Develop accounting policies and procedures	Ongoing
Ensure that accounts payable are paid on time	Daily
Ensure that accounts receivable are collected promptly	Daily
Ensure that all economical payable discounts are taken	Daily
Ensure that billings are issued promptly	Daily
Ensure that job costs are calculated	Ongoing
Ensure that bank reconciliations are completed	Monthly
Issue financial statements	Monthly

[3] Source: *Controllership: The Work of the Managerial Accountant*, 6th Edition, James Willson, Janice Roehl-Anderson, and Steven Bragg, copyright ©1999 John Wiley & Sons. This material is used by permission of John Wiley & Sons, Inc.

Maintain an orderly accounting filing system	Ongoing
Maintain the chart of accounts	Ongoing
Manage outsourced functions	Ongoing
Manage the accounting staff	Ongoing
Manage the budgeting process	Annual
Prepare the annual budget	Annual
Process payroll in a timely manner	Bi-weekly
Provide financial analyses as needed	Ongoing
Review systems for control weaknesses	Ongoing
Finance	
Arrange for banking services	Ongoing
Arrange for debt financing	Ongoing
Conduct public offerings	As needed
Invest excess cash	Daily
Invest pension funds	Monthly
Issue credit to customers	As needed
Maintain insurance coverage	Annual
Maintain lender relations	Ongoing
Manage the finance staff	Daily
Monitor cash balances	Daily

Assistant Controller, Transactions

Reports to: Controller

Responsibilities	Timing
Manage the accounts payable process	Ongoing
Manage the accounts receivable process	Ongoing
Manage the payroll process	Ongoing
Use best practices to increase transactional efficiency	Ongoing
Take all viable supplier discounts	Weekly
Ensure that payments are authorized and accompanying deliveries are received prior to payment	Daily
Issue invoices to customers in a timely manner	Daily
Obtain payment from customers in a timely manner	Daily
Create an efficient time keeping system	Ongoing
Issue payments to employees in a timely manner	Bi-weekly
Make payroll tax payments in a timely manner	Monthly

Assistant Controller, Financial Reporting

Reports to: Controller

Responsibilities	Timing
Create financial statements	Monthly
Create footnotes to financial statements	Monthly
Create SEC reports	Quarterly
Monitor changes in generally accepted accounting principles	Ongoing
Present financial results to the management team	Monthly
Create systems for efficient reporting process	Ongoing
Create the annual budget	Annual
Create internal management reports	Ongoing

Assistant Controller, Cost and Tax Accounting

Reports to: Controller

Responsibilities	Timing
Manage the cost and taxation staff	Ongoing
Devise tax strategies	Ongoing
Create tax data collection systems	As needed
Complete required tax forms in a timely manner	As needed
Update the company sales tax database as tax rates change	As needed
Negotiate with tax authorities over tax payment issues	As needed
Review adequacy of costing systems	Quarterly
Report on costing variances	Monthly
Report on overhead allocation variances	Monthly
Report on margins and break-even points	Monthly
Report on capital budgeting requests	Ongoing
Assist in development of the budget	Annual
Analyze new product margins	Ongoing

Accounts Payable Clerk

Reports to: Assistant Controller, Transactions

Responsibilities	Timing
Match supplier invoices to purchase orders and receiving documents	Daily
Take all viable supplier discounts	Daily
Obtain approvals for supplier invoices	Daily

Pay supplier invoices when due	Weekly
Research supplier requests for payment	As needed

Billings Clerk

Reports to: Assistant Controller, Transactions

Responsibilities	**Timing**
Issue invoices to customers	Daily
Contact customers about overdue invoices	Daily
Issue monthly customer statements	Monthly
Resolve billing discrepancies with customers	As needed
Process cash receipts	Daily
Recommend bad debt write-offs	As needed

Payroll Clerk

Reports to: Assistant Controller, Transactions

Responsibilities	**Timing**
Collect time cards from employees	Weekly
Obtain supervisory approval of time card discrepancies	Weekly
Obtain overtime approvals	Weekly
Process garnishment requests	As needed
Process employee advances and paybacks	As needed
Print and issue paychecks	Bi-weekly
Issue direct deposit tapes to the bank	Bi-weekly
Deposit payroll taxes	Monthly

General Ledger Accountant

Reports to: Assistant Controller, Financial Reporting

Responsibilities	**Timing**
Create a system of recurring journal entries	Annual
Calculate and enter all adjusting journal entries	Monthly
Provide detailed analysis of accounts to auditors	Annual
Create financial statements	Monthly
Assist in writing footnotes to financial statements	Monthly
Assist in completing SEC reports	Quarterly

Financial Analyst

Reports to: Assistant Controller, Financial Reporting

Responsibilities	**Timing**
Provide analysis of investment vehicles	Ongoing
Review financing options	Ongoing
Review capital expenditure proposals	Ongoing
Review acquisition candidates	Ongoing
Provide ratio analysis of company results	Monthly

Tax Accountant

Reports to: Assistant Controller, Cost and Tax Accounting

Responsibilities	**Timing**
Devise tax strategies for management approval	Ongoing
Create tax data collection systems	As needed
Complete required tax forms in a timely manner	As needed
Update the company sales tax database as tax rates change	As needed
Manage audits by taxation authorities	As needed
Negotiate with tax authorities over tax payment issues	As needed

Cost Accountant[4]

Reports to: Assistant Controller, Cost and Tax Accounting

Responsibilities	**Timing**
System Tasks	
Review adequacy of activity-based costing system	Quarterly
Review adequacy of data collection systems	Quarterly
Review system costs and benefits	Quarterly
Audit costing systems	Monthly
Analysis and Reporting Tasks	
Report on product target costing variances	Monthly
Report on activity-based costing overhead allocations	Monthly

[4] Source: *Cost Accounting: A Comprehensive Guide*, Steven Bragg, copyright ©2001 John Wiley & Sons. This material is used by permission of John Wiley & Sons, Inc.

Report on break-even points by product and division	Monthly
Report on margins by product and division	Monthly
Report on periodic variance analyses	Monthly
Report on special topics as assigned	Ongoing
Report on capital budgeting requests	Ongoing
Assist in development of the budget	Annual
Pricing Tasks	
Work with marketing staff to update product pricing	Ongoing

Bookkeeper

Reports to: Company Owner

Responsibilities	Timing
Calculate attendance bonus	Bi-weekly
Close software modules following the monthly close	Monthly
Compile 401(k) census information	Annual
Complete bank reconciliation	Monthly
Conduct job costing	Ongoing
Create financial statements	Monthly
Cut manual checks and enter them into the computer	Ongoing
Enter accounts payable into compute and cut checks	Weekly
Enter time cards and pay rate changes into computer	Weekly
Issue 401(k) payments to mutual fund	Monthly
Issue paychecks	Bi-weekly
Match accounts payable documents	Daily
Post accounts receivable payments	Daily
Process employee expenses	Ongoing
Reconcile petty cash	Monthly
Store backup information on fixed assets	Ongoing
Track warranty expense detail	Ongoing

Note that the last job description presented, the bookkeeper, was independent of the hierarchical structure assumed for all of the preceding positions. Rather than reporting to someone else in the accounting or finance department, this person usually reports directly to the business owner, because a bookkeeper is usually only used in very small businesses which only need one or two accounting positions.

2.5 ACTIVITIES CALENDAR

The general accounting manual can also include a set of activities calendars. This is a listing of what special events occur on certain days of the year, such as tax report submissions or investor letters. It is extremely useful as a memory jogger so that the accounting staff does not forget to complete certain nonrepetitive key activities. There is usually a summary-level activities calendar for the entire year; dates from this calendar are then transferred to a monthly calendar that is more detailed in nature, and which contains events that tend to be more repetitive within the month. These calendars may be split up by job position so that each person in the department has an uncluttered view of his or her responsibilities over the course of the year. Examples of annual and monthly activities calendars are shown in Exhibits 2.1 and 2.2.

2.6 ACCOUNTING POLICIES

A policy can be described as an anticipated or required course of action that is used to guide both present and future decisions. In short, it is a goal. The general outlines of many procedures will be guided by one or more corporate policies. Given the large number of procedures used in the accounting area, one would expect to see a reasonably large list of policies.

A complete set of accounting policies can be listed in the general accounting manual, or individual policies can be placed in the procedures manual near the procedures most closely related to each policy. The author's preference is to keep the policy list in the general accounting manual for easy access by readers, rather than spreading it out over many pages.

The following list represents a general overview of the types of policies that should be contained within the general accounting manual:

Accounts Payable[5]

- Any supplier invoice within 5% of the price indicated on the buyer's purchase order requires no additional authorization to pay.

Document Archival

- Use the following format to determine when to dispose of old records:

Type of Record	Retention
Accounts payable ledgers/schedules	7 years
Advertisement for a job opening	1 year
Capital stock records	Permanent
Checks (canceled)	7 years
Deeds, mortgages, bills of sale	Permanent

[5] Source: *Accounting Best Practices*, 2nd Edition, Steven Bragg, copyright ©2001 John Wiley & Sons. This material is used by permission of John Wiley & Sons, Inc.

January 1st Commissions 5th CO Sales Tax License 10th 1099 Forms 15th NM Sales Tax Report 15th GSA Sales Report 20th NV Sales Tax 29th Investor Letter	**February** 1st Commissions 28th Trademark Review	**March** 1st Commissions 15th 401(k) Enrollment	**April** 1st Commissions 15th GSA Sales Report 20th NV Sales Tax 29th Investor Letter
May 1st Commissions 31st Trademark Review	**June** 1st Commissions 15th 401(k) Enrollment	**July** 1st Commissions 15th NM Sales Tax Report 15th GSA Sales Report 20th NV Sales Tax 29th Investor Letter	**August** 1st Commissions 10th VETS-100 Report 31st Trademark Review
September 1st Commissions 15th 401(k) Enrollment	**October** 1st Commissions 15th GSA Sales Report 20th NV Sales Tax 29th Investor Letter	**November** 1st Commissions 30th Budget 30th Trademark Review	**December** 1st Commissions 15th 401(k) Enrollment 23rd Add incremental life insurance to paychecks in last payroll 27th Update Annual Pay Report 30th Issue W-9 Mailing

Exhibit 2.1. Annual Activities Calendar

Sunday	Monday	Tuesday	Wednesday	Thursday	Friday	Saturday
					1 Weekly Invoice Review **Pay Rent** Commission Calculation	2
3	4 Overtime Report Remaining Billable Hours Production Hours Not Billed Report Open Jobs Report	5 Review Job Costing **Colorado Sales Tax** **Verify Deductions**	6 **Verify Life Insurance** **Verify Medical Enrolls** **Verify Deductions**	7 Department Meeting Flash Report Sales Report	8 Weekly Invoice Review **Payroll Processing**	9
10	11 Overtime Report Remaining Billable Hours Production Hours Not Billed Report Open Jobs Report	12 Review Job Costing	13 Issue Vacation Notices	14 Department Meeting Flash Report Sales Report	15 Weekly Invoice Review Hand Out Paychecks Cash Forecast	16
17	18 Overtime Report Remaining Billable Hours Production Hours Not Billed Report Open Jobs Report	19 Review Job Costing	20	21 Department Meeting Flash Report Sales Report	22 Weekly Invoice Review **Payroll Processing** **Manager's Off-Site**	23
24	25 Overtime Report Remaining Billable Hours Production Hours Not Billed Report Open Jobs Report	26 Review Job Costing **Investor Letter**	27	28 Hand Out Paychecks **Cash Forecast** **Payroll Summary** Sales Report Flash Report Trademark Review		

Exhibit 2.2. Monthly Activities Calendar

Earnings per week	3 years
Financial statements	Permanent
General ledgers (year-end)	Permanent
Hiring records	1 year from date record made or personnel action taken, whichever is later
Insurance/pension/retirement plans	1 year after termination
Invoices to customers	7 years
Minute books, including bylaws and charter	Permanent
Payroll records—employment data	3 years from termination
Physical/medical examinations	Duration of employment, plus 30 years
Property records	Permanent
Sales and purchase records	3 years
Stock and bond certificates (canceled)	7 years
Subsidiary ledgers	7 years
Tax returns	Permanent
Time cards	3 years

Fixed Assets

- The minimum dollar amount above which expenses are capitalized is $2,000.
- Any member of the management committee can approve an expenditure for amounts of $5,000 or less if the item was already listed in the annual budget.
- Any capital expenditure exceeding $5,000 requires the approval of the president, plus all expenditures not already listed in the annual budget, regardless of the amount.
- Every production machine shall be assigned a salvage value of 25% of the purchase price.

Investments

- Retirement funds shall not be invested in the company's securities, or those of its subsidiaries or affiliates.
- No more than 10% of invested funds should be invested in any one security.
- No more than 15% of invested funds shall be invested in any one industry.
- The return on investment target for invested funds is to match the Standard & Poor's 500 Index.
- Investments must be made in marketable securities.
- Investment activity is prohibited in the areas of short sales, puts, calls, straddles, hedges, or margin purchases.

Logistics

- Any items arriving at the receiving dock without a purchase order number will be rejected.

Risk Management[6]

- The company will obtain insurance only from companies with an A.M. Best rating of at least B++.
- All self-insurance plans will be covered by an umbrella policy that covers all losses exceeding $50,000.
- No insurance may be obtained from captive insurance companies.
- The company must always have current insurance for the following categories, and in the stated amounts:
- Director's and officer's insurance, $5 million.
- Commercial property insurance, matching the replacement value of all structures and inventory.
- Business interruption insurance, sufficient for four months of operations.

Travel and Entertainment

- All reimbursements require a receipt.
- Employees must show all receipts for travel advances within one week of travel, or the advance will be considered a salary advance.
- Only coach air fares will be reimbursed.
- There is no movie reimbursement.
- There is no reimbursement for commuting miles.
- There is no reimbursement for lunch mileage.

2.7 PROCESS CYCLE DESCRIPTIONS

The accounting manual typically contains a great many procedures, but does not enumerate how they are linked together to form complete process cycles. A process cycle is the complete set of transactions associated with an activity. Showing a user how a specific procedure is incorporated into a process cycle makes it much easier to understand why the procedure is needed. It is also useful for both external and internal auditors, who can see what controls have been incorporated into specific procedures, and how these controls are linked into the process cycles. Consequently, a summary-level

[6] The risk management policies are from *Controllership: The Work of the Managerial Accountant,* 6th Edition, James Willson, Janice Roehl-Anderson, and Steven Bragg, copyright © 1999 John Wiley & Sons. This material is used by permission of John Wiley & Sons, Inc.

overview of all major process cycles is an extremely useful component of the accounting manual.

An example of a process cycle is the purchasing cycle. This begins with the ordering of goods by the purchasing department, continues with the receipt of those goods by the warehouse staff, and ends with payment for them by the accounts payable staff. Examples of other major process cycles are the billing cycle and order fulfillment cycle. There are also many lesser cycles that have a less pervasive influence throughout a company, such as cycles for quality, maintenance, and contracts.

A key aspect of nearly all process cycles is that the activities associated with them cross over multiple departmental boundaries. Whenever this happens, there is a potential loss of data that can affect the completion of the transactions. To continue with the purchasing cycle example, the purchase order generated by the purchasing department may never arrive at the receiving dock, resulting in the erroneous rejection of materials. Similarly, the received goods may never be entered in the inventory database, resulting in their sitting in a corner unused. Further, the receiving documentation may never be sent to the accounting department, resulting in the nonpayment of supplier billings. Thus, possible failures in the overall process cycles can occur as information moves between departments.

The best way to avoid these problems is for the controller to take over the review of process cycles by regularly examining the points in the cycles where errors are likely to occur. Though this function falls outside the boundaries of most individual departments, the controller is the person most frequently called upon to take on this task, given the accounting department's familiarity with systems in general and transactions in particular.

This section describes a number of procedures that are commonly used to spot problems in the transfer of information between departments for major process cycles. They are:

- Compare billings to the shipping log
- Review rush freight
- Review suppliers with no activity
- Delete old purchase orders
- Review suppliers with early payment discounts
- Review blanket purchase orders
- Review customers with no activity
- Review old open orders
- Review pricing errors
- Review small orders

Policy/Procedure Statement Brasto Publishing **Subject: Monthly Journal Entry Review**	Procedure No.: Page: Issue Date: Revision Date:	701 1 of 1 10/28/0X None

COMPARE BILLINGS TO THE SHIPPING LOG

1. PURPOSE AND SCOPE

This procedure is used by the accounts receivable clerk to verify that shipments are matched by the same number of invoices to customers so that no billings are missing or duplicated.

2. RESPONSIBILITIES

ACC RECV **Accounts Receivable Clerk**

3. PROCEDURES

3.1 ACC RECV **Obtain the Shipping Log**

Go to the warehouse and make a copy of the shipping log for the previous week. Alternatively (if available), access this information online through the receiving system and print out the shipping log.

3.2 ACC RECV **Verify Information**

Match the shipments listed on the shipping log to invoices issued during the same period. Note all exceptions in the shipping log for missing billings. Also, note on invoices any incorrect quantities that were billed, as well as "leftover" invoices for which there is no shipping record.

3.3 ACC RECV **Bill for Missing Invoices**

Using the list of shipments for which there are no corresponding invoices, go to the shipping department and obtain bills of lading for the unbilled shipments. If these are not available, determine which freight carrier shipped the items and obtain shipping traces on them. Then create invoices, mail a copy to the customer, and attach the proof of delivery to the company's copy of the invoice. File the company's copy in the accounting files.

3.4 ACC RECV **Issue Credits for Duplicate Invoices**

Using the list of invoices for which no corresponding shipment is recorded in the shipping log, go back to the company's copy of these invoices and see if there is any bill of lading or other proof of delivery attached to the invoice. If not, call the shipping department to verify that no such documentation exists there. If not, issue a credit to eliminate these invoices.

3.5 ACC RECV **Adjust Incorrect Invoices**

Using the list of invoices for which the quantity of product billed is different from the quantity shipped, go back to the company's copy of the invoice and check the attached bill of lading to determine the actual quantity shipped. If the quantity is different, verify this with the shipping department, and then either issue a credit (if the quantity billed was too high) or an additional invoice (if the quantity billed was too low).

Policy/Procedure Statement	Procedure No.:	702
Brasto Publishing	Page:	1 of 1
	Issue Date:	10/28/0X
Subject: Monthly Journal Entry Review	Revision Date:	None

REVIEW RUSH FREIGHT

1. PURPOSE AND SCOPE

This procedure is used by the financial analyst to determine the amount and type of any rush freight services used by a company to either receive or send materials.

2. RESPONSIBILITIES

ANALYST **Financial Analyst**

3. PROCEDURES

3.1 ANALYST **Access the Freight Account**

Go to the freight account in the computer for each department. If the total amount for the month is less than $100, ignore the account. Otherwise, write down the total department freight and go to the next step.

3.2 ANALYST **Access Detail Freight Amounts**

Go to the GLJE screen in the accounting software and call up the detail for each freight expenditure. This information should include the date of expenditure, the name of the authorizing person, and the name of the freight carrier.

3.3 ANALYST **Summarize Freight Information**

Enter this detailed freight information into the FREIGHT.XLS spreadsheet. List all the freight for each department and summarize the dollar amounts. The totals in this spreadsheet should match the freight expense totals for each department, as noted in the general ledger. List all rush freight charges in bold font; these charges are noted in the underlying expense detail as being either from a rush freight company, or designated as rush freight by a standard freight company.

3.4 ANALYST **Distribute Freight Information**

Distribute the freight report to each department manager, as well as the controller and chief operating officer.

3.5 ANALYST **Track Freight Expenses on a Graph**

Enter the total freight cost by department on a graph, showing the expense for the last 12 months for each department. The intention in using this chart is to show managers any improvement (or lack thereof) in their management of this expense. Distribute the graph to all department managers, the controller, and the chief operating officer.

Policy/Procedure Statement Brasto Publishing **Subject: Monthly Journal Entry Review**	Procedure No.: Page: Issue Date: Revision Date:	703 1 of 1 10/28/0X None

REVIEW SUPPLIERS WITH NO ACTIVITY

1. PURPOSE AND SCOPE

This procedure is used by the financial analyst to determine which suppliers are no longer used by the company. The logistics manager uses the resulting list to determine which suppliers can be removed from the company database.

2. RESPONSIBILITIES

ANALYST **Financial Analyst**

3. PROCEDURES

3.1 ANALYST **Extract Supplier Usage Information**

Go to the EXTRACTS screen in the accounting software and run an extract file that shows all suppliers currently in the database, as well as the last dates on which the company purchased supplies from them. This is the SUPPLIER extract, which dumps into an Excel file of the same name.

3.2 ANALYST **Summarize Supplier Usage Information**

Enter the Excel program and access the SUPPLIER spreadsheet. Sort the records based on the last date on which purchases were made from a supplier. Delete all suppliers from the spreadsheet for whom there are purchase dates within the last two years. Print the remaining list of suppliers on the spreadsheet. This list constitutes those suppliers with whom the company is no longer doing business.

3.3 ANALYST **Issue Supplier Report**

Give the supplier spreadsheet report to the purchasing manager, with a request to mark those suppliers who can be deleted from the list, and to return it to the financial analyst.

3.4 ANALYST **Delete Suppliers from Database**

Upon receipt of the approved list, go into the Suppliers screen in the accounting software. Call up each supplier record that was marked on the supplier report, and press Ctrl-F6 to delete each of those suppliers. File the report in the "Deleted Suppliers" folder, which is located in the front of the accounts payable records.

Policy/Procedure Statement	Procedure No.:	704
Brasto Publishing	Page:	1 of 1
	Issue Date:	10/28/0X
	Revision Date:	None
Subject: Monthly Journal Entry Review		

DELETE OLD PURCHASE ORDERS

1. PURPOSE AND SCOPE

This procedure is used by the financial analyst to determine which purchase orders are still open, but are not going to be filled. The logistics manager uses this information to close down old purchase orders.

2. RESPONSIBILITIES

ANALYST **Financial Analyst**

3. PROCEDURES

3.1 ANALYST **Extract Open Purchase Order Information**

Go to the EXTRACTS screen in the accounting software and generate an extract of all open purchase orders in the database. This information dumps into an Excel spreadsheet called PURCHORD and contains each purchase order number, supplier name, date on which it was created, and a flag to indicate if it is a blanket purchase order.

3.2 ANALYST **Summarize Purchase Order Information**

Enter the Excel program and access the PURCHORD spreadsheet. Sort the records based on the date of each purchase order. Delete from the spreadsheet all purchase orders for which the creation date is within the last six months. Also delete all purchase orders for which there is a blanket purchase order flag (as these may be open and valid for more than a year). Print the remaining list of purchase orders on the spreadsheet, which should thus include all old orders that may be subject to deletion.

3.3 ANALYST **Issue Open Purchase Order Report**

Forward the open purchase order spreadsheet to the purchasing manager, with a request to mark all purchase orders on the list that should be closed and then to return the list to the financial analyst.

3.4 ANALYST **Delete Open Purchase Orders**

Upon receipt of the approved list, go into the PURCHASE ORDER screen in the accounting software. Call up each purchase order record that was marked on the report and press Ctrl-F6 to delete each one. File the report in the "Deleted Purchase Orders" folder, which is located in the front of the accounts payable records.

Policy/Procedure Statement Brasto Publishing **Subject: Monthly Journal Entry Review**	Procedure No.: Page: Issue Date: Revision Date:	705 1 of 1 10/28/0X None

REVIEW SUPPLIERS WITH EARLY PAYMENT DISCOUNTS

1. PURPOSE AND SCOPE

This procedure is used by the financial analyst to determine how many suppliers currently allow early payment discounts by the company. The logistics manager uses this information to ask suppliers for new or larger discounts.

2. RESPONSIBILITIES

ANALYST **Financial Analyst**

3. PROCEDURES

3.1 ANALYST **Extract Discount Information**
Go to the EXTRACT screen in the accounting software and select the "Suppliers Extract" option. Select for all suppliers, and extract to an Excel file format.

3.2 ANALYST **Sort the Discount Information**
Sort the Excel file on the discount field so that the largest discounts are at the top and the smallest at the bottom.

3.3 ANALYST **Issue the Discounts Report**
Print out the report and issue it to the purchasing manager with a standard request to attempt to obtain discounts from more suppliers, as well as to increase the discount amounts from suppliers that already grant them.

3.4 ANALYST **Update Discounts Information**
If any changes to discounts are submitted by the purchasing manager, go to the SUPPLIER MASTER screen in the accounting software and update the discount field with the new information for those suppliers needing changes.

3.5 ANALYST **Record Discounts Statistics**
Go to the Process_Stats Excel file and enter the total number of supplier discounts for the month into the statistics page.

Policy/Procedure Statement Brasto Publishing **Subject: Monthly Journal Entry Review**	Procedure No.: Page: Issue Date: Revision Date:	706 1 of 1 10/28/0X None

REVIEW BLANKET PURCHASE ORDERS

1. PURPOSE AND SCOPE

This procedure is used by the financial analyst to determine how many blanket purchase orders are currently open, and with how many suppliers these are used. The resulting information is used by the logistics manager to increase the number of blanket purchase orders.

2. RESPONSIBILITIES

ANALYST **Financial Analyst**

3. PROCEDURES

3.1 ANALYST **Extract Blanket Purchase Order Information**

Go to the EXTRACT screen in the accounting software and select the "Blanket Purchase Orders Extract" option. Select for all purchase orders, and extract to an Excel file format.

3.2 ANALYST **Sort the Blanket Purchase Order Information**

Access Excel and call up the extract of blanket purchase order information. Format the spreadsheet based on a copy of the last blanket purchase order report that was issued in the previous month. Print the report.

3.3 ANALYST **Issue the Blanket Purchase Order Report**

Issue the blanket purchase order report to the purchasing manager with a request to add more blanket purchase orders than are currently recorded. The purchasing manager can enter any new blanket purchase orders directly; there is no need for the financial analyst to do so.

3.4 ANALYST **Record Blanket Purchase Order Information**

Go to the Process_Stats Excel file and enter the total number of blanket purchase orders for the month into the statistics page.

Policy/Procedure Statement Brasto Publishing **Subject: Monthly Journal Entry Review**	Procedure No.: Page: Issue Date: Revision Date:	707 1 of 1 10/28/0X None

REVIEW CUSTOMERS WITH NO ACTIVITY

1. PURPOSE AND SCOPE

This procedure is used by the financial analyst to determine which customers have not placed orders with the company. The sales manager uses this information to determine which customers can be removed from the customer database.

2. RESPONSIBILITIES

ANALYST **Financial Analyst**

3. PROCEDURES

3.1 ANALYST **Extract Customer Information**
Go to the EXTRACT screen in the accounting software and select the "Customers Extract" option. Select for all customers, and extract to an Excel file format.

3.2 ANALYST **Determine Inactive Customers**
Access Excel and call up the EXTRACT spreadsheet. Sort the report based on activity dates so that the oldest dates are at the top of the report. Review the fields in the report that list the last dates on which the company shipped anything to a customer or received payment from one. If the most recent date in either column is less than two years ago, delete the record. This will leave a list of customers with whom the company has had no business in at least two years.

3.3 ANALYST **Report on Inactive Customers**
Print the spreadsheet and issue it to the sales manager with a request to mark those customers who should be deleted from the accounting database.

3.4 ANALYST **Delete Inactive Customers**
Once the report is received back from the sales manager, go to the CUSTOMER MASTER screen in the accounting database and delete those customers who have been so marked by the sales manager in the report.

3.5 ANALYST **Record Customer Statistics**
Go to the Process_Stats Excel file and enter the total number of inactive customers for the month into the statistics page.

Policy/Procedure Statement		
Brasto Publishing	Procedure No.:	708
	Page:	1 of 1
	Issue Date:	10/28/0X
	Revision Date:	None
Subject: Monthly Journal Entry Review		

REVIEW OLD OPEN ORDERS

1. PURPOSE AND SCOPE

This procedure is used by the financial analyst to locate those customer orders that are still open but no longer need to be filled, so that they can be closed down.

2. RESPONSIBILITIES

ANALYST **Financial Analyst**

3. PROCEDURES

3.1 ANALYST **Extract Open Orders Information**

Go to the EXTRACT screen in the accounting software and select the "Open Orders Extract" option. Select for all open orders, and extract to an Excel file format.

3.2 ANALYST **Locate Old Open Orders**

Go to Excel and open the EXTRACT file. Sort it for orders that have been open for at least one month, and delete all but these records.

3.3 ANALYST **Report on Old Open Orders**

Add headings to the report, as well as a column for the names of the customer service staff who are responsible for each customer. Print the report and issue it to them, with a note to either close the orders or shift their due dates forward into a future time period.

3.4 ANALYST **Close Old Open Orders**

If the customer service staff cannot do so, assist them in closing the orders or shifting their due dates through the ORDER ENTRY screen in the accounting software.

3.5 ANALYST **Record Open Order Statistics**

Go to the Process_Stats Excel file and enter the total number of old open orders for the month into the statistics page.

Policy/Procedure Statement Brasto Publishing **Subject: Monthly Journal Entry Review**	Procedure No.: Page: Issue Date: Revision Date:	709 1 of 1 10/28/0X None

REVIEW PRICING ERRORS

1. PURPOSE AND SCOPE

This procedure is used by the financial analyst to determine the number of credits issued to customers that are based on pricing problems, and the nature of the pricing errors.

2. RESPONSIBILITIES

ANALYST **Financial Analyst**

3. PROCEDURES

3.1 ANALYST **Review Existing Credits**

Go to the EXTRACT screen in the accounting software and select the "Invoices Extract" option. Select for all invoices in the previous month, and extract to an Excel file format.

3.2 ANALYST **Extract Pricing Error Information**

Sort the Excel file for invoices with credit balances and delete all other invoices from the file. Then search the description field for each remaining credit for wording regarding a pricing error. Retain these records and delete all others. Print the spreadsheet.

3.3 ANALYST **Create Pricing Error Report**

Go to the Price_Error Excel spreadsheet and clear out the information in it from the previous month, except for headings and totals. Then enter the new credit information from the extract spreadsheet you just printed. This information includes the credit number, credit amount, customer name, correct price, actual price charged, the differences between the two, the quantity of product to which the incorrect pricing applies, the grand total pricing error, and the initials of the customer service person who made the entry. When finished, print the Price_Error report.

3.4 ANALYST **Distribute Report**

Distribute the report to the sales manager, controller, president, and chief operating officer.

3.5 ANALYST **Record Pricing Error Statistics**

Go to the process_Stats Excel file and enter the total number of pricing errors for the month into the statistics page.

Policy/Procedure Statement	Procedure No.:	710
Brasto Publishing	Page:	1 of 1
	Issue Date:	10/28/0X
Subject: Monthly Journal Entry Review	Revision Date:	None

REVIEW SMALL ORDERS

1. PURPOSE AND SCOPE

The procedure is used by the financial analyst to determine which customers habitually place small orders. This information is useful in determining pricing changes for customers, or whether some customers should be dropped.

2. RESPONSIBILITIES

ANALYST **Financial Analyst**

3. PROCEDURES

3.1 ANALYST **Extract Invoice Information**

Go to the EXTRACT screen in the accounting software and select the "Orders Extract" option. Select for all orders in the previous month, and extract to an Excel file format.

3.2 ANALYST **Select Small Order Information**

Go to Excel and open the ORDERS EXTRACT file. Sort on the order dollar amount, and delete all records except those that are equal to or less than $500.

3.3 ANALYST **Create Report**

Sort the Excel file again by customer name so that the number of small orders for each customer can be easily determined. Then print the report. Go to the Small_Order Excel file, which lists the grand total of small orders by customer for the last year in a grid format, and enter the data from the first spreadsheet into this format. Print the report.

3.4 ANALYST ISSUE THE REPORT

Issue the report to the sales manager, controller, president, and chief operating officer.

3.5 ANALYST **Update Small Order Statistics**

Go to the Process_Stats Excel file and enter the total number of small orders for the month into the statistics page.

2.8 ACCOUNTING PROCEDURES

It is extremely important to create an environment within the accounting department that results in the consistent processing of all accounting transactions so that resulting financial statements are comparable for all time periods and across all corporate divisions. Another result is error-free transactions that require little ongoing review or correction by the senior accounting staff, which results in a more efficient department. Further, both internal and external auditors will test the accuracy of these transactions from time to time, and will gain a high degree of confidence in the accuracy of company-reported transactions if they are consistently completed. In addition, consistent transaction usage results in better conformance with generally accepted accounting principles (GAAP), so a company will not require restatement of certain transactions for GAAP conformance purposes. For all of these reasons, it is critical to use a standard set of accounting procedures for all regular accounting transactions.

A complete set of accounting procedures may be included within the general accounting manual. However, if the business entity is a large one, there may be so many procedures that they are subdivided by job position or process cycle, and distributed separately.

In the next chapter, we will review the various types of procedures and how they are formatted, as well as examine a checklist of suggested procedures and a number of related examples.

Chapter 3

PROCEDURE STATEMENTS

3.1 INTRODUCTION

A procedure is a standard method for accomplishing a task, usually composed of a series of steps that are followed in a definite, regular order. A typical procedure identifies the purpose for completing it, as well as what job position is responsible for each task within it and how each task is to be completed.

A procedures manual usually only contains the most commonly used procedures, because the inclusion of every possible procedure would require a great deal of time and effort. The reason for this long delay is that, in addition to initiating, checking, approving, distributing, calculating, balancing, and other accounting activities, there are also many forms that each person completes on a regular basis, which may require input from multiple departments. Documenting all of this is a considerable task. Consequently, it is not uncommon to target for documentation only a few of the most important procedures for inclusion in the initial procedures manual, and then add more procedures to subsequent releases of the manual if there is a cost-effective reason for doing so.

In this chapter, we will review the format of a procedure, as well as the writing style and writing mechanics used to create its content. The chapter also covers the basic work steps needed to create a procedure, and a detailed list of possible procedures that may be worthy of inclusion in a procedures manual.

3.2 WRITING STYLE

Clarity and readability are much more important than style, perfect grammar, and a large vocabulary. One should ensure that readers can easily understand the contents of a procedure. To this end, consistent use of outlining and active verbs, and avoiding distracting grammar errors, will ensure overall readability.

A typical procedure is composed of a number of logical steps. If these steps are presented in a paragraph format, the reader can become confused about which steps to complete next. To avoid this problem, one should split the text into an outline format, which lets the reader easily move through the various processing steps of a procedure. Exhibit 3.1 shows three outline formats.

The standard outline format is the most flexible approach when there are many sublayers of activities within a procedure. For example, a major processing step for the accounts payable function is "Create Checks," which could be listed as Roman numeral "I." Within the check creation step may be several additional substeps, such as document matching, obtaining final approvals, and printing checks. There may be additional steps within these substeps. The resulting outline is:

I. Create checks.
   A. Match supporting documents.
      1. Obtain receiving documents.
      2. Obtain purchase orders.
      3. Obtain supplier invoices.
      4. Compare all documents and note variances.
         a. Contact supplier over quantity variances.
         b. Contact purchasing over pricing variances.

Standard Outline	Roman Numeral Outline	Arabic Numeral Outline
I.	I.	1.
A.	II.	10.
1.	IV.	50.
2.	V.	75.
a.	VI.	100.
b.	VII.	125.
B.	VIII.	150.
II.	XI.	175.

Exhibit 3.1: Different Types of Outline Formats

B. Obtain final approvals.

1. Obtain department manager approval if <$10,000.

2. Obtain president approval if <$100,000.

3. Obtain board approval if $100,000+.

C. Print checks.

An outline format makes it much easier to follow a long or complex procedure. If the procedure is shorter or has minimal complexity, then either the Roman numeral or Arabic numeral outlines listed in Exhibit 3.1 can be used. In all cases, one should line up the periods vertically within the outline, so that the text forms a pleasing straight vertical line down the left side of each text block.

No matter what type of outline is used, there must always be at least two of each type of character. For example, there cannot be I without a following II, an A without a following B, or a 1 without a following 2. If outline step "I. Create checks" was followed by "A. Match supporting documents," there must also be a step B. Otherwise, step A would be renamed "II. Match supporting documents."

Outlining is the written version of a flowchart. The mechanics of flowcharting are covered later in section 3.4.

Misspelling is much less of a problem with the advent of automated spell checkers. For example, Microsoft Word can be set to automatically check spellings as soon as they are typed. To set up this function, go to the Tools command in the Word menu, and select the Options command. This will bring up a tiled set of command boxes. Select the Spelling & Grammar box. Select the "Check Spelling as You Type" box, and click OK. Word will then put a wavy red line underneath any word for which there appears to be an incorrect spelling. One can then position the cursor over the word and press the right mouse button, which will bring up a range of alternate spellings from which a selection can be made.

One should use active verbs whenever possible to forcibly push the reader through the narrative of the procedure. The best way to illustrate the problem is with the following examples:

Inactive Version	**Active Version**
The reader is advised to regularly review documents for mistakes.	Review documents for mistakes.
The receiving log is compared by the accounts payable clerk to the on-hand inventory at month-end.	Verify that all receipts are present in the inventory.

By shifting the verb to the beginning of the sentence, one can create much more active and vibrant sentences. Accountants commonly use these active verbs:

Accrue	Cancel	Correct	Extend
Accumulate	Charge	Credit	File
Approve	Check	Decide	Issue
Authorize	Compare	Enter	Locate

Obtain	Reconcile	Review	Total
Prepare	Record	Run	Verify
Receive	Request	Send	Write off

A few common grammar rules also must be mentioned here. Microsoft Word can conduct a grammar check during the writing task, so one does not have to have a grammar and style book on hand at all times. To activate the grammar checker in Word, go to the Tools command in the Word menu, and select the Options command. This will bring up a tiled set of command boxes. Select the Spelling & Grammar box. Select the "Check grammar as you type" box, and click OK. Word will then put a wavy line underneath any sentence or portion of a sentence for which there appears to be incorrect grammar. One can then position the cursor over the indicated area and press the right mouse button to determine the type of problem. To avoid total reliance on the grammar checker, one should remember the following rules:

- *Abbreviations*. Spell out the abbreviations *lb.*, *oz.*, *ft.*, and *in.* as pound, ounce, foot or feet, and inches. However, some common abbreviations are permitted when used with numbers, such as 50 mph or 1800 rpm.
- *Almost, only, nearly*. Place these modifiers immediately before the words they modify. For example, change "this system nearly costs $10,000" to "this system costs nearly $10,000."
- *Ampersand*. Only use the ampersand (&) in organization names that have this abbreviation in their official titles.
- *Apostrophe*. To form a possessive, place the apostrophe before the final "s" for a singular noun; place it after the final "s" to make a plural noun possessive. Do not use it in numeric dates (such as 1990s), but use it when numerals are omitted from dates ('90s). Omit the apostrophe when an acronym is plural (VCRs).
- *Exclamation point*. When it doubt, leave it out. When using it, you are essentially shouting at the reader.
- *Of*. Avoid using "of" after the words *all, outside, inside*, and so on. Thus, *all of the books* can be reduced to *all the books*.
- *Quotation marks*. Always place quotation marks outside an ending comma, period, exclamation point, or question mark.
- *There is, there are*. Omit these stock phrases if they begin a sentence. Thus, *There is a problem with this journal entry* becomes *This journal entry has a problem*.

Accounting procedures are full of numbers. One should be aware of the rules for including numbers in sentences, and follow them consistently:

- Do not begin a sentence with a number. For example, state "17 facilities follow this procedure" as "Seventeen facilities follow this procedure."
- Spell out numbers one through nine, and use numerals for anything larger. For example, "Eight vice presidents follow the 23 procedures in this manual."

Follow this rule until you reach 1 million, and then describe the zeros in a number with words—for example, $32 million.

- Precede decimals of less than one with a zero, such as 0.7%.

A key issue when writing a procedure is one's ability to keep the resulting document as easy to read as possible. Clarity of writing can be quantified to some extent by using the readability scoring system in Microsoft Word. This scoring system itemizes the number of words per sentence, as well as the number of characters per word, to derive a readability index called the Flesch Reading Ease measure. A score of 100 indicates an extremely easy-to-read document; measurements closer to zero indicate increasing levels of reading difficulty. A score of 60 to 70 is considered acceptable for most documents. This measurement can also be converted into the Flesch-Kincaid Grade Score, which converts the Flesch Reading Ease measure into the comparable grade school level of education required to read the document. For example, a score of 7 indicates that someone with a seventh grade education can read the procedure.

To compile the readability information in a Word document, go to the Tools command in the menu bar, access the Options command, and select the Spelling & Grammar option. Then check the Show Readability Statistics box and click on the OK button to close the command box. Run the spell checker for the document; when the spell check is complete, a readability statistics box will appear. An example of this box is shown in Exhibit 3.2.

A reasonable target is a Flesch-Kincaid Grade Level score of no higher than 12, preferably closer to 8. If the score is too high, consider splitting long sentences into smaller ones; a paragraph containing just one sentence may indicate a sentence-length problem. Also, consider replacing any words exceeding two syllables with shorter synonyms. These steps can greatly increase a procedure's clarity.

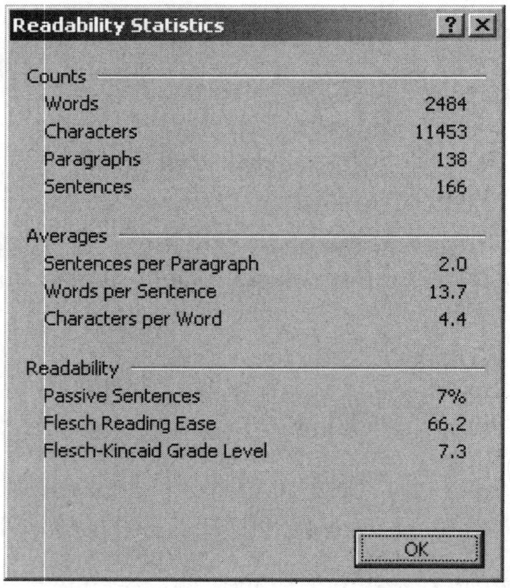

Exhibit 3.2. Readability Statistics Results for a Word Document

3.3 WRITING MECHANICS

The mechanics of writing include the paper, type style, hardware, method of reproduction, use of logos, numbering schemes, indexes, and headlining related to the completion of a procedure. These guidelines provide some rules for each of these items.

- *Color*. Use colors to denote different accounting purposes. Avoid a lack of contrast between colors, such as using blue ink on blue, brown on brown, or black on dark gray.
- *Distribution*. Note the job title or department to which the procedure is to be distributed. This will assist in distributing the procedure.
- *Issue date*. List the actual date on which the procedure was released. This tells a reader if the date on the procedure that he or she is reading matches the date of the most recent release.
- *Logos*. Include the company logo on all forms and procedures as often as possible. The logo tends to make the reader accept the material as *our* procedure, and lends an official status to the document.
- *Margins*. Use a one-inch margin on both sides of any page, as well as at the bottom. If the top margin contains a logo or other information, then use a top margin of a half inch; otherwise, use a one-inch margin at the top of the page.
- *Page numbering*. Number all pages in the form "Page 1 of 2" so that readers can see how many pages are supposed to be included in a procedure, and can thereby see if any are missing.
- *Paper*. Do not use paper that is so flimsy that text on the back side can be seen through it. To avoid this problem, consider using at least 24-pound bond paper. Most photocopy paper is adequate for one-sided printing.
- *Retrieval numbers*. Assign a permanent retrieval number to a document when it is first created, which (as the name implies) can be used to retrieve it from storage. This number also can be used as the identifying file name where the document is stored in the computer system. If not many documents are expected to be included in the procedures manual, then the retrieval number can be as short as three digits, and might be divided in the following manner to leave room for the documents of all departments:

Number Range	Department to Which Numbers Are Assigned
000–099	Accounting
100–199	Purchasing
200–299	Human Resources
300–399	Treasurer

Number Range	Department to Which Numbers Are Assigned
400–499	Sales
500–599	Engineering
600–699	Production/Materials Handling
700–799	Advertising/Public Relations
800–999	Reserved for future use

This scheme breaks down in larger organizations, where there may be many departments and a multitude of forms and procedures. In these cases, it is better to identify the department with a two-digit number, followed by a hyphen, followed by a three- or four-digit number that identifies the document. For example, here are the number ranges that could be used within the accounting department, with the department being assigned an overall code of 10:

Number Range	Functions to Which Numbers Are Assigned
10–000 thru 099	Accounting—Controller
10–100 thru 199	Accounting—Accounts Payable
10–200 thru 299	Accounting—Accounts Receivable
10–300 thru 399	Accounting—Budget
10–400 thru 499	Accounting—Cost Accounting
10–500 thru 599	Accounting—Payroll
10–600 thru 699	Accounting—Purchasing

- *Supercedes.* If a new procedure supercedes a previous one, note the retrieval number of the procedure being eliminated so that the recipient can purge it from the existing procedures manual.
- *Type size.* Use the standard Times New Roman font. Avoid using cursives that imitate handwriting, fancy Old English type, square-faced type, or all-capital type, because they are difficult to read.

3.4 FLOWCHARTING FOR A PROCEDURES MANUAL

(a) Introduction

Flowcharts are a valuable addition to any manual that describes the flow of steps in a process. In the following sections, we review when flowcharts should (and should not) be added to a manual, as well as their basic components and proper layout. A series of examples cover the more basic process flows for the major accounting transactions.

(b) When to Use Flowcharts

Flowcharts should only be used in a minority of situations where the subject matter is so complex that a lengthy written document may not convey the key information to a user without a number of repetitions. This situation most commonly arises when there are many decision points in a process, where a person can move down a number of alternative paths within a procedure. An example of a multidecision process is shown in Exhibit 3.3, where an employee must make several decisions to determine the correct outcome to a credit analysis situation.

By converting this example into the flowchart format shown in Exhibit 3.4, we can greatly simplify the decision-making process for the user of the procedure. However, this conversion can result in the loss of some detailed information that was included in the written procedure, as there is not sufficient room in the flowchart. In this instance, the underlined wording in Exhibit 3.3 relates to a method of reducing the amount of credit granted, which cannot fit into the existing flowchart format. To avoid this problem, the original written procedure can be simplified to avoid these "text overhang" problems; the size and complexity of the flowchart can be expanded to include all

Credit Approval Procedure:

Upon receipt of a request for credit, follow these sequential steps:

1. Is the credit request for less than $500? If so, grant the request at once.
2. If not, then go to the Dun & Bradstreet database and print out a Business Information Report on the prospective customer.
3. Is the average amount of payment days listed on the Business Information Report less than 40? If so, grant a credit level equal to the median amount listed on the report, <u>reduced by the impact of the top 10 percent of credit levels shown on the report</u>.
4. Is the average amount of payment days between 39 and 50? If so, reduce the credit level calculated in the last step by five percent for every payment day in excess of 40 days.
5. Is the average amount of payment days on the report 50 or higher? If so, reject the credit request.

Exhibit 3.3. Decision Points in a Procedure

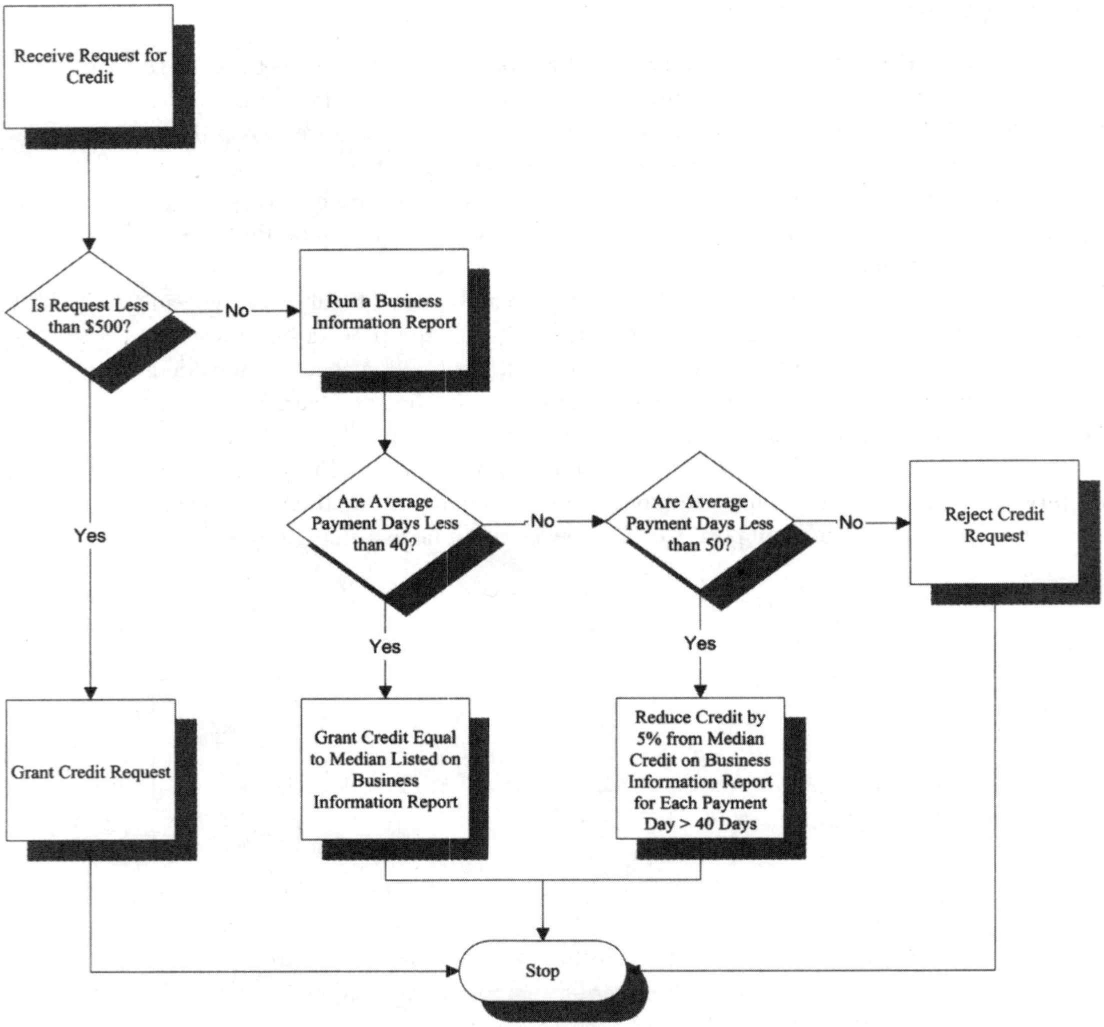

Exhibit 3.4. Decision Points in a Flowchart

possible text; or a reference notation can be added to the flowchart that will send the reader back to the written version of the procedure for additional information.

Besides bringing clarity to complex procedures, the flowchart is also very useful for constructing a written procedure. By plotting the steps in a flowchart format while producing the written procedure, one can more easily identify decision points and ensure that all possible variations have been accounted for. Thus, the flowchart introduces more rigor into procedure writing. When it is not intended for later inclusion in the accounting manual, a flowchart may be discarded after the written procedure has been completed.

The flowchart is of particular use for training new employees. An instructor can use it as a teaching tool to walk users through a procedure. The same reasoning applies if the workforce's primary language is not the same as the one in which a procedure has been written, or if the level of employee education is relatively low, because a flowchart is much easier to understand than a written procedure.

A flowchart can also be used as a disposable check-off sheet. For example, an extremely complex procedure can be made much easier for the person performing it if that person checks off each item on the flowchart as he or she progresses through the various procedural steps. This usage can become a formal one, where the user signs off on the flowchart when a procedure is completed to provide proof of completion.

There are also situations in which flowcharts are not worth the effort to construct. One such case is when the underlying procedure is so simple, or so well written, that few readers would refer to the flowchart for additional clarification. Another situation is when there are so many changes to the underlying procedure over time that there is some risk that the details in the accompanying flowchart will not be appropriately revised, resulting in conflicting instructions between the two documents. A final issue is that an excessive amount of flowcharting will result in a considerable increase in the size of an accounting manual; if there is an objective to create a leaner manual, then an editor may view a large number of flowcharts as being excessive duplication of existing written procedures and throw them out.

Despite these few problems, the selective use of flowcharts can greatly increase the user's level of comprehension of more complex procedures, and they remain highly recommended for that purpose.

(c) Flowcharting Symbols

Many symbols can be used to create a flowchart. However, one must focus on user comprehension—will they know what all of the symbols mean? Probably not—their training may not include flowchart symbols. Accordingly, only a few symbols should be used to describe the majority of flowchart activities. The key items are noted in Exhibit 3.5.

By far the most common flowchart symbol is the rectangle, which signifies a process step. If something can be described with a verb, then it is probably a process step. For example, "compare receiving log to supplier invoices" and "issue financial report to investors" are both valid process descriptions that might be found within a process symbol.

The next symbol in the exhibit is a diamond, which represents a decision point. A decision should be answered with a "yes" or "no." If a statement ends with a question mark, then it is probably a decision point. The flowline for a "yes" answer to the decision point should continue on the main flow of the flowchart from the decision symbol, which may be either down or to the right. The flowline for a "no" answer to the decision point will branch off to the side for separate treatment. An example of a decision point is "Document match OK?" Given the smaller text area in a decision symbol, the amount of text allowed is quite small, so brevity is crucial.

The terminator symbol is a long, narrow rectangle with rounded corners (as shown in the exhibit). It is intended to show where a process ends, but can also be used to show its beginning point. It is not normally used to signify end points for all the side junctions that branch from decision points, as this tends to clutter a flowchart too much. The text within a terminator symbol is simple enough—use "start" if the symbol signifies the beginning of a process, and "end" or "stop" at the end point.

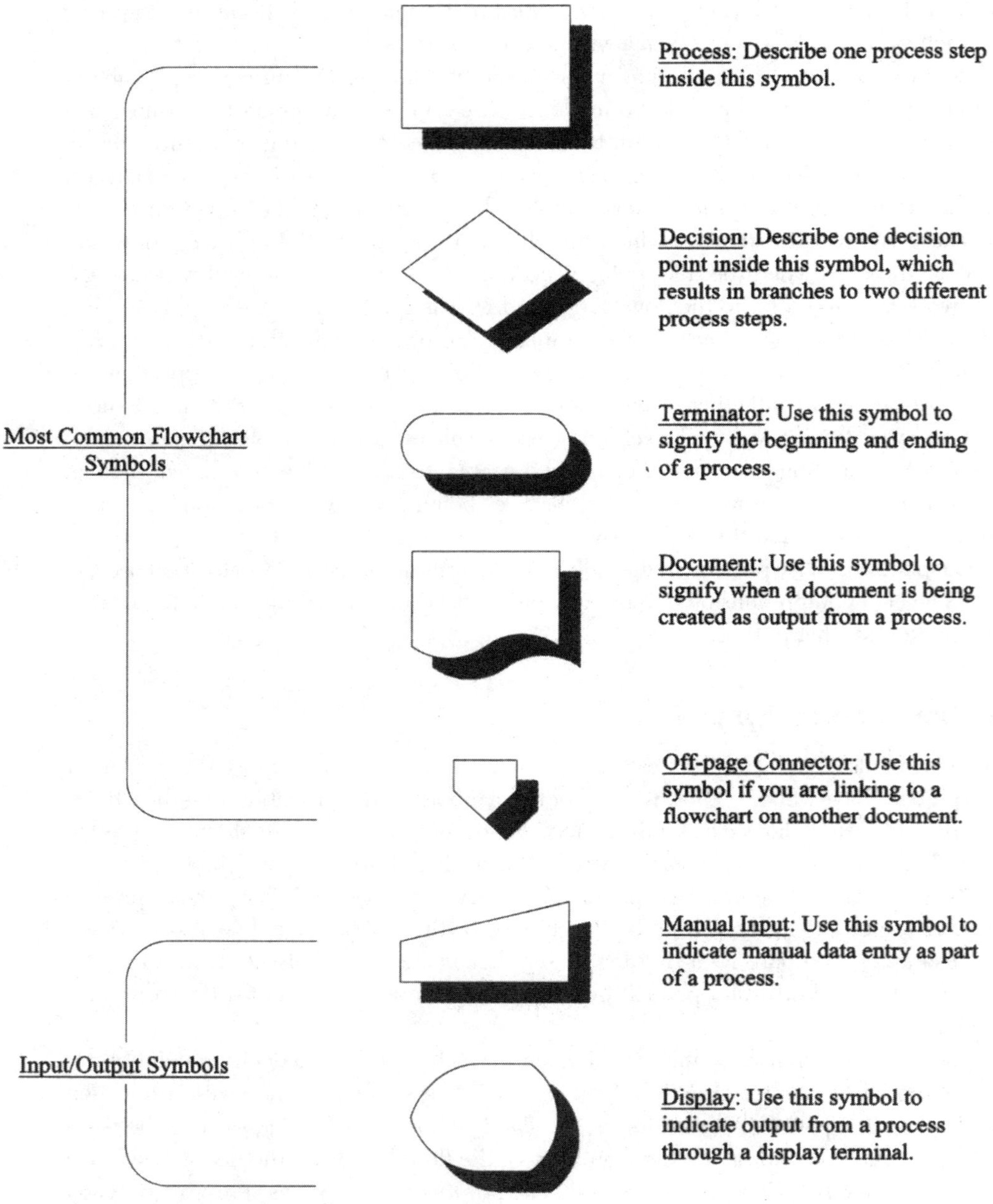

Exhibit 3.5. Common Flowcharting Symbols

The document symbol is a rectangle with a wavy bottom, as noted in the exhibit. It signifies instances when a document is being created as output from a process. It may also be used to signify when key documents are being added to a process, such as when a document is being taken out of a file and added to an information packet (such as in the accounts payable matching process). This symbol tends to be used too much, which adds an excessive number of symbols to a flowchart. In most cases, it is best to only add it to a chart when there are multipart documents being used, and the flowchart can clarify who gets which copy of the document. The text entered within this symbol should only identify the name of the document, such as "Customer Invoice (pink copy)."

The off-page connector is a square symbol with a pointed end. It is a cross-reference that signifies a shift in the flowchart to another flowchart, probably because either the existing flowchart is too large, or it logically links with another flowchart. This symbol can also be used to signify incoming linkages into a flowchart; a wide arrow symbol may also be used to represent incoming flows, but using the off-page connector in both roles eliminates a symbol, and so is the preferred approach. Each off-page connector should be uniquely identified with a letter or number, which should also be used at the point where it connects to another flowchart so that a reader can see the linkages between flowcharts.

The symbol for manual data input is a rectangle whose top line slopes up to the right (as shown in the exhibit). This signifies that the previous step (usually a process) has resulted in the manual entry of data, probably into a computer system. This symbol can frequently be replaced with a process symbol because action is implied in both cases.

The symbol for information that appears on a display is a two-dimensional representation of a cathode-ray tube, and is shown at the bottom of Exhibit 3.5. It should be used only in cases in which the process flow must describe the dissemination of information to the user from a computer terminal.

Of the symbols described here, by far the most common ones used are the process, decision, terminator, and off-page connector. The document symbol will appear from time to time, but the input/output symbols for manual input and data display are falling into disuse. The general rule when using any of these symbols is to keep the number of different types to an absolute minimum so that readers can spend their time interpreting the process flow that they represent, rather than guessing at what they are.

(d) Flow of the Flowchart

Having gone over the types of symbols to include in a flowchart, the next step is to understand the general layout and flow of the flowchart.

The general flow of information should be either from top to bottom or from left to right. A flowchart ideally should be attached to a set of documents that are printed in portrait mode, so the flowchart should also be in portrait mode; this means that the greatest amount of space on the page is from top to bottom, which makes this the most common direction of flow. Whenever a flowchart contains a decision point, there will be a second flow that juts out from one side of the decision symbol. These contingent flows can be charted to either side of the main flow, depending on space considerations; common practice tends to shift them to the right side of the flowchart (if constructing a top-down flowchart) or on the bottom (if constructing a left-to-right flowchart).

When using a decision symbol, the "yes" answer that flows out of the symbol should generally follow the main flow of the process, while "no" answers are shunted off into contingencies on either side of the main process flow. This type of standardization allows a user to follow the diagram more easily if he or she becomes accustomed to always having positive results associated with the main process flow—if there were to be a mix of "yes" and "no" answers in the main flow, then it would take much longer to comprehend the information contained within a flowchart. However, if this convention is used, then it must be followed 100% of the time, for a reader who is accustomed to it may easily pass over a decision point with a different process flow, which may result in an incorrect transaction.

A final point is to only address actions and decisions within a flowchart. By reducing or eliminating the presence of symbols related to inputs, outputs, obvious decisions, or process steps with no discernible activity, a greatly streamlined product that is clear and easily understandable will result. The only case in which this rule can be ignored is when multipart forms are used, as the flowchart format can be very useful for noting which form copies go to which users. To illustrate the points made in this section, Exhibit 3.6 shows a flowchart that follows no rules, and Exhibit 3.7 shows a much cleaner version that contains approximately the same information as Exhibit 3.6, but with standard formatting rules.

Exhibit 3.6 contains a number of excess symbols and improper formatting. For example, there are no fewer than three processes to schedule and hold a meeting—these can be consolidated into one symbol. In addition, there are two process symbols that instruct the user to wait for an outside entity to do something; this is certainly not an activity worthy of mention! There is also a form-signing decision symbol that only has a "no" flowline coming out of it (apparently there is no reason why a "yes" instance would occur!). There are also three cases where documents are listed as sources of information or forms for data entry by employees—these can be safely removed. An overall problem is that the flowchart winds about the page in a manner reminiscent of the Mississippi River; a straighter, top-down reconfiguration would be much more understandable. The result, the much cleaner version shown in Exhibit 3.7, imparts the same information, but does so with approximately half the symbols.

(e) Proper Use of Flowlines

Of particular interest is the use of flowlines within a flowchart. Flowlines are the lines that connect symbols within a flowchart and reveal the direction of process flow. If handled properly, flowlines can result in a clean presentation that does not confuse the reader. Here are a few key points to focus on when creating flowlines:

- *Merge those flowlines having the same destination.* If there are a number of flowlines coming from different points in a flowchart, all of which connect to the same symbol, then one can greatly reduce the number of lines appearing on the flowchart by merging them together at the earliest point so that only a single unified line arrives at the symbol. A "before and after" example of this concept is shown in Exhibit 3.8.
- *Add arrows to long flowlines.* If a flowline is so long that it extends beyond the page, or wraps around one or more symbols, a reader may not understand its direction. To avoid this problem, overlay the flowline with arrows at regular intervals.
- *Avoid crossed flowlines.* A process flow will be barely discernible if flowlines repeatedly cross over each other. There are several ways to avoid this problem. One is to use outgoing and incoming off-page connector symbols on either side of a potential cross-over point so that users can see where the flow is supposed to go. However, this method adds symbols to the flowchart, increasing the

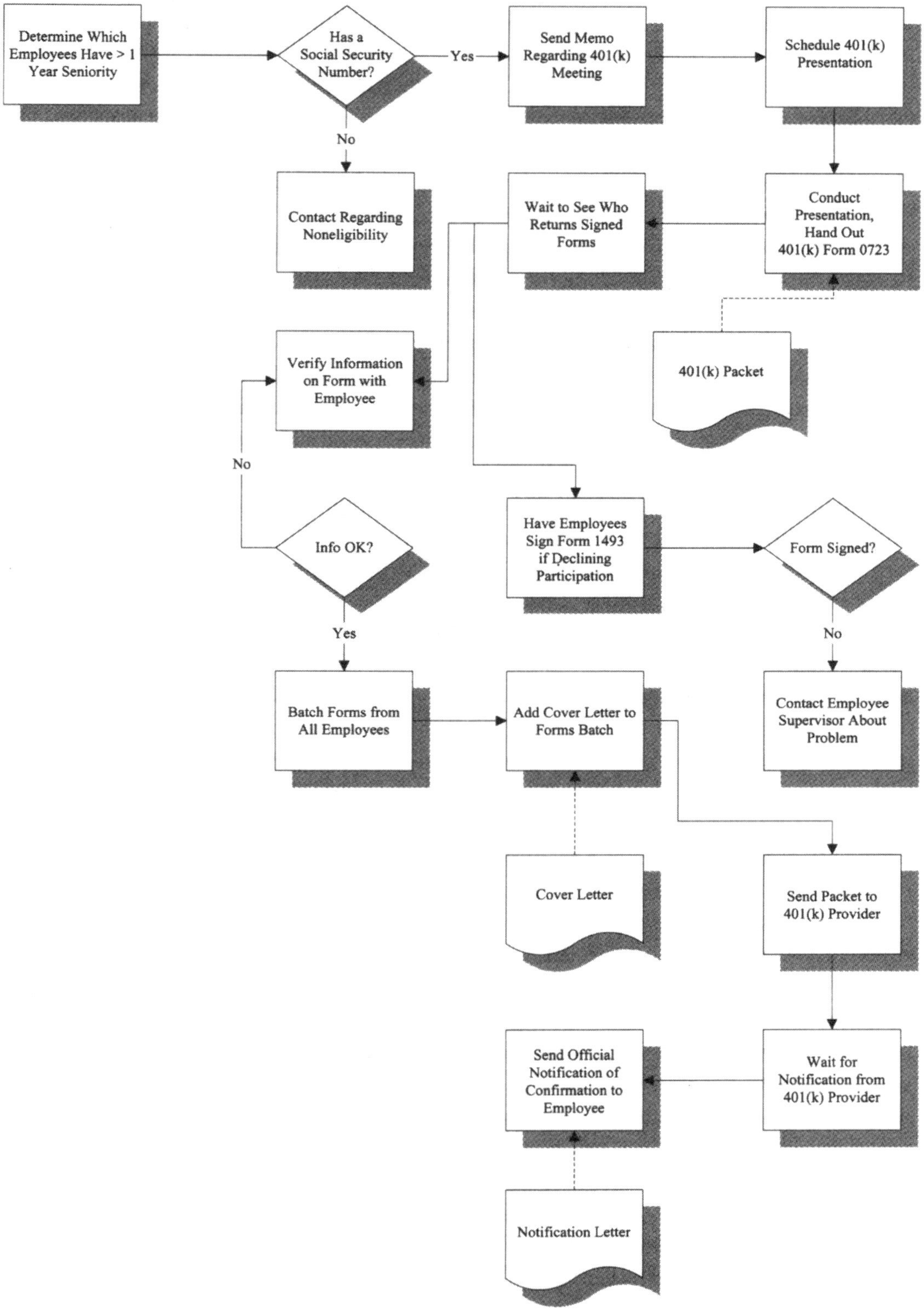

Exhibit 3.6. Poorly Designed Flowchart

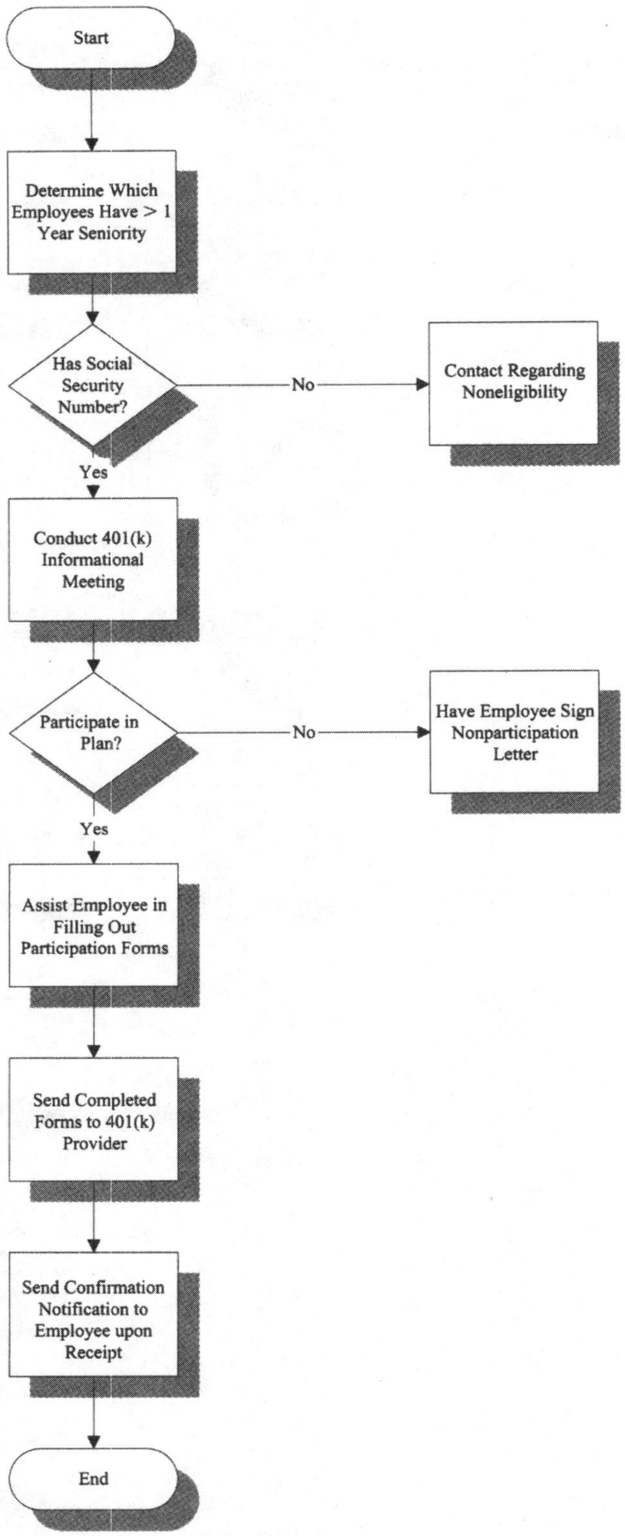

Exhibit 3.7. Properly Formatted Flowchart

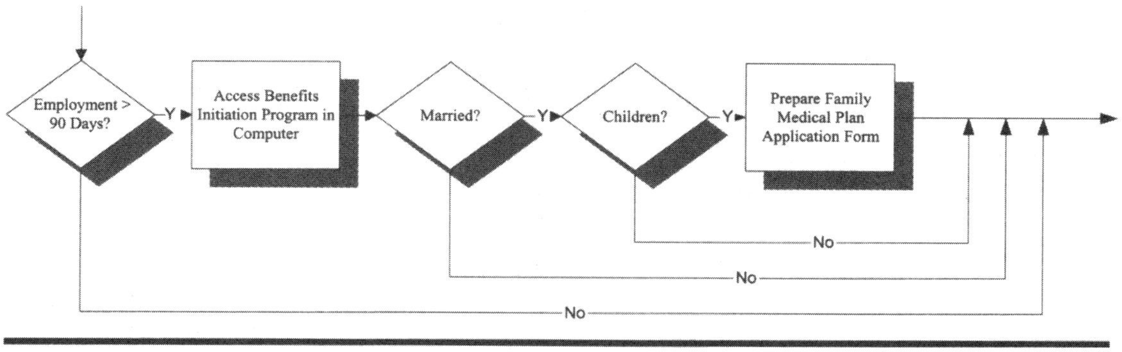

Example of Merged Flowlines:

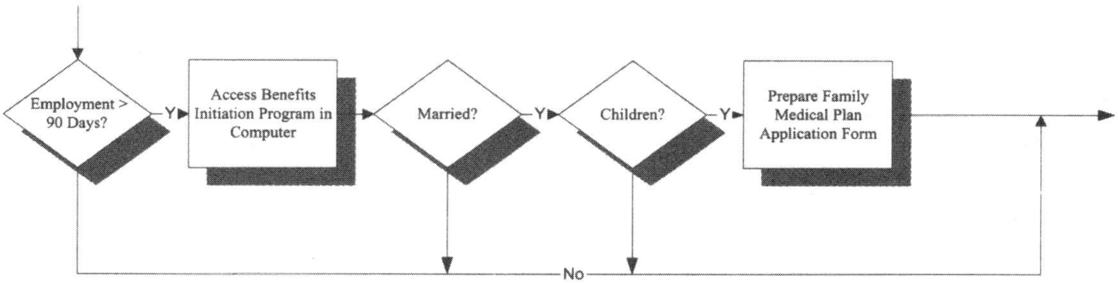

Exhibit 3.8. How to Merge Multiple Flowlines

overall level of clutter. Another approach is to duplicate process steps in different parts of a flowchart, rather than use a crossed line. However, this also results in an increase in symbols. A third solution is to allow the cross-over, but to use a "bubble" that makes the flowline look like it is "hopping" over the underlying flowline. Though less aesthetically pleasing, this approach is generally understandable to the reader. A final option is to see if one's flowcharting software has a rearrange feature that attempts to reconfigure the software to avoid crossed flowlines.

(f) Flowcharted Procedure Examples

This section contains a number of examples of flowcharts for the more common accounting transactions, such as accounts payable, billing, and cash receipts. These are vastly simplified formats, but can be used as the basis for constructing more detailed flowcharts that will more specifically apply to the transactions in one's own accounting system. Wherever possible, the discussion for each flowchart notes those areas that can be expanded upon when converting it to match a company's actual systems.

Exhibit 3.9 contains a flowchart of the accounts payable function. The top half of the flowchart is concerned with the matching of documentation related to a purchase, while the bottom half covers the printing, signing, and distribution of checks to suppliers.

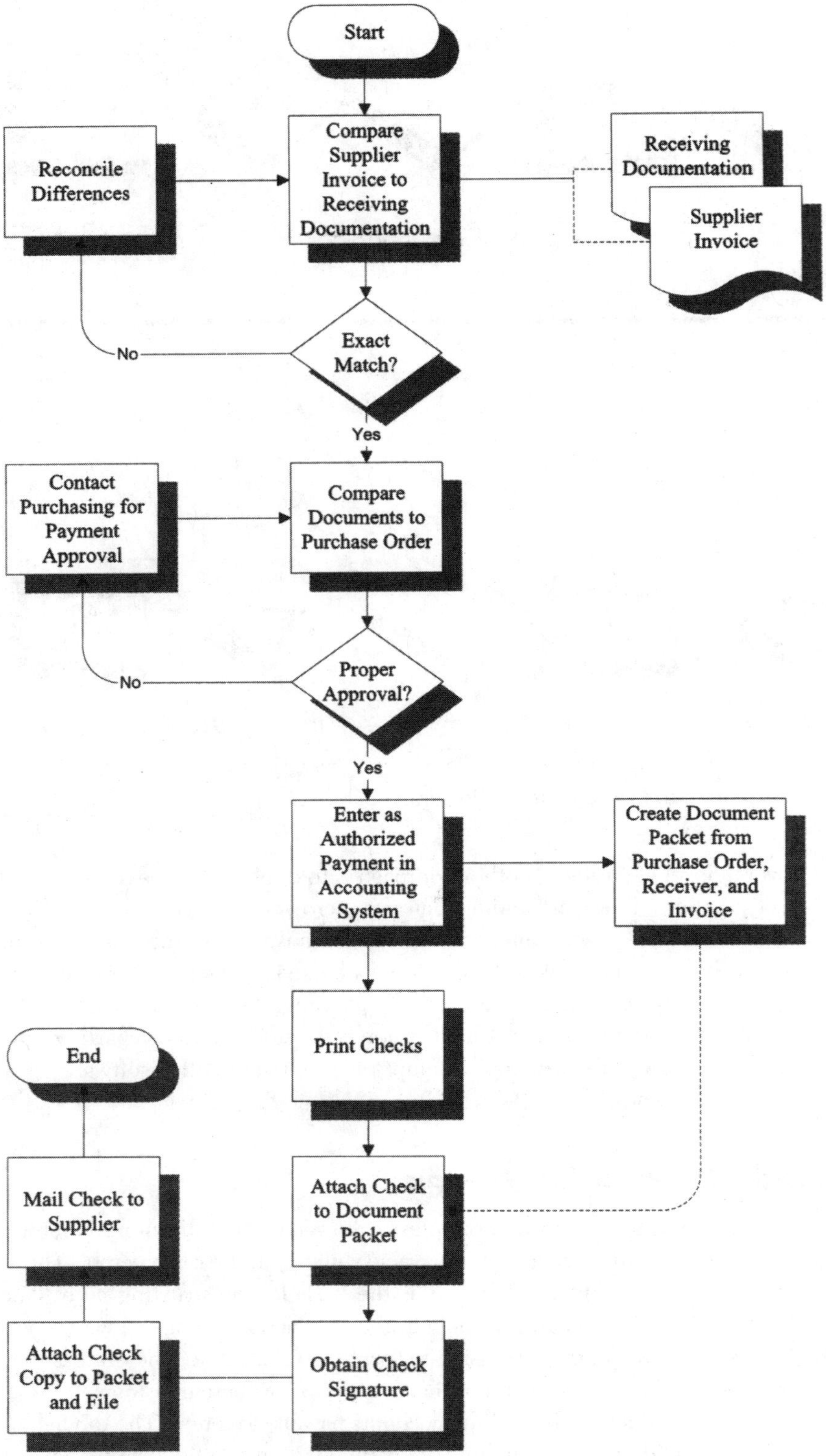

Exhibit 3.9. Accounts Payable Flowchart

A more comprehensive flowchart could also include an off-page connector that shows where the various documents are coming from that are being compared during the matching process. The flowchart can also be expanded to show what happens if an invoice is received but is not authorized by anyone and must be rejected. Also, steps can be added that relate to the various types of signature levels required for checks of different sizes. It may also be necessary to describe the handling of alternative forms of payment and their authorization, such as cash, wire transfers, or automated clearing house (ACH) payments. All of these additions will result in a much larger flowchart, so it may be useful to split it up into numerous smaller flowcharts that are linked with off-page connectors.

Exhibit 3.10 describes a typical billing transaction. Its top half describes the process of verifying invoice information, while the bottom half describes how this information is converted into an invoice. A more detailed version should also include some discussion of the approval process for unusual pricing that has been granted to a customer, as well as alternative forms of invoicing, such as electronic data interchange (EDI) or creating invoices at the point of delivery.

Exhibit 3.11 describes a simplified cash receipts procedure that assumes all cash is received either in the form of checks or ACH transfers. In reality, there are several other types of cash receipt, such as over-the-counter cash, credit card payments, lock box receipts, or wire transfers that should also be described. Also, since this is an area in which theft is always a possibility, there may be a need for some additional steps that describe extra control points.

The next flowchart (Exhibit 3.12) is unique, for it shows the applicability of using parallel activities during the financial statement closing process. Notice how the many closing steps can be greatly compressed by splitting them into separate streams of activities and allowing them to run side by side. In only one case, where accounts payable information feeds into the fixed assets activities, is there any dependence between separate sets of activities. This is a clear-cut case in which the use of a flowchart makes the overall comprehension of a series of processes much easier to understand.

Purchasing is a lengthy process that includes many steps, some of which can be added to Exhibit 3.13 to arrive at a more comprehensive presentation. The existing flowchart shows the general flow of requisitions to the purchasing staff, which puts large items out for bid and then places an order. Other tasks that can be added include the approval process for requisitions, the use of online catalogs to bypass many of the purchasing steps, and the use of procurement cards, plus the different process flow used for blanket purchase orders, not to mention the transmission of purchase orders by EDI. Given the large number of additions to this flowchart, it is generally presented in a multilayered format, with a multitude of off-page connector symbols linking the assemblage together.

3.5 FORMAT OF THE PROCEDURE

A procedure should follow a standard format to the greatest extent possible so that the same set of ancillary information—such as retrieval numbers and issue dates—can be uniformly included in all documents. This makes it easier to update procedures. A standard procedure format is shown in Exhibit 3.14. This layout shows a logo block where a

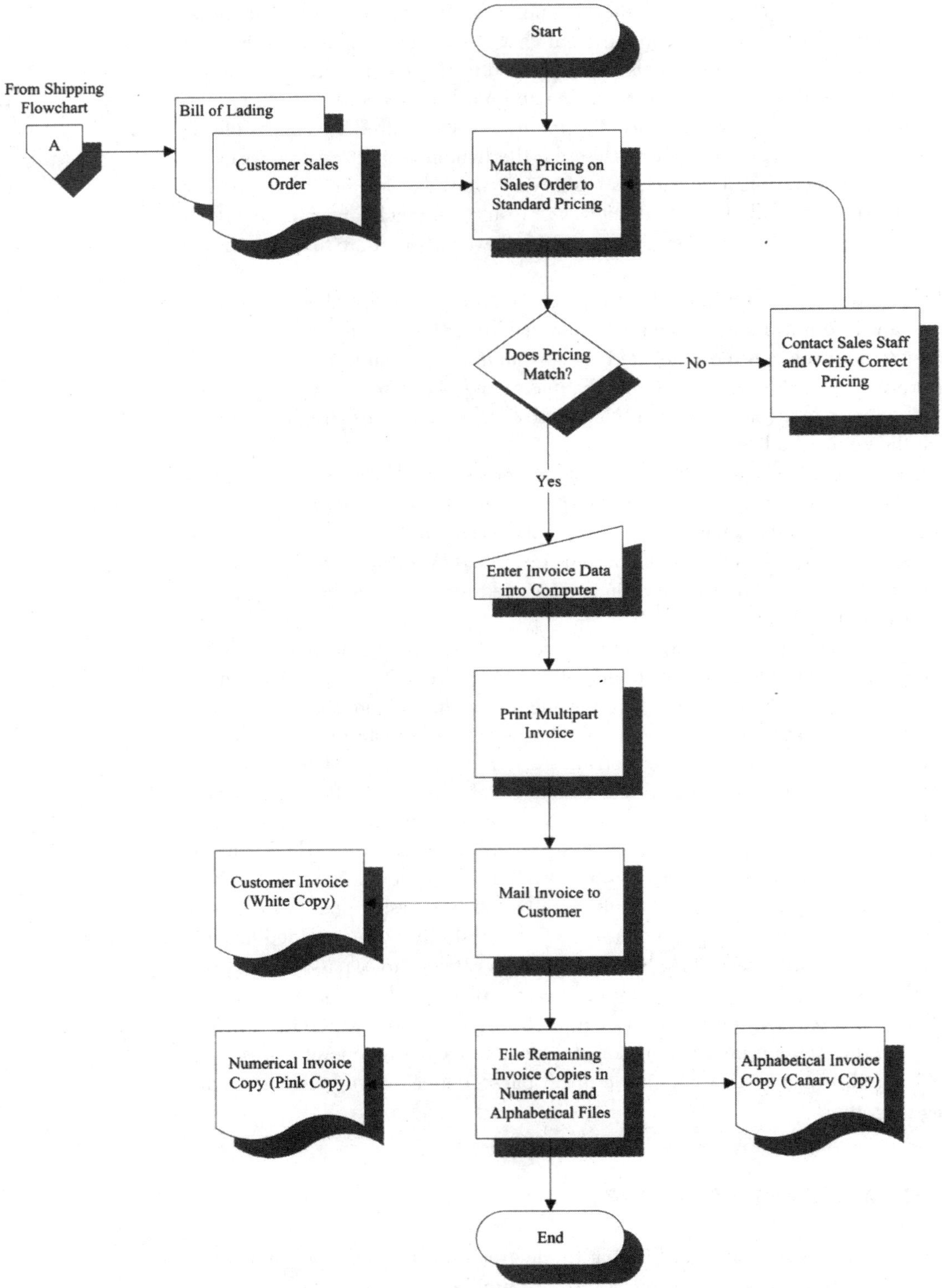

Exhibit 3.10. Billing Flowchart

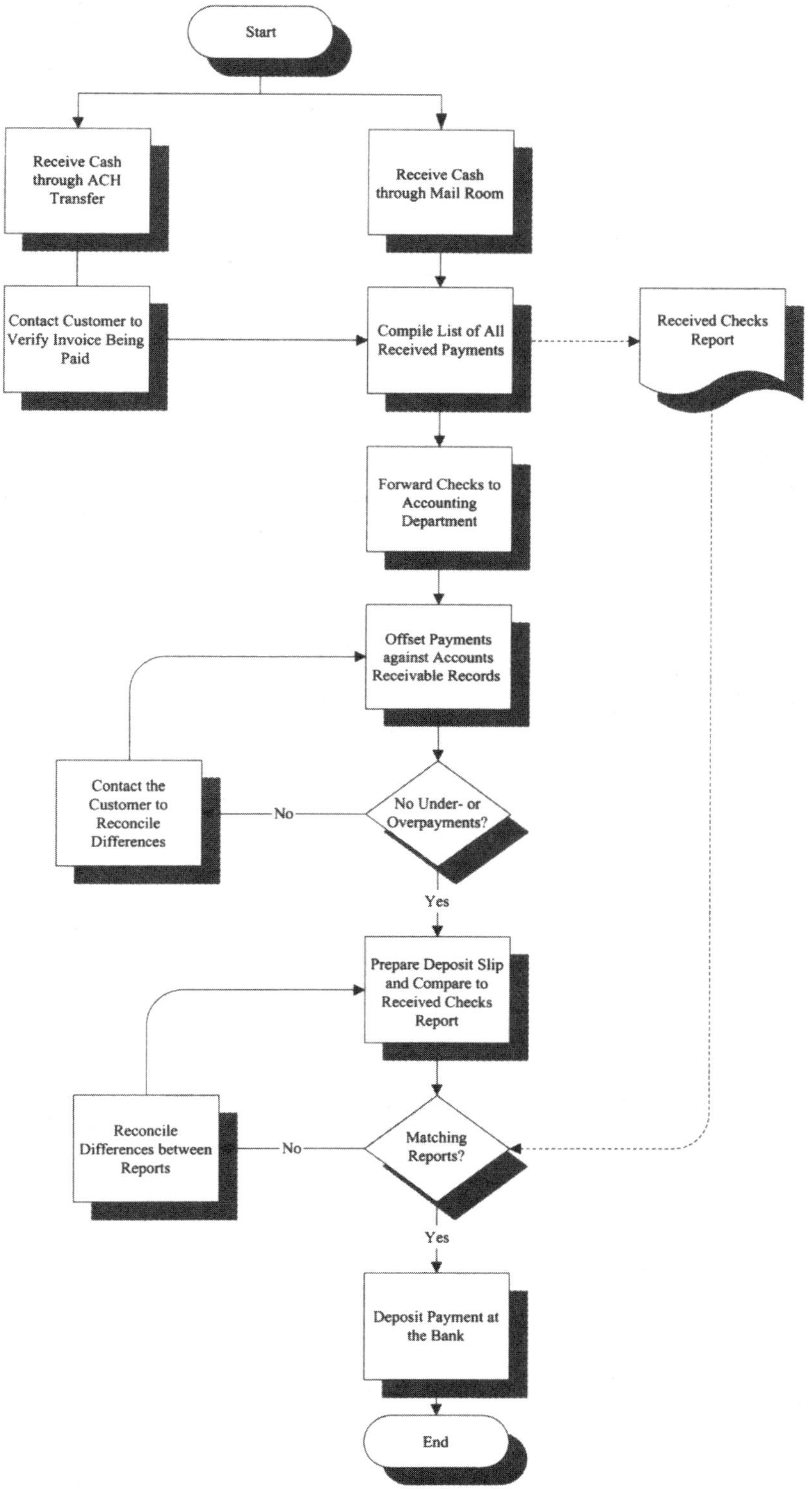

Exhibit 3.11. Cash Receipts Flowchart

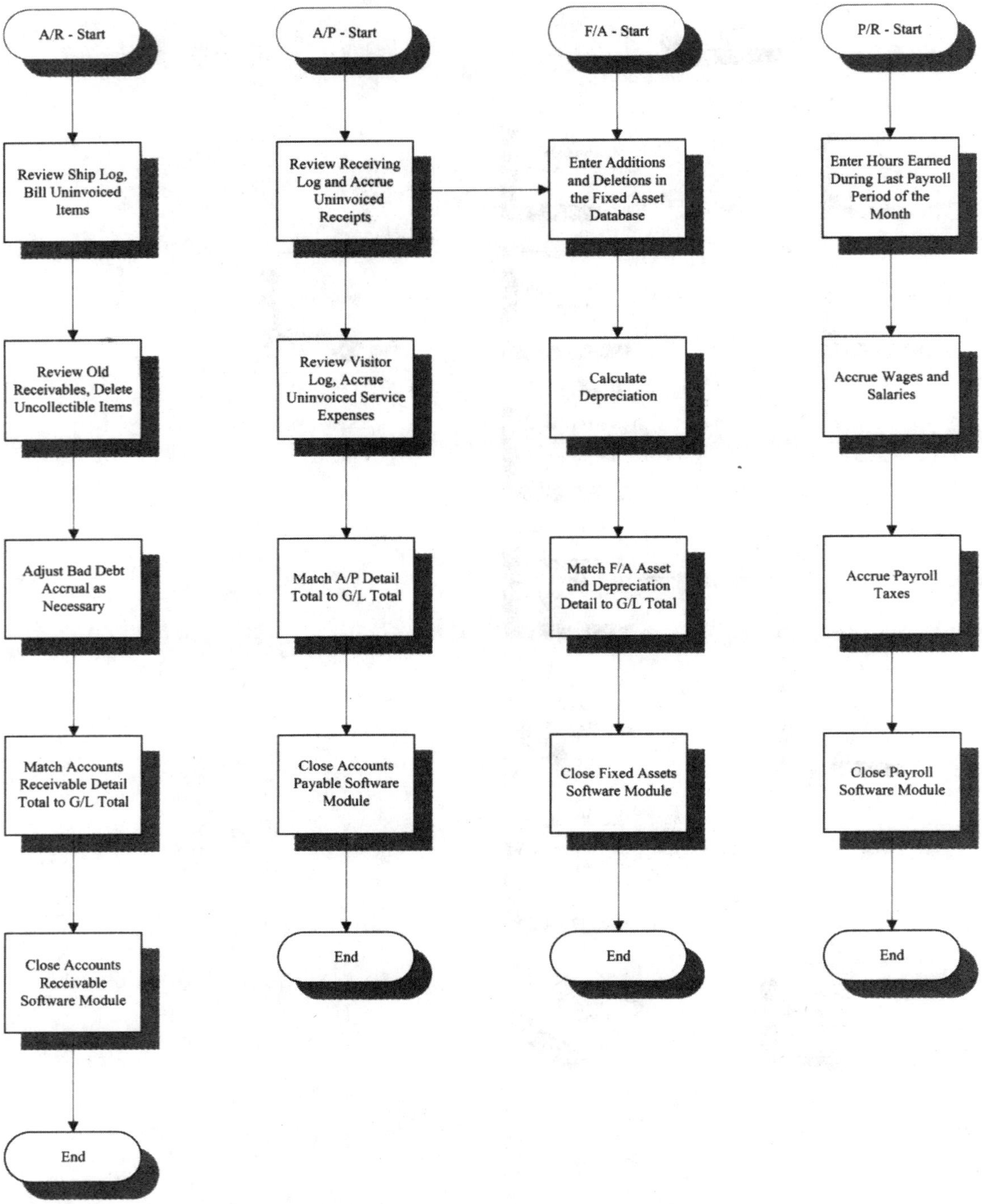

Exhibit 3.12. Financial Statement Closing Flowchart

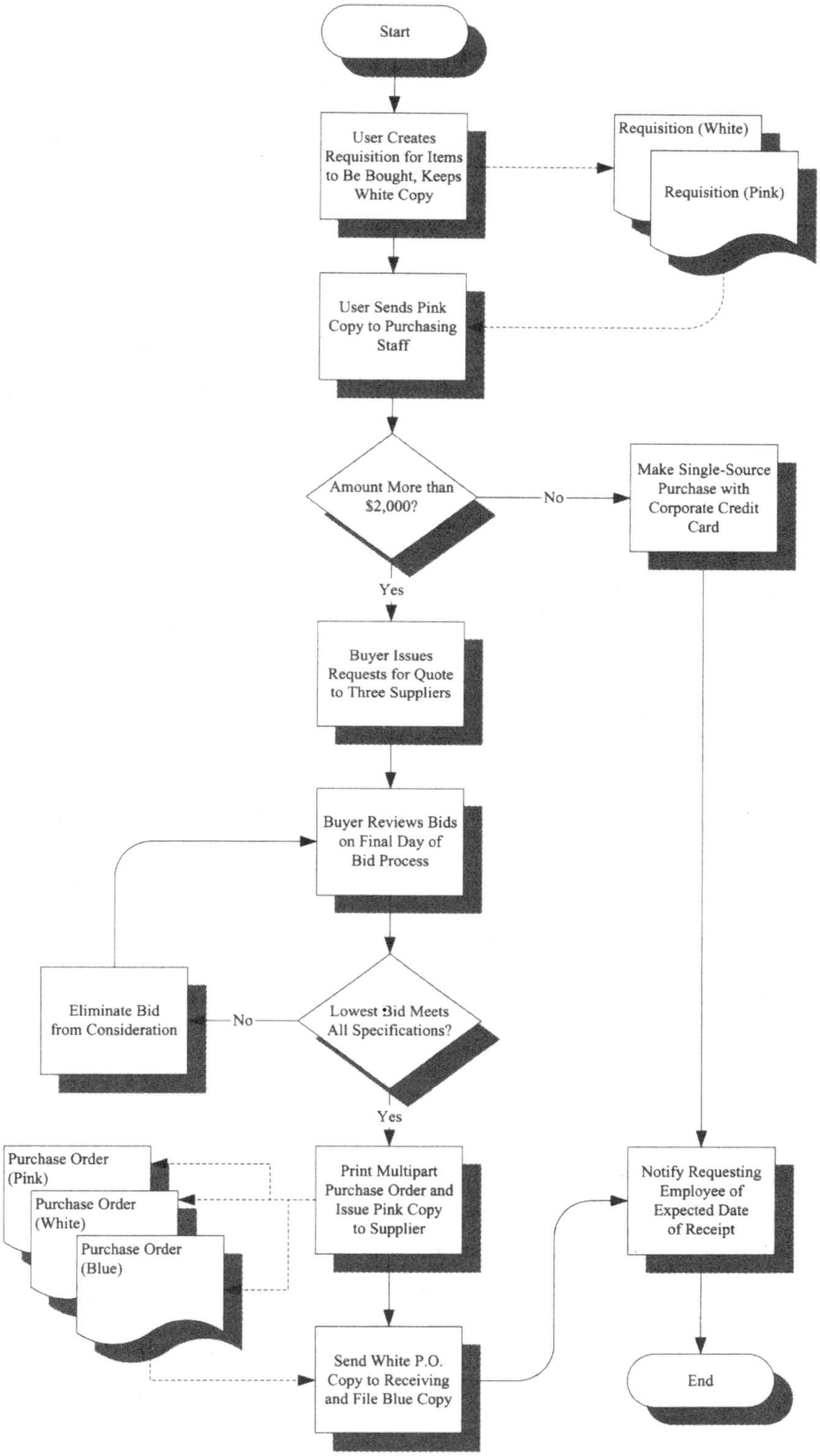

Exhibit 3.13. Purchasing Flowchart

3-Hole
Punched

1" Margin

Policy/Procedure Statement

LOGO

L. O. GRANT ORGANIZATION, INC.

- RETRIEVAL NO. (Assigned when released)
- PAGE (Style 1 of, 2 of, ...)
- ISSUE DATE (Month, day, year)
- ORIGINATOR (Person or Unit)
- SUPERSEDES (Retrieval No. of replaced statement, if applicable)

SUBJECT: (All capital letters) (Used for Indexing)

Background or Problem

Narrative explaining cause of problem and need for revision.

1" Margin

Revised Policy or Procedure

Narrative explanation, effective date, and enforcement.

Revised or New Form (If Applicable)

Uses of the form and general instructions.

Completing the Form (If Applicable)

Detailed instructions for completing each area of the form.

Summary

Name, address, telephone number where assistance can be obtained.

Attachments: (Use exact name of attachments)

Distribution: (Optional)

Exhibit 3.14. Standard Procedure Layout Specifications

company's logo should be copied into the document, as well as a header block in the upper right corner that contains a standard set of identification information. The main text area contains a brief header describing the procedure subject, as well as the detailed procedure (or instructions for completing a form) and some additional information.

Within the format shown in Exhibit 3.14, a procedure is laid out as a series of consecutively numbered tasks that accomplish a specific function. A procedure documents the flow of data and what each described work area does to that data to process it and pass it forward to the next work area. It is not a job description, job outline, policy, or form description.

The first part of the procedure is the header section, which includes a standard set of identification information. An example of a header is shown in Exhibit 3.15, where we see listed a company logo, retrieval number, page number, issue date, and the retrieval number of any document being superceded.

The narrative portion of a procedure begins immediately below the header block. Although the format of this section can vary considerably, the general narrative pattern for a procedure is an opening paragraph on the background of the subject and the intent of the procedure. This first paragraph may be labeled Background or Present Procedure. This paragraph is followed by a detailed itemization of the new procedure. If the user may require additional information, the bottom of the procedure can include a contact name or phone number to call. If there is an attachment to the procedure, such as a flow chart or form, it is described at the end of the procedure, and is identified using the exact header name used for the attachment. One can also include a distribution list that identifies the departments or positions to which the procedure should be sent.

The following four examples illustrate how general policies and procedures are developed, in what order the information is presented, and the probable distribution of each one; they also illustrate the considerable versatility of this system.

Example 1: Sales Department Reorganization

A company sells products to original equipment manufacturers (OEMs), to wholesale distributors, and to large retailers. This information is presented as background material at the beginning of the procedure narrative.

Sales have fallen off. The next section of the procedure describes what actions will be taken to deal with this problem, and how it will be implemented. This includes setting up separate sales teams for each customer type, which will require a different supporting management structure and account code system to record transactions. The procedure can also list the types of internal reports that will be generated to track

Policy/Procedure Statement Brasto Publishing **Subject: Monthly Journal Entry Review**	Retrieval No.: Page: Issue Date: Supercedes:	10-150 1 of 3 3/15/0X 10-148

Exhibit 3.15. Standard Procedure Header Format

this new system, and to whom the reports will be distributed (probably the executive officers, the entire sales force, and accounts payable manager).

Example 2: New Corporate Committee

The policy and procedure format is used to describe the creation of a new budgeting committee. The subject line would read *New Budget Committee*. The opening paragraph states the purpose of the committee and any expected benefits of having it.

The body of the document will describe how the committee is formed, what positions serve on it, the frequency and location of meetings, and its expected output. Distribution would be to all executive officers and department managers. This approach is quite useful in larger organizations where several committees function on a regular basis.

Example 3: Release of Financial Information

An organization may receive requests from outside entities, such as the press or credit reporting agencies, for financial information. Sometimes the person receiving the request is not fully qualified to give such information. The problem can be resolved by the use of a policy statement that defines the rules for release of such information and that also names the positions qualified to release such information.

The subject *Release of Financial Information* would define the contents of the policy. The opening paragraph would explain the problem and how it may adversely impact the organization. The second paragraph, which might be labeled *Policy for Release of Financial Information*, would set up a procedure under which any employee receiving a request for financial information would forward it to one of the authorized personnel noted in the procedure. There may be further information regarding specific restrictions on certain types of information, and under what circumstances legal counsel should be involved.

Example 4: New Receiving Report

A potential receiving problem has been discovered, so a new receiving procedure must be issued to address the problem. The company issuing the procedure buys large quantities of steel bars and rolls of sheet steel. Raw material inventories have been consistently short, and a review of existing procedures reveals that the receiving department always records the weights from the supplier-affixed mill tags on each roll received. The solution is to install scales at the receiving dock, weigh each item received, and enter both the mill tag weight and measured weight on the receiving report.

The background paragraph should explain the underlying problem of raw material shortages and the probable cause, and the next section would describe the revised weighing and reporting procedure, as well as the form alteration that creates space to report on actual received weights. Distribution would be to all accountants involved in inventory control, and the entire receiving department.

Once a set of procedures has been created, one should categorize them in a master index procedure so that one can easily determine what procedures are available, when they were created, where they can be located, and to whom they are issued. An example of such an index is shown in Exhibit 3.16.

Policy/Procedure Statement	Retrieval No.:	Index
Brasto Publishing	Page:	1 of 2
	Issue Date:	12/31/02
	Supercedes:	N/A
Subject: Cumulative Index through December 31, 2002		

Retrieval Number	Date	Distribution	Subject
10-000	3/15/02	Cash Clerk	Authorize a wire transfer payment
10-001	3/15/02	Cash Clerk	Process cash receipts
10-002	3/15/02	Cash Clerk	Process credit card payments
10-003	3/15/02	Cash Clerk	Process credit card refunds
10-004	3/15/02	Cash Clerk	Reconcile bank statement to book balance
10-005	3/15/02	Cash Clerk	Reconcile petty cash
10-101	4/30/02	Ledger Clerk	Accrue for earned vacation time
10-102	4/30/02	Ledger Clerk	Accrue for income taxes payable
10-103	4/30/02	Ledger Clerk	Accrue for unpaid wages
10-104	4/30/02	Ledger Clerk	Accrue for warranty expenses
10-105	4/30/02	Ledger Clerk	Calculate earnings per share
10-106	4/30/02	Ledger Clerk	Create journal entries
10-107	4/30/02	Ledger Clerk	Create the budget
10-108	4/30/02	Ledger Clerk	Calculate accruals
10-201	5/31/02	Treasury	Conduct a daily cash sweep
10-202	5/31/02	Treasury	Create borrowing base certificate
10-203	5/31/02	Treasury	Issue capital stock
10-204	5/31/02	Treasury	Issue dividends
10-205	5/31/02	Treasury	Pay for outstanding debt
10-206	5/31/02	Treasury	Prepare a cash forecast
10-207	5/31/02	Treasury	Process a letter of credit
10-301	6/30/02	Assets Clerk	Calculate depreciation on fixed assets
10-302	6/30/02	Assets Clerk	Conduct inventory of fixed assets
10-303	6/30/02	Assets Clerk	Enter fixed asset payments
10-304	6/30/02	Assets Clerk	Evaluate capital purchase proposals
10-305	6/30/02	Assets Clerk	Record gain/loss on sale of an asset
10-401	7/31/02	Inventory Clerk	Cycle count inventory
10-402	7/31/02	Inventory Clerk	Physical count inventory
10-403	7/31/02	Inventory Clerk	Track scrap transactions
10-501	8/31/02	Payroll Clerk	Calculate excess life insurance payments
10-502	8/31/02	Payroll Clerk	Calculate payroll taxes
10-503	8/31/02	Payroll Clerk	Calculate profit sharing
10-504	8/31/02	Payroll Clerk	Process payroll transactions
10-505	8/31/02	Payroll Clerk	Summarize timesheets

Exhibit 3.16. Procedures Index

3.6 WORK STEPS FOR CONSTRUCTING A PROCEDURES MANUAL

Constructing a procedures manual is a major project for all but the smallest organizations. These steps are designed to provide structure to the process and create boundaries over the number of procedures being produced, which will keep the organization from getting bogged down in an endless cycle of procedure creation and updating.

1. *Define the project.* The largest single problem with the construction of a procedures manual is that no one knows when to stop. Instead, new procedures keep pouring in from all parts of the company for the most mundane and inconsequential items, resulting in a massive manual that is never truly finished and is never issued. To avoid this, it is very important to define immediately the company functions for which procedures will (and will not) be written, as well as make a rough guess at the total number of procedures that will be generated. This keeps the project within boundaries that give it a reasonable expectation of completion.

2. *Obtain a project sponsor.* No project of any size is ever completed unless there is someone in upper management who believes strongly enough in the project to support it through budget battles and the allocation of other scarce corporate resources. The positions that are generally most interested in a procedures manual are the chief financial officer and chief operating officer, so these people should be approached first. If they are not interested, the controller is also acceptable, though this person tends to have less influence over other parts of the company, which may result in a manual that covers only the accounting and finance areas.

3. *Determine the size of the project team.* The only other item needed prior to making a budget request for funds is to determine the size of the project team, because the main expense is labor. To do so, take the previously estimated total number of procedures, multiply them by a generous estimated number of hours each, and factor in an overage percentage, resulting in an approximate number of man-hours for the work. Then determine the average pay rate per person, and multiply this amount by the total number of estimated hours to determine the total labor expense. It may also be necessary to budget for some travel to outlying company locations, as well as for office space for the team and the production and distribution costs of the manual.

4. *Obtain an approved budget.* Present the proposed budget through the usual budget process, using the project sponsor to obtain approvals when needed. If the approved budget level is inadequate, scale back the number of procedures to be written to reflect the number of paid hours available. If reduction is needed, give feedback to the project sponsor regarding the pared-down size of the manual so that there will be no surprises when it is eventually issued.

5. *Determine the number of procedures to be written.* A general estimate of the total number of procedures to be added to the manual was done initially, but now it is time to develop a master list of procedures. To do so, each department should be contacted and asked for a full list of the procedures they would like to have. List all these procedures together and determine the total number in the list. It is almost always far more than the budgeted number. Then work with the department managers to throw out the least important procedures. This can be a time-consuming process; some managers

will insist on having more than their share of procedures, so the project sponsor must intervene to decide which departments will be given more or less than their fair share of procedures. When complete, there should be a master list of procedures that the project team uses as its basis for all future planning.

6. *Prioritize the procedures.* Once the master list of procedures is complete, it is necessary to determine which are the most important. Though all of them may be completed, one should always complete a core set of procedures first, in case funds are cut off before the project is finished or a need arises for an advance release of the procedures before they have all been completed. The criteria for establishing importance can vary considerably, such as ranking one department over another if the department's work is considered more critical. Another method is to complete all of the procedures related to a specific process cycle, such as order fulfillment or purchasing, so that those activities are completely documented. The common approach is a political one, whereby each department receives an allocation of procedures; though not necessarily the best way to prioritize procedures, this method does allow all departments to participate in the process at about the same time, which increases the degree of user buy-in to the project and gives it a better overall chance of success.

7. *Establish a time line.* A set of due dates and milestones should be assigned to the project, to establish boundaries for when work is expected to be completed. For example, there should be regularly scheduled review dates to ensure that progress on procedures is acceptable. There should also be milestones for the completion of specific groups of procedures (usually for easily grouped clusters, such as by department or process cycle).

8. *Issue requests for existing procedures.* Based on the master list of prioritized procedures, send out requests to all department managers, asking for any existing documentation of targeted procedures. The returned information may include paper-based or electronic procedure formats, and may be in text or graphical mode. Whatever the format, it is wise to collect as much existing procedural information as possible, as this forms a foundation for subsequent interviews and, in many cases, also provides such complete information that there is little additional work to do, except for reformatting the material into a standard procedure layout.

9. *Undertake initial interviews.* Using any previously collected documentation, go to the departments that need procedures and obtain additional information through interviews. This should include multiple interviews whenever possible so that one cannot only verify information with different people, but also have the same interviewees review the interviewer's written notes for accuracy. As a general rule, the first interview *will* result in erroneous procedural information, so follow-up interviews are necessary to increase the level of information accuracy

10. *Send out preliminary procedures for review.* Once the procedures have been completed, send them out to the department managers for review. These people will probably pass along the documents to the experts within their organisations who are most able to determine if there are any inaccuracies in the information. It is helpful to determine in advance if other employees should also review the preliminary procedures. This is a key point for procedures that are used by multiple departments—simply

having one of the users review them does not cover the full range of possible users. Also, when sending procedures out for review, it is helpful to attach a review form to them, explaining how to review a procedure, as well as how to note changes to the document. There should also be a control document for tracking when procedures are sent for review, as well as when they were received back and who reviewed them. This document is most useful for determining which reviewers have not returned documents so that timely follow-up to complete the review process can be done.

11. *Update preliminary procedures.* Once the procedures have been reviewed and returned, input the changes into the procedures database. This step should include an independent review of the updated documents by an experienced editor who can verify that all required changes were made, as well as ensure that the documents use correct grammatical conventions. There should also be a control document for this stage of work, because procedure updates may be performed over a long period of time (depending on how long it takes to recover documents that are out for review), and some updates may be missed. By regularly examining the control document, on which are noted the procedures that have been updated, it is an easy matter to track down and update those still requiring this work

12. *Approve procedures.* Approvals should be kept to a minimum. If only accounting information is released, a three-step preparation and approval system generally works best. The system consists of origination, editing for accuracy and consistency, and officer approval. Origination is done best at the unit level, such as by the manager of payroll, payables, budgeting, and so forth. The controller should then review the proposed release for consistency and accuracy. Finally, the chief financial officer's staff should review the proposed release for possible legal conflicts, as well as conflicts with the procedures of other company segments. If approved, the procedure is released for general distribution.

13. *Assemble procedures manuals.* Once the procedures have been approved, they must be formatted properly. The typical format includes a company logo, the date of the procedure, the page number, the version number, and the index number. Once the procedures are formatted, the publisher must be notified of how many copies to print, which is based on the distribution list (see next item). Also, the type of binder must be determined, which may include inserts on the spine and cover itemizing the contents. Finally, depending on the size of the volume, it may be useful to include index tabs that delineate the procedures of each department. There are a wide range of prices, depending on the layouts, types of binders, inserts, and use of color, so try to match the budget to the options selected.

14. *Determine procedures distribution list.* Once the procedures writing is completed, it is time to determine who should receive the resulting manuals. This can be as simple as issuing a fixed number of manuals to each department head and giving them the responsibility for handing out the books. However, this tends to result in an uneven distribution of valuable documents, so it is generally best to determine, with the assistance of the department managers and the human resources coordinator, what job titles should receive a procedures manual. This approach makes it a simple matter to distribute manuals based on the job descriptions listed in the human resources database. It is also necessary to determine which parts of the manual go to each recipient. For a very large manual, possibly encompassing a multitude of binders, it can be cost-prohibitive

to distribute all of it to everyone, especially those who do not need it. Accordingly, the list of position titles to whom the manual should go must also include a description of exactly what part of the manual is to be sent.

15. *Distribute procedures manuals.* Once the procedures binders arrive from the printer, it becomes a simple matter to use the distribution list to send out procedures manuals to recipients, either through interoffice mail (if there is one location) or the postal service (if there are many locations). If there are multiple locations, it may be necessary to update the distribution list (see the preceding step) with mailing addresses for each recipient. All mailings should include a note asking the receiving organization to return the binder if the recipient no longer works for the company so that these expensive documents can be used elsewhere.

16. *Determine frequency of review.* Once the initial procedures documentation work is completed, it is time to determine how frequently the process should be repeated. Integral to the frequency question are the funds available, the likely need for additional new procedures (especially common if businesses are being added that are unrelated to existing ones), and the need for rapid updates. This last factor is most important if a company uses its procedures manual as a training tool for employees—if the actual procedure is no longer correctly reflected in the written procedures, the binder is of no further use as a training tool. A typical review cycle is once a year, with more frequent updates only if the department needing the update designates it as being on a rush basis (which can be limited by charging the rush update work back to the requesting department!).

17. *Obtain approval of budget continuations.* Once the frequency of procedures updates has been determined, one must make estimates of the continuing staff time and distribution costs that will be needed. Because these are the two main cost drivers for the process, it is then a simple matter to compile a budget request for the upcoming year that should encompass the project requirements. The main variables that may require an increase in funding are requests for a number of new procedures, more recipients of the expensive procedures binders, or the addition of new subsidiaries that also require new procedures writing.

18. *Write a project review.* Once the project is complete and the budget request has been submitted for the upcoming year, there is one step remaining—to review the entire process with participants to see whether any problems with the process came up that could be corrected the next time around. This is a frequently ignored step, as everyone involved wants to move on to other work. However, this is a critical step for reducing the work required to produce quality procedures when valuable staff time can be used elsewhere, and costs can be lowered in the future. In short, a carefully reviewed and documented project review is an excellent way to leave recommendations for the next project team assigned to updating procedures, making the process easier and less expensive in the future.

The exact process used to create or update a procedures manual will vary from company to company. Some businesses are so small that many of the preceding steps are unnecessary—a few people can gather a sufficient amount of information in a short time to rapidly assemble a reputable procedures manual. Other companies have so many far-flung divisions that the procedures writing chore becomes massive, with a full-time team to research and write procedures and an ongoing staff to handle updates. In this environment, the preceding process steps are clearly not sufficient for timely and successful completion of the project. Instead, these steps are designed to serve the needs of the majority of small- to medium-sized businesses with enough departments and procedures to require a formal documentation process.

3.7 SUGGESTED LIST OF PROCEDURES

The exact procedures chosen will depend on their criticality within a specific business, as well as how much they are needed as control points. Also important are the amount of resources consumed by them and the proportion of total time taken by an employee to complete them. Thus, the procedures chosen for inclusion in a procedures manual will vary considerably by company. A short list of the more common procedures can be used as the basis for a procedures manual:

Cash

- Authorize a wire transfer payment.
- Process cash receipts.
- Process credit card payments.
- Process credit card refunds.
- Reconcile bank statement to book balance.
- Reconcile petty cash.

Financial Statements

- Accrue for earned vacation time.
- Accrue for income taxes payable.
- Accrue for unpaid wages.
- Accrue for warranty expenses.
- Calculate earnings per share.
- Calculate overhead costs and application thereof.
- Create journal entries.
- Create the budget.
- Calculate accruals.
- Enter the budget into the financial statement report.

Financing

- Conduct a daily cash sweep.
- Create borrowing base certificate.

- Issue capital stock.
- Issue dividends.
- Pay for outstanding debt.
- Prepare a cash forecast.
- Process a letter of credit.
- Request additional debt from a revolving credit line.

Fixed Assets

- Calculate depreciation on fixed assets.
- Conduct inventory of fixed assets.
- Enter fixed asset payments.
- Evaluate capital purchase proposals.
- Record gain/loss on sale of an asset.

Inventory and Purchasing

- Cycle count inventory.
- Physical count inventory.
- Purchase under economic order quantity calculations.
- Purchase small tools and supplies.
- Receive deliveries from unqualified suppliers.
- Receive deliveries from qualified suppliers.
- Track scrap transactions.

Payroll

- Calculate excess life insurance payments.
- Calculate payroll taxes.
- Calculate profit sharing.
- Process payroll transactions.
- Summarize timesheets.

Payments

- Calculate commissions.
- Calculate royalties.
- Calculate sales taxes.
- Match receiving, purchasing, and supplier documents.

- Obtain authorization for non–purchase order acquisitions.
- Print 1099 forms.
- Process manual check payments.
- Review expense reimbursements.
- Void checks.

Sales

- Authorization of bad debts.
- Billings to employees.
- Calculation of allowance for bad debt reserve.
- Collection of overdue accounts.
- Create customer invoices.
- Issue credit to customers.
- Record sales returns.
- Record scrap sales.

Other

- Conduct due diligence review of an acquisition.

The preceding list is meant for just the accounting department, but the accountant may also be called upon to prepare procedures for other departments. Unfortunately, this project encompasses so many functional areas that it is difficult to determine where to start. The following is a sample listing, sorted by functional area, of the most common procedures that may be needed in a procedures manual for most companies. These are just the core procedures; additional procedures will be needed based on the special requirements of each company, which are determined mainly by the structure of the organization and the industry in which it is located.

Administration

- Copier and fax repairs
- Ordering office supplies
- Reception management
- Voice mail setup

Computer Systems

- Daily batch processing
- Database maintenance
- Database purging
- E-mail setup

- Password maintenance
- Programming request processing
- Restore from backup
- System backup
- System security maintenance
- Time clock backup

Engineering

- Bill of material creation
- Changing standard costs
- Effectivity date changes
- Engineering change notices
- Engineering document numbering
- Engineering document storage
- Project prioritization
- Project tracking
- Work order routing

Human Resources

- 401(k) change processing
- Birthday notifications
- Cafeteria plan change processing
- Forklift training
- Injury reports
- Last pay increase/review notification
- Life insurance change processing
- Medical insurance change processing
- Safety training
- Security review
- Training request

Logistics

- Capacity planning
- Cycle counting
- Floor stock location maintenance

- Master schedule maintenance
- Master scheduling
- Material returns to suppliers
- Opening, reviewing, and closing orders
- Order entry
- Order picking
- Physical inventory count
- Product recall receipts
- Production scheduling
- Purchase orders
- Purchasing for prototypes
- Receiving
- Resolving scheduling conflicts
- Returns to suppliers
- Running material requirements reports
- Scrap reporting
- Shipping
- Supplier master records, adding
- Staging
- Weekly planning meeting

Production

- Lock out/tag out
- Machine calibration
- Machine maintenance requests
- Machine preventive maintenance
- Machine shutdown check-off list
- Machine startup check-off list
- Maintenance on-call procedure
- Scrap reporting

Quality Assurance

- Corrective action reports
- First and last piece inspection

- Inspection equipment calibration
- Inspection equipment control
- Nonconforming material control
- Placing production on hold status
- Quality records maintenance
- Receiving returned goods
- Sample retention
- Temporary deviation

Sales

- Forecast management
- Price book maintenance
- Pricing changes
- Quoting
- Recall notifications
- Sales forecasting
- Special services quotes

3.8 OTHER USES FOR PROCEDURES MANUALS

The accounting department is not the only company function that can profit from the use of a properly created and maintained procedures manual. It is also useful in any situation where a department's operations can benefit from a set of consistently performed procedures. Examples of such areas are the Management Information Systems department (which needs a data processing manual to cover such issues as system backups, disaster recovery planning, and the timely production of scheduled reports) and the Human Resources department (which needs a manual dealing with all employee-related benefits, safety issues, and disciplinary concerns). Examples of procedure manuals for these two departments are included in later chapters of this book.

Chapter 4

MAINTAINING AND DISTRIBUTING ACCOUNTING MANUALS

4.1 INTRODUCTION

The process of creating an accounting manual does not end with the creation of policies and procedures, for even the best manual will be of no use if it is not properly organized and distributed in a manner that makes it thoroughly readable and instructive. In this chapter, we will explain why a master copy of the manual must be kept, even for years after it has been superceded. Also, we will review the mechanics of physically assembling the accounting manual, determining the best possible members for the distribution list, and ensuring that everyone receives and understands it. This can be a very complex process, especially in a multilocation organization. By the end of this chapter, it will become apparent that the distribution task is crucial to the overall success of an accounting manual.

The greatest innovation to come to the field of accounting manual design and maintenance in many years is the conversion of manuals to an electronic format. In this chapter, we will explore the various types and combinations of formats that can be used, as well as discuss why these changes are beneficial and how to create electronic manuals. The reader may be interested in overhauling the entire current system of accounting manual presentation to take advantage of current innovations.

4.2 MAINTAINING ACCOUNTING MANUALS

As soon as a new manual has been released, maintenance is not far behind. Accounting manual changes consist of adding or deleting something, changing a record, account, or procedure, or clarifying a previous release. Maintenance of documentation can vary considerably, from a minor change that may affect only a few people to a massive change such as the installation of new systems or major overhaul of existing systems.

There are three levels of change and several ways to announce or publish changes. Minor changes—such as adding or deleting one or a few account numbers, income or expense codes, or approval authorizations—can be reported by interoffice correspondence or memoranda to those departments or employees affected by the change. The memorandum would specify the change and the reason for it; the change would be related to a specific manual or prior release with enough information to enable the recipient to enter the change in his or her copy of the proper manual.

Intermediate changes, such as the replacement of a significant portion of a manual, the introduction of a new form, a significant change in an existing form, or a policy or procedural change that may affect most operations within the company, are disclosed through the policy/procedure statement (P/PS) system, possibly in conjunction with replacement sections of the manual as attachments.

A major change, such as a new accounting system, a new data processing system affecting users, or a replacement of several action or transaction forms, would require the rewriting and reissuance of the manual, or major sections thereof if the changed affected only one or two separate sections of a manual. These types of changes are noted in Exhibit 4.1 in relation to how they are used for each of the various manuals. In all cases, the determination that maintenance is required and the level of reporting changes are both subjective and judgmental. The person or group most closely related to each manual is probably the best source for determining the impact of an addition, deletion, or other change to that manual.

Each of the manuals discussed in this book require the levels and methods of reporting changes related to typical maintenance items:

General Accounting Manual

Typical minor changes consist of adding or deleting a few account codes, or a change in a form. In most cases, changes of this type only affect one or two employees or departments, so the logical method of reporting the change is a memorandum to the affected users.

The introduction of a new form or replacement of an existing form, changes in many account numbers, or changes in organizational structure with little impact on the general accounting procedures are best reported through the P/PS system. It is here that the background information can be reported, the changes can be described in any amount of detail desired, and the distribution can be handled in an effective manner. However, if several P/PS statements are issued over a short time period, you should consider reissuing the manual or major subsections—a major change.

A major change in the general accounting manual would be the introduction of many new accounts, a new general accounting system or major subsystem, a reorganization of a significant portion of the operations of the company, or substantial changes in data entry processing or processing methods and reports.

General Accounting Manual

- *Minor change.* Use memorandum to user departments.
- *Intermediate change.* Use policy/procedure statement.
- *Major change.* Reissue manual or major sections thereof.

Procedure Statements

- *Any change.* Issue new P/PS and supersede old P/PS if appropriate.

Period-End Manual

- *Any change.* Revise and publish new manual.

Budgeting Manual

- *Any change.* Revise and publish new manual.

Property Accounting Manual

- *Minor change.* Use memorandum to user departments.
- *Intermediate change.* Use policy/procedure statement.
- *Major change.* Reissue manual or major sections thereof.

Forms Manual

- *Minor change.* Use memorandum to user departments.
- *Intermediate change.* Use policy/procedure statement.
- *Major change.* Reissue manual or major sections thereof.

User Manual

- *Minor and intermediate changes.* Use memorandum to department users.
- *Major change.* Reissue manual annually or if substantial changes, such as a new accounting system, have been implemented.

Information Technology Manual

- *Minor change.* Use memorandum to user departments.
- *Intermediate change.* Use policy/procedure statement.
- *Major change.* Reissue Manual or major sections thereof.

Human Resources Manual

- *Any change.* Revise and publish new manual.

Exhibit 4.1. Maintenance Methods for Accounting Manuals

Procedure Statements

Policy and procedure statements are never updated; they are superseded and a new P/PS released. The heading of the new P/PS would indicate the retrieval number of the one superseded; the body of the new P/PS would only mention the superseded one in the background information section in general terms.

Period-End Manual

The period-end manual should be in a constant state of revision, because part of the closing procedure is to review completed tasks and see if increased efficiencies can be obtained by revising the timing or work instructions in the manual. Consequently, this manual should be incrementally revised and released in its entirety following most month-end closings, and completely overhauled at least once a year.

Budgeting Manual

The budgeting manual is typically updated just once a year and released as a new version as part of the budgeting process, usually toward the end of the current fiscal year. At this time, all older versions of the budgeting manual should be collected and destroyed so that no one uses budgeting procedures from an out-of-date version.

Property Accounting Manual

The property accounting manual is essentially a highly specific subset of the forms manual, relating strictly to the recording of transactions for fixed assets. As such, the same rules relating to the forms manual apply to the property accounting manual.

Forms Manual

The forms manual is a series of forms and instructions for completing accounting forms. Updating usually consists of replacing the instructions or the form, or both. The procedure is an exception to the rule that asking the user to update a manual by removing and replacing pages is to be avoided. If the forms manual has a known sequence, such as a form number or official title, inserting new pages is not burdensome. When issuing a new form or a replacement form, the covering memorandum should explain its purpose and location in the forms manual. If deleting a form from the accounting system, the interoffice memorandum is the only method available for informing holders of the forms manual of the deletion. If the forms manual has a published index, it should be reissued after two or three changes have been made to the contents of the manual.

User Manual

The user manual is a periodic-release type of manual, essentially to inform new employees following a period of employee turnover. However, if the manual remains substantially unchanged, maintenance is handled in the same manner as for the general accounting manual. Minor maintenance need not be reported because the people affected are informed through a memorandum or letter. If a new or replacement form included in the user manual is being issued, the holders of the user manual should be informed by memo or through the P/PS system. If the change is major—such as a new accounting system or substantial changes thereto, or a major policy change negates a large portion of the manual—then a new manual should be written and published and the holders notified to destroy the old manual. User manuals should be dated so that, if a user makes an inquiry to accounting, both parties would be referring to the same publication.

If newly hired employees need the user manual, they should receive the latest manual with updates noted or copies of the change letters or memos included. If the manual is used as the basis of a training session for new employees, the changes would be discussed as part of the instruction.

Information Technology Manual

Portions of this manual resemble the forms manual in style and content. Changes in record layouts, batch input or processing forms, and output report layouts are handled by asking each recipient of the manual to remove existing pages and insert record or report layouts. If there are many changes, or the system is being drastically altered or replaced, then a new manual should be compiled and issued, along with instructions to destroy the old manual.

Human Resources Manual

This manual contains a number of policies that directly impact the manner in which the company deals with its employees. For this reason, changes in the polices over time will have an impact on the benefits, pay, and hiring policies of the company, which will have a direct monetary impact on employees. Consequently, the human resources manual can be used as the basis for lawsuits by employees against the company when company actions deviate from the policies outlined in the manual. For this reason, it is very important to incorporate all suggested changes into the manual at one time, and then release the new manual to all recipients at the same time, being careful to collect and destroy all old manuals being replaced. Given the risk of lawsuits, at least one copy of each older version of the manual should be stored in a locked and fireproof location. Also, recipients should sign a document stating that they have received the new manual and turned in the old version so there is no chance of having old manuals treated as current ones.

Updating manuals is highly judgmental. Indications of the need for the release of new information to the holders of any manuals include an increase in transaction errors, a sudden disregard of company policy or procedure, or consistently faulty transaction coding indicating the preparer has not been informed of a change in the coding structure.

The preparer of the manuals or systems documentation should maintain a record of the distribution of each type of release if updates and new releases are to be distributed to the original recipients in an orderly manner. The minimum amount of information contained in a distribution record should be:

- Name of the released document
- Date published
- Retrieval number (if any)
- Distribution list

For small-issue releases, such as the general accounting manual, specific names and titles may be recorded. For larger, more general releases, the general name of the employee group may be listed. For example, if a P/PS were released to supervisors, department heads, and senior management, names would not be needed because the next release, even if it is an update of a previous publication, would be addressed the same way.

Large lists of names are difficult to maintain because of employee turnover in most organizations. At all times, the primary objective of releasing information is to get the information to the right department or designated level of personnel. The distribution list should be fairly definitive. For example, if a P/PS is used to announce a special change in the retirement plan for employees over 60 years old, the distribution list should have that description. Maintaining specific names is not important because it is unlikely that a similar release will be issued to exactly the same employees. Thus, designated group names become an important part of the distribution system.

4.3 RESPONSIBILITY FOR MAINTENANCE OF MANUALS

The person selected to document an accounting system should have a fairly comprehensive knowledge of modern accounting practices, some knowledge of the organization, and a strong desire to complete the assignment. In a very large organization, a specialist may be employed in a staff position, reporting to the controller or chief financial officer. This person should be given as much authority as an internal auditor, with full access to the officers and department managers, documents, and the current procedures in use. The position title should indicate the span of authority, such as Director of Systems Documentation.

Two specific employee types immediately come to mind: the recent college graduate with a major or minor in accounting, or an older person within two or three years of retirement—an excellent use of an experienced person with prior management-level experience in the accounting function.

In many organizations, the task of documenting accounting systems can be assigned to the controller, who can assign specific areas or tasks to knowledgeable supervisors reporting to him or her. The controller then becomes the editor, approver, and publisher of accounting manuals. In any case, the assignment should be closely allied with and monitored by the controller's office, for it is here, at the highest level of knowledge, that the working accounting procedures are controlled, changed when necessary, and maintained appropriately.

The following is a brief summary of the most appropriate documenters for each of the accounting manuals:

General Accounting Manual

The controller is the logical choice to develop this manual. Department or functional supervisors of payroll, payables, cash receipts, investments, cost accounting, fixed assets, and so on can be assigned specific documentation tasks related to their operation or to the general operations of accounting. The controller would supervise the editing, printing, and publishing. In a large organization, a staff position could be added to handle these tasks.

Procedure Statements

Because policy and procedure statements are the heart of an ongoing accounting operation, these should be under the controller's jurisdiction. Most P/PS statements are originated in departments, and the system of bringing the policy or procedure to the controller with the request to publish it is a most satisfactory solution.

Period-End Manual

The logical preparer of the period-end manual is the assistant controller in charge of financial statement preparation, working in conjunction with the director of internal audit or a knowledgeable audit manager, particularly if the person works closely with the external auditors to facilitate a speedy, effective financial audit of the organization. The audit specialist should be able to write effective programs of examination for specific audit functions. Effectively handled, a comprehensive pre-audit review and a detailed period-end manual can reduce the cost of an independent audit significantly.

Budgeting Manual

The budgeting manual is essentially the work instructions for the area over which the budgeting manager has full responsibility; accordingly, this person should be responsible for the manual. If a company is too small to employ a budgeting manager, then responsibility for the manual should shift back to the controller.

Property Accounting Manual

Property accounting forms and related instructions fall completely within the responsibility area of the fixed assets accountant, so this position should have responsibility for this manual. If there is no fixed assets accountant, then responsibility should shift back to the controller.

Forms Manual

Again, the controller is selected to centralize the accumulation of forms and forms descriptions. A small working task force can be organized to bring all current forms up to date and then describe how each form is to be completed and used. Once the total forms manual is in place, it is not difficult to make additions or deletions for the relatively infrequent changes in operating forms.

User Manual

This manual is ideally suited to be a cooperative department or functional project, headed by the controller or a staff assistant to the controller. Each department or functional area knows the forms in use, the proper data to be included, the approvals, and the related problems based on prior outside user questions and complaints. Each preliminary writer should be instructed to write only what is necessary for the user to know. It is not necessary to describe all the inner workings, controls, or procedures employed to edit, enter, summarize, and report the data or produce a final output report; this manual only covers basic input forms and procedures related to user-provided information required by forms.

Information Technology Manual

The writer of this manual should have some knowledge of basic business data processing. However, much of the required manual contents can be determined with extensive interviews of user personnel and computer analysts and programmers. Suppliers of packaged accounting systems should provide user documentation.

In most cases, this user documentation must be customized to an organization's specific methods and procedures.

Human Resources Manual

The bulk of the policies, procedures, and forms itemized in this manual will be compiled by the human resources staff, with the exception of a few instructions that may be generated in conjunction with the payroll function of the accounting department. Accordingly, responsibility for this manual will largely fall upon the human resources manager, in conjunction with some assistance from the payroll staff.

The following is a job description showing the traits desirable in an employee who will be assigned the writing and compiling tasks, and the criteria for selecting an outside consultant who may be employed to produce specific accounting manuals.

Documenter Job Description

- Degree in accounting
- Large-company business experience
- Knowledge of internal accounting controls
- Good writing ability (style)
- Desire to spend several years in this job
- Good interviewing techniques

Consultant Selection Criteria

- Significant experience in writing documentation for accounting, data processing, or similar operations
- Well-designed plan to use internal employees as much as possible for start-up materials
- Good, readable writing style. (Review several recent reports or actual documentation prepared by the consultant who will be assigned to the job).
- Full understanding of the exact requirements of the specific manuals that he or she will complete.

Outside consultants may require that office space, photocopying, and printing services be provided.

4.4 SPECIFICATIONS FOR MAINTENANCE OF MANUALS

There should be printed instructions for maintaining each type of manual. The instructions should include five categories of information. The first category is *mechanics*, which refers to the size of paper used for different types of forms and reports, as well as the method by which a manual is bound. The second category is *content*, which refers to the types of forms, tables, policies, procedures, and other instructions to be contained within the manual. The third category is *updating*, which refers to what types of information should be updated on a regular basis. The fourth category is *numbering and indexing*, which describes the numbering schemes used to identify documents within each manual. The final category is *normal distribution and retention*, which notes who receives each manual and what happens to old manuals when they are replaced by new ones. Here are examples of the maintenance instructions for all of these categories, applied to each of the accounting manuals:

1. Mechanics

- *General Accounting Manual*. Printed on 8½ by 11 white paper on one side only, and punched for a three-ring binder.
- *Procedure Statements*. Printed on 8½ by 11 white paper on one side only, and punched for a three-ring binder, but corner stapled when issued. Use a standardized first sheet with company name and logo.
- *Period-End Manual*. Printed on 8½ by 11 white paper, corner-stapled.
- *Budgeting Manual*. Printed on 8½ by 11 white paper, corner-stapled.
- *Property Accounting Manual*. Printed on 8½ by 11 white paper on one side only, and punched for a three-ring binder.
- *Forms Manual*. Printed on 8½ by 11 white paper on one side only, and punched for a three-ring binder.
- *User Manual*. Printed on 8½ by 11 white paper, corner-stapled. May be prepunched for a three-ring binder. The index is printed on the cover of the manual. May be printed on both sides of paper, but printing on only one side is recommended.
- *Information Technology Manual*. Batch control forms and report descriptions typed on 8½ by 11 white paper and punched for a three-ring binder. Tables, data dictionary, and output reports are usually printed by computer on standard 14 by 11 continuous paper and bound into computer output binders.
- *Human Resources Manual*. Printed on 8½ by 11 white paper on one side only. It should be permanently bound so that pages cannot be added or deleted.

2. Content

- *General Accounting Manual*. Minimum contents are the chart of accounts, description of the numbering scheme, and definitions of accounting codes. Optional items are the basic accounting forms if no forms manual is maintained; major accounting principles followed; and layouts of all major financial statements and schedules.
- *Procedure Statements*. Each statement stands alone and is referenced to a former P/PS only if it supersedes that P/PS. The P/PS announces policy additions or changes, major procedures, new forms, and any other significant management pronouncement affecting company operations.

- *Period-End Manual.* This manual contains a list of all accounting procedures required to close the books at the end of the fiscal year or period and specifies the person assigned to complete each procedure, schedule, or financial statement and related information.
- *Budgeting Manual.* This manual contains a list of all accounting procedures required to prepare a budget near the end of the fiscal year and specifies the person assigned to complete each budgeting procedure or schedule.
- *Property Accounting Manual.* This manual contains a sample property accounting form and related descriptive information for each type of fixed asset maintained by a company.
- *Forms Manual.* Each form is described in a three-pages-per-form layout. The first page describes the mechanics of the form, number of copies, use of each copy, retention and filing information, how obtained for use, and which department controls the distribution of blank forms. The second page contains numbered instructions for completing the form. The last page is a copy of the actual form with every space for entering data numbered for reference to the instructions.
- *User Manual.* Included are the index, major forms prepared outside of accounting, departmental procedures such as reporting time and attendance, expense reporting, a list of accounting personnel and the areas handled by each, and instructions for reading reports furnished by accounting for departmental use.
- *Information Technology Manual.* Tables are needed for reference and updating purposes. Descriptions of reports and the reports themselves (generally reduced copies of larger-format reports) are optional.
- *Human Resources Manual.* This manual is composed of all human resources policies and procedures.

3. Updating

- *General Accounting Manual.* Major updating is required if major changes in systems or new computer application programs are installed. It is reissued by section after several minor updates have been published. Minor updating is by P/PS, memorandum, or letter. Minor updates are defined as adding, changing, or deleting one or two new accounts or object codes, changing the definition of an account code, or adding a new accounting form or schedule.
- *Procedure Statements.* There is no updating of policies or procedures. Each P/PS is complete as issued with the problem or background information stated, the policy or procedure defined, the effective date if required, and instructions for compliance.
- *Period-End Manual.* A new manual is prepared before each period-end.
- *Budgeting Manual.* A new manual is prepared one or two months prior to the beginning of the annual budgeting process.

- *Property Accounting Manual.* No updating is required unless the form is revised or discontinued, in which case a new set of form uses and descriptions is issued through the P/PS system to those involved in its preparation and use.
- *Forms Manual.* No updating is required unless the form is revised or discontinued, in which case a new set of form uses and descriptions is issued through the P/PS system to those involved in its preparation and use.
- *User Manual.* Updating materials usually consist of interoffice correspondence, information releases, or P/PS. When a significant system change occurs, a new manual is prepared and distributed.
- *Information Technology Manual.* The forms and descriptions are replaced when computer changes require changes in forms used for data entry. Generally, there is very little updating of batch control forms or reports unless significant systems changes are made to the related programs.
- *Human Resources Manual.* Updates are only included in an entirely new release of the manual, which should occur at least once a year.

4. Numbering and Indexing

- *General Accounting Manual.* The manual is numbered sequentially by section, beginning with "1" in each section. Because both the chart of accounts and definitions are in account number order by type of account, indexing consists only of a list of sections by title.
- *Procedure Statements.* The use of retrieval numbers used in sequential order is recommended. Retrieval number groups should be assigned a permanent four- or five-digit series. A new index should be issued after every 10 P/PS statements are issued. The minimum interval for new indexing is annually. A superseded P/PS should be included on the next index with "purged" or "superseded" as the subject, and not printed at all in the following index. The index itself does not use a retrieval number.
- *Period-End Manual.* The pages are numbered consecutively. No indexing is usually required because of the manual's limited size and sequence by major accounting operation of balance sheet, operating accounts, and statements and schedules.
- *Budgeting Manual.* The pages are numbered consecutively. No indexing is usually required because of the manual's limited size.
- *Property Accounting Manual.* All forms should include a number and revision date. If not, the form is described by the actual name of the form as printed in the heading.
- *Forms Manual.* All forms should include a number and revision date. If not, the form is described by the actual name of the form as printed in the heading. Indexing is normally done by principal area of use, such as payroll forms, accounts payable forms, and so on. Under each section, the name and number of the form is shown. Sequential page numbers may be used, in which case the index would show the locations as consecutive pages.

- *User Manual.* Pages are numbered consecutively. An index of contents should be on the cover of the manual with consecutive page number references.
- *Information Technology Manual.* Batch control forms and output reports are usually identified with a program number. These numbers can be used to index the materials. Tables are described by title and number, and a simple index of the titles is usually sufficient as they are used only by accountants experienced with the data processing systems.
- *Human Resources Manual.* Pages are numbered consecutively.

5. Normal Distribution and Retention

- *General Accounting Manual.* Distribution is to accounting staff and outside department personnel who initiate a large volume of variable accounting transactions. Retention is mandatory.
- *Procedure Statements.* Each P/PS is issued to the accounting staff, to all outside departments affected by the policy or procedure, or to anyone with the need to know. Permanent retention is assumed until a P/PS is superseded by a replacement P/PS.
- *Period-End Manual.* Distribution is to every person assigned to complete one or more listed tasks. It is retained until the books are closed and the statements published. One copy should be filed with the year-end working papers. All other copies should be discarded when a new period-end manual is issued.
- *Budgeting Manual.* Distribution is to every person assigned to complete one or more listed tasks. Old copies of the manual should be destroyed whenever a new version is released.
- *Property Accounting Manual.* Distribution is generally limited to those involved with recording transactions related to fixed assets. As changes are made to forms contained within the manual, both the forms and their related descriptions should be replaced. Recipients of this manual should retain it indefinitely, with updates occurring in a piecemeal fashion.
- *Forms Manual.* Each functional area within and outside the accounting department should receive information about the forms they prepare, edit, approve, complete, or process. It is expected that recipients of the forms manual retain it indefinitely. This manual is usually updated piecemeal rather than replaced in its entirety.
- *User Manual.* As the manuals are intended for users who need the information for supplying coded forms and data to accounting, retention by the users is required. Distribution is made to those operating units or departments that provide accounting information on forms or that turn around documents such as time reports and clock cards. An office copy should be provided for clerical use in each department.
- *Information Technology Manual.* Because of its complexity, the contents of this manual are distributed only within the accounting and information technology

staffs, usually one reference copy in each department. These documents are retained until a new report is printed and checked for accuracy, at which time the replaced tables and forms are destroyed.

- *Human Resources Manual*. This manual is distributed to those dealing with either human resources or payroll issues. It is only updated as a new and complete volume. When replacement occurs, the old versions should be collected and destroyed; employees should sign statements saying that they have received the new replacement manuals. At least one copy of manuals being replaced should be stored in a locked and fireproof location.

4.5 PHYSICAL CONSTRUCTION OF THE MANUAL'S BINDER

Before issuing an accounting manual, the subset of policies, procedures, forms, and flowcharts that have previously been developed must be assembled into a cohesive whole. We will address this task as two parts: the binder and the contents.

The first part seems simple enough—just buy a boxful of binders. However, there are some subtleties to the purchase of a binder that should be considered:

- *Use a loose-leaf binder*. Any accounting manual will start to go out of date the moment it is released for general use, just because a company's systems are always changing to reflect alterations in the business. Accordingly, the accounting manual should be stored in a binder that can be easily opened so that pages can be inserted or removed at any time in the future.
- *Buy the slant-ring version of the binder*. If there is a choice, it is better to purchase binders in the slant-ring style. This is because the slant ring version holds more pages than the standard circular rings, and also tends to result in less page jamming. These features easily outweigh its slight increase in cost.
- *Buy binders that are too large*. When first creating an accounting manual, it is quite likely that the number of documents created will not cover all possible topics, if only because there will be pressure to release some sort of document to help the accounting department as soon as possible. The trouble is that the binder purchased for this first release may not be sufficiently large to encompass the additional pages that will be added during future releases. Accordingly, the binder purchased should be much wider than the size needed to hold the pages produced for the first release.
- *Base binder size on the ring width*. Less-expensive binders are likely to cost less because their manufacturer has scrimped on the size of the ring within the binder, while still creating a binder that has an impressively wide spine. A purchaser of such a binder will find that the binder will hold fewer pages than expected. A much better way to predict the page capacity of a binder is to base it on the inside diameter of the ring; one inch of ring diameter will hold roughly 200 pages of paper (though this will vary if heavier-weight paper types are used).
- *Buy a stiff binder*. A stiff binder cover is preferred, because this type of binder is more likely to be stood up on end for storage, and so will be more visible to

the user. Alternatively, a soft binder is more likely to be stored horizontally, and so may be buried under a stack of other papers, which makes it invisible to the user, and so less likely to be used.

- *Buy binders with plastic overlay covers.* It is not acceptable to issue an accounting manual that is completely unidentified by any type of marking; it will certainly be shuffled in with other user binders that are similarly unmarked, and will never be used at all. Instead, there should be plastic overlay covers on the front, back, and spine. The exact type of identification sheets used within these overlays is up to the manual development team; a suggestion is to use a different color insert for different types of binders. For example, the accounting manual may have a blue cover, and the human resources manual may be red. This makes it easier for the manual development team to differentiate the manuals as it prepares them for delivery to recipients.
- *Use clearly visible index tabs.* Avoid index tabs that are flush with the edge of a page, for these will not be clearly visible to the user. Instead, any type of index tab that stands out clearly is preferred. Some users may prefer a particular type that is color-coded by topic, but users will probably not understand the color scheme if there are many topics (which require many colors).
- *Reference procedure numbers on index tabs.* It is very common to group procedures by department or function on index tabs. However, this approach may not work if department names or processes change over time, which will require the distribution of new tabs, and possibly a heavily reorganized manual. Instead, the tabs should identify clusters of procedures by the range of their identifying numbers.

Though a seemingly minor topic, this section included eight points that primarily targeted the type of binder to use for an accounting manual. These are subtle items, but can make the difference between a professional-looking and heavily used manual and one that is undistinguished and rarely used.

4.6 CREATION AND STORAGE OF THE MASTER MANUAL COPY

With all binders completed, it is now necessary to create a complete master document for this issue of the accounting manual. There are several reasons for doing so. One is that the distribution process may take place over several weeks or months, depending on how the roll-out plan has been developed (such as providing training alongside a new manual, which tends to result in a much slower, though more thorough, roll-out). When there is a long interval between the first and last mailing, there is some danger that the later recipients will receive documents that contain newer changes than those that were sent to the earlier recipients; this can result in differences in transactional processing throughout the company. Another problem is that the company may choose to bring suit against an employee for improperly completing a procedure or following a policy. If so, the employee may use the defense of having relied on an earlier or later version of the manual. It is difficult to counteract this defense unless there is a master copy of the manual on hand that relates to the period under discussion.

Given these points, one should address the following steps to create a master copy of the manual:

1. *Assign the same release date to all documents.* All new pages that are to be inserted in the manual should be given the expected release date for the manual, rather than the earlier date when they were actually created. This avoids the contention that some other date on a document indicates that there was a separate, earlier release of documents.

2. *Update the revision history.* If the manual contains a list of dates when each document was updated, be sure to include any new revision dates on this list. This is especially useful for legal reasons, allowing a company to prove a complete history of when new documents were issued to employees.

3. *Verify that old page versions are replaced.* If new versions of documents have been created for this most recent master copy, then verify (several times) that the old pages have been taken out of the manual and replaced with the new ones. It is not acceptable to send out the manual with duplicate or missing pages because this confuses readers.

4. *Create multiple tables of contents.* Once all of the pages have been inserted or deleted, create two tables of contents for the manual. One should be in order by the subject topic, as shown in Exhibit 4.2. A reader can look up a topic in this table, then use the related document number to find it within the manual. This is the table of contents that will be used most heavily, and so should be the first of the two tables. The second of the tables should itemize the manual's contents by sequential document number. An example is shown in Exhibit 4.3. This table reflects the actual order in which the manual is organized; this may be of some use to employees who are already familiar with the general grouping of documents within the manual, allowing them to find documents more readily with this type of presentation.

5. *Update the existing tables of contents.* If the manual already exists and is only being updated, then the previous step can be eliminated. Instead, the document design team only needs to verify that all of the latest document changes have been properly reflected in the two tables of contents.

C	Document Number
Cash, Petty	0307
Cash, Receipts	0329
Cash, Reconciliation	0305
Cash, Deposits	0300
Cash, Electronic Funds Transfer	0372
Cash, Wire Transfer	0399
D	
Deposits, Cash	0300

Exhibit 4.2. Table of Contents Sorted Alphabetically by Subject Topic

Document Number	Procedure Description
0300	Cash, Deposits
0305	Cash, Reconciliation
0307	Cash, Petty
0329	Cash, Receipts
0372	Cash, Electronic Funds Transfer
0399	Cash, Wire Transfer
0423	Billing, to Service Customers
0569	Collections
0721	Finance Charge Deductions

Exhibit 4.3. Table of Contents Sorted Numerically by Subject Identifier

6. *Lock up the master copy.* Once the set of documents is complete, the primary issue remaining is to ensure that no one changes its contents without formal approval. The physical copy should be locked up, preferably in a fireproof safe. The electronic copy of the manual should be given password protection in the computer system so that only authorized personnel can change it. This does not mean that the preceding master copy should be thrown out when the new one is completed. On the contrary, and as noted at the beginning of this section, there are legal reasons for keeping older copies of the manual. Accordingly, older master copies should be clearly labeled with their dates of completion, and kept in storage. The legal department should notify the manuals team of the dates on which these older copies can be safely destroyed.

4.7 CREATION AND MAINTENANCE OF THE DISTRIBUTION MAILING LIST

The most expensive way to distribute a manual is to do a bulk mailing to every employee in the organization. This can be prohibitively expensive if there are many employees. It also does not make much sense from the perspective of subsequently updating the information contained within it, as many employees cannot be bothered with replacing pages in their manuals. As noted in the last section, updating a manual is also an issue from a legal perspective, because there is a risk that employees will base their actions on old versions of a manual. A better and much less expensive approach is to create a list of positions within the company that are most likely to use the manual, and which will be responsible for making its contents available to other employees. This usually means that supervisors are the ones most likely to be on the mailing list for a manual.

Once the mailing list has been determined, it can be converted into a matrix, such as the one shown in Exhibit 4.4. This one has converted the names of recipients to their job titles, because employee departures and hires would otherwise render the mailing list obsolete very rapidly. The matrix also lists the type of manual that each person should receive. By subdividing the total number of manuals into subsets for each recipient, a company can reduce the cost of creating an excessive number of manuals. Of particular note is that there is a date listed in the matrix for each manual that has been sent

Recipient Job Title	Accounting Manual	Budgeting Manual	Human Resources Manual	Information Technology Manual	Period-End Close Manual
Assistant Controller	11/03				04/03
Budget Manager	11/03	03/03			04/03
CFO	11/03	03/03	08/02	07/02	04/03
CIO		03/03	08/02	07/02	
Controller	11/03	03/03	08/02		04/03
Development Manager				07/02	
Engineering Manager		03/03	08/02		
H/R Manager		03/03	08/02		
Production Manager		03/03	08/02		

Exhibit 4.4. Mailing List Matrix

to each person on the mailing list. This is the date of the most recent update sent, and is of great value to the manuals design team in determining who has not yet received the most recent update to a manual.

With this mailing list matrix in hand, a company can easily determine what manual has been issued to a specific job position, as well as the last date on which it was updated, which greatly aids in the process of sending out updated information.

4.8 PHYSICAL DISTRIBUTION PROCESS

With all of the distribution materials now ready, as well as the list to recipients, how do we go about actually distributing the manuals? The first step is to create a cover letter that goes with the manual, describing why the manual is being sent out and what changes have been made to it since the last release. Some time should go into writing this part of the letter: A vivid description of key changes is the best way to get the reader to immediately review the attached materials. If only a partial release is being issued, then the letter should also include a detailed listing of exactly what pages in the old manual are being replaced. If training classes related to the manual have been developed at this time, the letter should also include a list of training dates and locations. In addition, it should also list the name and phone number of a person on the manuals development team who can be called if the recipient thinks there is a problem with it. This letter should be mail merged with the distribution list to personalize it with the names of recipients.

The manual development team has now completed all of the materials needed to distribute the manuals. At this point it can shift the physical distribution process to the company mailroom, which is better equipped to handle the distribution task. However, many smaller organizations do not have a mailroom, so the development team must handle this chore as well. If so, the following steps should be followed:

1. *Match cover letters to manuals*. If there are several different manuals, such as an accounting manual and a human resources manual, then the staff must match up the

cover letter for each person to the correct types of manuals. This may require double checking to avoid mistakes.

2. *Securely package manuals.* Internal deliveries may require minimal packaging, especially if the sturdiest possible binders have already been obtained to hold manual documents. However, anything designated for external delivery may receive rough handling, and should be packaged accordingly.

3. *Route local deliveries through internal mail stops.* If there is an internal company delivery system, then the development team should determine the correct mail stop for each recipient, address the packages to be delivered, and send them on their way.

4. *Route external deliveries through a delivery verification service.* If any documents are being sent outside the company delivery system, then the development team will want to verify that they were received by the person to whom they were sent. This requires mailing through a service, such as Federal Express (FedEx) or United Parcel Service (UPS), that will record the name of the person to whom a package was delivered. An alternative is to contact all recipients a few days after the mailing date to verify receipt of the package.

Manuals are primarily being sent to people in management positions, so it is critical that they share this information with their staff. Some managers are not good at this task, which results in a group of employees who are not well versed in the most current procedures. There are several ways in which the manuals development team can go straight to the employees to notify them that a new manual has been issued, and that they should see their supervisors to review it. One approach is to include this information in a bulletin that can be posted on company bulletin boards and other public places. Another alternative is to include a notice in the company newsletter, such as this:

> **Human Resources Employees:** A new human resources manual was issued to all managers in the Human Resources department on October 3rd. Since this manual contains extensive updates to existing policies, procedures, and forms, we strongly recommend that you talk to your supervisor about reviewing it.

Another alternative is to maintain a copy of the most recent version of the manual in a public place, such as the copy room (convenient for making copies of the most pertinent pages) or the cafeteria. The only problem with this approach is that the manuals can suffer from extensive use and will need to be replaced with great frequency.

4.9 ISSUANCES TO NEW EMPLOYEES

New employees may be hired at any time, and it is most unlikely that they will arrive on precisely the same dates when new manuals are released. Consequently, they may be left without any knowledge of a company's policies and procedures for quite some time. There are several ways to avoid this problem.

One approach is to create a form for use by the human resources department, which it forwards to the manuals development group whenever a new employee is hired. This should serve as sufficient notification that a manual should be sent to that person, who should also be added to the ongoing mail list for future updates.

Another approach is to have the human resources staff send a notification to the new employee's supervisor as a reminder to go over the supervisor's copy of the manual. A further step may be to require the supervisor to sign a document attesting to the completion of such training, and to send it back for inclusion in the employee's file.

Yet another approach is to schedule all new employees for training in the use and contents of company manuals as part of their new employee indoctrination. This may include the scheduling of later classes that cover the manuals in greater detail. If this approach is used, then the human resources staff should also maintain a database that lists who has attended these classes, in case reminder messages must be sent out.

4.10 MANUAL RETRIEVAL

Some companies go to great lengths to determine the location of manuals that have been left behind by departing employees, even going to the extreme of withholding final paychecks until the manuals are turned in or deducting their cost from final paychecks. The reasons given are that the company manual is a confidential document that should not be revealed to outsiders, and that it is a valuable document that is difficult to reproduce.

One should seriously discount both of these arguments. If an employee wants to disseminate the contents of a manual to all possible competitors, all that is needed is an hour on the local copier—and there is very little that a company can do to stop this sort of behavior. As for retrieving valuable manuals for later use, how would an incoming employee feel about being given a hand-me-down accounting manual that is laced with notes and scribbles? It is better to throw out all "pre-owned" manuals and issue new ones, even if there is a modest attendant cost.

The only reason why a manual should be retrieved when an employee leaves is that it is less likely to be maintained with new document updates, and so will eventually contain less-than-accurate information. Consequently, there should be a notation in the exit interview form that reminds the interviewer to inquire if the manual has been turned in. This is a much more reasonable approach than forcing departing employees to pay for unreturned manuals.

4.11 BENEFITS OF USING ELECTRONIC MANUALS

Why switch to an electronic manual? Among the excellent reasons for doing so are reductions in the costs of preparing, updating, and (especially) distributing accounting manual information to users. In addition, and perhaps most importantly, a properly designed mix of electronic presentations can make it much easier for users to find the procedural information that they need, which will greatly enhance the overall comprehension and usage of the information contained within the accounting manual. Some of the main benefits are:

- *Cannot lose the manual.* In a large accounting department where there are many potential users of a set of accounting manuals, it is more the rule than the exception for some of the manuals to be missing as people take them for reference purposes. This is a problem for anyone who needs a quick answer to a procedural problem. However, by using an electronic manual, all users can access the same data all of the time, and the manual cannot be lost.

- *Faster access to desired information*. A traditional accounting manual will contain a table of contents, and in rare cases an index too. These forms of reference may not be sufficient for allowing a user to rapidly locate the precise procedural information needed within a short period of time. An electronic document, on the other hand, may include pull-down help screens that contain needed information, or indexes of related information that can be accessed throughout the document, or imbedded hypertext that can be clicked to shift a user to related information. It may also be possible to conduct searches of the entire document based on a few key words. Given all of these alternatives for accessing information, it is much easier for a user to find specific information with an electronic manual than it is with a paper-based one.
- *Greater frequency of updates*. A traditional system for updating documentation will require that changes be gradually accumulated until there are enough to justify the cost of sending out replacement pages to the existing manuals. It may be a number of months before this takes place, so all procedural changes that have been requested in the meantime will be put on hold. By switching to electronic manuals, this issue is eliminated and incremental adjustments can be made to the documents at once; revised documents can be posted for electronic distribution. The only issue here is that users may not know that changes have been made to the electronic documents unless a notification, such as an e-mail, is sent to them that describes the change; they can then access the relevant text within the electronic documents and print or download the changes that they need.
- *Instant data access*. When using an electronic manual, the speed with which data can be accessed will usually be an improvement over the use of a paper-based manual. A few clicks of a mouse will bring the relevant text to a user's computer, whereas the user of a traditional manual takes substantially more time to locate it in the manual, refer to its table of contents, and then access the appropriate information. A side benefit of having instant data access is that users will be more inclined to access the information in the manual when they are not certain about a particular procedure, rather than guessing at the correct approach. Thus, greater adherence to corporate policies and procedures becomes more likely.
- *Provides an additional help capability*. A traditional accounting manual tends to be a rather dry collection of policies, procedures, and forms. However, when an electronic manual is used, it is also possible to employ drop-down menus that provide access to help information, as well as hypertext that can send a user to definitions or examples that are tied directly to the information currently being reviewed. Though adding this feature to an electronic document certainly increases the time required to create it, the resulting presentation will result in a much higher degree of user comprehension.
- *Reduced cost of distribution*. If documents can be made available for downloading by users, they can be accessed when needed without any need for

expensive shipping and handling charges. The only case where there would still be some cost of distribution is in acquiring equipment for employees who must access the information but do not currently have any computer access.

- *Reduced documentation tracking cost.* When a set of expensive paper-based manuals are issued to a user, the issuing entity must keep track of who has received them so that it can issue revision documents at regular intervals. If there are many such recipients, this can become an administrative hassle, because over time the recipients will change their locations within the company, and probably will not always contact the manuals development group to inform them of this fact. By switching to electronic manuals, one can avoid the necessity for tracking mailing addresses. Nonetheless, one should still trace the e-mail addresses of clusters of probable users so that notices can be sent out when changes are made to the electronic documents. This does not mean that the e-mail addresses of *specific* individuals must be tracked, but rather that the e-mail addresses of all likely users of a manual can be clumped together for a group notification; for example, all accounts receivable personnel should receive notification if a portion of the manual that applies to them is altered, but not any other members of the organization.
- *Send comments to the maintainer of the manual.* Anyone can send a memo back to the documentation design team in regard to suggestions for improvements to the accounting manual—however, it takes time to write a memo and post it through the interoffice mail or postal service. Given the effort required, most design teams do not hear back from users of its manuals. However, when an e-mail button is added to the presentation of an electronic manual, it is a simple matter for a user to fire off a request for changes. The result is a stream of productive comments from users back to the design team.

Many of the advantages listed here are related to logistics—how to get the most recent production (e.g., product updates) to customers (e.g., users of the manuals) with the lowest possible distribution cost. The basic work of collecting information about a process flow and writing procedures about it does not change at all, just the compilation, presentation, and distribution of the resulting information (unless help facilities are added to the basic text).

4.12 DISADVANTAGES OF USING ELECTRONIC MANUALS

Though the just-noted advantages of using electronic manuals are powerful ones, there are also several problems that one should be aware of. In some instances, these may be sufficiently important to curtail the use of electronic manuals:

- *Cost of reprinting electronic documents.* Though the manuals development staff may save a significant amount of money from no longer having to print accounting manuals, this does not mean that paper costs are completely eliminated. On the contrary, every user of an electronic manual may feel compelled to print it out, either due to a greater comfort level with paper-based documents or because access to the electronic manual is relatively limited. This may result in a greater reprinting cost on a company-wide basis than was previously the case for the manuals development staff.

- *Duplicate use of both paper-based and electronic manuals.* There may be cases where some continued use of the existing paper-based manuals must continue, in addition to the use of electronic manuals. One reason for this situation is when long-term employees who use the old manuals are unwilling to try something new. Another reason is that some employees may not have ready computer access to the electronic documentation. Whatever the reason may be, this situation will call for the retention of most existing systems (and costs) required to create, distribute, and update the paper-based manuals, as well as new systems (and costs) for the electronic versions.
- *More complex formatting requirements.* As will be noted in the "Accounting Manual in Multiple Formats" section later in this chapter, there are a variety of ways in which an electronic manual can be formatted—frequently calling for more than one format at the same time. For example, it may be necessary to insert some procedures into the "Help" fields attached to the company accounting software, as well as a separate version that is formatted to be downloaded and printed out by users, while yet a third version is set up with interactive links and online demonstrations, with the intention of being used more frequently by first-time users. All of the formats have a different use, and may greatly increase the utility of the electronic manual, but they also call for a much greater formatting effort on the part of the manuals development staff.
- *Methods of electronic access required.* Though it is increasingly unlikely in today's interconnected world, some potential users of electronic manuals may not have ready access to the computers or intranet/Internet connections that they need to gain access to electronic manuals. If this is a problem, the cost of properly equipping these employees may greatly exceed any benefits that might otherwise be gained from the use of electronic manuals. On the other hand, this may just be one more reason to give computer access to these employees, and tip the scales in favor of doing so.
- *No access if the computer system is down.* Though greater computer reliability makes system outages an increasingly small problem, there are times when a glitch in the network or in a computer will keep users from accessing electronic manuals. The likelihood of this issue can be further reduced with the use of battery backups for all computers and network servers, as well as fiber optic cabling in environments where manufacturing emissions can interrupt the flow of data through cables. If problems remain, then it may be necessary to add a paper-based manual to the mix of options available to users.

One of the key problems noted here is that electronic documents may not completely replace the existing paper-based manuals for a variety of reasons. As a result, a separate system is used to maintain the electronic manual, as well as its predecessor. This will result in greater costs than was previously the case, so a manager should carefully analyze the impact of this conversion to determine if costs will indeed rise as a result of the changeover.

4.13 BASIC ELECTRONIC MANUAL

In its most basic form, what is an online accounting manual? It is essentially a direct restatement of the existing paper-based manual, with no enhancements such as interactive tutorials, help menus, or sound or video clips. Despite the lack of these additional features, a basic online accounting manual can be quite an attractive option, because it requires limited skill to transfer documents to the online format. The files are either posted directly to the company intranet, or else they are incorporated into the help screens used in the corporate accounting software. By using this approach, a company can have its manuals available to the company as a whole with very little effort.

In these formats, a user is expected to either download the necessary files and review them on his or her computer, or review them on the screen when accessed through the accounting system. Though this is a reasonable approach to accessing the necessary information, and will present information that is similar to what users have come to expect, it does not result in an enhanced learning environment where new tools are added to the basic manual files. Consequently, the most rudimentary online manual should be treated as a jumping-off point, from which many other features can be added to make the electronic manual a real pleasure for users to access and browse through. These additional features are described in some of the following sections.

4.14 ACCOUNTING MANUAL ON AN INTRANET, EXTRANET, OR THE INTERNET

One may have heard of a number of different terms that relate to the centralized storage and dissemination of information (for our purposes, the accounting manual)—the Internet, intranet, and extranet. What are they, and how can they be used as a storage medium for the electronic manual?

The Internet is based on the use of hypertext, which allows anyone with access to an Internet browser to jump between information links on many different computers, located anywhere on the planet. It is an extraordinarily open form of communication, but can subject a user to a potential overflow of information, as there may be millions of possible locations in which data is stored.

An intranet is essentially the same thing as the Internet, in that hypertext is used and browser software is sufficient for general access. However, outside users are restricted from access by a corporate firewall. Also, incoming files may be rejected (or at least screened for viruses) by the firewall software. Thus, a company has a much greater ability to control the type and volume of information flowing through an intranet. It is on an intranet that most electronic manuals will be found, rather than being posted for general access on the Internet. The reason for this restricted level of access is partially because outsiders have no real need to see an accounting manual, and also some information contained within the manual may be considered confidential.

An extranet is simply a collection of intranets that are mutually accessible to users, though the amount of access may be restricted between the intranets. Users are also generally given access from the extranet to the Internet. This concept is most commonly used for sharing information with business partners (either customers or suppliers). There is some limited applicability for electronic manuals within an extranet, but only for those policies, procedures, and forms that must be accessed by business partners to understand how to conduct transactions with a corporation.

For the purposes of the discussion in the following sections, we will assume that a company has installed its electronic manual on the corporate intranet, as this is the most likely location for it to be positioned.

4.15 ELECTRONIC MANUAL WITH EMBEDDED HYPERTEXT

One of the chief advantages of creating an electronic manual is the use of embedded hypertext. This is text located anywhere within a document that contains linkages to other parts of the document, such as help screens and tutorials. By clicking on hypertext, a user can be shifted instantly to related information that is crucial to his or her understanding of the information being reviewed. This greatly enhances the speed with which a user can access the most relevant information pertaining to the issue at hand.

An alternative use for hypertext is to send a user to an e-mail screen so that he or she can send a message directly to the manuals development staff in regard to any issues that should be fixed in the electronic manual. This greatly improves the speed with which feedback about problems will be given to preparers.

Another use for hypertext is to send a user to an area of the manual that contains explanations of highly technical information contained within a procedure. For example, the content from a relevant FASB (Financial Accounting Standards Board) pronouncement related to the proper treatment of foreign exchange rates for month-end reporting can be linked via hypertext to a procedure that deals with this issue. It is even possible to have some outside expert maintain the section of the manual that deals with technical issues, and store it on a Web server at some other physical location—the hypertext links will still access the relevant data. This approach is particularly useful in those cases where a company cannot afford to pay for its own staff of in-house experts, instead providing linkages to the data provided by an outside entity.

The sample text shown in Exhibit 4.5 contains a series of hypertext links, which are noted in bold and underlined. Key words that require explanatory definitions are provided with hypertext links, as are technical topics. At the bottom of the text, the user is also provided with hypertext links to several related topics, plus links that will send the user to an e-mail feedback form or to an interactive tutorial regarding the current topic.

There are several key issues related to the text in Exhibit 4.5. First, though the topic of inventory valuation is quite a long and complex one, we have reduced it into a very small and readable snippet that provides just a brief overview of the process. By doing so, a reader can easily access the key information related to the topic without having to scroll down beyond a single computer screen of information. Second, the additional information that makes up this topic is accessed through hyperlinks; by using this formatting method, we allow the user to go directly to those related topics that are of most importance while by-passing all other topics that are of less relevance. Finally, by adding a series of related topics at the bottom, we prevent the user from having to guess at what other information might be available in the electronic manual—instead, the linkages are made available for the easiest possible access.

The hypertext linkages noted in Exhibit 4.5 are re-created in graphical form in Exhibit 4.6, where we see that the hypertext links allow a user to switch between

Inventory Valuation Overview

To value inventory, one must establish a clear **period-end cut-off** so that transactions occurring after the cut-off are not mistakenly included within the valuation calculation. To aid in this effort, all items on the receiving or shipping docks should be clearly identified as being either included within or excluded from the counting process. Next, **counting procedures** must be created for use by counting teams that make use of specific prenumbered **forms**. The **count teams** must be selected from a group of employees who are knowledgeable in the characteristics of the inventory. The teams must then be educated in the use of count procedures, and then set to count specific sections within the inventory area. Once the count is complete and audited, the **count sheets** are entered into the computer system and costed using the existing **LIFO** cost database. Next, the inventory valuation is sorted by total dollar amount and checked to see if any obvious **costing anomalies** are present; if so, the unit quantities, units of measure, and costs for these items are reviewed and corrected, if necessary. Next, the inventory is reviewed for **obsolescence** issues, with the cost of obsolete items being eliminated from the inventory valuation. Finally, **lower of cost or market** rules are applied to the inventory to further reduce the valuation, if necessary.

Related Topics:

Average Costing

- **Consignment inventory**

FIFO

- **Generally accepted accounting principles**
- **Inventory controls**
- **Perpetual inventory system**
- **Valuation of supplies**

Other Items:

- **Access the Inventory Valuation Tutorial**
- **Contact the Manuals Development Team**

Exhibit 4.5. Embedded Hypertext

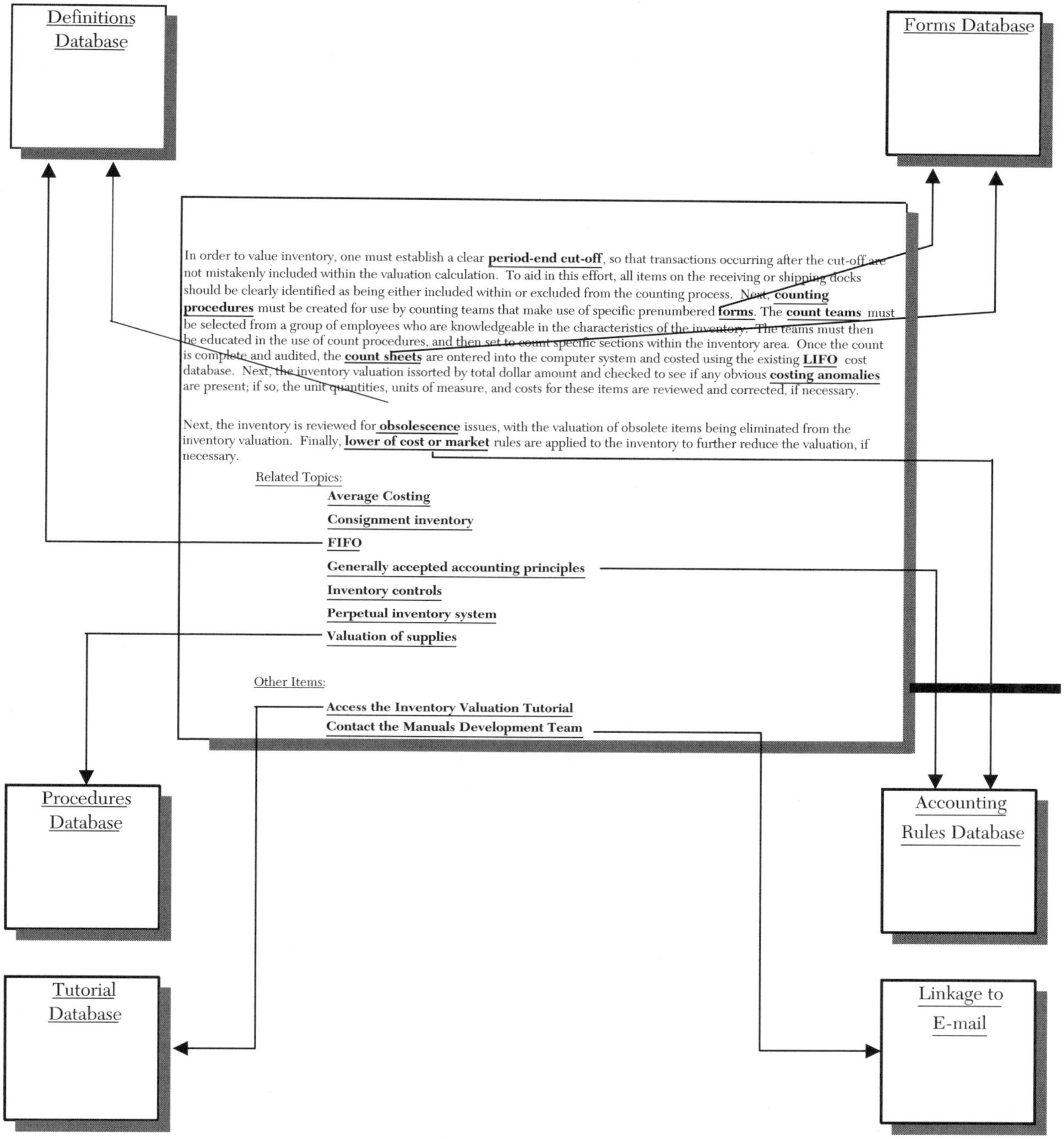

Exhibit 4.6. Hypertext Links Graphical Representation

several different files—including files for forms, definitions, procedures, tutorials, and accounting rules. To improve the readability of the presentation, not all linkages are traced to related databases. Based on the number of files shown in Exhibit 4.6, it is evident that hypertext linkages can be an effective way to cross-reference information from a wide variety of information sources.

Unfortunately, it is also possible to misuse links—which adds to a user's confusion. For example, an excessive proliferation of links will give a user so many choices for where to go for extra information that it takes an excessively long time to explore every possible item of related information. Also, links to only slightly related topics will not assist user comprehension of a topic. This later issue is best resolved through clear writing skills so that only the most relevant information is included in a manual. The most common problem with hypertext linkages is when they are not adjusted to reflect ongoing changes in the documentation. For example, a new definition that is added to the definitions database will not be of much use to readers if it is not referenced anywhere with hypertext links, because no one will be aware of its presence. Similarly, if information is deleted but the related hypertext links are not, users can become confused. Thus, constant maintenance of hypertext links to reflect changes in related information sources is mandatory.

4.16 ELECTRONIC MANUAL WITH ADVANCED INDEXING FEATURES

A standard paper-based manual will assist the reader in finding information by listing the names of all policies, procedures, and forms in the table of contents—and that is all. A more advanced manual may also list the names of related procedures as part of a cross-references section. However, this may not be sufficient for a user who is trying to find the usage for a particular word, or whose concept of a topic is different from the title already given to it.

These problems can be avoided through the use of more advanced alphabetical indexes. When used with an electronic manual, there is no reason to create an abbreviated table of contents that may only include a few dozen items. Instead, we can create a much larger version with hundreds of entries. For example, Exhibit 4.7 lists a traditional table of contents for a portion of an accounting manual.

These are obviously highly aggregated topics that do not give a user much information about the precise types of information that he or she is searching for. However, an

- Accounts Payable Processing
- Billing Processing
- Cash Receipts Processing
- Financial Statement Preparation
- Inventory Valuation

Exhibit 4.7. Traditional Table of Contents for an Accounting Procedures Manual electronic manual can be outfitted with a multilevel table of contents that allows for a much greater level of detail. By clicking on one of the major category headings, an additional set of more detailed topics will be revealed beneath it—and even more levels of detail, if necessary. As an example, Exhibit 4.8 shows sublevels of contents for just the "Accounts Payable Processing" category of the table of contents.

The above list does not have to appear in a massive pull-down table of contents listing on a computer screen. Instead, it is much easier to only have the main categories appear, and then click on each one to "drill down" to greater levels of detail. Another approach is to set up a search feature that allows a user to type in a few key phrases. The system will respond with a short list of topical entries, possibly drawn from several different parts of the table of contents. For example, an entry of "Documentation Matching" in such a search field would result in a list of topics from the policies, procedures, *and* tutorials sections of the table of contents. The search feature is especially useful when a user finds that information could be listed under a myriad of similar headings, and does not want to spend the time manually combing through all of them.

The multilayered table of contents, when combined with a data search field, allows users to locate relevant information much more rapidly in an electronic manual than can be managed with an identical paper-based manual.

4.17 ELECTRONIC MANUAL WITH BUILT-IN HELP INFORMATION

A traditional paper-based accounting manual does not hold out much hope for a user who reads through the standard policy and procedures formats, but simply does not "get it." They usually have to consult with a more experienced employee who can assist them with overcoming information that is not sufficiently clearly presented or for which they do not possess enough background information. However, this can require a significant amount of employee time. A better approach is to use some of the help features of an electronic manual.

Hypertext itself, as discussed in the last section, is a tremendous improvement over traditional manuals in that it provides a reader with a multitude of information sources. Simply by making use of all possible hypertext links, a user will be much more likely to find the answers to most issues.

Another approach is to install a list of frequently asked questions (FAQ) that is linked to each topic in the database. The linkage is through a hypertext connection, and will reference a reader to a separate file that is constantly being updated with the answers to questions that have repeatedly cropped up in the past. This file may be updated by the in-house training staff. Or a linkage can be to an Internet Web site maintained by the provider of whatever software packages that a company may be using; the provider can update the FAQ based on queries that their customer service staff has received. The use of an online FAQ list is highly recommended, for it will cover the vast majority of user comprehension problems that continually arise. Only a small minority of other user questions will then have to be answered by other means.

Another help feature is a comprehensive database of explanations that can be accessed at any time from the menu of the electronic manual. This database can include either a search feature or detailed table of contents, as long as it brings a user straight to an explanation of the current problem area. Much of the information contained within

Accounts Payable Processing

- Definitions
  - Discount
  - Electronic Funds Transfer
  - Matching
  - Receiving Documentation
  - Routing Number
  - Vendor
  - Voucher
  - Wire Transfer
- Flowcharts
  - The Accounts Payable Process Flow
- Forms
  - Check Request
  - Purchase Order
  - Requisition
  - Three-Way Matching Verification
  - Voucher
- Policies
  - Early Payment
  - Cash Payment
  - Approvals
  - Check Signing
  - Documentation Matching
- Procedures
  - Cash Payment
  - Check Payment
  - Credit Memo Processing
  - Documentation Matching
  - Electronic Funds Payment
  - Supplier Invoice Cancellation
  - Supplier Invoice Data Entry
- Tutorials
  - Documentation Matching
  - Payment Methods
  - Supplier Invoice Data Entry

Billing Processing . . .

Exhibit 4.8. Expanded Table of Contents

this help database will duplicate the information contained within a well-designed electronic manual with a plethora of hypertext links, so many companies will prefer to avoid the expense of creating this feature and will instead focus their efforts on ensuring that this help information is more fully integrated into the basic manual. This is a valid response, since the creation of a full-blown help database is a significant effort; realistically, only the minority of employees whose questions have not already been answered by the FAQ section of the database will use it.

A final feature can be added for those users whose questions are not answered through any other feature of the electronic manual. These are usually the most difficult questions that either cannot be anticipated or represent such a small minority of issues that it is not worth adding explanatory information to the electronic manual that will address them. In these instances, the manual can include a phone number to the company help desk (or to the company expert on a specific informational area), an e-mail message box that will send the request to an appropriate party, or an e-mail message box that will page the company help desk staff and require them to call the user back at once. Any of these options will allow for a relatively rapid response to the most difficult employee questions.

The additional help options noted here will result in an electronic manual that is much more likely to provide users with the explanations they need to increase their comprehension of the information contained within an accounting manual. Even better, it means that users are much more likely to use the manual, because they will come to realize that it is the most complete resource of accounting information for them. This in turn leads to more wide-ranging acceptance of the policies and procedures contained within it, and therefore fewer transactional exceptions.

4.18 ELECTRONIC MANUAL WITH BUILT-IN TUTORIALS

A beginning user of a procedure will have a much higher degree of comprehension if the electronic manual goes beyond the typically dry listing of steps to follow, and additionally contains a tutorial that shows exactly how to create a transaction. This requires the addition of a button to the existing layout that takes the user to a separate tutorials database where he or she can peruse a multiscreen, step-by-step procedure. Such a tutorial should include exact representations of the computer screens that will be used to create each transaction, as well as added notes that discuss key features of each step in the process. The user should be able to shift backward and forward in the tutorial at will to find the steps that are most critical to comprehension.

The amount of effort required to create a tutorial is considerable, so they should be limited only to the most important processes that will be needed by a number of users. If a process is only to be used by a small number of people, then it will be more cost-effective to give them personalized training, rather than spend far more time creating a computer-based training environment for them.

There are software packages available that also allow one to create interactive question-and-answer sessions with users, as well as final quizzes to test user comprehension. Given their added cost, these packages are generally not appropriate for smaller corporations. Another alternative is the computer-based training movie; this is created by software that replicates on-screen the actions of someone who is walking through a standard set of activities while explaining each action through a microphone. The resulting movie will show a user exactly what is being done to process a transaction (or some other activity) while the accompanying voice recording explains what is going on. Just as is the case with a movie that is inserted into a video cassette recorder, this movie format contains on-screen buttons for rewind, pause, play, and fast forward. Each movie is easily created—just plot out the steps to be followed during the movie, practice them a few times, then press the "record" button and start recording the movie. The audio portion of the movie can be added concurrently or at a later time. The required software is generally in the $50 to $150 range, and may require a download to individual computers where the software will be resident. The software that is currently available for making computer-based movies includes ScreenCam by Lotus (www.lotus.com), HyperCam by Hyperionics (www.hyperionics.com), Camtasia Recorder and Producer by TechSmith (www.techsmith.com), and CameraMan by MotionWorks (www.mwg.com).

The key point to remember for online tutorials is to create them only for high-volume applications, given the significant labor time required to develop them.

4.19 WRITING TIPS FOR ELECTRONIC MANUALS

The writing format for a traditional paper-based accounting manual does not work well for an electronic manual, because the size of the reading area (the computer screen) is considerably smaller than the printed page. Also, the paper-based format does not take advantage of the many features that can be added to an electronic document, as have been described over the past few sections of this chapter. Instead, some of the following writing tips should be used:

- *Use a consistent format.* There are a great many features that can be added to an electronic manual, such as help buttons, hypertext, references to a glossary, access buttons to send an e-mail to a procedure writer, tutorials, and so on. However, the trouble with this feature-rich environment is that the screen can become excessively cluttered. To avoid this problem, the design team should determine a standardized format that it will use for all screens in the electronic manual, so a user will always find the same reference points at the same spot on any screen being viewed. This does not mean that some good potential features must be left out of the standard format, but that the format should be constructed in such a way that they are compressed into a readable format that does not excessively clutter the screen. This is a sufficiently important topic that the design team should consult with users to see what potential formats yield the greatest benefit to them.
- *Keep the message short.* The electronic manual is ideally suited for delivering short snippets of information to the user—preferably within a single computer screen so that a minimum amount of scrolling is needed. If the text is excessively long, users will tend to jump around through the presented material and will not absorb it as well. Accordingly, the anticipated documentation should be carefully structured in advance so that topics are kept short; and heavy use should be made of hypertext so that users can easily jump to related topics.

This can be a difficult transition for a procedure writer to make, and requires a great deal more structure to one's writing than was previously the case. A good way to truncate the length of presented text is to divide it into segments, each of which only deals with a single main idea. If a secondary idea is also contained within the text, then split it off and cross-reference it with hypertext.

- *Cross-reference heavily*. One of the main writing tips for the electronic manual is to break down information into a large number of small text messages, so it makes sense to spend a great deal of time ensuring that a reader is able to easily collect a sufficient amount of information about a topic through the use of hypertext links. By creating many cross-references, related topics can be easily clustered together for rapid perusal. This is a major part of the work required to create an online manual, and is worth the extra effort of having users verify that the cross-references used in the manual are sufficiently comprehensive.
- *Continually review references to new text*. When any new information is entered into an electronic manual, no one will know that it is now available until it is added to the online help screen, table of contents, and hypertext linkages of the manual. It is essentially invisible, inaccessible knowledge until these changes take place. Consequently, a great deal of attention must be paid to these reference sources.
- *Avoid dangling hypertext links*. Information may be deleted from a manual when it is out of date, no longer relevant, or attached to a process that is no longer in use. When this happens, the manual design team should verify that all hypertext linkages to it have been eliminated so that users will not attempt to access information that is no longer provided.
- *Reinforce topics with glossaries and tutorials*. Whenever there is the slightest doubt that a reader may not understand the content of a message, add hypertext links to an online glossary that explains key words or provide links to online tutorials that will walk an employee through a particularly important transaction. Because these tools are available, use them to the greatest possible extent.

The writing tips noted here will result in an electronic document that requires more preplanning of the final document than had previously been the case for a paper-based manual. The accounting topic will now be broken down into a much larger number of small topics, which must then be carefully reassembled into a highly readable presentation structure. This does not mean that the chore of assembling an electronic manual is meant to be a daunting one—only that extra effort in this area will result in a vastly more rewarding experience for anyone using it, much more so than would be the case for even the most perfectly designed paper-based manual.

4.20 EXAMPLE OF COMPREHENSIVE ELECTRONIC MANUAL FEATURES

A number of features have been mentioned in this chapter that can be added to an electronic manual. The exact layout and content of the resulting electronic manual is entirely

Inventory Valuation Overview

Keyword Search **Table of Contents** **Glossary** **Help** **Tutorial** **Contact Help Desk**	To value inventory, one must establish a clear **period-end cut-off** so that transactions occurring after the cut-off are not mistakenly included within the valuation calculation. To aid in this effort, all items on the receiving or shipping docks should be clearly identified as being either included within or excluded from the counting process. Next, **counting procedures** must be created for use by counting teams that make use of specific prenumbered **forms**. The **count teams** must be selected from a group of employees who are knowledgeable in the characteristics of the inventory. The teams must then be educated in the use of count procedures, and then set to count specific sections within the inventory area. Once the count is complete and audited, the **count sheets** are entered into the computer system and costed using the existing **LIFO** cost database. Next, the inventory valuation is sorted by total dollar amount and checked to see if any obvious **costing anomalies** are present; if so, the unit quantities, units of measure, and costs for these items are reviewed and corrected, if necessary. Next, the inventory is reviewed for **obsolescence** issues, with the cost of obsolete items being eliminated from the inventory valuation. Finally, **lower of cost or market** rules are applied to the inventory to further reduce the valuation, if necessary.

Exhibit 4.9. Inventory Valuation Overview: Full Electronic Format

up to the discretion of the manual development team. Nonetheless, an example of a fully developed format is noted in Exhibit 4.9, more to provide a starting point for further development than as the best possible layout. The exhibit contains the text from Exhibit 4.5 but goes on to surround it with additional linkages to other features of the electronic manual.

In Exhibit 4.9, a sidebar has been added that contains a number of links to various types of information, such as the help desk, the table of contents, and a tutorial. They are itemized in order, so the most commonly used ones are listed at the top. An alternative approach is to list these items in alphabetical order and let users scan through the list to find what they need. It is also possible to include this information in a top bar that contains drop-down menus. The worst place to itemize these linkages is at the bottom of the text, because users may not realize that they must scroll down some distance to gain access to the links and so may not realize they are available at all.

If a particular screen does not contain all of the linkages used in the master layout (e.g., there is no tutorial available), then the format should remain the same, for two reasons. First, users should become used to having information available to them in the exact same spots on the screen, every time. Second, there may eventually be a need to include a linkage in the missing location; leaving it initially blank will allow the development staff to more easily fill in the linkage at a later date.

4.21 USING THE PDF FORMAT FOR ELECTRONIC FILES

One problem with the use of electronic files for the distribution of manuals is that users may not have the required type of software to read them. This problem has been avoided by Adobe with its Adobe Acrobat software by making the reader version a free download (available at its www.adobe.com site). One must only pay for the software if it is to be used to *create* documents. The resulting portable document file (PDF) file format has become extremely popular.

- A document can be created in one's favorite file format and then be converted into the PDF format with no loss of formatting.
- Web pages in the PDF format look exactly line Web pages with the latest Web technology, such as cascading style sheets and javascript.
- Text stored in the PDF format can be saved to the rich text format (RTF) for later importing into word processing software for further editing and formatting.
- PDF files can be opened in the Windows, Mac OS, and UNIX operating environments.
- A PDF file is compact in size, so it can be quickly downloaded, frequently faster than the document formats in which a file was originally designed.
- Such features as text boxes, check boxes, list boxes, radio buttons, digital signature fields, and more can be added to a document within Acrobat.
- Acrobat allows one to develop PDF forms containing fields that can change depending upon user input. Users can use this feature to fill in information on a PDF form and then submit it electronically.
- Reviewers can add comments and position them at the location of the requested changes. Many types of changes can be added, such as electronic sticky notes, text, audio, stamps, graphic or text markups, and attached files. Also, comments from multiple reviewers can be merged into a single, consolidated PDF file to facilitate the review process.
- A PDF file can also be set to allow no changes by users to the document.
- Any links on PDF file pages are active, so additional Web pages can be downloaded as needed without returning to a Web browser.
- A variety of navigational elements allow readers to locate specific information more quickly within a PDF document, such as thumbnails (automatically generated miniature page previews), bookmarks, links, and full-text indexes.

This wide array of benefits has made Acrobat the preferred software for the development of any document that will be widely distributed electronically.

4.22 MAINTAINING AN ELECTRONIC MANUAL

There are several key differences between the maintenance of a paper-based manual and one that is constantly accessed electronically by employees:

- *Constant maintenance*. A traditional procedure maintenance system uses batch processing of procedural changes—that is, changes are accumulated until the pile reaches an impressive height, and then all the changes are incorporated at once, resulting in a small number of procedure distributions per year. With an electronic manual, there is no need to wait to make changes, as there is no distribution cost. Accordingly, changes are made to the manual as soon as they are received. This calls for more daily attention to the task, rather than a short-term project orientation.
- *Additional training*. A small amount of additional training is needed to access the online procedure database and alter existing information. Though this is not a major item, some training is required for everyone associated with ongoing procedure maintenance.
- *Less review time*. Because changes can be made to the database at any time, there is some pressure to make immediate changes to the database, though this can result in incorrect procedures. This is different from the traditional approach, which involves a mass mailing of proposed changes to users, who can comment on them for some time before they are incorporated into the existing manual.
- *Stratified review system*. Given the high speed of procedure updating, there is an increased need for a stratified review system, whereby minor changes or any changes to minor procedures can bypass the traditional lengthy review process; larger changes should still be screened before permanent alterations are made.
- *Database access issues*. The procedures staff finds itself dealing with complaints from users regarding their access to the database. Though the procedures staff has no control over who gets access to the computer network, it will nonetheless find itself in the midst of user requests for more access, which it must forward to the computer system department for action, perhaps with recommendations regarding the real need of each applicant for the desired computer workstation.

Thus, the administrator of an online procedures manual will find that changes are made to procedures more frequently. More training and review systems are needed to ensure that the changes are the correct ones and that they are entered correctly. Though it may not seem to be in this person's job description, issues surrounding user access to the database will occupy a portion of his or her time.

Chapter 5

ACCOUNTING PROCEDURES

5.1 INTRODUCTION

This chapter begins with a series of 10 process flowcharts, which itemize all the procedures that a typical accounting department can expect to be involved with; there are even additional procedures listed for the purchasing, shipping, and receiving departments, because these three areas initiate paperwork that eventually flows to the accounting department. By creating flowcharts first, one can identify all activities and thereby ensure that a procedure is written for each one. Also, each box in the flowcharts contains an identifying index number for each procedure, which is later listed as the procedure number in the header for each procedure. Thus, one can first refer to a process flowchart for the specific procedure needed, then trace the index number to the detailed procedure (which is also listed here, sorted in order by process flowchart designation). The process flowcharts are:

- Acquisitions (Exhibit 5.1)
- Billing (Exhibit 5.2)
- Budget (Exhibit 5.3)
- Credit (Exhibit 5.4)
- Financial Statements (Exhibit 5.5)
- Fixed Assets (Exhibit 5.6)
- Funds Management (Exhibit 5.7)
- Internal Audit (Exhibit 5.8)
- Payroll (Exhibit 5.9)
- Purchasing Cycle (Exhibit 5.10)

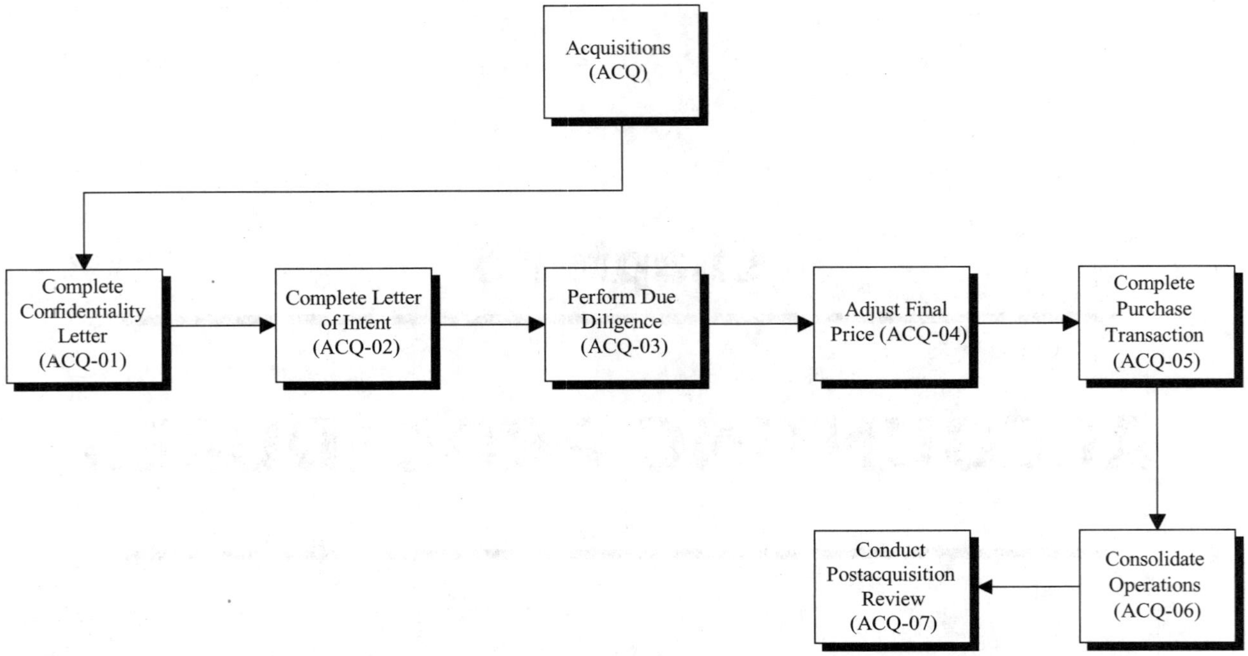

Exhibit 5.1. Acquisitions Flowchart

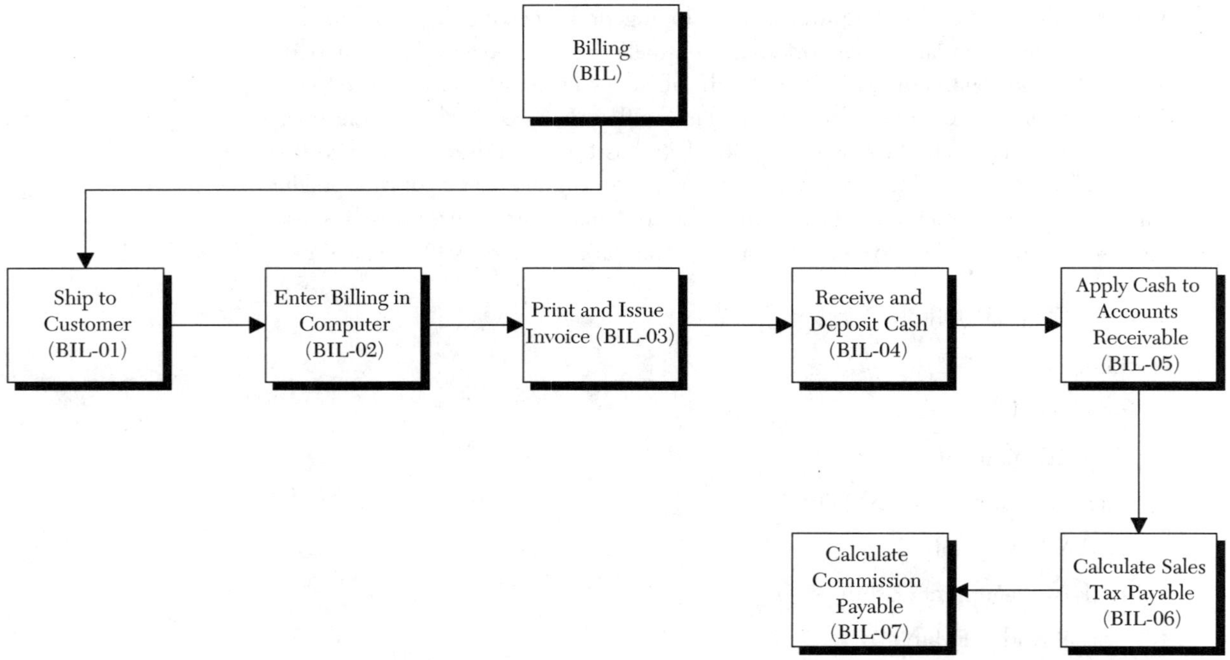

Exhibit 5.2. Billing Flowchart

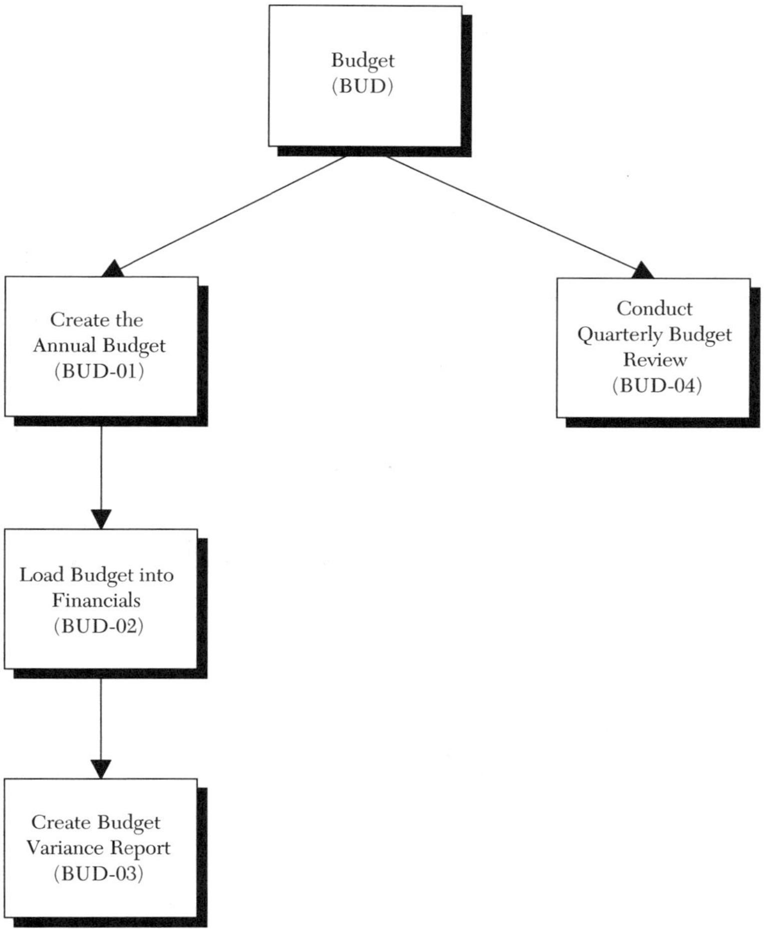

Exhibit 5.3. Budget Flowchart

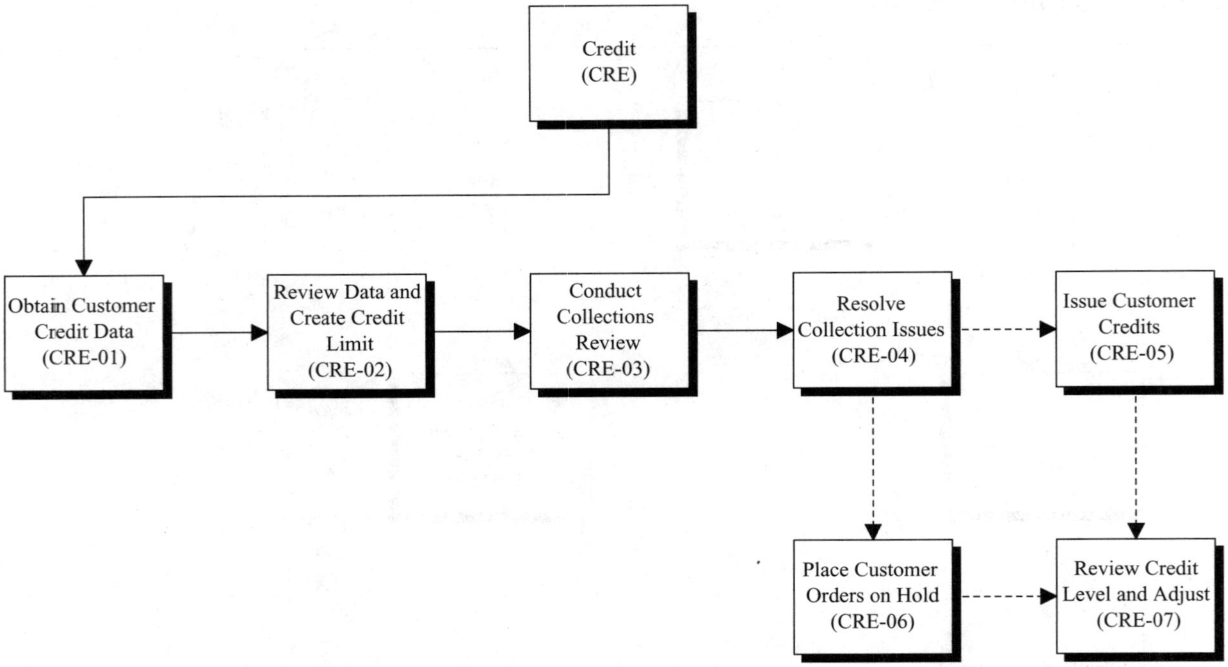

Exhibit 5.4. Credit Flowchart

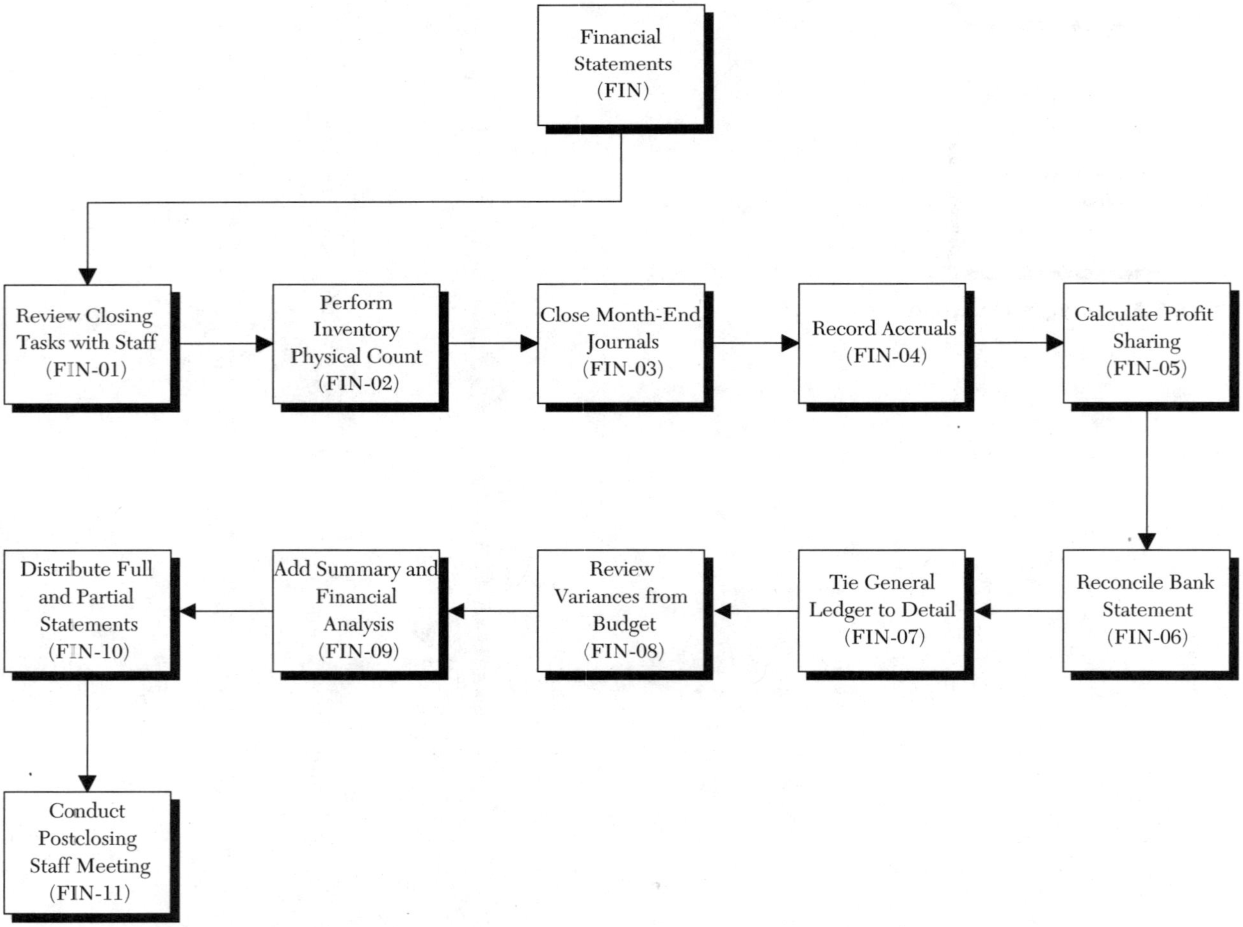

Exhibit 5.5. Financial Statements Flowchart

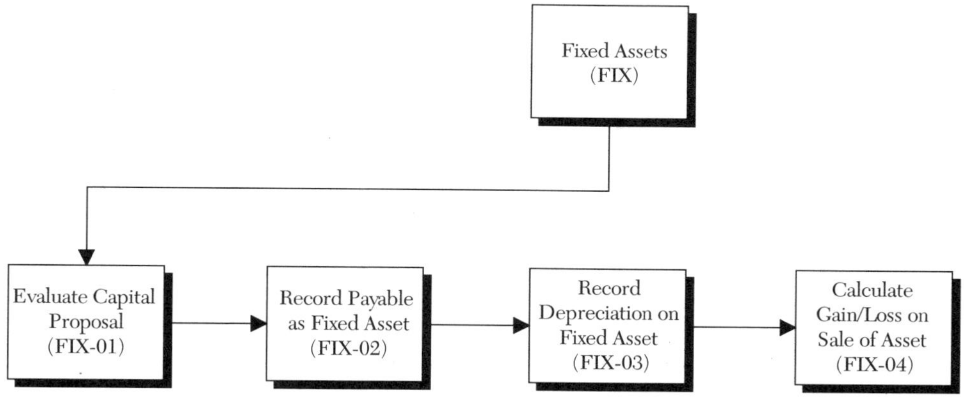

Exhibit 5.6. Fixed Assets Flowchart

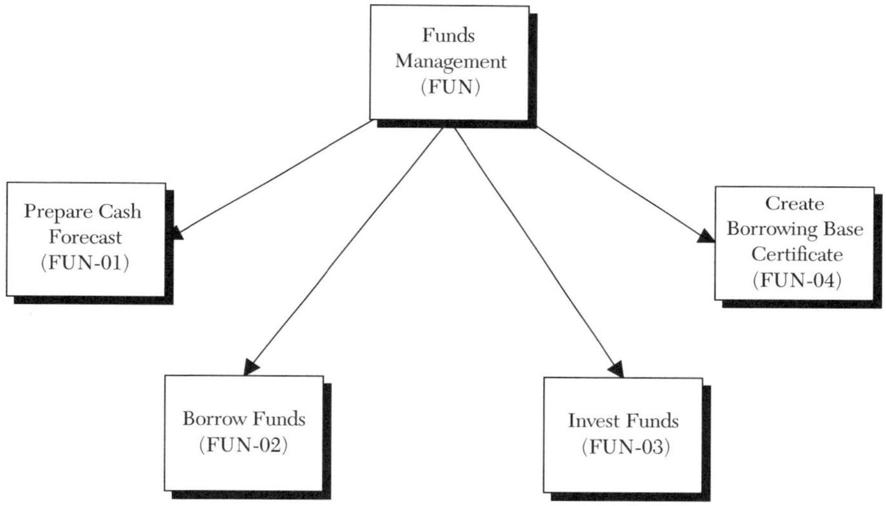

Exhibit 5.7. Funds Management Flowchart

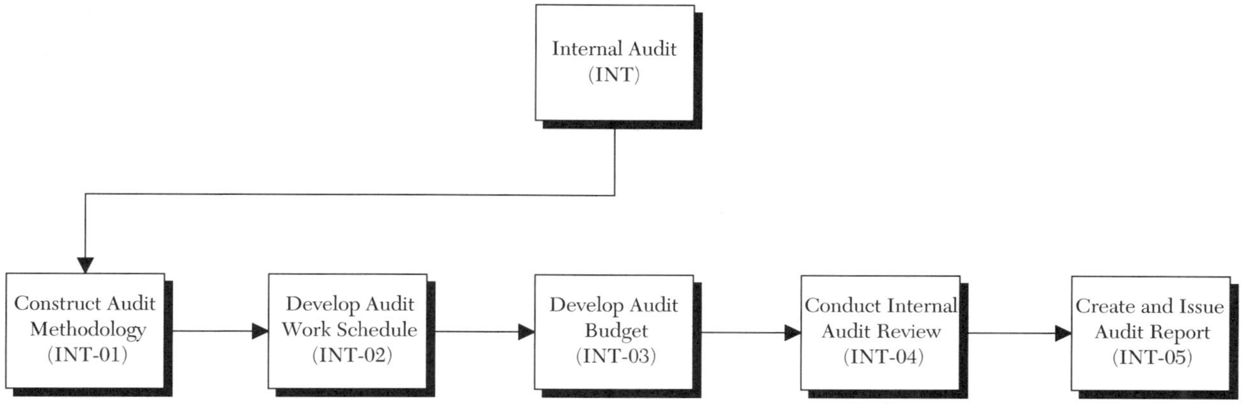

Exhibit 5.8. Internal Audit Flowchart

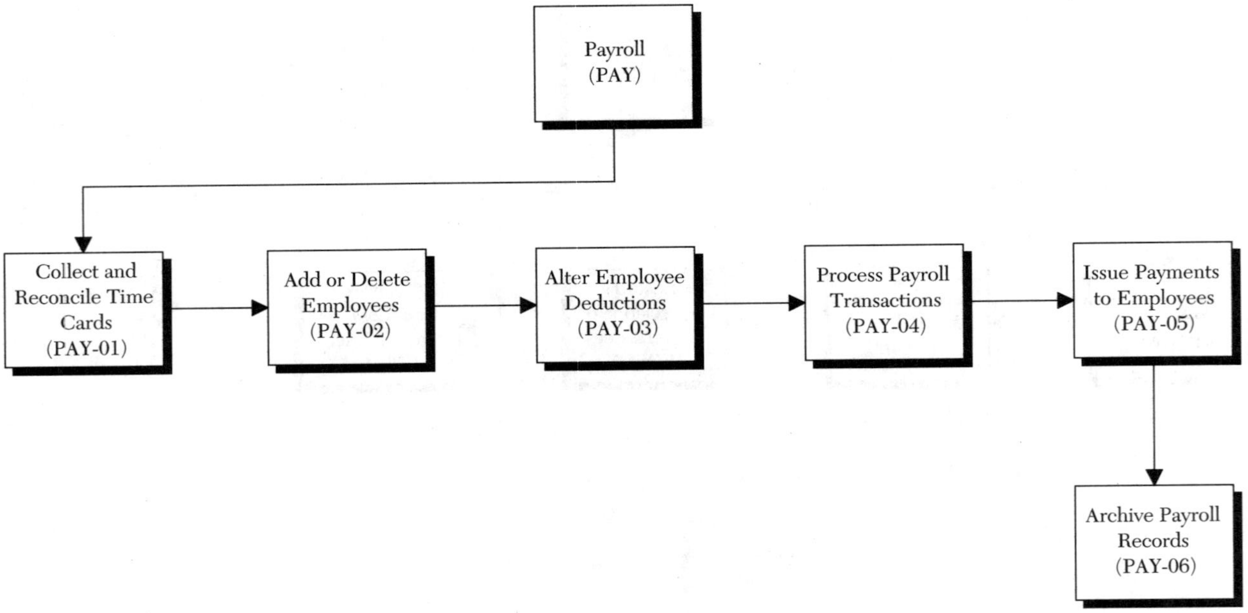

Exhibit 5.9. Payroll Flowchart

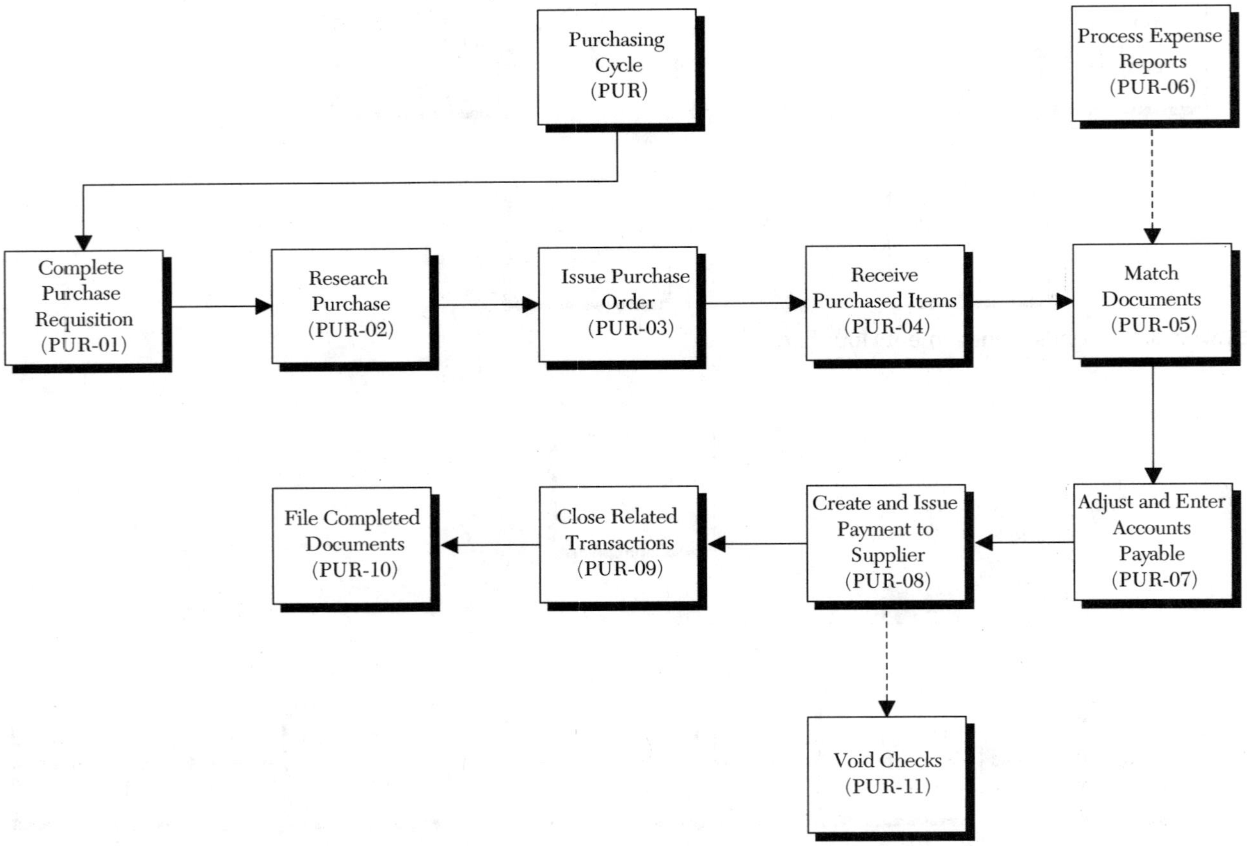

Exhibit 5.10. Purchasing Cycle Flowchart

Some organizations may want to fill out these procedures with additional sections pertaining to the definition of any technical terms included in the procedure, as well as references to related documents or policies.

The exact procedures used here are designed for specific software packages and company procedures, and so are not meant for exact copying by a user. Instead, it is best to review the general layout and terminology used in each procedure, and then use this information to design a customized set of procedures for one's own specific circumstances. The following procedures are included in this chapter:

1. **Acquisitions (ACQ)**
   - Complete confidentiality letter (ACQ-01)
   - Complete letter of intent (ACQ-02)
   - Perform due diligence (ACQ-03)
   - Adjust final price (ACQ-04)
   - Complete purchase transaction (ACQ-05)
   - Consolidate operations (ACQ-06)
   - Conduct postacquisition review (ACQ-07)
2. **Billing (BIL)**
   - Ship to customer (BIL-01)
   - Enter billing in computer (BIL-02)
   - Print and issue invoice (BIL-03)
   - Receive and deposit cash (BIL-04)
   - Apply cash to accounts receivable (BIL-05)
   - Calculate sales tax payable (BIL-06)
   - Calculate commission payable (BIL-07)
3. **Budget (BUD)**
   - Create the annual budget (BUD-01)
   - Load budget into financials (BUD-02)
   - Create budget variance report (BUD-03)
   - Conduct quarterly budget review (BUD-04)
4. **Credit (CRE)**
   - Obtain customer credit data (CRE-01)
   - Review data and create credit limit (CRE-02)
   - Conduct collections review (CRE-03)

- Resolve collections issues (CRE-04)
- Issue customer credits (CRE-05)
- Place customer orders on hold (CRE-06)
- Review credit level and adjust (CRE-07)

5. **Financial Statements (FIN)**
   - Review closing tasks with staff (FIN-01)
   - Perform physical inventory count (FIN-02)
   - Close month-end journals (FIN-03)
   - Record accruals (FIN-04)
   - Calculate profit sharing (FIN-05)
   - Reconcile bank statement (FIN-06)
   - Tie general ledger to detail (FIN-07)
   - Review variances from budget (FIN-08)
   - Add summary and financial analysis (FIN-09)
   - Distribute full and partial statements (FIN-10)
   - Conduct postclosing staff meeting (FIN-11)
6. **Fixed Assets (FIX)**
   - Evaluate capital proposal (FIX-01)
   - Record payable as fixed asset (FIX-02)
   - Record depreciation on fixed asset (FIX-03)
   - Calculate gain/loss on sale of asset (FIX-04)
7. **Funds Management (FUN)**
   - Prepare cash forecast (FUN-01)
   - Borrow funds (FUN-02)
   - Invest funds (FUN-03)
   - Create borrowing base certificate (FUN-04)
8. **Internal Audit (INT)**
   - Construct audit methodology (INT-01)
   - Develop audit work schedule (INT-02)
   - Develop audit budget (INT-03)
   - Conduct internal audit review (INT-04)
   - Create and issue audit report (INT-05)

9. **Payroll (PAY)**
   - Collect and reconcile time cards (PAY-01)
   - Add or delete employees (PAY-02)
   - Alter employee deductions (PAY-03)
   - Process payroll transactions (PAY-04)
   - Issue payments to employees (PAY-05)
   - Archive payroll records (PAY-06)

10. **Purchasing Cycle (PUR)**
    - Complete purchase requisition (PUR-01)
    - Research purchase (PUR-02)
    - Issue purchase order (PUR-03)
    - Receive purchased items (PUR-04)
    - Match documents (PUR-05)
    - Process expense reports (PUR-06)
    - Adjust and enter accounts payable (PUR-07)
    - Create and issue payment to supplier (PUR-08)
    - Close related transactions (PUR-09)
    - File completed documents (PUR-10)
    - Void checks (PUR-11)

Though budgeting procedures are included in this chapter to provide a complete set of accounting procedures, they are also dealt with again in Chapter 7, which is solely concerned with that topic.

Policy/Procedure Statement Brasto Publishing **Subject: Complete Confidentiality Agreement**	Retrieval No.: Page: Issue Date: Supercedes:	ACQ-01 1 of 1 10/28/0X N/A

1. PURPOSE AND SCOPE

This procedure is used by the chief financial officer to complete the confidentiality letter that must be signed by both parties prior to taking additional steps to complete an acquisition.

2. RESPONSIBILITIES

CFO **Chief Financial Officer**

3. PROCEDURES

3.1 CFO **Locate Boilerplate Letter Format**

1. Call up the confidentiality letter format, which is located in the N:\ACQUIRE subdirectory.
2. Print the letter.
3. Forward the letter to corporate counsel and schedule a meeting to go over special confidentiality issues related to the target company.

3.2 CFO **Alter Letter to Match Current Situation**

1. Alter the format of the confidentiality letter.
2. Have the altered letter reviewed by corporate counsel.
3. Reprint extra copies and send to president for signature.

3.3 CFO **Have Letter Signed**

1. Have president sign all copies of confidentiality letter.
2. Store one copy of letter in acquisitions file.
3. Forward all other copies to president of target company by traceable express delivery.

3.4 CFO **File Letter**

Upon receipt of signed copies from target company, store them in the acquisition file, replacing the earlier, unsigned, copy.

Complete Confidentiality Agreement

Policy/Procedure Statement	Procedure No.:	ACQ-02
Brasto Publishing	Page:	1 of 1
	Issue Date:	10/28/0X
	Supercedes:	N/A
Subject: Complete Letter of Intent		

1. PURPOSE AND SCOPE

This procedure is used by the chief financial officer to ensure the completion of the letter of intent that is used to notify the management of a target company that the acquiring company is making a bid.

2. RESPONSIBILITIES

CFO **Chief Financial Officer**

3. PROCEDURES

3.1 CFO **Locate Boilerplate Letter Format**

1. Call up the letter of intent format, which is located in the N:\ACQUIRE subdirectory.
2. Print the letter of intent.
3. Update the letter based on the preliminary purchase terms already discussed with the target company.
4. Forward the letter to corporate counsel and schedule a meeting to go over legal issues related to the letter of intent.

3.2 CFO **Have Letter Signed**

1. Schedule a meeting with the president to review the terms of the letter.
2. Obtain the signature of the president on two copies of the letter of intent.

3.3 CFO **Issue and File Letter Copies**

1. Put an unsigned copy of the letter of intent in the acquisitions file.
2. Send the other two (signed) copies to the president of the target company by traceable express mail.
3. Upon receipt of the signed copy from the target company, replace the unsigned copy in the acquisitions file with the signed copy.

Complete Letter of Intent

Policy/Procedure Statement	Retrieval No.:	ACQ-03
Brasto Publishing	Page:	1 of 3
	Issue Date:	10/28/0X
	Supercedes:	N/A
Subject: Perform Due Diligence		

1. PURPOSE AND SCOPE

This procedure helps outline the general business fundamentals of a potential acquisition target. This procedure is used by the controller.

2. RESPONSIBILITIES

CONTROLLER **Controller**

3. PROCEDURES

3.1 CONTROLLER

Review Sales and Marketing

- What is the current customer concentration?
- What is the profitability by customer?
- Does the typical customer purchase the complete product line?
- What are sales by geographic region?
- Which of the various lines have resulted in the greatest market penetration?
- What is the seasonality of sales?
- Has the target received any requests to expand its market geographically? Who has asked, and what product lines were requested?
- What is the organizational structure of the sales and marketing team?
- What types of outside sales representative relationship(s) do they have?
- What is the commission structure?
- What was the unit sales volume by product for last year, and current projections for the upcoming year?
- What types of agreements exist with customers in regard to price changes in response to changes in raw material prices?
- What customer agreements "lock in" pricing for fixed time periods?
- What is the return merchandise history for the last 18 months across all product lines?
- Have there been any recent product recalls?

3.2 CONTROLLER

Review the Competition

- Who are the primary competitors?
- What is their share of the market?
- What information is available on competitors in regard to sales volume, distribution, and products?

3.3 CONTROLLER

Review New Products

- What new products are being developed? What is the time line for the introduction of these products?
- What products have been introduced in the past year? What is their sales performance so far?
- What proportion of sales are from products that have been on the market for at least five years?

Perform Due Diligence (1 of 3)

Policy/Procedure Statement Brasto Publishing **Subject: Perform Due Diligence**	Procedure No.: Page: Issue Date: Supercedes:	ACQ-03 2 of 3 10/28/0X N/A

3.4 CONTROLLER

Review Product Designs

- Which organization has been responsible for product development? What are the skills and composition of the staff?
- What kind of design software do they use?
- Are there any existing patents for design or function on existing products? When are they due to expire?
- Have existing design patents within the industry affected product options?

3.5 CONTROLLER

Review Finance and Accounting

- What transfer costs are used between subsidiaries?
- Review the accounts receivable aging for old items and investigate.
- Review the accounts payable aging and investigate old unpaid items.
- Are operations matching budgeted performance levels?
- What depreciation schedule do they use for major assets?
- What leases are current?
- How long does the facility lease run? Is there an option to renew it?
- Obtain a copy of the building lease.
- Obtain a copy of the asset list.
- Obtain detailed financial statements for the last two years.
- Obtain a list of all loans, as well as the detailed agreements for them.
- Obtain a copy of the current business plan and financial projections.
- Obtain the most current credit report. What are the average payable days?
- Obtain a listing of the inventory. What proportion of the inventory has not been used recently? Are there any clearly obsolete items?
- What are the percentages of the cost of goods sold attributable to direct labor, materials, and overhead?
- What costs comprise the overhead expense?
- What costs go into the overhead allocation calculation?
- Are expenses being sufficiently accrued for?
- Are liabilities (such as pensions, taxes, warranties, insurance, litigation, and environmental remediation claims) underfunded?
- Does the company's bank want to continue funding any existing debt?

3.6 CONTROLLER

Review Legal and Tax Issues

- Are there any outstanding legal issues? Has there been a history of legal problems?
- What type of corporation structure is involved (partnership, Sub S, or C)?
- Are there any carryover tax credits?
- Obtain a list of all stockholders, and their proportions of ownership.
- Are there any potential environmental problems?
- Has OSHA recently reviewed the facility? What was the result?
- Is the facility unionized?

Perform Due Diligence (2 of 3)

Policy/Procedure Statement Brasto Publishing **Subject: Perform Due Diligence**	Retrieval No.: Page: Issue Date: Supercedes:	ACQ-03 3 of 3 10/28/0X N/A

3.7 CONTROLLER

Review Computer Systems Issues

- What type of software is used for accounting and manufacturing activities?
- Describe the network layout.
- Does the company use electronic data interchange?
- Obtain a list of all computers currently in use, including model numbers and age.

3.8 CONTROLLER

Review General Management Issues

- Obtain a copy of the current organization chart.
- Obtain a listing of salaries and employment agreements for key employees.
- Obtain a copy of the current benefit plan.

3.9 CONTROLLER

Review Logistics Issues

- What mode of transport do they use? Is there any in-house freight delivery service?
- What shipping range do they believe is competitive for their products?
- Are there any long-term supply contracts that the company is locked into that have unfavorable rates?

3.10 CONTROLLER

Review Manufacturing Issues

- What products are currently being produced?
- What types of manufacturing automation are in use?
- What percentage of machines are currently used?
- What percentage of the facility square footage is currently used?
- What brand and age of machines are being used? How soon before they need replacement?
- Do they use machine monitoring systems? What kind are used?
- Is there an active preventive maintenance system in place?

Policy/Procedure Statement	Procedure No.:	ACQ-04
Brasto Publishing	Page:	1 of 1
	Issue Date:	10/28/0X
	Supercedes:	N/A
Subject: Adjust Final Price		

1. PURPOSE AND SCOPE

This procedure is used by the chief financial officer as a set of guidelines that covers the maximum price to which the company will adjust its bid based on due diligence findings.

2. RESPONSIBILITIES

CFO **Chief Financial Officer**

3. PROCEDURES

3.1 CFO **Review Policy for Maximum Price Guidelines**

1. Summarize the controller's due diligence report and note all areas in which purchase price adjustments are necessary, based on variances from the original information on which the original letter of intent was based.
2. Refer to the company policy on maximum pricing guidelines, in case any pricing requires upward adjustment.
3. Document all downward pricing adjustments, along with exact calculations, and store this information in the acquisitions file.

3.2 CFO **Calculate Final Price Based on Due Diligence Results**

1. Summarize all pricing adjustments in a standard report format, as noted in the N:\ACQUIRE\PRICE.DOC file.
2. Schedule a meeting with the president to review all pricing adjustments and the final price.
3. Obtain the president's approval of the final pricing offer.

3.3 CFO **Communicate Price to Target Company**

1. Create a cover letter to the president of the target company, explaining all pricing adjustments. Include the pricing adjustment summary sheet. Include an offer termination date in the cover letter.
2. Copy the packet and store it in the acquisitions file.
3. Send the packet to the target company by traceable express mail.

Policy/Procedure Statement	Retrieval No.:	ACQ-05
Brasto Publishing	Page:	1 of 1
	Issue Date:	10/28/0X
	Supercedes:	N/A
Subject: Complete Purchase Transaction		

1. PURPOSE AND SCOPE

This procedure is used by the chief financial officer to ensure that all legal and financial documentation has been completed for an acquisition.

2. RESPONSIBILITIES

CFO **Chief Financial Officer**

3. PROCEDURES

3.1 CFO **Review Checklist of All Purchase Documentation**

Extract the standard checklist of purchase documentation from the N:\ACQUIRE subdirectory, file name CHECKLIST.DOC.

3.2 CFO **Verify That All Checklist Items Have Been Completed**

1. Ensure that the environmental testing report has been completed and reviewed for problems.
2. Verify that there are no legal attachments to any target company assets.
3. Ensure that all property taxes have been paid by the target company or put in escrow through the date of the acquisition.
4. Verify that bridge loans for the acquisition have been approved by lenders.
5. Ensure that the auditors have completed their investigative audit of the target company.
6. Verify that the appraised value of all assets matches the summary total against which the original price was based.

3.3 CFO **Follow Up on Missing Checklist Items**

1. Draft a list of all checklist issues that have not yet been completed.
2. Assign responsibility for all tasks, and schedule due dates.
3. Follow up to ensure that all checklist items are complete.

3.4 CFO **Complete Purchase Transaction**

1. Prepare all purchase documentation and submit it to all parties for review.
2. Incorporate any final changes into the documentation.
3. Schedule a meeting with representatives from the target company, as well as all legal advisors, to sign the purchase documentation.

Policy/Procedure Statement Brasto Publishing **Subject: Consolidate Operations**	Procedure No.: Page: Issue Date: Supercedes:	ACQ-06 1 of 1 10/28/0X N/A

1. PURPOSE AND SCOPE

This procedure is used by the chief financial officer to ensure that the proper steps are followed in consolidating the operations of an acquired entity into those of the company.

2. RESPONSIBILITIES

CFO **Chief Financial Officer**

3. PROCEDURES

3.1 CFO **Assign Consolidation Project Team**

1. Determine the available staff and management group available for assignment to the consolidation project team.
2. Select the team from this group, based on past experience and management skill.
3. Meet with the team leader to determine the dates and locations for the consolidation project.

3.2 CFO **Setup Consolidation Guidelines and Deadlines**

1. Review the team leader's recommendations for deadlines and revise as necessary.
2. Review with the team leader the standard set of consolidation activities, as listed in the N:\ACQUIRE\GUIDE.DOC file, and revise it as necessary, depending on the conditions at the target company.
3. Create a list of milestone dates and meetings to review progress.
4. Meet with the entire consolidation team to review the project plans.

3.3 CFO **Conduct Milestone Progress Reviews**

1. Meet with the consolidation team on the previously specified dates to review progress.
2. Address the need for changes in the composition of the team to ensure that due dates are met, or else modify the due dates.
3. Issue a written communication to the team leader regarding expectations for the next milestone meeting.

Consolidate Operations

Policy/Procedure Statement	Retrieval No.:	ACQ-07
Brasto Publishing	Page:	1 of 1
	Issue Date:	10/28/0X
Subject: Conduct Postacquisition Review	Supercedes:	N/A

1. PURPOSE AND SCOPE

This procedure is used by the chief financial officer to ensure that solutions are found to any problems encountered during the acquisition process.

2. RESPONSIBILITIES

CFO **Chief Financial Officer**

3. PROCEDURES

3.1 CFO **Conduct Postacquisition Review**

1. Schedule a review meeting with members of the consolidation team.
2. Issue an agenda of discussion items in advance of the meeting.
3. Review all issues that arose during the latest consolidation that related to increased costs or delayed deadlines, as well as new initiatives for correcting both problems, plus concerns raised by team members.

3.2 CFO **Assign Responsibilities for Resulting Projects**

1. Specify who is responsible for projects that will improve the consolidation process the next time. Set up deadlines and precisely define expectations.
2. Agree to the date and subject matter for a follow-up meeting regarding these issues.

Policy/Procedure Statement	Procedure No.:	BIL-01
Brasto Publishing	Page:	1 of 1
	Issue Date:	10/28/0X
Subject: Ship to Customer	Supercedes:	N/A

1. PURPOSE AND SCOPE

This procedure is used by the shipping supervisor to ensure that the proper paperwork and computer transactions are completed when product is shipped to a customer.

2. RESPONSIBILITIES

SHIPPING **Shipping Supervisor**

3. PROCEDURES

3.1 SHIPPING **Print Daily Shipping List**

Go to the REPORTS screen in the computer system and access the Shipping List report. Enter today's date and press ENTER. The report will print.

3.2 SHIPPING **Verify That all Shipments Are Available**

1. Go to the INVENTORY menu and select the ON HAND screen. Verify that all finished goods listed on the shipping list are also noted on the screen as being on hand and available for shipment.
2. If the required quantities are not available, contact the customer service staff to ascertain customer wishes regarding partial orders, or contact the production scheduling staff to ensure that the production department will complete the missing products as soon as possible.
3. Mark all other items on the shipping list as being ready for delivery.

3.3 SHIPPING **Prepare Shipments**

1. Using the shipping list, remove all targeted items from the warehouse bins and relocate them to the shipping area.
2. Contact freight carriers regarding pickup times.
3. Prepare bills of lading and packing slips for all shipments.
4. Load shipments on trucks for delivery.

3.4 SHIPPING **Complete Related Paperwork**

1. Complete the shipping log.
2. Send copies of the bills of lading and packing slips to the accounting department by interoffice mail. Include a copy of the day's shipping log, which should match all other documentation sent.

3.5 SHIPPING **Complete Related Computer Transactions**

Go to the INVENTORY menu in the computer system. Access the SHIP screen and enter the customer, ship date, part number, and quantity shipped for each shipment sent out that day.

Ship to Customer

Policy/Procedure Statement Brasto Publishing **Subject: Enter Billing in Computer**	Retrieval No.: Page: Issue Date: Supercedes:	BIL-02 1 of 2 10/28/0X N/A

1. PURPOSE AND SCOPE

This procedure is used by the accounts receivable clerk to complete daily billings to customers.

2. RESPONSIBILITIES

ACC RECV **Accounts Receivable Clerk**

3. PROCEDURES

3.1 ACC RECV **Shipping Paperwork**

Find the shipping paperwork in the "shippers" box in the mail room. The paperwork should include a handwritten shipping log, as well as white and green copies of the bills of lading. Separate these documents into different piles.

3.2 ACC RECV **Verify Bills of Lading**

Verify that there is a bill of lading for every order listed on the shipping log, and also that all bills of lading are listed on the log. Then put the bills of lading in order, first by customer number and then by order number (if there is more than one order per customer). Next, check the "carrier" column of the shipping log. Most orders will have "Customer Pickup" listed next to them. Any accompanying freight sheet is filled out by the shipping department. These are usually turned in ahead of time and kept in a file. Pull out the appropriate sheets, because they are needed for invoicing.

3.3 ACC RECV **Review Freight Sheets**

Review the freight sheets. If the bill of lading reads "Packing List" on the top, the order has already been picked by the shipping department. If it reads "Customer Order Picklist" and the shipment quantities are handwritten in the blanks, the order still must be picked. To pick an order, go to SHIP in the software, enter an "I" for the issue type, and then enter the customer number. If the quantity showing on the screen for an item matches the quantity handwritten in the bill of lading, press ENTER to pick that item. If the quantities differ, type the handwritten quantity into the order and press ENTER. Put a "P" (for "picked") next to the quantity shipped. Pick all of the items on the order, and then press HOME and proceed to the next order.

3.4 ACC RECV **List All Picked Orders**

List all picked orders by typing INRV. The resulting list should include all the orders in the stack, plus any orders shipped out today. In this step, go through the list and choose only those orders that were shipped the previous day and for which there are bills of lading. Choose the orders by typing an "A" in the far right column. Those orders that you do not wish to invoice must have a "U" in that column. It may be difficult to determine the order numbers for some shipments, because there may be more than one sequence number for the same customer order number. You may need to look at all of the orders with a particular order number to find the correct one. To pick one, make sure the item numbers and quantities match the bill of lading.

Policy/Procedure Statement Brasto Publishing **Subject: Enter Billing in Computer**	Procedure No.: Page: Issue Date: Supercedes:	BIL-02 2 of 2 10/28/0X N/A

3.5	ACC RECV	**Check Pricing** Check the pricing for each order and verify that there is a charge for pallets and shipping. Go to the IVIE screen and enter the customer order number and sequence number to check prices. Each customer has a price sheet in the price book that lists current prices for all of the items it orders. The price sheet will also tell you whether or not to charge that customer for pallets. This is also where the freight sheet is used. Check the freight code on the order and make sure that it matches what the shipping department has written on the freight sheet. If the code is "prepaid," do not charge the customer for freight. If it is "prepay and add," you must add the amount on the freight sheet to the invoice. If the order was sent collect, there will be no freight sheet, because the customer is arranging and paying for its own freight.
3.6	ACC RECV	**Verify Checking Pricing** After reviewing pricing, go back to the IVRV screen to verify that all orders to be printed have an "A" status, and those that should not print have a "U" status. Also, verify that the sequence numbers are correct.

Enter Billing in Computer (2 of 2)

Policy/Procedure Statement Brasto Publishing **Subject: Print and Issue Invoice**	Retrieval No.: Page: Issue Date: Supercedes:	BIL-03 1 of 1 10/28/0X N/A

1. PURPOSE AND SCOPE

This procedure is used by the accounts receivable clerk to print and issue invoices to customers as well as to file.

2. RESPONSIBILITIES

ACC RECV **Accounts Receivable Clerk**

3. PROCEDURES

3.1 ACC RECV **Print Invoice Batch**

1. Go to the ACCOUNTS RECEIVABLE menu in the computer system and select the BILLING BATCH screen. Select the "All Unprinted" option.
2. Turn on the printer and verify that the invoice stock is correctly positioned in it.
3. Using the RUN TEST option, run a sample invoice to ensure that the line settings are correct.
4. Using the RUN FULL BATCH option, print all invoices in the batch.

3.2 ACC RECV **Prepare and Send Invoices**

1. Burst all invoices, with the pink copies going in the TO FILE bin, the white copies going in the TO CUSTOMER bin, and the goldenrod copies going in the NUMERICAL bin.
2. Stuff envelopes with the white invoice copies.
3. Affix postage to the envelopes and put them in the interoffice mail, marked for outside delivery.

3.3 ACC RECV **File Invoice Copies**

1. Attach the pink invoice copies to the billing of lading and packing slip copies, and file by customer.
2. File the goldenrod copies in numerical order.

Policy/Procedure Statement	Procedure No.:	BIL-04
Brasto Publishing	Page:	1 of 1
	Issue Date:	10/28/0X
Subject: Receive and Deposit Cash	Supercedes:	N/A

1. PURPOSE AND SCOPE

This procedure is used by the cash clerk to receive cash from a variety of sources and deposit it into the company bank account.

2. RESPONSIBILITIES

CASH **Cash Clerk**

3. PROCEDURES

3.1 CASH **Total and Record Cash**

1. Summarize all cash on an adding machine tape.
2. Enter all checks received on a deposit slip, as well as cash receipts in a lump sum. Verify that the deposit slip total and the adding machine tape total are the same. If not, recount the cash.

3.2 CASH **Prepare and Issue Deposit**

1. Give the deposit slip and attached checks and cash to the second cash clerk, who compares the check total to the summary sheet forwarded from the mail room. Reconcile any differences.
2. Split all remittance advices from the checks, and copy all checks that have invoice numbers written on them. Verify that this packet of information matches the total that is to be sent to the bank in the deposit.
3. Send the completed deposit to the bank by courier.

3.3 CASH **Forward Information**

Send the remittance advice packet to the accounts receivable staff, which will apply it to outstanding accounts receivable.

Receive and Deposit Cash

Policy/Procedure Statement		
Brasto Publishing	Retrieval No.:	BIL-05
	Page:	1 of 1
	Issue Date:	10/28/0X
	Supercedes:	N/A
Subject: Apply Cash to Accounts Receivable		

1. PURPOSE AND SCOPE

This procedure is used by the accounts receivable clerk to apply cash received from customers to open accounts receivable balances.

2. RESPONSIBILITIES

ACC RECV **Accounts Receivable Clerk**

3. PROCEDURES

3.1 ACC RECV **Summarize Cash Receipts**

Add up all daily cash receipts and match the paper tape of the summarization to the individual payments to ensure that the total is correct.

3.2 ACC RECV **Enter Total Cash Amount**

Go to the accounting software and enter the APPLY screen. At the top of the screen, enter today's date and the total amount to be applied.

3.3 ACC RECV **Apply Individual Payment Amounts**

For each customer payment, enter the customer number, individual check amount, the check number and date, and then TAB to the detail section of the screen. The list of all open invoices for each customer will appear. Click on each invoice being paid and enter any discounts taken. After identifying all invoices paid by each customer, click on the "Next Payment" button at the bottom of the screen. Continue in this fashion until all receipts have been entered.

3.4 ACC RECV **Verify Amounts Applied**

At the top of the screen is a running total that increases as each check is applied. If the total amount applied through the software does not match the grand total you initially entered in the screen, there is an entry problem. Click on the "Print Receipt Report" button to obtain the detail for all entries made, and determine where the error lies. Fix the error, and then press the "Post Cash" button to transfer all the receipts information to the general ledger.

3.5 ACC RECV **File Receipt Documentation**

Staple the cash receipts report to the daily cash receipts, and file the set of documents in the applied cash filing cabinet.

Apply Cash to Accounts Receivable

Policy/Procedure Statement Brasto Publishing **Subject: Calculate Sales Tax Payable**	Procedure No.: Page: Issue Date: Supercedes:	BIL-06 1 of 1 10/28/0X N/A

1. PURPOSE AND SCOPE

This procedure is used by the assistant controller to calculate state and local sales taxes on monthly sales.

2. RESPONSIBILITIES

ASST CNTLR	**Assistant Controller**
ACCT PAY	**Accounts Payable Clerk**
CONTROLLER	**Controller**

3. PROCEDURES

3.1 ASST CNTLR — **Print Invoice Register**
Go to the "Accounts Receivable Reports" screen in the accounting software. Print out the Sales Tax Register for the preceding month. This report itemizes invoices by the state in which items were sold.

3.2 ASST CNTLR — **Summarize Invoice Totals by Taxing Region**
The report is subtotaled for each state. Extract these subtotals from the report and list the amounts on a separate sheet of paper.

3.3 ASST CNTLR — **Insert Invoice Summary Totals into Tax Documents**
Go to the tax forms file and remove a sales tax reporting form for each state in which the company recorded a sale in the previous month. Transfer the sales totals to these documents and fill out all other required fields on the forms.

3.4 CONTROLLER — **Obtain Independent Review of Tax Filings**
Take the completed sales tax forms and invoice registers to the controller, who should verify that the correct amounts have been transferred from the registers to the forms, and that all other information on the forms is correct. The controller should then sign the forms and return everything to the assistant controller.

3.5 ACCT PAY — **Obtain Check Payment for Tax Filings**
Attach a payment request form to each tax form and take them to the accounts payable clerk. This person enters the requests into the computer system for inclusion in the next check run.

3.6 ASST CNTLR — **Issue Tax Payment**
Once the check run is complete, the accounts payable clerk removes the sales tax payments from the run, attaches them to the tax forms, and mails them to the appropriate taxation authorities.

3.7 ASST CNTLR — **File Tax Records**
File the company's copy of each tax return in the sales tax files, along with the invoice register that provides backup information for each return.

Calculate Sales Tax Payable

Policy/Procedure Statement Brasto Publishing **Subject: Calculate Commission Payable**	Retrieval No.: Page: Issue Date: Supercedes:	BIL-07 1 of 1 10/28/0X N/A

1. PURPOSE AND SCOPE

This procedure is used by the accounts payable clerk to calculate monthly commission payments. The accounting department is responsible for this procedure.

2. RESPONSIBILITIES

ACCT PAY	**Accounts Payable Clerk**
CONTROLLER	**Controller**

3. PROCEDURES

3.1 CONTROLLER — **Access the Commissions Report**

The controller prints out the commissions report that lists sales by customer detail and gives it to the accounts payable clerk. To print this report, go to the ACCOUNTS RECEIVABLE REPORTS menu and access the "Sales by Salesperson" report. Select the dates for the month for which commissions are being calculated. Then click the "Printer" icon to generate the report.

3.2 ACCT PAY — **Calculate Commissions**

To calculate commissions, access the COMMISSION.XLS report, which is located in the C:/FILES/COMMISSIONS subdirectory. Create a new workbook for each month. Summarize the sales for each customer and cluster them based on the sales code noted in the original report, identifying the salesperson. Then multiply the sales for each person by the commission rate.

3.3 ACCT PAY — **Print the Commissions Report**

Print a copy of the commission report for each salesperson and e-mail it to them for review. Also submit a master copy to the controller for review and approval. Following approval, print commission checks for the sales staff, staple a copy of the commission report to each check receipt, and issue the checks. File the calculations and reports in the commissions file.

Calculate Commission Payable

Policy/Procedure Statement	Procedure No.:	BUD-01
Brasto Publishing	Page:	1 of 2
	Issue Date:	10/28/0X
	Supercedes:	N/A
Subject: Create the Annual Budget		

1. PURPOSE AND SCOPE

This procedure is used by the controller to guide the process of updating the annual budget.

2. RESPONSIBILITIES

CONTROLLER **Controller**

3. PROCEDURES

3.1 CONTROLLER

Update Expenses

As of mid-November, issue to each department of listing of its expenses that are annualized based on actual expenses through October of the current year. The listing should include the personnel in each department and their current pay levels. Request a return date of 10 days in the future for this information, which should include estimated changes in expenses.

3.2 CONTROLLER

Update Revenue

As of mid-November, issue to the sales manager a listing of revenue by month by business unit, through October of the current year. Request a return date of 10 days in the future for this information, which should include estimated changes in revenues.

3.3 CONTROLLER

Update Capital Expenditures

As of mid-November, issue a form to all department heads, requesting information about the cost and timing of capital expenditures for the upcoming year. Request a return date of 10 days in the future for this information.

3.4 CONTROLLER

Update Automation

As of mid-November, issue a form to the manager of automation, requesting estimates of the timing and size of reductions in headcount in the upcoming year that are due to automation efforts. Request a return date of 10 days in the future for this information. Be sure to compare scheduled headcount reductions to the timing of capital expenditures, as they should track closely.

3.5 CONTROLLER

Update the Budget Model

This task should be completed by the end of November.

- Update the numbers already listed in the budget with information as it is received from the various managers. This may involve changing "hard-coded" dollar amounts or flex budget percentages. Be sure to keep a checklist of who has returned information so you can follow up with those who have not.
- Update the "Last Year" cells on the right side of the budget model, using annualized figures.
- Verify that the indirect overhead allocation percentages shown on the budgeted factory overhead page are accurate.
- Verify that the FUTA, SUTA, FICA, medical, and workers' compensation amounts listed at the top of the staffing budget page are still accurate.

Create the Annual Budget (1 of 2)

Policy/Procedure Statement Brasto Publishing **Subject: Create the Annual Budget**	Retrieval No.: Page: Issue Date: Supercedes:	BUD-01 2 of 2 10/28/0X N/A

- Add job titles and staffing levels to the staffing page as needed, along with new average pay rates based on projected pay levels made by department managers.
- Run a depreciation report for the upcoming year, add the expected depreciation for new capital expenditures, and add this amount to the budget.
- Revise the loan detail budget based on projected borrowings through the end of the year.

3.6 CONTROLLER **Review the Budget**
Print out the budget and circle any budgeted expenses or revenues that are significantly different from the annualized amounts for the current year. Go over the questionable items with the managers who are responsible for those items.

3.7 CONTROLLER **Revise the Budget**
Revise the budget, print it again, and review it with senior management. Incorporate any additional changes.

3.8 CONTROLLER **Issue the Budget**
Bind the budget and issue it to the management team.

Create the Annual Budget (2 of 2)

Policy/Procedure Statement Brasto Publishing **Subject: Load Budget into Financials**	Procedure No.: Page: Issue Date: Supercedes:	BUD-02 1 of 1 10/28/0X N/A

1. PURPOSE AND SCOPE

This procedure is used by the controller to enter all data from the budget model into the financial statement database in the computer system.

2. RESPONSIBILITIES

CONTROLLER **Controller**

3. PROCEDURES

3.1 CONTROLLER **Locate Budget Model**

1. Call up the completed budget model, which is located in the N:\BUDGET\BUDGET.XLS file.
2. Print the budget.
3. Verify that there is a valid account number for every budget line item in the budget model.
4. Highlight the budget numbers that must be input into the financial statement database.

3.2 CONTROLLER **Access Computer Input Screen**

1. Call up the accounting software package, and access the BUDGET menu. Then access the INPUT BUDGET screen from that menu.
2. Enter the appropriate budget year to be entered, as well as the budget version.

3.3 CONTROLLER **Enter Budget Information**

1. Enter the account number for each budget line item.
2. Enter the budget in each month on the screen for that account number.
3. Verify that the months entered and the amounts are correct, and then press ENTER.
4. Repeat for all account numbers.

3.4 CONTROLLER **Verify Entered Information**

1. Go to the BUDGET menu and access the REPORTS screen.
2. Select the BUDGET report and enter the correct budget year and version. Print the report.
3. Compare the entered amounts to the amounts listed on the budget model. Go back to step 3.3 to correct any incorrectly entered budget numbers.

Load Budget into Financials

Policy/Procedure Statement	Retrieval No.:	BUD-03
Brasto Publishing	Page:	1 of 1
	Issue Date:	10/28/0X
	Supercedes:	N/A
Subject: Create Budget Variance Report		

1. PURPOSE AND SCOPE

This procedure is used by the financial analyst to calculate and report on the extent of actual financial results from budgeted expectations.

2. RESPONSIBILITIES

FINL ANALYST **Financial Analyst**

3. PROCEDURES

3.1 FINL ANALYST **Locate Budget Variance Spreadsheet**

Call up the budget variance spreadsheet, which is located in the N:\FINANCIALS\VARIANCE.XLS file.

3.2 FINL ANALYST **Enter New Year Budget**

1. Enter all expense line items from the budget model into the variance model.
2. Verify that the same managers listed in the variance report from last year are still responsible for expense line items this year.
3. Send the preliminary variance report to the controller to verify the accuracy of the format and numbers.

3.3 FINL ANALYST **Enter Year-to-Date Actual Amounts**

1. Enter both year-to-date and last month actual expenses in the report.
2. Verify that the expense totals match the numbers in the financial statements.
3. Sort the report by responsible manager and subdivide the report so that each manager only receives the listing of accounts for which they are responsible.

3.4 FINL ANALYST **Issue Variance Report**

1. Schedule meetings with all department managers who are receiving the report.
2. Go over all negative variance items, and record their responses regarding actions to take to correct problems.
3. Include manager comments in the final variance report, and issue it to senior management.

Policy/Procedure Statement	Procedure No.:	BUD-04
Brasto Publishing	Page:	1 of 1
	Issue Date:	10/28/0X
	Supercedes:	N/A
Subject: Conduct Quarterly Budget Review		

1. PURPOSE AND SCOPE

This procedure is used by the controller to review with other department managers the comparison of actual to budgeted financial results for their departments for the last quarter.

2. RESPONSIBILITIES

CONTROLLER **Controller**

3. PROCEDURES

3.1 CONTROLLER **Prepare Quarterly Budget Report**

1. Extract the most recent budget variance report, which is located in the N:\FINANCIALS\VARIANCE.XLS file.
2. Print copies of the report and issue it to those managers who are listed as being responsible for expense line items.

3.2 CONTROLLER **Conduct Manager Interviews**

1. Meet with managers to verify their intentions regarding currently negative variances.
2. Record these comments on the report.
3. Supply managers with any additional requested information, such as added detail regarding expenses, or copies of actual supplier invoices.

3.3 CONTROLLER **Report Results to General Manager**

1. Highlight all negative variances on the budget report, and sort it by the names of responsible managers.
2. Issue the completed budget variance report to the general manager.

Conduct Quarterly Budget Review

Policy/Procedure Statement Brasto Publishing **Subject: Obtain Customer Credit Data**	Retrieval No.: Page: Issue Date: Supercedes:	CRE-01 1 of 1 10/28/0X N/A

1. PURPOSE AND SCOPE

This procedure is used by the credit clerk to obtain credit information about prospective customers.

2. RESPONSIBILITIES

CREDIT **Credit Clerk**

3. PROCEDURES

3.1 CREDIT **Obtain Credit References**

1. Pull the standard credit references form from the forms cabinet.
2. Fax the form to the customer who is requesting credit.

3.2 CREDIT **Contact Credit References**

1. Verify with each customer reference the maximum and average amounts of credit granted and used, as well as any issues with slow payment.
2. Obtain the names of other credit references from these references, if possible, and record the answers to the same questions from them.

3.3 CREDIT **Obtain Credit Information from Other Sources**

1. Contact Dun & Bradstreet's automated credit reporting system, enter the customer's phone number at the prompt, and specify that you want to receive the Business Information Report.

Obtain Customer Credit Data

Policy/Procedure Statement Brasto Publishing **Subject: Review Data and Create Credit Limit**	Procedure No.: Page: Issue Date: Supercedes:	CRE-02 1 of 1 10/28/0X N/A

1. PURPOSE AND SCOPE

This procedure is used by the controller to help adjust customer credit limits.

2. RESPONSIBILITIES

CONTROLLER **Controller**

3. PROCEDURES

3.1 CONTROLLER **Access the Customer Account**
Access the CREDIT file. Enter into it any new customer names, which can be obtained from the CUSTOMER screen (F7 to print).

3.2 CONTROLLER **Annualize the Sales Report**
Take sales from the "Access Sales" report that lists sales by customer, and annualize the numbers. This information goes into the "Annualized Sales" column in the report.

3.3 CONTROLLER **Extend Formula Columns**
The next two columns are formulas. Extend them to any new customers that have been added.

3.4 CONTROLLER **List the Current Credit Limit**
List the current credit limit in the "Current Credit" column. This information comes from the CUSTOMER screen.

3.5 CONTROLLER **Compare Average Credit Levels**
Compare the 45-day and 90-day average credit levels to annualized sales, and enter new credit limits in the "Suggested Credit" column.

3.6 CONTROLLER **Enter Changes**
Enter the changes into the "Limit" field in the CUSTOMER master screen.

Review Data and Create Credit Limit

Policy/Procedure Statement		
Brasto Publishing	Retrieval No.:	CRE-03
	Page:	1 of 1
	Issue Date:	10/28/0X
Subject: Conduct Collections Review	Supercedes:	N/A

1. PURPOSE AND SCOPE

This procedure is used by the accounts receivable clerk to manage the collections process.

2. RESPONSIBILITIES

ACC RECV **Accounts Receivable Clerk**

3. PROCEDURES

3.1 ACC RECV **Print Accounts Receivable Aging**

Go to the accounting software and access the ACCOUNTS RECEIVABLE screen. Print the accounts receivable aging, making sure that the aging date buckets are set at 10, 30, and 60 days. This bucket configuration will separate out all invoices that are 40 days old and older, which is the primary grouping of invoices that require collections activity.

3.2 ACC RECV **Note Old Receivables**

Go through the printed aging and circle or highlight all invoices that are more than 40 days old. These are the invoices requiring specific collections activity.

3.3 ACC RECV **Contact Customers**

Go to the ACCOUNTS RECEIVABLE REPORTS menu and print the Customer Master Report. This contains a list of all customers, their main accounts payable contacts, phone numbers, and fax numbers. Use the information on this report to contact customers with overdue invoices. Determine why payment has not been made. If a customer states that a payment is on the way, verify exactly which invoices are being paid and then inquire about any overdue invoices that continue to be open after the payment.

3.4 ACC RECV **Maintain Contact Log**

Go to the customer contact log book and write down in it, for each customer, the date of contact, who was contacted, and what information was gained. Use this information as a reference whenever calling the customer again in the future. Also if there is new customer contact information as a result of the day's calls, update the "Customer Master Report" with this information.

3.5 ACC RECV **Review Accounts with Credit Department**

If, as a result of the day's phone calls, it is necessary to alter a customer's credit status to more properly reflect his or her ability to pay, then go to the credit department and review the customer's credit situation with the credit manager. If new credit terms are decided upon, contact the customer to let him or her know about the revised situation.

Conduct Collections Review

Policy/Procedure Statement Brasto Publishing **Subject: Resolve Collection Issues**	Procedure No.: Page: Issue Date: Supercedes:	CRE-04 1 of 1 10/28/0X N/A

1. PURPOSE AND SCOPE

This procedure is used by the collections clerk to determine the causes of collection problems and find solutions to them.

2. RESPONSIBILITIES

COLLECT **Collections Clerk**

3. PROCEDURES

3.1 COLLECT **Summarize Collection Issues**

1. Contact the customer regarding why it has not paid each invoice on time. Note the reasons in the collections contact log.
2. Based on the previous history of reasons given by the customer, ascertain if there is a correctable internal problem causing the collection issue, or if the problem lies with the customer.

3.2 COLLECT **Correct Internal Problems**

1. Summarize all internal problems for all collection customers to determine which problems recur most frequently. Sort the list in declining order of frequency.
2. Meet with the assistant controller to determine what actions to take internally that will correct these problems.
3. The internal controller meets with the controller regarding these issues, who meets with other department heads to determine a course of action.
4. The controller regularly follows up on these issues and consults with the collections staff to see if problem areas are declining in frequency.

3.3 COLLECT **Increase Collection Activities**

If the problem is deemed to be with the customer, then meet with the assistant controller to determine the best course of action, which can include a reduction in credit terms for future orders, an increased number of collection calls, dunning letters, or referral to an attorney or collection agency.

Resolve Collection Issues

Policy/Procedure Statement	Retrieval No.:	CRE-05
Brasto Publishing	Page:	1 of 1
	Issue Date:	10/28/0X
	Supercedes:	N/A
Subject: Issue Customer Credits		

1. PURPOSE AND SCOPE

This procedure is used by the accounts receivable clerk to determine the correct method for processing a credit memo.

2. RESPONSIBILITIES

ACC RECV **Accounts Receivable Clerk**

3. PROCEDURES

3.1 ACC RECV **Receive Request for Credit Memo**

A request for a credit memo must be submitted on the "Credit Memo" form. If someone requests this information without the proper form, give that person a blank form along with a sample form and request that it be filled out completely. Once this is done, file the form in the "To Do" box until the end of the week, when the credit memos are batched for further processing.

3.2 ACC RECV **Obtain Approval for Credit**

Take the batch of credit memos to the controller for approval. The controller signs each one if they are approved. If not, send the credit memos back to the requestors with a note explaining why they cannot be granted. If more information is needed on the form, make the recipient aware of the need for more information.

3.3 ACC RECV **Create Credit Memo**

Go to the INVOICES screen in the accounting software and enter the identification number of the customer who is receiving the credit memo. Enter a new invoice, using a negative balance that equals the amount of the requested credit. Be sure to enter an explanation on the invoice, noting whether this is a credit to be issued to the customer or an internal credit to be filed away. Print the credit memos during the daily printout of invoices.

3.4 ACC RECV **Distribute Credit Memo**

When bursting the invoices after the print run is complete, separate the credit memos and put them in a separate stack. If they are marked as internal invoices, file all copies into customer folders and do not send them to the customers. If they are marked as external credit memos, send the white copy to the customer, put the goldenrod copy in the customer's file, and put the pink copy in the credit memos file.

Issue Customer Credits

Policy/Procedure Statement Brasto Publishing **Subject: Place Customer Orders on Hold**	Procedure No.: Page: Issue Date: Supercedes:	CRE-06 1 of 1 10/28/0X N/A

1. PURPOSE AND SCOPE

This procedure is used by the collections clerk to freeze customer orders currently active in the computer system that have not yet been shipped.

2. RESPONSIBILITIES

COLLECT **Collections Clerk**

3. PROCEDURES

3.1 COLLECT **Create Hold Transaction**

Go to the ORDERS menu in the computer system, and access the CUSTOMER screen. Go to the "Status" field and enter an "H." *Note*: To switch back to regular shipment status, enter an "R" in this field.

3.2 COLLECT **Notify Customer and Employees of Hold Status**

1. Issue an e-mail to the customer service representative and the sales manager to inform them that the customer is on Hold status.
2. Call the accounts payable person at the customer and inform him or her of the change in shipment status.

Policy/Procedure Statement Brasto Publishing **Subject: Review Credit Level and Adjust**	Retrieval No.: Page: Issue Date: Supercedes:	CRE-07 1 of 1 10/28/0X N/A

1. **PURPOSE AND SCOPE**
   This procedure is used by the credit clerk to revise credit levels based on internal collection experience, and to adjust those levels based on this information.

2. **RESPONSIBILITIES**
   CREDIT **Credit Clerk**

3. **PROCEDURES**

3.1 CREDIT **Summarize Internal Collection Experience**

1. Obtain all collections contact information about a specific customer from the collections clerk.
2. Compare this information to externally obtained credit data.
3. Obtain additional verbal information from the collections clerk, such as that person's opinion of the correct credit level.

3.2 CREDIT **Determine New Credit Level**

Using the credit setting policy as the chief guideline, alter the customer's credit level. However, because this policy is based on historical information, the credit clerk should also base the decision on forward-looking information, such as information from other creditors regarding a general inability to pay, or a prospective bankruptcy filing.

3.3 CREDIT **Adjust Credit Level in Computer System**

1. Go to the ORDERS menu in the computer system and access the CUSTOMER screen. Alter the dollar amount in the "Credit" field.
2. Contact the sales and customer service staffs to inform them of this change.

Review Credit Level and Adjust

Policy/Procedure Statement Brasto Publishing **Subject: Review Closing Tasks with Staff**	Procedure No.: Page: Issue Date: Supercedes:	FIN-01 1 of 1 10/28/0X N/A

1. PURPOSE AND SCOPE

This procedure is used by the controller to assign closing responsibilities to various members of the accounting staff.

2. RESPONSIBILITIES

CONTROLLER **Controller**

3. PROCEDURES

3.1 CONTROLLER **Schedule Staff Meeting**

1. Schedule a meeting with all accounting staff who are involved in the month-end closing process, specifying a time and place.
2. Issue an agenda to this group prior to the meeting.

3.2 CONTROLLER **Hold Meeting**

Review with this group the order in which tasks will be completed, as well as who is responsible for completing each one. Emphasize changes to the schedule that were agreed on at the end of the last month's closing process.

Review Closing Tasks with Staff

Policy/Procedure Statement		
Brasto Publishing	Retrieval No.:	FIN-02
	Page:	1 of 3
	Issue Date:	10/28/0X
	Supercedes:	N/A
Subject: Perform Physical Inventory Count		

1. PURPOSE AND SCOPE

This procedure is used to create a structured approach to a physical inventory count.

2. RESPONSIBILITIES

CONTROLLER **Controller**

3. PROCEDURES

3.1 CONTROLLER

Preparation for the Count

Take the following steps one week before the physical count:

1. Contact the printing company and order a sufficient number of sequentially numbered count tags. The first tag number should always be "1000." The tags should include fields for the product number, description, quantity count, location, and the counter's signature.
2. Review the inventory and mark all items lacking a part number with a brightly colored piece of paper. Inform the warehouse manager that these items must be marked with a proper part number immediately.
3. Clearly mark the quantity on all sealed packages.
4. Count all partial packages, seal them, and mark the quantity on the tape.
5. Prepare "Do Not Inventory" tags and use them to mark all items that should not be included in the physical inventory count.
6. Issue a list of count team members, with a notice regarding where and when they should appear for the inventory count.

3.2 CONTROLLER

One Day before the Count

1. Remind all participants that they are expected to be counting the next day.
2. Notify the warehouse manager that all items received during the two days of physical counts must be segregated and marked with "Do Not Inventory" tags.
3. Notify the manager that no shipments are allowed for the duration of the physical count.
4. Notify the warehouse manager that all shipments for which the paperwork has not been sent to accounting by that evening will be included in the inventory count on the following day.
5. Notify the warehouse manager that all shipping and receiving documentation from the day before the count must be forwarded to the accounting department that day, for immediate data entry. Likewise, any pick information must be forwarded at the same time.
6. Notify all outside storage locations to fax in their inventory counts.

3.3 CONTROLLER

Morning of the Physical Inventory Count

1. Enter all transactions from the previous day.
2. Assemble the count teams. Issue counting instructions to them, as well as blocks of tags, for which they must sign. Give each team a map of the warehouse with a section highlighted on it that they are responsible for counting. Those teams with forklift experience will be assigned to count the top racks; those without this experience will be assigned the lower racks.

Policy/Procedure Statement Brasto Publishing **Subject: Perform Physical Inventory Count**	Procedure No.: Page: Issue Date: Supercedes:	FIN-02 2 of 3 10/28/0X N/A

3. Call all outside storage warehouses and ask them to fax in their counts of company-owned inventory.
4. The count supervisor assigns additional count areas to those teams that finish counting their areas first.
5. The tag coordinator assigns blocks of tags to those count teams that run out of tags, tracks the receipt of tags, and follows up on missing tags. All tags should be accounted for by the end of the day.
6. The data entry person enters the information on the tags into a spreadsheet, and then summarizes the quantities for each item and pencils the totals into the cycle count report that was run earlier in the day.
7. The count supervisor reviews any unusual variances with the count teams to ensure that the correct amounts were entered.
8. Review the test count with an auditor, if necessary. Give the auditor a complete printout of all tags, as well as the cycle counting spreadsheet, showing all variances.

3.4 CONTROLLER

Job Descriptions

- The *count supervisor* is responsible for supervising the count, which includes assigning count teams to specific areas and ensuring that all areas have been counted and tagged. This person also waits until all count tags have been compared to the quantities listed in the computer, and then checks the counts on any items that appear to be incorrect.
- The *tag coordinator* is responsible for tracking the blocks of count tags that have been issued, as well as for accounting for all tags that have been returned. When distributing tags, mark down the beginning and ending numbers of each block of tags on a tracking sheet, and obtain the signature of the person who receives the tags. When the tags are returned, put them in numerical order and verify that all tags are accounted for. Once the verification is complete, check off the tags on the tracking sheet as having been received. Once returned tags have been properly accounted for, forward them to the extension calculation clerk.
- The *extension calculation clerk* is responsible for summarizing the amounts on the tags (if there are multiple quantities listed) to arrive at a total quantity count on each tag. This person also compares the part numbers and descriptions on each tag to see if there are any potential identification problems. This person forwards all completed tags to the data entry person.
- The *data entry person* is responsible for entering the information on all count tags into the computer spreadsheet. When doing so, enter all the information on each tag into a spreadsheet. Once a group of tags has been entered, stamp them as having been entered, clip them together, and store them separately. Once all tags are entered in the spreadsheet, sort the data by part number. Print out the spreadsheet and summarize the quantities by part number. Transfer the total quantities by part number to the cycle count report. If there are any significant variances between the counted and cycle count quantities, bring them to the attention of the count supervisor for review.

Perform Physical Inventory Count (2 of 3)

Policy/Procedure Statement Brasto Publishing **Subject: Perform Physical Inventory Count**	Retrieval No.: Page: Issue Date: Supercedes:	FIN-02 3 of 3 10/28/0X N/A

3.5 CONTROLLER

Time and Place

The count begins at 7:30 AM and ends at 4:30 PM on the first day of the count. If the count continues to a second day, it will begin at the same time, and count teams will be released whenever the counts have been completed. On both days, all count teams should meet at the warehouse gate.

3.6 CONTROLLER

Counting Responsibility

1. Count the bin locations assigned to you. These will be marked on a map of the warehouse with a highlighter. When you have counted all of the items in your assigned area, return to the count supervisor, who will assign additional count areas to you.
2. For each item counted in a separate bin location, enter the product code and date on the part of the inventory tag that is labeled "Pallet" and tape it to the inventory item. Rip off the other part of the tag and mark on it the product code, description, location, and quantity counted. Also initial the tag or list the number of your count team. Keep this part of the tag and return it to the tag coordinator when you run out of tags. This person will ensure that all of the tags assigned to you have been returned. If some are missing, you must locate and return them to the tag coordinator.
3. If there are many boxes of the same item to count, list the individual amounts on a tag, and an extensions calculation person will add them up for you. For example, if there are 18 boxes of 300 and a partial box of 12, just enter (18 × 300) + 12 on the tag.

3.7 CONTROLLER

General Information

- Do not count any item that has a "Do Not Inventory" tag on it.
- Scales will be provided to all count teams. The warehouse supervisor is available for training in the use of scales.
- Use a pen (not a pencil) to enter information on count tags. To make a quantity correction, put a line through the old quantity, write the new quantity next to it, and initial the change.
- ALL tags must be accounted for! If you do not use some, return them to the tag coordinator.

Perform Physical Inventory Count (3 of 3)

Policy/Procedure Statement Brasto Publishing **Subject: Close Month-End Journals**	Procedure No.: Page: Issue Date: Supercedes:	FIN-03 1 of 3 10/28/0X N/A

1. PURPOSE AND SCOPE

This procedure establishes roles and responsibilities for closing the fiscal period in the general ledger.

2. RESPONSIBILITIES

CONTROLLER	**Controller**
ASST CNTLR	**Assistant Controller**
LOG MGR	Logistics Manager
ACC PAY	Accounts Payable Clerk
ACC RECV	Accounts Receivable Clerk

3. PROCEDURES

3.1 CONTROLLER

Background

The assistant controller is responsible for coordinating the closing of the general ledger at the end of each accounting period. The controller is responsible for reviewing recommended changes to the procedures described here.

3.2 ASST CNTLR

Complete Early Activities

1. Complete the depreciation journal entry, using the fixed asset base from the previous month.
2. Review the general ledger accounts through this point in the month and adjust any obvious mistakes.

3.3 LOG MGR

Reviewing Pricing Variances

1. Go to the computer system and print out the purchase price variance report.
2. Examine all variances noted on this report and alter any standard prices that require adjustment, based on the actual prices noted.

3.4 ASST CNTLR

Notify Departments of the Closing

1. Notify the receiving staff that all paperwork must be completed for month-end.
2. Notify the shipping staff that all shipment paperwork must be completed for month-end.
3. Notify the accounts payable staff that all expenses must be recorded in the system by the due date.
4. Notify all accounting system users that the system will go down at a specified time for month-end processing.

3.5 ACC PAY

Process Accounts Payable

1. Notify all employees that expense reports must be turned in by the last business day of the month.
2. Enter all manual checks into the computer system.

Close Month-End Journals (1 of 3)

Policy/Procedure Statement	Retrieval No.:	FIN-03
Brasto Publishing	Page:	2 of 3
	Issue Date:	10/28/0X
Subject: Close Month-End Journals	Supercedes:	N/A

3. Review the receiving log to see if there are any expensive items received at month-end for which an invoice has not been received from a supplier. If so, accrue the estimated expense based on the cost noted in the purchase order.
4. Verify that all recurring supplier invoices have been entered into the accounts payable system. If not, then an accrual must be made for these expenses. The expenses should include the following:
   - Electricity
   - Gas
   - Telephones
   - Waste pickup and disposal
   - Water
5. Match all accounts payable documentation and enter it into the system as either vouchered or unvouchered.
6. Print out summary and detail reports for the vouchered and unvouchered accounts payable and forward them to the assistant controller.

3.6 ACC RECV

Process Billings

1. Verify with the shipping staff that all shipping documentation for shipments through the end of the month have been forwarded to the accounting department.
2. Verify that all special service charges have been billed.
3. Verify that freight charges have been included in all billings.
4. Run the final month-end billings and mail them to customers.
5. Print customer statements and mail them to customers.
6. Print the month-end journals for cash receipts, taxes, and invoices. Verify that the totals are correct. File these reports.

3.7 ASST CNTLR

Make Adjustments and Journal Entries

1. Verify that all remaining batches to be submitted for entry in the general ledger are authorized and that there are no errors in the batch totals. Process the batches.
2. Accrue for the following expenses:
   - Unpaid payroll
   - Vacation expenses
   - Sales tax expenses
   - Prepaid rent
   - Unbilled purchases
   - Prepaid insurance
3. Allocate the following costs to departments:
   - Utility expenses
   - Services
   - Accounting
4. Reverse all inter-company transactions.
5. Make journal entries for depreciation and amortization expenses.

Close Month-End Journals (2 of 3)

Policy/Procedure Statement	Procedure No.:	FIN-03
Brasto Publishing	Page:	3 of 3
	Issue Date:	10/28/0X
	Supercedes:	N/A
Subject: Close Month-End Journals		

6. Review the detailed balances in all balance sheet accounts and adjust the ending balances with journal entries, depending on which assets and liabilities should be retained in these accounts.

3.8 CONTROLLER

Issue Financial Statements

1. Create a preliminary set of financial statements.
2. Compare all actual expenses to budgeted amounts and review items that vary significantly from the budget. Use journal entries to alter ending balances in those cases where amounts are recorded in the wrong accounts.
3. Record the income tax expense accrual.
4. Print out the final financial statements.
5. Issue the statements to all employees on the approved distribution list. Also send the statements to the bank, other lenders and investors, as noted on the approved distribution list.
6. Close the books for the month and roll forward all balances to the next month.

Close Month-End Journals (3 of 3)

Policy/Procedure Statement	Retrieval No.:	FIN-04
Brasto Publishing	Page:	1 of 1
	Issue Date:	10/28/0X
Subject: Record Accruals	Supercedes:	N/A

1. PURPOSE AND SCOPE

This procedure is used by the general ledger clerk to record standard accruals in for the current reporting period.

2. RESPONSIBILITIES

GL CLERK — **General Ledger Clerk**

3. PROCEDURES

3.1 GL CLERK — **Locate List of Standard Accruals**

1. Obtain the list of standard accruals, which is located in the N:\CLOSING\ACCRUALS.XLS file.
2. Verify that explanations and completion dates are included in the file for each accrual.

3.2 GL CLERK — **Verify Accruals**

1. Meet with the assistant controller and review each accrual, verifying that each one is still needed.
2. Review the journal entry records from the last reporting period to see if additional recurring entries should be made.
3. Compare accrual amounts to actual expenses to see if the amounts accrued are still valid.
4. Make any alterations to the accruals file.

3.3 GL CLERK — **Enter Accruals in Computer System**

1. Go to the LEDGER menu in the computer system and access the ACCRUALS screen.
2. Enter the standard accrual number for each entry, which brings up the standard accounts and dollar amounts on the screen.
3. Verify the amounts and press ENTER to accept each accrual for the new reporting period.
4. For new accruals, clear the screen and enter the account numbers, amounts, and the number of periods over which to repeat the entry, and press ENTER.

Policy/Procedure Statement	Procedure No.:	FIN-05
Brasto Publishing	Page:	1 of 1
	Issue Date:	10/28/0X
Subject: Calculate Profit Sharing	Supercedes:	N/A

1. PURPOSE AND SCOPE

This procedure is used by the assistant controller to calculate the correct amount of profit-sharing expense accrual to be charged to the financial statements each month.

2. RESPONSIBILITIES

ASST CNTLR **Assistant Controller**

3. PROCEDURES

3.1 ASST CNTLR **Determine Estimated Monthly Profit**

Complete the preliminary financial statements. This should include all adjustments and accruals in all revenue and expense areas, as well as comparisons of budgeted amounts to actual.

3.2 ASST CNTLR **Locate Profit Sharing Calculation**

Go to the formula page of the procedures manual and locate the formula for profit sharing. In brief, it requires an accrual of 10% of pretax profits for the compensation of the management team, and 10% of the after-tax profits for the compensation of everyone else in the company.

3.3 ASST CNTLR **Determine Profit-Sharing Accrual**

Calculate the profits for the management team first, which will reduce the overall profit level for the second calculation, which is after-tax profits for the other employees.

3.4 ASST CNTLR **Record Profit-Sharing Accrual**

Record the profit-sharing calculation in the general ledger, with the expense being debited to the "Profit Sharing" account and the credit to "Accrued Expenses."

3.5 ASST CNTLR **File the Profit-Sharing Calculation**

Insert the profit-sharing calculation into the journal entries book, alongside the related entry.

Policy/Procedure Statement Brasto Publishing **Subject: Reconcile Bank Statement**	Retrieval No.: Page: Issue Date: Supercedes:	FIN-06 1 of 2 10/28/0X N/A

1. PURPOSE AND SCOPE

This procedure helps the accounts payable clerk compare his or her internal cash records to those of the bank and reconcile any differences between the two.

2. RESPONSIBILITIES

ACC PAY **Accounts Payable Clerk**

3. PROCEDURES

3.1 ACC PAY **Entries**

During the month, enter each lockbox or deposit amount in its entirety, print the batch total, and store the batch total report with the lockbox or deposit record. Take the following steps to apply cash:

- Go to the CASH APPLICATION screen. Enter the customer's check number and the total amount of the payment.
- Enter the specific invoice number being paid, as well as any discounts taken. Repeat the process until all the cash has been applied for all the invoices paid by each customer.
- Use a journal entry to record cash receipts for items not related to invoices.

3.2 ACC PAY **Manual Checks**

During the month, enter manual checks into the computer system as soon as they are issued.

3.3 ACC PAY **Journal Entry**

Make a journal entry to record all payroll payments for the preceding month.

3.4 ACC PAY **Bank Statement**

When the bank statement arrives, create the outstanding checks list for both accounts payable and payroll checks. To do so, go to the RECONCILIATION screen and press the ENTER key when each open check is highlighted on the screen that the bank statement shows has having been processed. Once this step is complete, print the list of checks that have not cleared.

3.5 ACC PAY **Outstanding Checks**

Subtract the total amount of outstanding checks from the ending bank balance. The net amount is the number that the general ledger cash balance should match.

3.6 ACC PAY **General Ledger Balance Reconciliation**

Reconcile the general ledger to the bank balance with the following steps:

- Make a separate journal entry for each wire transfer noted on the bank statement, unless these cash flows are already accounted for through the accounts payable or accounts receivable systems.
- Make a separate journal entry for each special expense or revenue item on the bank statement, such as a monthly account processing fee.

Reconcile Bank Statement (1 of 2)

Policy/Procedure Statement Brasto Publishing **Subject: Reconcile Bank Statement**	Procedure No.: Page: Issue Date: Supercedes:	FIN-06 2 of 2 10/28/0X N/A

- If a manual check is discovered during the reconciliation process that was not already entered in the computer system, then record the item with a journal entry.
- Print out the general ledger detail for the cash account and compare it to the bank statement. Cross out matching items on both statements. Any remaining items that do not match must still be reconciled. If all items reconcile and the bank statement still does not match, then the only remaining possible solution is that the beginning bank reconciliation was incorrect.

Reconcile Bank Statement (2 of 2)

Policy/Procedure Statement Brasto Publishing **Subject: Tie General Ledger to Detail**	Retrieval No.: Page: Issue Date: Supercedes:	FIN-07 1 of 1 10/28/0X N/A

1. PURPOSE AND SCOPE

This procedure is used by the general ledger clerk to verify that general ledger summary balances equal the totals for subsidiary journals.

2. RESPONSIBILITIES

GL CLERK **General Ledger Clerk**

3. PROCEDURES

3.1 GL CLERK **Locate Summary Balances in General Ledger**

1. Print the summary level general ledger report, using the GL option in the REPORTS screen.
2. Highlight any balance sheet accounts with an ending balance.

3.2 GL CLERK **Compare to Subsidiary Journal Totals**

1. For all account balances exceeding $1,000, compare the general ledger ending balance to the amount shown in the subsidiary-level journal.
2. If there is no journal, then compare the balance to the manually maintained listing that is located in the N:\GL\DETAIL.XLS file.

3.3 GL CLERK **Investigate Variances**

1. For any accounts for which the general ledger balance does not match the supporting detail, print out the detail level general ledger for those accounts, using the GL DETAIL option in the REPORTS screen.
2. Compare the detail in the general ledger to the detail in the subsidiary journal to find any differing items.
3. Investigate the reasons for these variances, and make correcting journal entries if necessary.

Tie General Ledger to Detail

Policy/Procedure Statement Brasto Publishing **Subject: Review Variances from Budget**	Procedure No.: Page: Issue Date: Supercedes:	FIN-08 1 of 1 10/28/0X N/A

1. PURPOSE AND SCOPE

This procedure is used by the financial analyst to determine the amount and reason for actual revenue and expense variances from budgeted levels.

2. RESPONSIBILITIES

FINL ANALYST **Financial Analyst**

3. PROCEDURES

3.1 FINL ANALYST **Print Budget versus Actual Financial Statements**

Print the financial statements. To do so, go to the REPORTS screen and select the FINLS, FULL option.

3.2 FINL ANALYST **Identify Key Variances**

1. Review the complete set of financial statements and circle all items for which there is a negative variance between the budget and actual expenses of at least $1,000 for the month, or $1,000 per month (cumulatively) for the year-to-date.
2. Note the name of the responsible manager next to these negative variances.

3.3 FINL ANALYST **Investigate Key Variances**

1. Review the circled variances with the responsible managers to determine the reasons for their occurrence.
2. If necessary, also print out the detailed list of transactions that created the ending expense totals, and investigate the largest ones to ascertain their nature.

3.4 FINL ANALYST **Report on Key Variances**

1. Prepare a report that identifies the reasons for the largest negative variances.
2. Meet with the controller to go over this variance information.
3. Revise the report as necessary and forward it to the assistant controller, who will include it in the financial statements.

Review Variances from Budget

Policy/Procedure Statement	Retrieval No.:	FIN-09
Brasto Publishing	Page:	1 of 1
	Issue Date:	10/28/0X
	Supercedes:	N/A
Subject: Add Summary and Financial Analysis		

1. PURPOSE AND SCOPE

This procedure is used by the assistant controller to ensure that all standard notes and analyses are included in the financial statement package.

2. RESPONSIBILITIES

ASST CNTLR **Assistant Controller**
CONTROLLER **Controller**

3. PROCEDURES

3.1 ASST CNTLR **Compile Footnotes to Financial Statements**

Go to the footnotes file from the last set of financial statements, and update them based on any subsequent changes. Most of this information is boilerplate and requires no changes, but any text in red is intended for monthly updates.

3.2 ASST CNTLR **Compile Numerical Notes to Financial Statements**

1. Update the numerical notes to the financial statements, which are located in an electronic spreadsheet at N:\FINANCIALS\FINANCIAL.XLS.
2. The updates should include the historical year-to-year comparison, the monthly balance sheet and income statement, ratios, and breakeven analysis. These are all located on separate worksheets within the same spreadsheet.

3.3 ASST CNTLR **Compile Written Commentary on Financial Statements**

Based on the variance and numerical analyses already completed, update the written commentary from the previous month's financial statements. The file is located in N:\FINANCIALS\ COMMENTARY.DOC.

3.4 CONTROLLER **Review Completed Financial Statements**

1. Using the previous month's financial statements as a guide, assemble them for the newest month in the same order, being sure to number all pages and refer to them in the table of contents.
2. Create separate financial statements for individual departments, which are to be released to department managers. Refer to the distribution list from the previous month to see who gets which pages of the financial statements.

3.5 ASST CNTLR **Assemble Financial Statements**

Copy and bind the financial statements.

Add Summary and Financial Analysis

Policy/Procedure Statement Brasto Publishing **Subject: Distribute Full and Partial Statements**	Procedure No.: Page: Issue Date: Supercedes:	FIN-10 1 of 1 10/28/0X N/A

1. PURPOSE AND SCOPE

This procedure is used by the controller to ensure that the correct full and partial monthly financial reports are issued to the standard list of recipients.

2. RESPONSIBILITIES

CONTROLLER **Controller**

3. PROCEDURES

3.1 CONTROLLER **Determine Report Distribution**

Mark the cover of each financial statement with the name of the person to whom it is being released, using the distribution list from the previous month.

3.2 CONTROLLER **Distribute Financial Reports**

1. Distribute the financial statements to the appropriate individuals.
2. If the financial statements are considered confidential, then have each recipient sign for his or her copy.
3. Send statement copies to external entities via registered mail or traceable express mail.

Policy/Procedure Statement	Retrieval No.:	FIN-11
Brasto Publishing	Page:	1 of 1
	Issue Date:	10/28/0X
Subject: Conduct Postclosing Staff Meeting	Supercedes:	N/A

1. PURPOSE AND SCOPE

This procedure is used by the controller to ensure that the standard set of topics are covered during the postclosing review of all closing activities.

2. RESPONSIBILITIES

CONTROLLER **Controller**

3. PROCEDURES

3.1 CONTROLLER **Schedule Staff Meeting**

1. Schedule a staff meeting with all personnel involved in the closing process.
2. Issue an agenda to all participants prior to the meeting.

3.2 CONTROLLER **Hold Meeting**

1. Review the results of the most recent closing, as well as problems encountered, and opportunities for further reducing time delays and errors in completing the statements.
2. Assign responsibilities for all resulting projects, as well as due dates.
3. Issue a follow-up memo confirming responsibilities and due dates.

Policy/Procedure Statement Brasto Publishing **Subject: Evaluate Capital Proposal**	Procedure No.: Page: Issue Date: Supercedes:	FIX-01 1 of 1 10/28/0X N/A

1. PURPOSE AND SCOPE

This procedure is used by the financial analyst to verify the assumptions, cash flows, and net present value of all capital proposals.

2. RESPONSIBILITIES

FINL ANALYST **Financial Analyst**

3. PROCEDURES

3.1 FINL ANALYST **Verify Assumptions**

1. Review each submitted capital expenditure form to ensure that all fields have been completed. If not, return the form to the sender with a note regarding the missing information.
2. Review all assumptions, which are noted at the bottom of the form. If these vary significantly from assumptions used for previous approved capital budgets, or if there are reasonable grounds for doubt, review them with the originating person, and modify them if necessary, including all underlying numerical data.

3.2 FINL ANALYST **Verify Cash Flows**

1. Review all itemized cash flows with the project manager, purchasing staff, sales staff, and anyone else with a reasonable degree of knowledge regarding the amount or timing of the cash flows.
2. Adjust the amount or timing of cash flows in the capital expenditure analysis based on the preceding cash flow review.

3.3 FINL ANALYST **Calculate Net Present Value**

1. Obtain the cost of capital from the controller, and use this to discount the stream of cash flows noted in the capital expenditure proposal.
2. If the project seems unusually risky, also recalculate the net present value using a higher discount rate, to be determined by the controller.

3.4 FINL ANALYST **Issue Recommendation**

1. If the net present value is positive, then issue a favorable project recommendation to the controller and project sponsor.
2. If the net present value is negative, state the amount by which it is negative and the internal rate of return so that the project sponsor can rework the assumptions and possibly arrive at a positive net present value.

Policy/Procedure Statement Brasto Publishing **Subject: Record Payable as Fixed Asset**	Retrieval No.: Page: Issue Date: Supercedes:	FIX-02 1 of 1 10/28/0X N/A

1. PURPOSE AND SCOPE

This procedure is used to process fixed asset transactions by the accounts payable clerk.

2. RESPONSIBILITIES

ACC PAY **Accounts Payable Clerk**

3. PROCEDURES

3.1 ACC PAY **Add Assets**

Go to the EDIT menu and choose "Add Assets." Enter information in the "General Information" section: you must use an asset number to add an asset. Then click on the bottom half of the screen to enter information about the cost basis. To save the new asset, go to the menu and choose "Save Asset."

3.2 ACC PAY **Delete Assets**

Select the Asset you want to delete. From the EDIT menu, choose "Delete Asset" and then confirm the deletion.

3.3 ACC PAY **Edit Assets**

Select an asset in the schedule folder and then go to the VIEW menu and choose "Asset Detail." Click on the field to make any changes. From the EDIT menu, choose "Save Asset."

3.4 ACC PAY **Find an Asset**

From the EDIT menu, pick "Find Asset." Enter the asset number and press ENTER. Then, depending on your search criteria, pick either "Next Asset," "Previous Asset," "First Asset," or "Last Asset" from the EDIT menu.

3.5 ACC PAY **Print a Report**

From the TOOLS menu, choose "Reports." Select a report from the list and click OK.

3.6 ACC PAY **Sell an Asset**

Select the asset for which you want to record sales information and click the "Disposal" tab. Click on the "Disposal" check box to enter information for this asset. Enter the asset number. Use the 'TAB' key to move to the "Disposal Date" field. Then enter the disposal date, followed by the sale price.

Policy/Procedure Statement Brasto Publishing **Subject: Record Depreciation as Fixed Asset**	Procedure No.: Page: Issue Date: Supercedes:	FIX-03 1 of 1 10/28/0X N/A

1. PURPOSE AND SCOPE

This procedure is used by the general ledger accountant to ensure that the correct depreciation type and period is used for each capitalized asset.

2. RESPONSIBILITIES

GL ACCT **General Ledger Accountant**

3. PROCEDURES

3.1 GL ACCT **Determine Type of Asset**

1. Compare the type of asset to the company policy statement on asset types in the accounting policy manual.
2. Go to the fixed assets register and enter the asset under the correct asset category, using the ADD ASSET screen.

3.2 GL ACCT **Determine Type and Length of Depreciation Method**

1. In the ADD ASSET screen, set the number of years of depreciation in accordance with the standard listed in the company policy statement on asset types.
2. Set the first-year depreciation at the half-year convention.
3. Set the depreciation method as the sum-of-years-digits, which is standard for all depreciation for all assets.
4. Use the PRINT option at the bottom of the screen to verify this entry.

3.3 GL ACCT **Calculate Depreciation**

Print the depreciation register from the REPORTS screen and verify the system has calculated the depreciation expense for the newly added asset correctly.

Record Depreciation as Fixed Asset

Policy/Procedure Statement	Retrieval No.:	FIX-04
Brasto Publishing	Page:	1 of 1
	Issue Date:	10/28/0X
	Supercedes:	N/A
Subject: Calculate Gain/Loss on Sale of Asset		

1. **PURPOSE AND SCOPE**

   This procedure is used by the assistant controller to calculate the gain or loss on the sale or disposal of any capital assets.

2. **RESPONSIBILITIES**

   ASST CNTLR **Assistant Controller**

3. **PROCEDURES**

3.1 ASST CNTLR **Determine Which Assets Are Being Disposed Of**

Receive documentation from the purchasing department regarding the sale of assets. This should include a signed Asset Disposition form that authorized someone to sell an asset. If the document is not signed by an authorized person, return it with a note asking for the appropriate signature. The document should be accompanied by a copy of the bill of sale, and a copy of the check or other document that shows proof of the amount paid.

3.2 ASST CNTLR **Find Assets in Fixed Assets Listing**

Once the sale documentation is complete, go to the fixed asset database and call up the record for the asset being sold. The easiest way is to conduct a search based on the name of the asset, though the documentation may contain the asset number, which can also be used to find the correct record.

3.3 ASST CNTLR **Extract Cost and Depreciation Figures**

Write down the original asset cost and total accumulated depreciation, which is located in the record in the fixed asset database.

3.4 ASST CNTLR **Determine Gain or Loss**

Subtract the sale amount and accumulated depreciation from the original asset cost. If there is a positive amount left over, this is a loss on the sale of the asset. If there is a negative amount left over, this is a gain on the sale of the asset.

3.5 ASST CNTLR **Record Journal Entry**

Obtain a journal entry form and complete it for the gain or loss transaction. The asset's original cost goes in the "Credit" column, while the accumulated depreciation amount goes in the "Debit" column. The sale amount is a debit to cash. If there is a gain, this is recorded as a credit. A loss is recorded as a debit.

3.6 ASST CNTLR **Record Change in Fixed Asset Database**

Access the fixed asset database and record the sale of the asset. Print the fixed asset database after this transaction is recorded and compare the total for the account to the general ledger to ensure that the information is recorded in the same amounts in both locations.

3.7 ASST CNTLR **File the Gain or Loss Calculation**

File a copy of the gain or loss calculation in the journal entry book, and also in the permanent file documenting the addition or removal of fixed assets.

Calculate Gain/Loss on Sale of Asset

Policy/Procedure Statement Brasto Publishing **Subject: Prepare Cash Forecast**	Procedure No.: Page: Issue Date: Supercedes:	FUN-01 1 of 1 10/28/0X N/A

1. PURPOSE AND SCOPE

This procedure is used to allow the accounts payable clerk to access information on the current day's cash balances and to recommend changes to the disposition of cash. The accounting department uses this procedure.

2. RESPONSIBILITIES

ACC PAY **Accounts Payable Clerk**

3. PROCEDURES

3.1 ACC PAY **Access the Cash Spreadsheet**

Access the CASH.XLS spreadsheet, which is located in the C:\FILES\CASH subdirectory.

3.2 ACC PAY **Making the Cashday Report**

Copy the current day's cash balance, computer check-run amount, payroll transfers, cash balance, and line of credit information from this report. Enter it into the CASHDAY.XLS file, which is located in the same subdirectory. The information goes into the "Ending Balance," "Computer Checks," "Payroll," and "Line of Credit" columns in the CASHDAY.XLS report. Print out the daily "CashFax Plus" report from the bank. Copy the collected balance amount into the "Collected Balance" column in the CASHDAY.XLS report. Also summarize the one-day and two-day floats into the "Float" field in the CASHDAY.XLS report.

3.3 ACC PAY **Print the Report and Recommend a Cash Transfer**

1. Add a cash transfer recommendation to the bottom of the CASHDAY.XLS report. The recommendation is based on the following rules:
   - Any excess in the collected balance over $100K should be transferred back to the line of credit, unless there is a payroll due within the next three days or if accounts payable checks are due for collection within three days.
   - Any shortfall in cash should be transferred to the checking account from the line of credit if accounts payable checks have been floating for five days, or if payroll is due the next day.
   - All transfers in or out are in increments of $1,000.
2. Issue the report to the controller and chief financial officer.

Policy/Procedure Statement Brasto Publishing **Subject: Borrow Funds**	Retrieval No.: Page: Issue Date: Supercedes:	FUN-02 1 of 1 10/28/0X N/A

1. PURPOSE AND SCOPE

This procedure is used by the chief financial officer to borrow funds from the line of credit.

2. RESPONSIBILITIES

CFO **Chief Financial Officer**

3. PROCEDURES

3.1 CFO **Determine Required Borrowing Level**

1. Review the short-term cash forecast with the financial analyst and determine the immediate cash need from that report.
2. Alter the expected amount based on any unusual cash flows not noted on the standard report.
3. Verify that there is a sufficient amount left on the line of credit to borrow.

3.2 CFO **Complete Borrowing Forms**

1. Extract a copy of the bank borrowing form from the forms cabinet and fill it out, entering the amount determined in the first step.
2. Have an authorized signer sign the borrowing form.

3.3 CFO **Borrow Funds**

1. Fax the form to the bank.
2. Call the bank to verify receipt of the fax.

3.4 CFO **Record Borrowing Information**

Send the borrowing form to the general ledger accountant for proper recording in the general ledger.

Borrow Funds

Policy/Procedure Statement	Procedure No.:	FUN-03
Brasto Publishing	Page:	1 of 1
	Issue Date:	10/28/0X
Subject: Invest Funds	Supercedes:	N/A

1. PURPOSE AND SCOPE

This procedure is used by the chief financial officer to invest funds in accordance with the corporate investment policy.

2. RESPONSIBILITIES

CFO **Chief Financial Officer**

3. PROCEDURES

3.1 CFO **Determine Amount of Funds to Invest**

1. Review the short-term cash forecast with the financial analyst and determine the amount of funds that are not immediately needed for operations.
2. Adjust the forecast based on unusual cash flows not noted in the standard report format.

3.2 CFO **Determine Appropriate Investment Instrument**

Using the corporate investing policy and the size of the investable cash amount as guidelines, select the appropriate investment vehicle. For the short-term cash investments, select the most liquid investments on the investing policy.

3.3 CFO **Invest Funds**

1. Extract a copy of the investment form from the forms cabinet and fill it out, entering the amount determined in the first step.
2. Have an authorized signer sign the investment form.
3. Fax this form to the company's investment firm.
4. Call the firm to verify receipt of the fax.

3.4 CFO **Record Investment**

Send the investment form to the general ledger accountant for proper recording in the general ledger.

Invest Funds

Policy/Procedure Statement Brasto Publishing **Subject: Create Borrowing Base Certificate**	Retrieval No.: Page: Issue Date: Supercedes:	FUN-04 1 of 1 10/28/0X N/A

1. PURPOSE AND SCOPE

This procedure is used by the controller to update the borrowing base certificate at the end of each month, and to send it both to file and all lenders requiring it.

2. RESPONSIBILITIES

CONTROLLER **Controller**

3. PROCEDURES

3.1 CONTROLLER **Locate Borrowing Base Certificate File**

Call up the borrowing base certificate from the N:\FINANCIALS\BORROW.XLS file.

3.2 CONTROLLER **Update Borrowing Base Information**

1. Alter the date of the month to reflect the date for which the certificate is being submitted.
2. Alter the month-end balance of accounts receivable and inventory, as well as overdue accounts receivable and obsolete inventory, on the report.
3. Alter the amount of currently borrowed funds on the report.
4. Review the report and sign it.

3.3 CONTROLLER **Issue Borrowing Base Certificate**

Mail the borrowing base certificate to the lender, along with the detail reports for accounts receivable and inventory that tie to the amounts listed on the certificate.

Create Borrowing Base Certificate

Policy/Procedure Statement	Procedure No.:	INT-01
Brasto Publishing	Page:	1 of 1
	Issue Date:	10/28/0X
Subject: Construct Audit Methodology	Supercedes:	N/A

1. PURPOSE AND SCOPE

This procedure is used by the internal audit manager to determine the auditing methodology to be used for each audit.

2. RESPONSIBILITIES

AUDIT MGR **Internal Audit Manager**

3. PROCEDURES

3.1 AUDIT MGR **Compile List of Methodologies**

Consult audit textbooks and the company's external auditors or consultants for copies of audit methodologies.

3.2 AUDIT MGR **Compare Pros and Cons of Methodologies**

Itemize the differences between the methodologies, not only in terms of investigation techniques and levels, but also reporting formats and control systems.

3.3 AUDIT MGR **Create Ranking Criteria**

1. Develop a ranking criteria based on the company's perceived levels of importance when selecting an audit methodology.
2. Develop a weighting system for each ranking criterion, which reflects the greater importance given to some criteria.

3.4 AUDIT MGR **Rank Methodologies**

1. Score each methodology based on the ranking criteria and weighting system.
2. Select the "winning" methodology based on the ranking system.

3.5 AUDIT MGR **Train Staff in Methodology**

1. Develop training materials for using the audit methodology.
2. Perform "dry runs" of training classes with trainers.
3. Schedule the internal audit staff for training sessions.
4. Conduct training.
5. Incorporate staff comments into revisions of the training materials.

Policy/Procedure Statement Brasto Publishing **Subject: Develop Audit Works Schedule**	Retrieval No.: Page: Issue Date: Supercedes:	INT-02 1 of 1 10/28/0X N/A

1. PURPOSE AND SCOPE

This procedure is used by the internal audit manager as a guideline in constructing the audit work schedule for all audit teams for the upcoming year.

2. RESPONSIBILITIES

AUDIT MGR **Internal Audit Manager**

3. PROCEDURES

3.1 AUDIT MGR **Compile List of Audit Requests**

1. Send an e-mail to all department managers to ask if anyone has requests for specific internal audits.
2. Review the recommendations of the external auditors to see if they have spotted weaknesses in the existing control systems.
3. Review the results of previous audits to see if there are control problems that may still exist.
4. Itemize those areas that have not been audited for a long time.
5. Summarize this information into a list of possible audits.

3.2 AUDIT MGR **Obtain Audit Priorities List from Audit Committee**

Review this list with the audit committee, and also gain their input regarding additional review areas.

3.3 AUDIT MGR **Assemble Final Audit List**

1. Finalize the list of audits, noting approximations of resources and time requirements.
2. Sort the report by priority level.

3.4 AUDIT MGR **Obtain Audit Committee Approval**

1. Present the audit list to the audit committee.
2. Make any final adjustments recommended by the audit committee, and obtain their approval.

Develop Audit Works Schedule

Policy/Procedure Statement	Procedure No.:	INT-03
Brasto Publishing	Page:	1 of 1
	Issue Date:	10/28/0X
Subject: Develop Audit Budget	Supercedes:	N/A

1. PURPOSE AND SCOPE

This procedure is used by the internal audit manager to develop a budget for all scheduled audits for the upcoming year.

2. RESPONSIBILITIES

AUDIT MGR **Internal Audit Manager**

3. PROCEDURES

3.1 AUDIT MGR

Determine Cost of Each Approved Audit

Determine the cost of each internal audit, which should include the salary cost of audit staff, allocated department overhead costs, travel costs, and the cost of any outsourced audit services.

3.2 AUDIT MGR

Create Detailed and Summary Budgets

Summarize the costs of all audits in a summary report, and sort the list in descending dollar order. List the original audit priorities assigned by the audit committee next to each audit so that the audit committee can evaluate the cost of each audit in comparison to its perceived value.

3.3 AUDIT MGR

Obtain Audit Committee Approval

1. Present the audit budget to the audit committee.
2. Modify the audit budget and list of approved audits in accordance with the wishes of the audit committee.
3. Gain final approval of the budget.

Policy/Procedure Statement	Retrieval No.:	INT-04
Brasto Publishing	Page:	1 of 1
	Issue Date:	10/28/0X
	Supercedes:	N/A
Subject: Conduct Internal Audit Review		

1. PURPOSE AND SCOPE

This procedure is used to determine the reliability of those accounting systems whose failure would have a direct impact on billings to customers or expenses incurred.

2. RESPONSIBILITIES

ACC PAY	**Accounts Payable Clerk**
ACC RECV	**Accounts Receivable Clerk**

3. PROCEDURES

3.1 ACC PAY

Verify Receiving Documentation

1. Take a sample of ____ supplier payments and verify that there is either a signed purchase order attached to the supplier invoice, or the signature of an authorized manager.
2. For the same sample, verify that there is a receiving document attached to the supplier invoice.

3.2 ACC RECV

Verify All Accounts Receivable Credits

Take a sample of ____ credits in the accounts receivable journal, and trace the credits back to supporting documentation. Verify that there is an explanation for each credit, as well as an authorized signature on the documentation.

3.3 ACC PAY

Verify Expense Reports

Verify that submitted expenses meet company guidelines for approved travel and entertainment expenses. Take a sample of ____ expense reports and verify that all reported expenses are in accordance with company reimbursement policies.

3.4 ACC PAY

Review Freight Revenue

Verify that customers are charged the correct amount for freight.

1. Take a sample of ____ shipments from the shipping log. If the bill of lading states "Prepay," then verify that the customer is one that is not normally charged for freight.
2. If the bill of lading states "Prepay and Add," verify that there is a freight amount charged on the corresponding invoice. If not, record this as an error.
3. If the invoice does not include a freight charge, trace the amount charged back to the list of standard freight rates by customer. If the rate invoiced does not match the amount on the list of standard rates, record this as an error.

3.5 ACC RECV

Review Invoicing

Verify that all items shipped are invoiced and vice versa. Also, verify that all invoices are printed within one day of shipment. Take a sample of ____ shipments from the shipping log. Trace each shipment back to an invoice, verifying the quantity invoiced. Also, take a sample of ____ invoices and trace them back to the shipping log, verifying that a shipment occurred and that the quantity invoiced is correct.

3.6 ACC RECV

Review Pricing

Verify that customers are being charged the correct prices. Take a sample of ____ invoices and trace the prices for all line items back to the original quote to the customer. Be careful to refer to the sales manager for any subsequent updates to customer quotes.

Policy/Procedure Statement Brasto Publishing **Subject: Create and Issue Audit Report**	Procedure No.: Page: Issue Date: Supercedes:	INT-05 1 of 1 10/28/0X N/A

1. PURPOSE AND SCOPE

This procedure is used by the audit staff to create audits for issuance to management and the audit committee regarding internal control issues discovered by them, along with recommended solutions.

2. RESPONSIBILITIES

AUDIT STAFF **Internal Audit Staff**

3. PROCEDURES

3.1 AUDIT STAFF **Obtain Audit Report Format**

Obtain the boilerplate format of the internal audit report, which is located at N:\INTERNAL\REPORT.DOC.

3.2 AUDIT STAFF **Create Preliminary Audit Report**

1. Assemble all findings from the internal audit and enter them into the standard report format.
2. Add supporting documentation and graphics to the report.
3. Add recommendations to the report.

3.3 AUDIT STAFF **Obtain Report Reviews**

1. Have the report reviewed by the internal audit manager.
2. Adjust the report based on any review comments.

3.4 AUDIT STAFF **Issue Report**

1. Review the audit report with the manager of the department whose area was reviewed, with an emphasis on the accuracy of the information presented.
2. Make final revisions and forward to the internal audit manager.
3. Send a copy of the report to the manager of the department whose area was reviewed.
4. Present the report to the internal audit committee.

Create and Issue Audit Report

Policy/Procedure Statement Brasto Publishing **Subject: Collect and Reconcile Time Cards**	Retrieval No.: Page: Issue Date: Supercedes:	PAY-01 1 of 1 10/28/0X N/A

1. PURPOSE AND SCOPE

This procedure is used by the payroll clerk to assemble time cards for all hourly employees, as well as to locate and resolve time punching errors.

2. RESPONSIBILITIES

PR CLERK **Payroll Clerk**

3. PROCEDURES

3.1 PR CLERK **Obtain Time Cards**

Obtain time cards from all company locations. Check off the receipts against the standard list of company locations, and contact the factory manager of each location from which no cards have been received.

3.2 PR CLERK **Review Time Cards**

1. Add up the time on all time cards, circling those time punches that have no clock-ins or clock-outs. Note the total time on all error-free time cards and forward them to the payroll clerk for data entry into the payroll system.
2. Any time card containing overtime hours must also be initialed by a manager; those cards missing this approval must be returned and signed.

3.3 PR CLERK **Resolve Time Card Discrepancies**

1. Review all time cards containing discrepancies with the responsible factory managers. They must initial all time cards for which there is an assumed clock-in or clock-out.
2. List the total time worked at the top of these time cards.
3. Forward the cards to the payroll clerk for data entry into the payroll system.

Collect and Reconcile Time Cards

Policy/Procedure Statement Brasto Publishing **Subject: Add or Delete Employees**	Procedure No.: Page: Issue Date: Supercedes:	PAY-02 1 of 1 10/28/0X N/A

1. PURPOSE AND SCOPE

This procedure is used by the payroll clerk to add or delete employees from the payroll system.

2. RESPONSIBILITIES

PR CLERK **Payroll Clerk**

3. PROCEDURES

3.1 PR CLERK **Obtain Addition or Deletion Documentation**

1. Receive documentation from the human resources department regarding the addition to or deletion from the payroll database of employees. Review the documentation for correct start or stop dates, extra pay, and (especially) the correct authorization signatures.
2. If any information is missing, return it to the sender for correction.

3.2 PR CLERK **Update Payroll Database**

1. Go into the payroll software and access the EMPLOYEE menu. Go to the ADD screen if adding an employee. Enter the employee name and social security number, pay rate, and start date. If deleting an employee go into the DELETE screen from the same menu, enter a "Y" in the "Terminate" field, and enter the final pay date, as well as the amount of any bonus payments.
2. Print the "Updates" report from the option at the bottom of the screen to verify that the correct entries were made.

3.3 PR CLERK **File Documentation**

Consult the document destruction policy to determine the date at which the filed documents can be destroyed for any terminated employees. Mark this date on the employee's folder and forward it to the document archiving area.

Add or Delete Employees

Policy/Procedure Statement	Retrieval No.:	PAY-03
Brasto Publishing	Page:	1 of 1
	Issue Date:	10/28/0X
	Supercedes:	N/A
Subject: Alter Employee Deductions		

1. PURPOSE AND SCOPE

This procedure is used by the payroll clerk to alter employee deductions in the payroll system.

2. RESPONSIBILITIES

PR CLERK **Payroll Clerk**

3. PROCEDURES

3.1 PR CLERK

Obtain Deduction Information

1. Obtain employee payroll deduction information from the human resources department.
2. Verify that all information on the deduction forms are clear, and that each one is authorized by the employee.

3.2 PR CLERK

Update Payroll Database

1. Go into the payroll software and access the EMPLOYEE menu. Go to the DEDUCT screen; enter the deduction code and the amount of the deduction for each documented deduction. Be sure to enter a deduction termination code for deductions that are of limited duration.
2. Verify that deductions are correctly allocated to each payroll period so that the total amount of each deduction is accurate on a monthly or annual basis.
3. Print the "Updates" report from the option at the bottom of the screen to verify that the correct entries were made.

3.3 PR CLERK

File Documentation

Return all employee documentation to the human resources department so that they can file it in employee folders.

Policy/Procedure Statement	Procedure No.:	PAY-04
Brasto Publishing	Page:	1 of 2
	Issue Date:	10/28/0X
Subject: Process Payroll Transactions	Supercedes:	N/A

1. PURPOSE AND SCOPE

This procedure is used to guide the human resources coordinator or accounting staff through the payroll process.

2. RESPONSIBILITIES

HR COORD **Human Resources Coordinator**

3. PROCEDURES

3.1 HR COORD **Follow Processing Steps**

1. Review all "Request for Time Off" forms that have been submitted during the most recent pay period.
2. Compare time-off requests to the accrued amounts for each employee, as noted in the payroll detail report for the last pay period. Notify employees if they do not have enough accrued vacation time available to fulfill their requests. Then process the portion of time they *do* have available into the payroll.
3. Collect all requests for employee transfers to different departments, and enter this information into the MASTER CONTROL screen in the payroll software.
4. Enter all manual check payments for the current period into the payroll software, using the MANUAL PAYMENT screen.
5. Collect all requests for pay changes. Verify that there are authorized signatures on the pay change forms. Then enter the changes into the MASTER CONTROL screen in the payroll software.
6. Collect all information regarding terminated employees. Calculate final payments due (if they have not already been paid with manual checks), and enter these final amounts into the CUSTOM PAYMENTS screen in the payroll software.
7. Compare the garnishments file to the detailed payroll records from the last payroll period to see if any changes are needed to current employee deductions. If so, make those changes in the MASTER CONTROL screen in the payroll software.
8. On the Friday before the next payroll, clear out all old records from the electronic time clocks that relate back to the previous pay period. Review all electronic time cards for the current period and notify employees if they have incomplete time cards (such as having clocked in but never clocked out).
9. Manually transfer the totals from the electronic time clocks to the payroll processing software. To do this, enter the grand totals of regular and overtime hours into the HOURLY PAY BY EMPLOYEE screen.
10. Verify all data entry by printing the "Payroll Audit" report and comparing all entered data to the source documents. If there are problems, go back and make the changes, and then print this report again to ensure that all payroll data is correct.
11. Go to the PROCESS PAYROLL screen and process all employee pay. Be sure to match the check number on the check stock to the check number appearing in the computer.
12. Use a signature stamp to sign the checks. Then stuff them into envelopes, along with any special employee notices, and sort them by department.

Process Payroll Transactions (1 of 2)

Policy/Procedure Statement Brasto Publishing **Subject: Process Payroll Transactions**	Retrieval No.: Page: Issue Date: Supercedes:	PAY-04 2 of 2 10/28/0X N/A

13. Back up the payroll database twice. Leave one copy on-site and send the other copy to the off-site storage location.
14. Reset the software to begin processing the payroll for the next pay period.
15. For any off-site locations, send payroll checks by guaranteed overnight delivery.
16. Retrieve the check register from the data center and review it for possible errors. Then file it in the payroll data storage area.

3.2 HR COORD **Process Deductions**

1. Move the cafeteria plan amount noted on the payroll summary from the corporate checking account to the cafeteria plan account.
2. Move the 401(k) amount noted on the payroll summary to the 401(k) fund management firm from the corporate checking account.
3. Update the corporate life insurance payment by adjusting it for the total number of employees now on the payroll, as noted in the payroll summary.
4. Issue a check to the United Way based on the amount shown on the payroll summary as having been deducted from employee paychecks.
5. Pay garnishments to the various court authorities. Verify that the amounts paid out match the deductions shown on the payroll summary.

Process Payroll Transactions (2 of 2)

Policy/Procedure Statement	Procedure No.:	PAY-05
Brasto Publishing	Page:	1 of 1
	Issue Date:	10/28/0X
Subject: Issue Payments to Employees	Supercedes:	N/A

1. PURPOSE AND SCOPE

This procedure is used by the payroll clerk to determine the locations of all employees in the company, and to issue paychecks or deposit advices to them.

2. RESPONSIBILITIES

PR CLERK **Payroll Clerk**

3. PROCEDURES

3.1 PR CLERK **Print Payroll Checks**

1. Go to the payroll software and access the PRINT option from the PAYMENTS menu.
2. Print the payroll test register and review it to ensure that all paychecks have been correctly calculated.
3. Insert check stock into the printer.
4. Use the TEST option to print a sample check and verify that the line spacing is correct. Repeat as necessary.
5. Print the entire batch of checks.
6. Reset the printer and print all deposit advices for the employees who use direct deposit.
7. Print the check register.
8. Review the file of direct deposits, and export it to tape.

3.2 PR CLERK **Issue Direct Deposit Data to Bank**

1. Include the direct deposits tape in a courier package to the bank.
2. Verify that the bank has received the tape, and that there are no errors in it.

3.3 PR CLERK **Distribute Payment Notifications**

1. Have all checks signed by an authorized check signer.
2. Stuff all pay checks and deposit advices in envelopes.
3. Batch the envelopes by supervisor and deliver them to supervisors for delivery to employees.

Issue Payments to Employees

Policy/Procedure Statement Brasto Publishing **Subject: Archive Payroll Records**	Retrieval No.: Page: Issue Date: Supercedes:	PAY-06 1 of 1 10/28/0X N/A

1. PURPOSE AND SCOPE

This procedure is used by the payroll clerk to properly label and archive all payroll records once they have been processed through the payroll system.

2. RESPONSIBILITIES

PR CLERK **Payroll Clerk**

3. PROCEDURES

3.1 PR CLERK **Index Payroll Records**

1. Extract the personnel folders from the on-site files for all inactive employees.
2. Batch all the time cards for prior work periods.
3. Referring to the corporate document destruction policy, mark each item with the legally mandated earliest destruction date.

3.2 PR CLERK **Archive Payroll Records**

1. Box the records by destruction date, mark each box with an index number, and record the index number in the master index, along with the contents of each box.
2. Send the boxes to the archiving center for storage.

Archive Payroll Records

Policy/Procedure Statement Brasto Publishing **Subject: Complete Purchase Requisition**	Procedure No.: Page: Issue Date: Supercedes:	PUR-01 1 of 1 10/28/0X N/A

1. PURPOSE AND SCOPE

This procedure is used by all employees as the first step in requisitioning purchases through the purchasing department.

2. RESPONSIBILITIES

ALL **All Employees**

3. PROCEDURES

3.1 ALL **Obtain Requisition Document**

Obtain a multipart purchase requisition form, which is available from all department secretaries.

3.2 ALL **Compete Purchase Requisition**

1. On the form, fill in the type of item requested, a recommended supplier and part number, and the due date.
2. Obtain the approval signature of the department manager.
3. Remove the pink copy from the form for your records, and forward the remainder of the form to the purchasing department by interoffice mail for further purchasing work.

Complete Purchase Requisition

Policy/Procedure Statement Brasto Publishing **Subject: Research Purchase**	Retrieval No.: Page: Issue Date: Supercedes:	PUR-02 1 of 1 10/28/0X N/A

1. **PURPOSE AND SCOPE**
This procedure is used by the purchasing staff to determine the best price and delivery terms for requisitioned goods.

2. **RESPONSIBILITIES**
PURCH STAFF **Purchasing Staff**

3. **PROCEDURES**

3.1 PURCH STAFF **Determine Purchase Research Rules**
Based on the estimated expense of the item to be purchased, consult the company policy on purchasing research rules to determine the minimum required level of pricing research required.

3.2 PURCH STAFF **Conduct Research**
1. Based on the rules noted in the last step, obtain the minimum number of supplier bids regarding prices and delivery dates.
2. Select from this list the best option, with price being the overriding factor for general and administrative purchases, and delivery time being the overriding factor for production purchases. Use other guidelines for purchases in the case of quality-sensitive purchases.

Policy/Procedure Statement		
Brasto Publishing	Procedure No.:	PUR-03
	Page:	1 of 1
	Issue Date:	10/28/0X
Subject: Issue Purchase Order	Supercedes:	N/A

1. PURPOSE AND SCOPE

This procedure is used by the purchasing staff to create and issue purchase orders to suppliers.

2. RESPONSIBILITIES

PURCH STAFF **Purchasing Staff**

3. PROCEDURES

3.1 PURCH STAFF **Create Purchase Order**

1. Go to the PO screen with the PURCHASING menu. Enter Alt-F8 to obtain a new purchase order number.
2. Enter the supplier number, or press F4 for a list of valid suppliers.
3. Enter the account number to which the purchase is to be charged, and then enter either the internal part number or its description.
4. Enter the unit price and the number of units to be purchased.
5. Enter the date at which the item is due at the receiving dock.
6. Press ENTER to store the purchase order, and press F7 to print it.

3.2 PURCH STAFF **Issue Purchase Order to Supplier**

1. If the supplier is set up for electronic data interchange (EDI), then switch to the EDI screen within the PURCHASING menu and enter the number of the purchase order. A confirming EDI message will arrive through the system once the supplier has accessed the purchase order.
2. If EDI is not set up, then burst the purchase order, with the white copy going to the supplier, the pink copy staying in the purchasing department files, the blue copy going to accounting, and the goldenrod copy going back to the person who requisitioned the item.

3.3 PURCH STAFF **Distribute Purchase Order Internally**

1. Send the goldenrod copy through the interoffice mail to the person who originated the requisition.
2. File the pink copy in the pending file.
3. Send the blue copy to the accounts payable staff through the interoffice mail.

Issue Purchase Order

Policy/Procedure Statement	Retrieval No.:	PUR-04
Brasto Publishing	Page:	1 of 1
	Issue Date:	10/28/0X
	Supercedes:	N/A
Subject: Receive Purchased Items		

1. PURPOSE AND SCOPE

This procedure is used by the receiving staff to ensure that all paperwork and computer systems are properly updated as part of a receipt from a supplier.

2. RESPONSIBILITIES

RECV STAFF **Receiving Staff**

3. PROCEDURES

3.1 RECV STAFF **Receive Materials**

1. Verify that there is a company purchase order number on the packing slip attached to a receipt. If not, contact the purchasing staff and inquire about the validity of the item. If it was not ordered through regular channels, then reject the shipment.
2. If keeping the shipment, verify the condition and quantity of the receipt.

3.2 RECV STAFF **Process Computer Entries**

Go to the RECEIPTS screen in the computer system and call up the purchase order number. Enter the number of items received and the confirm the date on which it was received. Press ENTER to log in the entry.

3.3 RECV STAFF **Process Receiving Paperwork**

Enter the quantity received, the supplier name, and a description of the items received in the receiving log. At the end of the day, attach all bills of lading and packing slips to a copy of the shipping log, and forward it to the accounts payable staff for further processing.

Policy/Procedure Statement	Procedure No.:	PUR-05
Brasto Publishing	Page:	1 of 1
	Issue Date:	10/28/0X
Subject: Match Documents	Supercedes:	N/A

1. PURPOSE AND SCOPE

This procedure is used by the accounts payable clerk to ensure that all documents related to a payment are properly authorized and matched.

2. RESPONSIBILITIES

AP CLERK **Accounts Payable Clerk**

3. PROCEDURES

3.1 AP CLERK **Receive and File Documents**

1. When receiving bills of lading and packing slips from the receiving department, file them in the "Unmatched Receivers" box.
2. When receiving purchase orders from the purchasing department, file them in the "Unmatched Purchase Orders" box.
3. When receiving invoices from suppliers, file them in the "Unmatched Invoices" box.

3.2 AP CLERK **Match Documents**

1. Alphabetize all the preceding documents by supplier name. Then take a supplier invoice and match it to a supporting company purchase order, verifying that the quantity authorized is the quantity billed. If there is no purchase order, then take it to either the purchasing department or the responsible department manager for authorization.
2. If the invoice and purchase order match, then match the receiving documentation to them that prove there was a delivery in the correct amount. If the paperwork is missing, review the shipping log to see if it ever arrived, or call the supplier and request a proof of delivery.
3. Once a set of documents is matched, forward it to the accounts payable clerk for entry into the computer system.

Match Documents

Policy/Procedure Statement	Retrieval No.:	PUR-06
Brasto Publishing	Page:	1 of 1
	Issue Date:	10/28/0X
Subject: Process Expense Reports	Supercedes:	N/A

1. PURPOSE AND SCOPE

This procedure helps the accounts payable clerk expedite the payment of expense reports. This is to be used any time an expense report is being submitted for payment.

2. RESPONSIBILITIES

ACC PAY **Accounts Payable Clerk**

3. PROCEDURES

3.1 ACC PAY **Access a Blank Expense Report**

Access the EXPRPT.XLS file, which is located in the C:\FILES subdirectory.

3.2 ACC PAY **Fill Out the Form**

Enter all travel expenses in the top part of the form, which is entitled "Business Travel." Enter all meal information in the middle part of the form, which is entitled "Meals and Entertainment." Enter all remaining expenses in the bottom of the form, which is entitled "Other Expenses." For company policies regarding the allowability of certain expenses, review the policies list at the bottom of the form. Be sure to attach receipts for all expenses exceeding $10.

3.3 ACC PAY **Complete the Form**

Copy the expense form and all receipts, and retain the copy for your records. Sign the form and have your supervisor review and sign it as well.

3.4 ACC PAY **Submit the Expense Report**

Have your supervisor forward the expense report to the accounts payable department for payment.

Process Expense Reports

Policy/Procedure Statement	Procedure No.:	PUR-07
Brasto Publishing	Page:	1 of 2
	Issue Date:	10/28/0X
	Supercedes:	N/A
Subject: Adjust and Enter Accounts Payable		

1. PURPOSE AND SCOPE

This procedure guides the accounts payable clerk in paying supplier invoices.

2. RESPONSIBILITIES

ACC PAY **Accounts Payable Clerk**

3. PROCEDURES

3.1 ACC PAY **Match Receiving Reports to the Purchase Order**

1. Receive purchase orders from the receptionist, who is in charge of entering this information.
2. Collect all receiving documents from the receiving staff, which is located in the warehouse.
3. Match all receiving reports to purchase orders and supplier invoices. If there is an invoice without an accompanying purchase order, call the supplier and ask who ordered the item being billed. While doing so, also point out to the supplier that all purchases require a purchase order.
4. If any receiving documents cannot be immediately matched to an invoice or purchase order, file them away for comparison at a later date.

3.2 ACC PAY **Enter Received Amount into the Computer**

Go to the PORV function in the computer and enter the purchase order number that is displayed on the packing slip. Find the correct line item and then press ENTER. Input the quantity received. Tab forward to the "Transport Via" field and enter the carrier's name. Tab again to the "Packing Slip" field and enter that number, which is listed on the packing slip. Then press ENTER.

3.3 ACC PAY **Prepare a Problem List**

Prepare a list of problems and give them to the purchasing manager to correct. Typical problems include pricing errors, incorrect quantities, or a missing proof of delivery.

3.4 ACC PAY **Enter Invoice into the Accounting System**

Enter the supplier number in the APIE screen to access the supplier record. Also enter the invoice number, invoice date, and purchase order number. Enter freight charges and taxes, if any. Purchases orders are listed on the left side of the screen. Find the purchase order number that matches the amount, and press ENTER.

3.5 ACC PAY **Run the Accounts Payable Report**

Enter the APRQ screen and print the report. This lists all accounts payable entered into the computer database. Use a highlighter to manually select invoices on the list that must be paid in the current payment period. Add up the amount and verify with the controller that it is acceptable to pay it out, based on current cash levels.

Adjust and Enter Accounts Payable (1 of 2)

Policy/Procedure Statement Brasto Publishing **Subject: Adjust and Enter Accounts Payable**	Retrieval No.: Page: Issue Date: Supercedes:	PUR-07 2 of 2 10/28/0X N/A

3.6 ACC PAY

Process Checks

1. Access the APRQ screen. Access each line item and select those to be paid by typing a "Y" in the last field. Press Ctrl-ENTER to distribute the payments to the general ledger.
2. Wait until the "Process Complete" message appears at the bottom of the screen.
3. Go to the APCW screen and enter "C" in the "Pay Form" field. The payment date should be today's date.
4. Verify the check number to be printed.
5. Load check stock into the printer. Verify that the check number on the check stock matches the number showing in the computer. If they do not match, change the number in the computer to match the number on the check stock.
6. Press ENTER to print checks. When finished processing, press Ctrl-ENTER to distribute to the general ledger.
7. Remove the signature stamp from the safe and use it to stamp all checks.
8. Send the front copy of the check to the supplier.

3.7 ACC PAY

File Documents

File the check copy, invoice, and related information in the supplier file.

Adjust and Enter Accounts Payable (2 of 2)

Policy/Procedure Statement Brasto Publishing **Subject: Create and Issue Payment to Supplier**	Procedure No.: Page: Issue Date: Supercedes:	PUR-08 1 of 1 10/28/0X N/A

1. PURPOSE AND SCOPE

This procedure is used by the accounts payable clerk to print a check or issue an electronic payment authorization, and ensure that either one is sent to the supplier.

2. RESPONSIBILITIES

AP CLERK — **Accounts Payable Clerk**

3. PROCEDURES

3.1 AP CLERK — **Print Checks**

1. Go to the PAYMENT menu in the accounting software and access the PRINT CHECKS option.
2. Scan the list of open and approved accounts payable and put a "*" in the "Pay" field to signify that these items will be paid in the upcoming check run.
3. Print the "Preliminary Check Register" once all line items are selected and verify that the correct items have been selected.
4. Put check stock in the printer and use the TEST option to correct the line spacing.
5. Use the PRINT BATCH option to print all checks on the printer.
6. Switch to regular paper when complete, and print the Check Register.

3.3 AP CLERK — **Transmit to Supplier**

1. Burst all check stock and retain the back copy.
2. Use the check stamp to sign all checks.
3. Stuff the check into envelopes, affix postage, and mail to suppliers.
4. Attach check copies to the matched packets of supplier invoices, purchase orders, and receivers.
5. File the packets by supplier name.
6. File the check register in the accounting reports cabinet.

Create and Issue Payment to Supplier

Policy/Procedure Statement Brasto Publishing **Subject: Close Related Transactions**	Retrieval No.: Page: Issue Date: Supercedes:	PUR-09 1 of 1 10/28/0X N/A

1. PURPOSE AND SCOPE

This procedure is used by the accounts payable clerk to close any purchase orders in the computer system related to a paid supplier invoice.

2. RESPONSIBILITIES

AP CLERK — **Accounts Payable Clerk**

3. PROCEDURES

3.1 AP CLERK — **Find Open Transactions after Matching**

1. Go to the OPEN PO screen in the computer system and select the REPORTS option, which prints out a list of all open purchase orders.
2. Review the list of open purchase orders to see if there are any orders that have been partially completed as a result of prior supplier deliveries.
3. Highlight these partial purchase orders.

3.2 AP CLERK — **Obtain Closing Permissions**

Forward the updated open purchase orders report to the purchasing manager, with a note to mark all purchase orders that can be closed out.

3.3 AP CLERK — **Close Related Transactions**

1. Go to the PURCHASE menu and access the CLOSE PO screen.
2. Enter the purchase order number to be closed out.
3. Reduce the quantity ordered so that it matches the quantity already received.
4. Press ENTER to close the purchase order.

Close Related Transactions

Policy/Procedure Statement Brasto Publishing **Subject: File Completed Documents**	Procedure No.: Page: Issue Date: Supercedes:	PUR-10 1 of 1 10/28/0X N/A

1. PURPOSE AND SCOPE

This procedure is used by the accounts payable clerk to ensure that all documentation related to a supplier payment is appropriately grouped together and filed in the correct location.

2. RESPONSIBILITIES

AP CLERK **Accounts Payable Clerk**

3. PROCEDURES

3.1 AP CLERK **Assemble and Attach Documentation**

Combine all paid supplier invoices with a copy of the checks from which they were paid, as well as a copy of the authorizing purchase order and proof of receipt.

3.2 AP CLERK **File Documents**

1. Create storage files for each supplier, and sort them alphabetically.
2. File the packets of accounts payable documents in the supplier files, sorted by date.

File Completed Documents

Policy/Procedure Statement	Retrieval No.:	PUR-11
Brasto Publishing	Page:	1 of 1
	Issue Date:	10/28/0X
Subject: Void Checks	Supercedes:	N/A

1. PURPOSE AND SCOPE

This procedure is used by the accounts payable clerk to void out any checks that have been created but are not to be issued as payments.

2. RESPONSIBILITIES

ACC PAY — **Accounts Payable Clerk**

3. PROCEDURES

3.1 ACC PAY — **Obtain Approval to Void a Check**

Take the check to be voided to the Controller and request a sign-off on the face of the check, indicating that it is to be voided. Write the reason for the voiding on the back of the check.

3.2 ACC PAY — **Physically Void the Check**

Take the check to the stamping machine and stamp the word "void" on the check with sufficient force to punch holes in the check, outlining the word.

3.3 ACC PAY — **Record Voided Check in the Computer System**

Go to the Accounts Payable module in the accounting software and access the CHECK PAYMENTS screen. Enter the check number to call up the correct item, and put a "V" in the "Check Status" field.

3.4 ACC PAY — **Verify That Voided Check Is Removed from Outstanding Check List**

Go to the Accounts Payable module in the accounting software and access the CLEARED CHECKS screen. Call up the check number for the check that has just been voided, and verify that it has been removed from the list of outstanding checks. If not, go back to the previous step and verify that the check has been listed as void in the accounting database.

3.5 ACC PAY — **Store Voided Check**

File the voided check in the voided check folder for the current year, which is kept with the cleared checks that are returned by the bank.

Void Checks

Chapter 6

PERIOD-END MANUAL

6.1 INTRODUCTION

The users of a company's financial statements—investors, lenders, and management—wish to see accurate results from the latest reporting period as soon as possible. In past years, these have been conflicting goals, under the premise that a rapid financial closing required the use of so many estimates that the results would be less accurate than those achieved after a prolonged wait. However, by using a carefully designed period-end closing manual, the accounting department can create accurate financial statements in short order. The author regularly issues 20-page financial statements within two days of the period-end, primarily by closely following a tight production schedule that is itemized in a closing procedure.

6.2 PERIOD-END MANUAL

The keys to the success of this manual include its constant review and updating to achieve continual improvements in the closing process; careful delineation of the tasks required of each person; and shifting of closing tasks forward into the accounting period to be closed. By paying constant attention to these mechanics, it is possible to close the accounting records and achieve a high degree of accuracy within just a few days of the end of an accounting period.

An example of the period-end closing manual is shown in Exhibit 6.1. This manual is the master copy that is maintained by the controller, showing the work tasks of every person who is involved in the closing process. The left column of the exhibit shows the number of days either before or after the date of the month-end; for example, the first

Policy/Procedure Statement		
Brasto Publishing	Retrieval No.:	10-250
	Page:	1 of 3
	Issue Date:	4/30/0X
	Supercedes:	N/A
Subject: Period-End Closing Activities		

Days from Month-End	*Responsibility*	*Task Description*
−4	Controller	1. Review closing schedule and distribute to staff.
−4	General Ledger Accountant	1. Verify that recurring journal entries are still correct for the current reporting period. 2. Review financial statements with the most recent information and investigate unusual variances. 3. Set up journal entry forms for the coming close.
−4	Cost Accountant	1. Audit bills of material and adjust for any inaccuracies found.
−2	Payables and Receivables Clerks	1. Review the contract schedule and verify that all contractual agreements have been either paid to suppliers or billed to customers.
−2	Cost Accountant	1. Complete all allocation bases.
−1	Cost Accountant	1. Conduct an inventory audit to determine the inventory accuracy level.
−1	Controller	1. Complete footnotes.
−1	General Ledger Clerk	1. Go online and complete a preliminary bank reconciliation. 2. Accrue estimated bank charges and the interest income and interest expense.
−1	General Ledger Accountant	1. Review financial statements with the most recent information and investigate unusual variances.
−1	Accounts Receivable Clerk	1. Conduct a preliminary review of the shipping log to ensure that all deliveries have been billed.
0	General Ledger Accountant	1. Process the period-end closing program in the computer. 2. Print and distribute all period-end reports.
0	Cost Accountant	1. Verify the quantities and descriptions of all offsite inventories that are on consignment. 2. Complete a physical inventory count if the inventory record accuracy is below 95%.
+1	General Ledger Accountant	1. Compare all period-end reports to general ledger balances and reconcile differences. 2. Complete the preliminary bank reconciliation. 3. Cancel all outstanding checks more than 90 days old. 4. Complete a petty cash reconciliation.

Exhibit 6.1. Period-End Closing Procedure

Policy/Procedure Statement Brasto Publishing **Subject: Period-End Closing Activities**	Retrieval No.: Page: Issue Date: Supercedes:	10-250 2 of 3 4/30/0X N/A

Days from Month-End	*Responsibility*	*Task Description*
+1	Payroll Clerk	1. Accrue for unpaid wages. 2. Accrue for unused vacation and sick time. 3. Prepare a detailed list of withheld taxes and pension deductions, tying back to individual payrolls, identified by date. 4. Prepare accrual for the amount of any company-paid matching funds to be deposited in pension account.
+1	Accounts Receivable Clerk	1. Complete billings to all customers. 2. Close the accounts receivable module. 3. Review accounts receivable aging with the controller and determine the amount of a bad debt accrual. 4. Review old accounts receivable and write off selected balances with controller approval. 5. Prepare a detailed schedule of other accounts receivable.
+1	Financial Analyst	1. Prepare a detailed list of short-term investments, showing the name of the investment, the date purchased, the face amount, interest rate, and total accrued interest.
+2	Controller	1. Review the bank reconciliation.
+2	Accounts Payable Clerk	1. Review cut-off information and accrue for any missing supplier invoices based on purchase order costs. 2. Accrue for any unpaid medical or dental insurance, or other employee benefits. 3. Review the repairs and maintenance account to see if any items charged here should be shifted to a fixed asset account. 4. Close the accounts payable module.
+2	Cost Accountant	1. Review inventory balances and conduct a reasonableness test of quantities on hand and costs in comparison to previous periods. 2. Conduct sample test counts for all inventory classes exceeding 10% of total inventory value. 3. Print inventory reports and issue to distribution list. 4. Close the inventory module.
+2	Fixed Assets Clerk	1. Review asset sales and disposals, and update fixed asset records accordingly. 2. Record gains and losses on the sale of assets. 3. Update the fixed assets schedule and calculate depreciation. 4. Verify that depreciation totals do not exceed the totals of asset valuations less salvage values. 5. Reconcile the general ledger fixed asset and accumulated depreciation balances to the detail ledger balances, and correct any variances. 6. Close the fixed asset module.

Exhibit 6.1. Continued

Policy/Procedure Statement	Retrieval No.:	10-250
Brasto Publishing	Page:	3 of 3
	Issue Date:	4/30/0X
Subject: Period-End Closing Activities	Supercedes:	N/A

Days from Month-End	*Responsibility*	*Task Description*
+2	General Ledger Clerk	1. Complete all remaining accruals. 2. Summarize prepaid assets and compare to balances from the previous period. Review balances with the controller and determine the extent of prepaid write-downs for the period. 3. Review the construction in progress account to see if any projects can be finalized; if so, shift to a fixed assets account and initiate depreciation.
+3	General Ledger Clerk	1. Update detailed schedules for all balance sheet accounts. 2. Trace all journal entries to the summary-level general ledger, and investigate all variances.
+3	Financial Analyst	1. Complete all operating data for inclusion in the financial statements.
+3	Controller	1. Consolidate incoming entries from subsidiaries. 2. Complete a preliminary set of financial statements.
+3	Tax Manager	1. Accrue for income taxes expense.
+4	Controller	1. Finalize the financial statements and issue to the distribution list. The following reports should be included in the statements: a. Balance sheet b. Income statement c. Statement of cash flows d. Income statements by department e. Key operating statistics
+4	Financial Analyst	1. Calculate the borrowing base certificate and send it to the lender, along with a set of financial statements.
+5	General Ledger Clerk	1. Review variances too small to be checked during the closing process.
+6	Controller	1. Review the size of the cut-off level used to eliminate variance investigations. 2. Review the closing schedule for the next month. 3. Review job assignments for the next month's closing schedule. 4. Review the closing schedules for subsidiaries for the next month. 5. Review the contents and layout of the financial statements, and plan for changes in advance of the next close.
+7	All Staff	1. Review problems with the last close and agree on necessary changes to be made for the next close.

Source: *Accounting Best Practices,* 2nd Edition, Steven Bragg, copyright ©2001 John Wiley & Sons. This material is used by permission of John Wiley & Sons, Inc.

Exhibit 6.1. Period-End Closing Procedure (Continued)

task listed is −4 days from the month-end, which is four days prior to that date. The next column lists the job title of the person responsible for each task, and the third and final column describes the task that must be completed on that date.

The procedure shown in Exhibit 6.1 is based on several underlying assumptions, which may call for a change in the contents of the procedure if the assumptions are incorrect. They are:

- *That bills of material are used to cost the inventory.* The procedure requires the cost accountant to verify the accuracy of a selection of bills of material in advance of the period-end. By doing so, one can gain some confidence that the costs assigned to work-in-process and finished goods inventories are reasonably accurate, and will require minimal further review or adjustment subsequent to the period-end. If there are no bills of material, or if they are not used to assign costs to inventory, or if they contain significant inaccuracies, then the procedure must include additional (and time-consuming) steps to review costed inventory valuations subsequent to the end of the period.
- *That there are standardized overhead allocations.* The procedure requires the cost accountant to complete the calculation of overhead allocation bases two days before the period-end date. This is possible if one uses a one-month delay in the allocation period so that allocations can be completed in advance. If such a system is not used, the allocation calculation must be delayed until after the accounts payable module is closed subsequent to period-end.
- *That there is an accurate perpetual inventory system.* The procedure requires the cost accountant to review the accuracy of the inventory with an audit prior to the period-end. If the accuracy level is high, then the controller does not need to conduct a physical inventory count (which can seriously delay the completion of the financial statements). There may not even be a need for a formal accuracy review by the cost accountant as long as cycle counts are regularly performed and yield high accuracy levels. If there is no perpetual inventory system or cycle counting procedure in place, then this procedure step must be replaced by a physical inventory count after the period-end.
- *That the bank reconciliation can be completed online.* Many larger banks now make daily account balance and detailed transaction information available online. This allows one to complete a running bank reconciliation so that there are no surprises at the end of the accounting period. The author completes bank reconciliations on all accounts by 8 AM every morning, so the period-end bank reconciliation is a nonevent. If a company does not have such account access, it must wait up to a week after period-end to obtain a mailed statement from the bank; this places the controller in the uncomfortable position of either delaying the close until the statement is received, or of issuing financial results before that date and hoping that there will be no significant changes contained within the statement.
- *That a receiving log is used.* The procedure requires the accounts payable clerk to accrue for any supplier invoices not yet received by reviewing the receiving log to see what deliveries have been received for which there is no

accompanying invoice. This is a particularly easy step in an integrated computerized accounting system that links purchase order numbers to specific receipts, allowing the computer to present an accrual list to the clerk. If this capability is not present, then the controller must authorize a lengthy manual analysis of receipts, or wait a number of days for supplier invoices to be received, or accrue based on a guess of the amount received (which can be incorrect to a significant degree).

The procedure assumes that the accounting staff will issue financial statements on the fourth day after the period-end. However, this is merely a sample target, which will not be reached at once, and which can be surpassed after a number of months of attention to the underlying processes. One can easily use the basic text of Exhibit 6.1 for a tailored procedure, changing the due dates to match the reality of one's current closing process.

Of particular note in this procedure are the steps listed on days six and seven. They require the controller and his or her staff to review the just-completed closing process to see what steps can be made more efficient, thereby contributing to the ongoing reduction of time required to complete the closing process.

6.3 CLOSING PROCEDURE BY POSITION

Each member of the accounting staff is interested only in those tasks requiring his or her involvement. The other activities listed in the Exhibit 6.1 procedure only contribute to one's knowledge of how other employees' activities may interact with one's tasks. Accordingly, it is common to see the closing procedure broken down into smaller procedures, with each accounting position receiving a procedure only dealing with those tasks for which it is responsible. The procedures listed in the following exhibits show the same tasks in Exhibit 6.1, but itemized by position:

- Closing procedure for the accounts payable clerk (Exhibit 6.7)
- Closing procedure for the accounts receivable clerk (Exhibit 6.3)
- Closing procedure for the controller (Exhibit 6.4)
- Closing procedure for the cost accountant (Exhibit 6.5)
- Closing procedure for the fixed assets clerk (Exhibit 6.6)
- Closing procedure for the general ledger clerk (Exhibit 6.2)

Policy/Procedure Statement Brasto Publishing **Subject: Accounts Payable Closing Activities**	Retrieval No.: Page: Issue Date: Supercedes:	10-251 1 of 1 4/30/0X N/A

Days from Month-End	*Responsibility*	*Task Description*
−2	Accounts Payable Clerk	1. Review the contract schedule and verify that all contractual agreements have been either paid to suppliers or billed to customers.
+2	Accounts Payable Clerk	1. Review cut-off information and accrue for any missing supplier invoices based on purchase order costs. 2. Accrue for any unpaid medical or dental insurance, or other employee benefits. 3. Review the repairs and maintenance account to see if any items charged here should be shifted to a fixed asset account. 4. Close the accounts payable module.
+7	Accounts Payable Clerk	1. Review problems with the last close and agree on necessary changes to be made for the next close.

Exhibit 6.2. Closing Procedure for the Accounts Payable Clerk

Policy/Procedure Statement Brasto Publishing **Subject: Accounts Receivable Closing Activities**	Retrieval No.: Page: Issue Date: Supercedes:	10-252 1 of 1 4/30/0X N/A

Days from Month-End	*Responsibility*	*Task Description*
−2	Accounts Receivable Clerk	1. Review the contract schedule and verify that all contractual agreements have been either paid to suppliers or billed to customers.
−1	Accounts Receivable Clerk	1. Conduct a preliminary review of the shipping log to ensure that all deliveries have been billed.
+1	Accounts Receivable Clerk	1. Complete billings to all customers. 2. Close the accounts receivable module. 3. Review accounts receivable aging with the controller and determine the amount of a bad debt accrual. 4. Review old accounts receivable and write off selected balances with controller approval. 5. Prepare a detailed schedule of other accounts receivable.
+7	Accounts Receivable Clerk	1. Review problems with the last close and agree on necessary changes to be made for the next close.

Exhibit 6.3. Closing Procedure for the Accounts Receivable Clerk

Policy/Procedure Statement		
Brasto Publishing	Retrieval No.:	10-253
	Page:	1 of 1
	Issue Date:	4/30/0X
Subject: Controller Closing Activities	Supercedes:	N/A

Days from Month-End	*Responsibility*	*Task Description*
−4	Controller	1. Review closing schedule and distribute to staff.
−1	Controller	1. Complete footnotes.
+2	Controller	1. Review the bank reconciliation.
+3	Controller	1. Consolidate incoming entries from subsidiaries. 2. Complete a preliminary set of financial statements.
+4	Controller	1. Finalize the financial statements and issue to the distribution list. The following reports should be included in the statements: a. Balance sheet b. Income statement c. Statement of cash flows d. Income statements by department e. Key operating statistics
+6	Controller	1. Review the size of the cut-off level used to eliminate variance investigations. 2. Review the closing schedule for the next month. 3. Review job assignments for the next month's closing schedule. 4. Review the closing schedules for subsidiaries for the next month. 5. Review the contents and layout of the financial statements, and plan for changes in advance of the next close.
+7	Controller	1. Review problems with the last close and agree on necessary changes to be made for the next close.

Exhibit 6.4. Closing Procedure for the Controller

Policy/Procedure Statement Brasto Publishing **Subject: Cost Accountant Closing Activities**	Retrieval No.: Page: Issue Date: Supercedes:	10-254 1 of 1 4/30/0X N/A

Days from Month-End	*Responsibility*	*Task Description*
−4	Cost Accountant	1. Audit bills of material and adjust for any inaccuracies found.
−2	Cost Accountant	1. Complete all allocation bases.
−1	Cost Accountant	1. Conduct an inventory audit to determine the inventory accuracy level.
0	Cost Accountant	1. Verify the quantities and descriptions of all off-site inventories that are on consignment. 2. Complete a physical inventory count if the inventory record accuracy is below 95%.
+2	Cost Accountant	1. Review inventory balances and conduct a reasonableness test of quantities on hand and costs in comparison to previous periods. 2. Conduct sample test counts for all inventory classes exceeding 10% of total inventory value. 3. Print inventory reports and issue to distribution list. 4. Close the inventory module.
+7	Cost Accountant	1. Review problems with the last close and agree on necessary changes to be made for the next close.

Exhibit 6.5. Closing Procedure for the Cost Accountant

Policy/Procedure Statement		
Brasto Publishing	Retrieval No.:	10-255
	Page:	1 of 1
	Issue Date:	4/30/0X
	Supercedes:	N/A
Subject: Fixed Assets Closing Activities		

Days from Month-End	*Responsibility*	*Task Description*
+2	Fixed Assets Clerk	1. Review asset sales and disposals, and update fixed asset records accordingly. 2. Record gains and losses on the sale of assets. 3. Update the fixed assets schedule and calculate depreciation. 4. Verify that depreciation totals do not exceed the totals of asset valuations less salvage values. 5. Reconcile the general ledger fixed asset and accumulated depreciation balances to the detail ledger balances, and correct any variances. 6. Close the fixed asset module.
+7	Fixed Assets Clerk	1. Review problems with the last close and agree on necessary changes to be made for the next close.

Exhibit 6.6. Closing Procedure for the Fixed Assets Clerk

Policy/Procedure Statement	Retrieval No.:	10-256
Brasto Publishing	Page:	1 of 1
	Issue Date:	4/30/0X
Subject: General Ledger Closing Activities	Supercedes:	N/A

Days from Month-End	*Responsibility*	*Task Description*
−4	General Ledger Clerk	1. Verify that recurring journal entries are still correct for the current reporting period. 2. Review financial statements with the most recent information and investigate unusual variances. 3. Set up journal entry forms for the coming close.
−1	General Ledger Clerk	1. Go online and complete a preliminary bank reconciliation. 2. Accrue estimated bank charges and the interest income and interest expense. 3. Review financial statements with the most recent information and investigate unusual variances.
0	General Ledger Clerk	1. Process the period-end closing program in the computer. 2. Print and distribute all period-end reports.
+1	General Ledger Clerk	1. Compare all period-end reports to general ledger balances and reconcile differences. 2. Complete the preliminary bank reconciliation. 3. Cancel all outstanding checks more than 90 days old. 4. Complete a petty cash reconciliation.
+2	General Ledger Clerk	1. Complete all remaining accruals. 2. Summarize prepaid assets and compare to balances from the previous period. Review balances with the controller and determine the extent of prepaid write-downs for the period. 3. Review the construction in progress account to see if any projects can be finalized; if so, shift to a fixed assets account and initiate depreciation.
+3	General Ledger Clerk	1. Update detailed schedules for all balance sheet accounts. 2. Trace all journal entries to the summary-level general ledger, and investigate all variances.
+5	General Ledger Clerk	1. Review variances too small to be checked during the closing process.
+7	General Ledger Clerk	1. Review problems with the last close and agree on necessary changes to be made for the next close.

Exhibit 6.7. Closing Procedure for the General Ledger Clerk

6.4 SOFT CLOSE

Some organizations avoid the hassle of closing the books every month, instead focusing on a quarterly close. This is most common for entities that are publicly held, and which are therefore required by law to provide complete quarterly financial statements. Even in these cases, it is useful to complete a "soft close" at the end of those months that are not at the end of a quarter so that management has some idea of the company's financial results as it approaches its quarterly reporting period. It is especially useful if a company is closely tracked by outside analysts who may ask the company for information about expected results as the end of each quarter approaches.

A soft close requires somewhat less work than the normal period-end close, because inventory counts are usually avoided and accruals are more roughly estimated. An example of the procedure for a period-end soft close is noted in Exhibit 6.8.

A comparison of the soft close procedure to the earlier period-end procedure reveals that the soft close contains less than half the number of closing steps. Here are some of the items that one can avoid through the soft close:

- *Petty cash reconciliation*. Though there can be a control problem if petty cash is not reconciled regularly, any adjustments to the account (even if the entire balance is missing) will still be too small to impact the income statement; thus, one can avoid it.
- *Cancel old checks*. Canceling checks that have exceeded a set amount will merely increase the amount of cash and accounts payable, and will have no impact on the income statement at all. Also the dollar amount of cancelled checks tends to be a small number. Consequently, avoiding this step has little impact on the financial statements.
- *Bad debt write-off*. There is no point in writing off uncollectible accounts receivable during the closing period, as the amount is offset by the bad debt allowance. Thus, there is no impact on the income statement at all, and the accounts receivable balance net of the reserve for bad debts will be unchanged. This does not mean that write-offs will only occur at the end of a quarter, but that the write-off process can occur at other times besides the closing period.
- *Detailed balance sheet schedules*. Though it is good practice to maintain a detailed schedule of the contents of every balance sheet account, one can review these both before and after the closing period to ascertain their accuracy, thereby avoiding this time-consuming task during the soft close. However, if the accounting department has a history of having incorrect schedules, this may have to be reviewed during the close for accounts with larger balances.
- *Bill of material (BOM) accuracy review*. The soft close substitutes a review of BOM accuracy with a cost of goods sold calculation that is based on the historical cost of goods sold percentage. This figure is the most likely to be inaccurate, because the mix of products sold may vary in the current month from that of the periods from which the historical average was taken. If this appears to be the case, one may still have to use bills of material to derive a standard cost of goods sold, which can be used as a cross-check of the historical cost of goods sold percentage.

Policy/Procedure Statement Brasto Publishing **Subject: Soft Close Activities**	Retrieval No.: Page: Issue Date: Supercedes:	10-257 1 of 1 4/30/0X N/A

Days from Month-End	*Responsibility*	*Task Description*
−1	Controller	1. Review closing schedule and distribute to staff.
−1	General Ledger Accountant	1. Verify that recurring journal entries are still correct for the current reporting period. 2. Review financial statements with the most recent information and investigate unusual variances. 3. Set up journal entry forms for the coming close.
+1	General Ledger Accountant	1. Complete the online bank reconciliation. 2. Accrue estimated bank charges and the interest income and interest expense.
+1	Payroll Clerk	1. Accrue for unpaid wages. 2. Accrue for unused vacation and sick time.
+1	Accounts Receivable Clerk	1. Complete billings to all customers. 2. Review accounts receivable aging with the controller and determine the amount of a bad debt accrual.
+2	Controller	1. Review the bank reconciliation.
+2	Accounts Payable Clerk	1. Review cut-off information and accrue for any missing supplier invoices based on purchase order costs. 2. If no purchase order system in use, accrue based on history of recurring supplier invoices. 3. Accrue for any unpaid medical or dental insurance, or other employee benefits. 4. Review the repairs and maintenance account to see if any items charged here should be shifted to a fixed asset account.
+2	Cost Accountant	1. Allocate overhead costs at the historical rate. 2. Charge cost of goods sold at the historical percentage, comparing to the mix of products sold at their standard costs for verification.
+2	Fixed Assets Clerk	1. Review asset sales and disposals, and update fixed asset records accordingly. 2. Record gains and losses on the sale of assets. 3. Update the fixed assets schedule and calculate depreciation.
+2	General Ledger Clerk	1. Complete all remaining accruals. 2. Review the construction in progress account to see if any projects can be finalized; if so, shift to a fixed assets account and initiate depreciation.
+3	Financial Analyst	1. Complete all operating data for inclusion in the financial statements.
+3	Controller	1. Consolidate incoming entries from subsidiaries. 2. Complete a preliminary set of financial statements.
+3	Tax Manager	1. Accrue for income tax expense.
+4	Controller	1. Finalize the financial statements and issue to the distribution list. The following reports should be included in the statements: a. Balance sheet b. Income statement c. Statement of cash flows d. Income statements by department e. Key operating statistics

Exhibit 6.8. Period-End Soft Close Procedure

- *Physical inventory count.* As long as historically derived cost of goods sold percentage is used to calculate the cost of goods sold for the soft close, there is no need to determine the actual amount of the ending inventory. This can be a very time-consuming step, so it is one of the most common tasks that is dropped from the soft close. If there is an ongoing problem with the accuracy of the inventory, then the controller can always conduct an inventory review at any other time besides the soft close to determine the extent of any variances from the inventory book balance and incorporate this variance into the results for the following accounting period.
- *Elimination of prepaid expenses.* Unless there is a large quantity of prepaid expenses on the balance sheet, the incremental shifting of these items to expenses will rarely have a significant impact on the income statement, so it can be avoided for a soft close. Even if the decision is made to reduce the amount of prepaid expenses amount, this task can easily be completed during some other time than the closing process.
- *Pension and payroll tax accruals.* Though the expense associated with a company's contribution to the employee pension plan and all payroll taxes must certainly be recorded as part of the soft close, there is no need to spend time verifying the exact amount of the liability that has not yet been sent to the pension plan or government entity. This later calculation only impacts the balance sheet, so it can be avoided for the soft close.
- *Software module closing.* Though some accounting software packages will require users to close out the current month before shifting to the next one, others will allow several periods to be kept open at the same time. This can save a small amount of time during the soft close, as some time for processing and report printing is usually associated with a module closing.

The number of tasks just described that can be skipped in a soft close is considerable. However, these deductions from the standard closing procedure must only be made in light of the accuracy of records within the accounting department. In particular, using a historical cost of goods sold percentage can yield surprising results when the quarterly "hard" close must be completed, because the historical percentage may have no bearing on the different mix of sales, production operating costs, and changes in overhead costs that have occurred since the last hard close. If this appears to be the case, be sure to cross-check the figure with a compilation of product standard costs from a company's bills of material.

6.5 YEAR-END CLOSE

The year-end close results in information that may be subject to an audit, if a company has outside lenders who require audited results or if the owners or management insist upon this extra step. In any case, the year-end audit will require the accounting department to integrate a number of extra steps into its standard closing procedure. An example of this more comprehensive procedure is shown in Exhibit 6.9, with the additional closing steps noted in bold print.

Policy/Procedure Statement	Retrieval No.:	10-258
Brasto Publishing	Page:	1 of 4
	Issue Date:	4/30/0X
Subject: Year-End Closing Activities	Supercedes:	N/A

Days from Month-End	*Responsibility*	*Task Description*
−4	Controller	1. Review closing schedule and distribute to staff. **2. Assist the auditors in conducting a controls review.** **3. Assist the auditors in planning their overview of the physical inventory**.
−4	General Ledger Clerk	1. Verify that recurring journal entries are still correct for the current reporting period. 2. Review financial statements with the most recent information and investigate unusual variances. 3. Set up journal entry forms for the coming close.
−4	Cost Accountant	1. Audit bills of material and adjust for any quantity inaccuracies found. **2. Conduct annual update of standard costs in bills of material to reflect actual costs**. **3. Audit the scrap rates in bills of material and adjust to match actual scrap rates**.
−2	Payables and Receivables Clerks	1. Review the contract schedule and verify that all contractual agreements have been either paid to suppliers or billed to customers.
−1	General Ledger Clerk	1. Go online and complete the bank reconciliation. 2. Accrue actual bank charges and the interest income and interest expense.
−1	Payroll Clerk	**1. Prepare payroll checks that include as recognized income to employees the amount of company-paid life insurance that exceeds the federally mandated maximum value**.
−1	General Ledger Clerk	1. Review financial statements with the most recent information and investigate unusual variances.
−1	Accounts Receivable Clerk	1. Conduct a review of the shipping log to ensure that all deliveries have been billed.
0	General Ledger Clerk	1. Process the period-end closing program in the computer. 2. Print and distribute all period-end reports.
0	Cost Accountant	1. Verify the quantities and descriptions of all off-site inventories that are on consignment.
+1	General Ledger Clerk	1. Compare all period-end reports to general ledger balances and reconcile differences. 2. Complete the preliminary bank reconciliation. 3. Cancel all outstanding checks more than 90 days old. 4. Complete a petty cash reconciliation.

Exhibit 6.9. Year-End Closing Procedure

Policy/Procedure Statement Brasto Publishing **Subject: Year-End Closing Activities**	Retrieval No.: Page: Issue Date: Supercedes:	10-258 2 of 4 4/30/0X N/A

Days from Month-End	*Responsibility*	*Task Description*
+1	Payroll Clerk	1. Accrue for unpaid wages. 2. Accrue for commissions earned but not paid. 3. Accrue for unused vacation and sick time. 4. Prepare a detailed list of withheld taxes and pension deductions, tying back to individual payrolls, identified by date. 5. Prepare accrual for the amount of any company-paid matching funds to be deposited in pension account. **6. Prepare a listing of employees and their annual pay, and set aside for the auditors.**
+1	Accounts Receivable Clerk	1. Complete billings to all customers. 2. Close the accounts receivable module. 3. Review accounts receivable aging with the controller and determine the amount of a bad debt accrual. 4. Review old accounts receivable and write off selected balances with controller approval. 5. Prepare a detailed schedule of other accounts receivable. **6. Print the year-end aged accounts receivable listing and set aside for the auditors.** **7. Print the bad debt accrual calculation and set aside for the auditors.** **8. Assist auditors in sending receivable confirmations to customers.**
+1	Financial Analyst	1. Prepare a detailed list of short-term investments, showing the name of the investment, the date purchased, the face amount, interest rate, and total accrued interest. Set aside a copy for the auditors.
+1	Cost Accountant	**1. Conduct a physical inventory count.**
+2	Controller	1. Review the bank reconciliation. **2. Compile a list of all current contracts, with attached contracts, and set aside for auditors.** **3. Assist auditors in sending legal opinion letters to company lawyers.**
+2	Accounts Payable Clerk	1. Review cut-off information and accrue for any missing supplier invoices based on purchase order costs. 2. Accrue for any unpaid medical or dental insurance, or other employee benefits. 3. Review the repairs and maintenance account to see if any items charged here should be shifted to a fixed asset account. **4. Print the accounts payable listing for year-end and set aside for the auditors.**

Exhibit 6.9. Continued

Policy/Procedure Statement Brasto Publishing **Subject: Year-End Closing Activities**	Retrieval No.: Page: Issue Date: Supercedes:	10-258 3 of 4 4/30/0X N/A

Days from Month-End	*Responsibility*	*Task Description*
+2	Cost Accountant	1. Print inventory reports and issue to distribution list. 2. Close the inventory module.
+2	Fixed Assets Clerk	1. Review asset sales and disposals, and update fixed asset records accordingly. 2. Record gains and losses on the sale of assets. 3. Update the fixed assets schedule and calculate depreciation. 4. Verify that depreciation totals do not exceed the totals of asset valuations less salvage values. 5. Reconcile the general ledger fixed asset and accumulated depreciation balances to the detail ledger balances, and correct any variances. **6. Calculate depreciation as per tax regulations, and set aside for the auditors.** 7. Close the fixed asset module.
+2	General Ledger Clerk	1. Complete all remaining accruals. 2. Summarize prepaid assets and compare to balances from the previous period. Review balances with the controller and determine the extent of prepaid write-downs for the period. 3. Review the construction in progress account to see if any projects can be finalized; if so, shift to a fixed assets account and initiate depreciation.
+3	General Ledger Clerk	**1. Update detailed schedules for all balance sheet accounts and set aside for the auditors.** 2. Trace all journal entries to the summary-level general ledger, and investigate all variances.
+3	Accounts Payable Clerk	**1. Record any late supplier invoices.** **2. Compile all legal invoices for the year and set aside for the auditors.** **3. Close the accounts payable module.**
+3	Cost Accountant	1. Compile allocation bases through the final month and allocate overhead. **2. Document allocation methodology and set aside for auditors.**
+3	Tax Manager	1. Accrue for income taxes expense.
+3	Financial Analyst	1. Complete all operating data for inclusion in the financial statements.
+3	Controller	1. Consolidate incoming entries from subsidiaries. 2. Complete a preliminary set of financial statements. **3. Complete financial footnotes.**
+4	Controller	1. Finalize the financial statements and issue to the distribution list. The following reports should be included in the statements: a. Balance sheet b. Income statement

Exhibit 6.9. Year-End Closing Procedure (Continued)

Policy/Procedure Statement Brasto Publishing **Subject: Year-End Closing Activities**		Retrieval No.: Page: Issue Date: Supercedes:	10-258 4 of 4 4/30/0X N/A
Days from Month-End	*Responsibility*	*Task Description*	
+4	Controller (Continued)	c. Statement of cash flows **d. Stockholders' equity statement** e. Income statements by department f. Key operating statistics	
+4	Financial Analyst	1. Calculate the borrowing base certificate and send it to the lender, along with a set of financial statements.	
+5	General Ledger Clerk	1. Review variances too small to be checked during the closing process.	
+6	Controller	**1. Review all documents required by the auditors, comparing them to the check-off list supplied by the auditors.**	
+7	Controller	1. Review the size of the cut-off level used to eliminate variance investigations. 2. Review the closing schedule for the next month. 3. Review job assignments for the next month's closing schedule. 4. Review the closing schedules for subsidiaries for the next month. 5. Review the contents and layout of the financial statements, and plan for changes in advance of the next close.	
+8	All Staff	1. Review problems with the last close and agree on necessary changes to be made for the next close.	

Exhibit 6.9. Continued

As shown in the procedure, the accounting staff must allocate additional time prior to the close to work with the auditors in reviewing control systems and planning the year-end physical inventory count.

The payroll staff must record on the final employee paychecks of the calendar year the amount of any company-paid life insurance that exceeds (at the time of this writing) $50,000, discounted by a factor that is based on each employee's age. If the year-end close does not fall on the calendar year-end, this step can be avoided. The auditors will also want to see a list of all employees and their annual pay, which is used for control testing. The payroll staff should have this information on hand for them.

The accounts receivable clerk is much busier than usual at this time, having to set aside a final accounts receivable aging for the auditors, write down the reasoning for the final bad debt accrual of the year, and assist the auditors in issuing to customers a selection of confirmations of year-end balances owed.

The cost accountant will have to conduct a physical inventory count for all company locations, and allow for extra time for the auditors to conduct test counts. This must be done as soon after the year-end as possible. This person must also fully document the allocation methodology used for the allocation of overhead costs, and have this information available for the auditors. In addition, the cost accountant usually updates the bills of material with a comprehensive review of costs; this is not necessary for the audit, but the year-end close is frequently used as the time to update bills.

The accounts payable clerk must run a final accounts receivable detail report for the auditors. This position may be required to hold the books open for at least a week subsequent to the date of the year-end to wait for extra supplier invoices to reach the company through the mail. Though Exhibit 6.9 shows that only a three-day wait is used, the books may be held open much longer. If this is not done, then the auditors will probably review supplier invoices that are received subsequent to the closing and require the company to include them in the results for the prior year. This position must also compile all the legal invoices that were received in the past year, which the auditors will review to see if there are any legal disclosures that they must make in the footnotes to the financial statements.

If the company is also hiring the auditors to complete its annual tax return, the fixed assets clerk or the tax manager can calculate the tax depreciation on all depreciable assets and forward this information to the auditors.

The controller must compile a list of current contracts as well as the underlying contract detail, and have this information available for the auditors' review. This person must also create a preliminary set of footnotes, which the auditors will amplify upon if their work reveals extra information that must be included. The controller should also conduct the final review of documents that have been set aside for the auditors and ensure that they are complete.

The volume of extra tasks required for the year-end close can make this a much longer closing process than usual. The procedure in Exhibit 6.9 shows the financial statements being produced one day later than usual, but it is quite common for this process to take one or more weeks of extra time to complete.

An alternative format to the year-end procedure is to break down the various tasks by job position and then convert them into flow charts. An example of this approach is shown in Exhibit 6.10. Though this method will make the tasks of each person quite easy to view, it does not show the due dates for each task, nor does it show the interrelationships between the tasks performed by each person. Consequently, it should only be used if the controller continues to use the master year-end closing procedure so that he or she has access to information about the entire process.

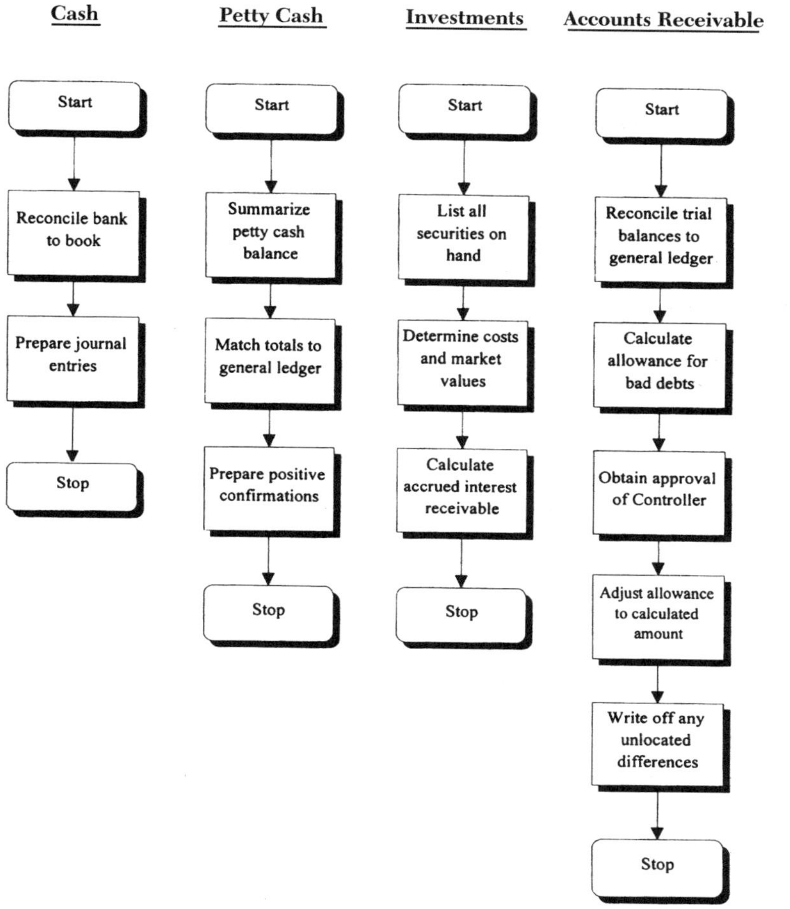

Exhibit 6.10. Closing Tasks by Position, in a Flowchart Format (Continued)

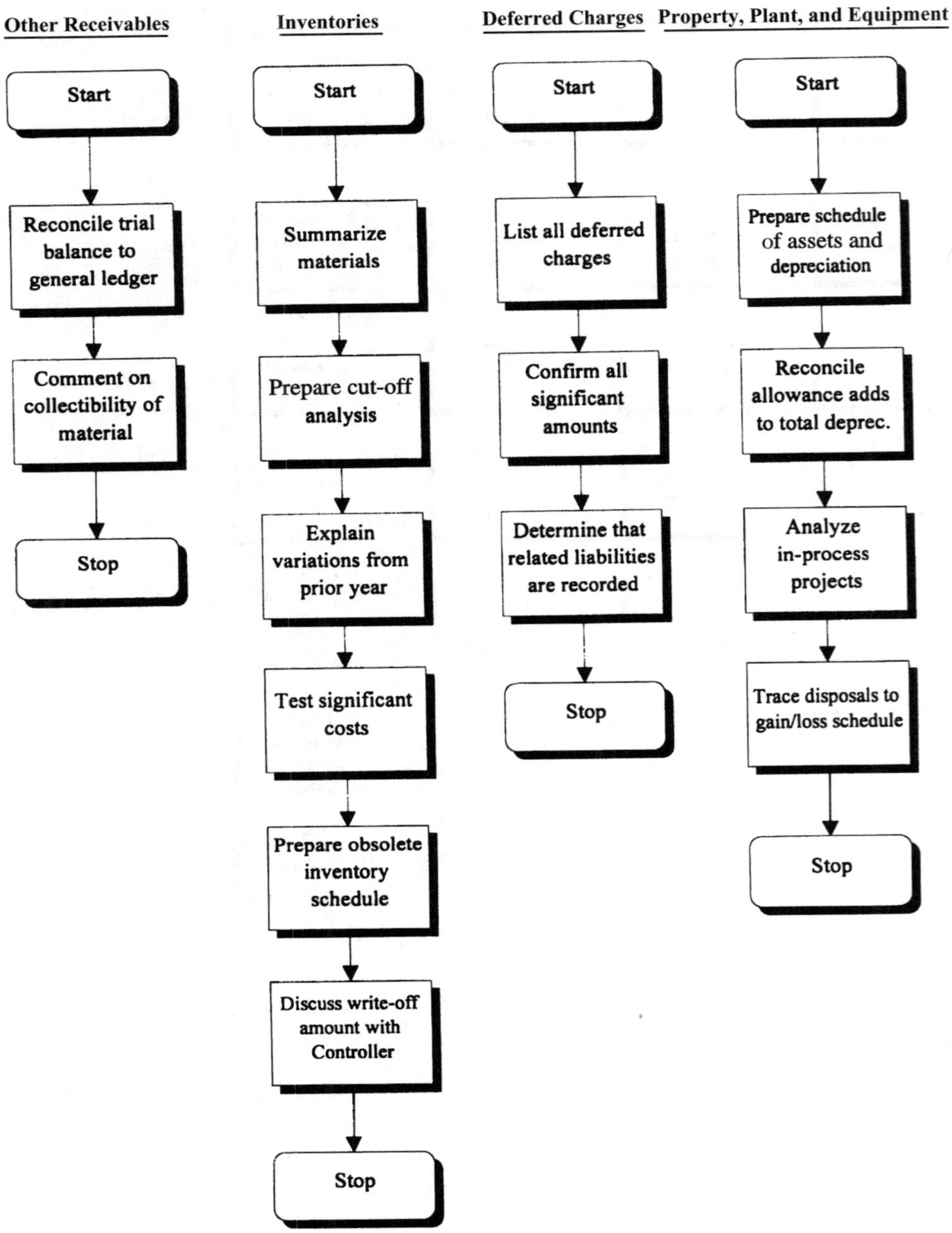

Exhibit 6.10. Closing Tasks by Position, in a Flowchart Format (Continued)

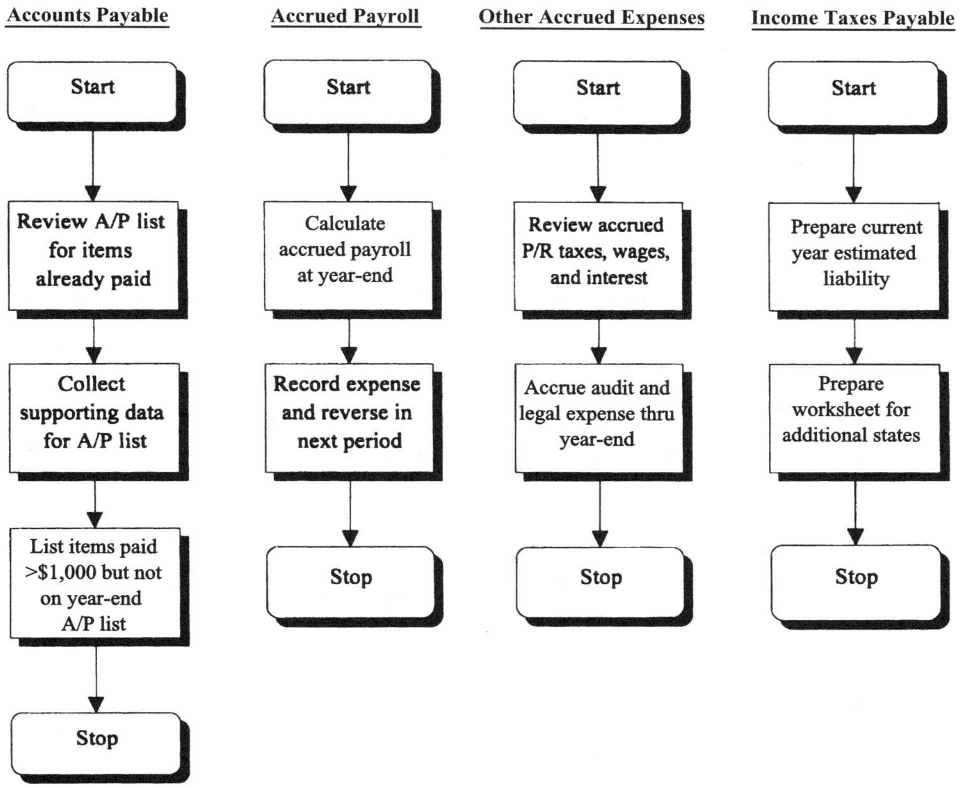

Exhibit 6.10. Continued

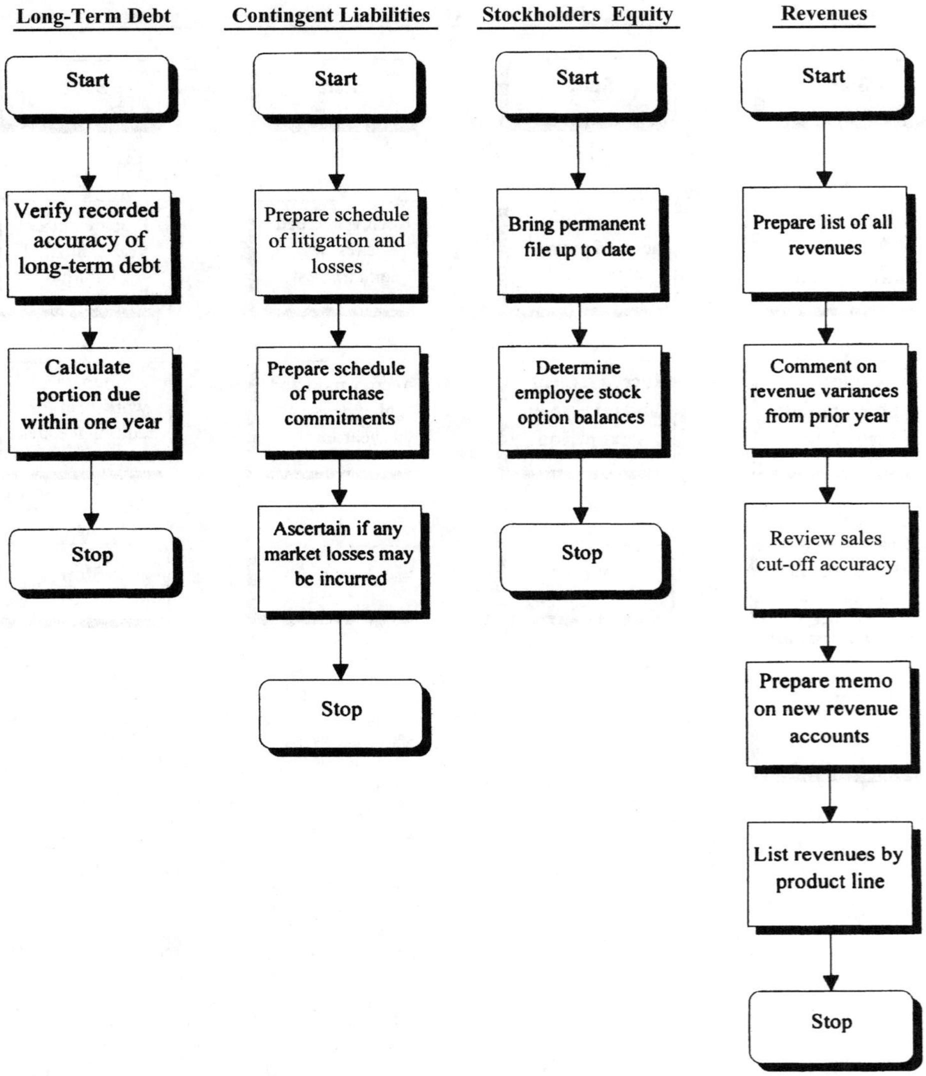

Exhibit 6.10. Closing Tasks by Position, in a Flowchart Format (Continued)

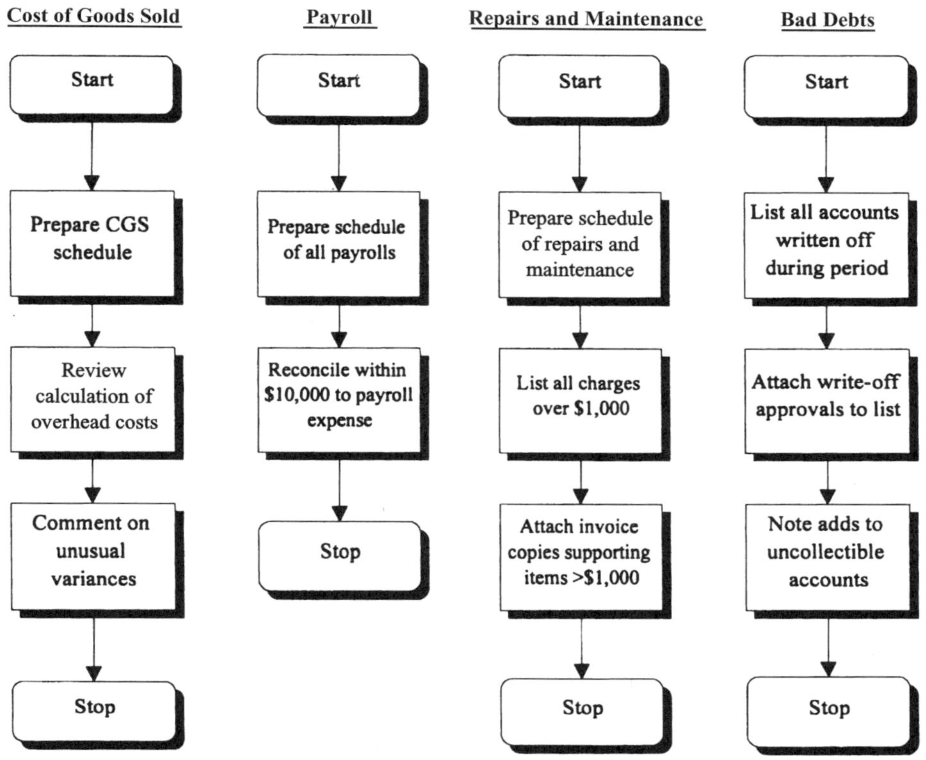

Exhibit 6.10. Continued

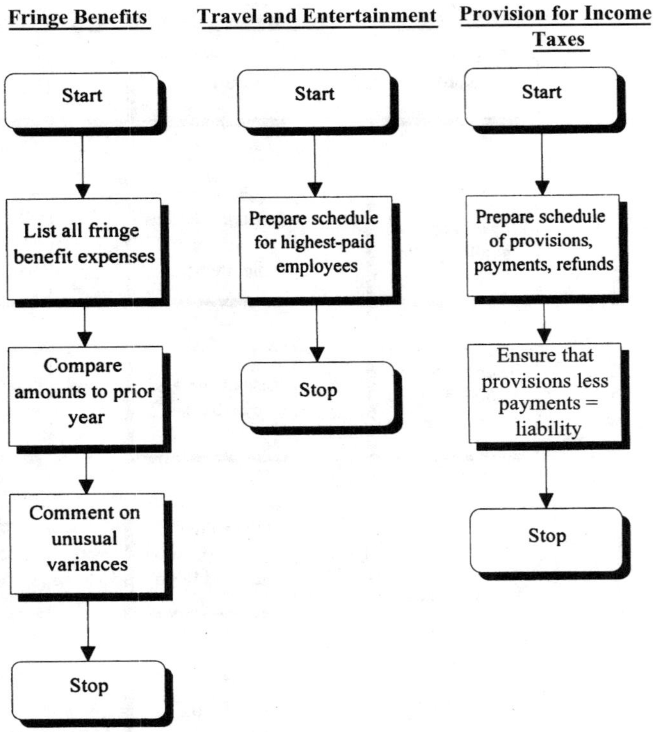

Exhibit 6.10. Closing Tasks by Position, in a Flowchart Format (Continued)

Chapter 7

BUDGETING MANUAL[1]

7.1 INTRODUCTION

Budgeting is one of the most important activities that an accountant can engage in, for it provides the basis for the orderly management of activities within a company. A properly created budget will funnel funding into those activities that a company has determined to be most essential, as defined in its strategic plan. Furthermore, it provides a bridge between strategy and tactics by itemizing the precise tactical events that will be funded, such as the hiring of personnel or acquisition of equipment in a key department. Once the budget has been approved, it also acts as the primary control point over expenditures, because it should be compared to purchase requisitions before purchases are so the level of allowed funding can be ascertained. In addition, the results of specific departments can be compared to their budgets, which is an excellent tool for determining the performance of department managers. For all of these reasons, a comprehensive knowledge of the budgeting process is crucial for the accountant.

In this chapter, we look at the system of budgets and how they are linked together, review a sample budget, cover the key elements of flex budgeting, address the processes required to construct a budget, and finish with coverage of the control systems that can be used if a budget is available.

7.2 SYSTEM OF INTERLOCKING BUDGETS

A properly designed budget is a complex web of spreadsheets that account for the activities of virtually all areas within a company. As noted in Exhibit 7.1, the budget begins

[1]Adapted with permission from Bragg, *Accounting Reference Desktop* (John Wiley & Sons), pp. 258–91.

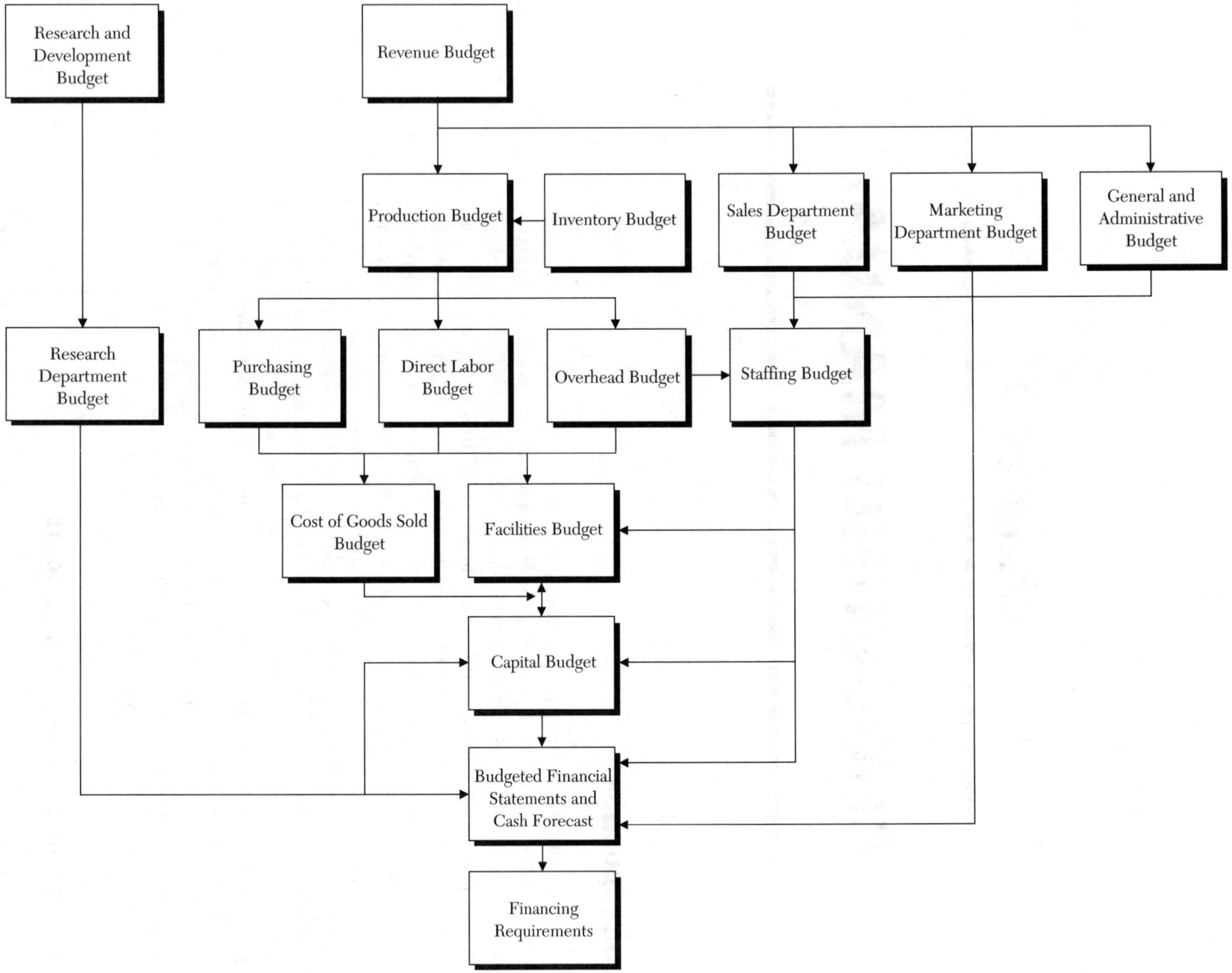

Exhibit 7.1. System of Budgets

in two places, with both the revenue budget and research and development budget. The revenue budget contains the revenue figures that the company believes it can achieve for each upcoming reporting period. These estimates come partially from the sales staff, which is responsible for estimates of sales levels for existing products within their current territories. Estimates for the sales of new products that have not yet been released, and for existing products in new markets will come from a combination of the sales and marketing staffs, who will use their experience with related product sales to derive estimates. The greatest fallacy in any budget is to impose a revenue budget from the top management level without any input from the sales staff, as this can result in a company-wide budget that is geared toward a sales level that is most unlikely to be reached.

A revenue budget requires prior consideration of a number of issues. For example, a general market share target will drive several other items within the budget, as greater market share may come at the cost of lower unit prices or higher credit costs. Another issue is the compensation strategy for the sales staff; a shift to higher or lower commissions for specific products or regions will be a strong incentive for the sales staff to alter their selling behavior, resulting in some changes in estimated sales levels. Yet another consideration is which sales territories are to be entered during the budget period—those with high target populations may yield very high sales per hour of sales effort, while the reverse will be true if the remaining untapped regions have smaller target populations. It is also necessary to review the price points that will be offered during the budget period, especially in relation to the pricing strategies that are anticipated from competitors. If there is a strategy to increase market share as well as to raise unit prices, the budget may fail due to conflicting activities. Another major factor is the terms of sale, which can be extended, along with easy credit, to attract more marginal customers; conversely, they can be retracted to reduce credit costs and focus company resources on a few key customers. A final point is that the budget should address any changes in the type of customer to whom sales will be made. If an entirely new type of customer will be added to the range of sales targets during the budget period, then the revenue budget should reflect a gradual ramp-up that will be required for the sales staff to work through the sales cycle of the new customers.

Once all of these factors have been ruminated upon and combined to create a preliminary budget, the sales staff should also compare the budgeted sales level per person to the actual sales level that has been experienced in the recent past to see if the company has the existing capability to make the budgeted sales. If not, the revenue budget should be ramped up to reflect the time it will take to hire and train additional sales staff. The same cross-check can be conducted for the amount of sales budgeted per customer to see if historical experience validates the sales levels noted in the new budget.

Another budget that initiates other activities within the system of budgets is the research and development budget. This is not related to the sales level at all (as opposed to most other budgets), but instead is a discretionary budget that is based on the company's strategy to derive new or improved products. The decision to fund a certain amount of project-related activity in this area will drive a departmental staffing and capital budget that is, for the most part, completely unrelated to the activity conducted by the rest of the company. However, there can be a feedback loop between this budget and the cash budget, because financing limitations may require management to prune some projects from this area. If so, the management team must work with the research and development manager to determine the correct mix of projects with both short-range and long-range payoffs that will still be funded. This is as much an art as a science, though the process can be helped along by a capital budgeting evaluation.

The production budget is largely driven by the sales estimates contained within the revenue budget. However, it is also driven by the inventory-level assumptions in the inventory budget. The inventory budget contains estimates by the materials management supervisor regarding the inventory levels that will be required for the upcoming budget period. For example, a new goal may be to reduce the level of finished goods inventory from 10 turns per year to 15. If so, some of the products required by the revenue budget can be bled off from the existing finished goods inventory stock, requiring smaller production requirements during the budget period. Alternatively, if there is a strong focus on improving the level of customer service, then it may be necessary to keep more finished goods in stock, which will require more production than is strictly called for by the revenue budget. This concept can also be extended to work-in-process (WIP) inventory, where the installation of advanced production planning systems, such as manufacturing resources planning or just-in-time, can be used to reduce the level of required inventory. Also, just-in-time purchasing techniques can be used to reduce the amount of raw materials inventory that is kept on hand. All of these assumptions should be clearly delineated in the inventory budget so that the management team is clear about what systemic changes will be required to effect altered inventory turnover levels. Also, one should be aware that any advanced production planning system takes a considerable amount of time to install and tune, so it is best if the inventory budget contains a gradual ramp-up to different planned levels of inventory.

Given this input from the inventory budget, the production budget is used to derive the unit quantity of required products that must be manufactured to meet revenue targets for each budget period. This involves a number of interrelated factors, such as the availability of sufficient capacity for production needs. Of particular concern should be the amount of capacity at the bottleneck operation. This tends to be the most expensive capital item, so it is important to budget a sufficient quantity of funding to ensure that this operation includes enough equipment to meet the targeted production goals. If the bottleneck operation involves skilled labor rather than equipment, the human resources staff should be consulted regarding its ability to bring in the necessary personnel in time to improve the bottleneck capacity in a timely manner.

Another factor that drives the budgeted costs contained within the production budget is the anticipated size of production batches. If the batch size is expected to decrease, then more overhead costs should be budgeted in the production scheduling, materials handling, and machine setup staffing areas. If longer batch sizes are planned then there may be a possibility of proportionally reducing overhead costs in these areas. This is a key consideration that is frequently overlooked but can have an outsized impact on overhead costs. If management attempts to contain overhead costs in this area while still using smaller batch sizes, then it will likely run into larger scrap quantities and quality issues that are caused by rushed batch setups and the allocation of incorrect materials to production jobs.

Step costing is also an important consideration when creating the production budget. Costs will increase in large increments when certain capacity levels are reached. The management team should be fully aware of when these capacity levels will be reached so that it can plan appropriately for the incurrence of added costs. For example, the addition of a second shift to the production area will call for added costs in the areas of supervisory staff as well as an increased pay rate and higher maintenance costs. The inverse of this condition can also occur, where step costs can decline suddenly if capacity levels fall below a specific point.

Production levels may also be impacted by any lengthy tooling setups or changeovers to replacement equipment. These changes may halt all production for extended periods and so must be carefully planned for. This is the responsibility of the industrial engineering staff. The accountant would do well to review the company's history of actual equipment setup times to see if the current engineering estimates are sufficiently lengthy, based on past history.

The expense items included in the production budget should be driven by a set of subsidiary budgets, which are the purchasing, direct labor, and overhead budgets. These budgets can simply be included in the production budget, but they typically involve such a large proportion of company costs that it is best to lay them out separately in greater detail in separate budgets. Comments on these budgets are as follows:

Purchasing budget

The purchasing budget is driven by several factors, first of which is the bill of materials that comprises the products that are planned for production during the budget period. These bills must be accurate, or else the purchasing budget can include seriously incorrect information. In addition, there should be a plan for controlling material costs, perhaps through the use of concentrated buying through few suppliers, or perhaps through the use of long-term contracts. If materials are highly subject to market pressures, are a large proportion of total product costs, and have a history of sharp price swings, then a best-case and worst-case costing scenario should be added to the budget so that managers can review the impact of costing issues in this area. If a just-in-time delivery system from suppliers is contemplated, then the purchasing budget should reflect a possible increase in material costs caused by the increased number of deliveries from suppliers. It is also worthwhile to budget for a raw material scrap and obsolescence expense; there should be a history of costs in these areas that can be extrapolated based on projected purchasing volumes.

Direct labor budget

One should not make the mistake of budgeting for direct labor as a fully variable cost. The production volume from day to day tends to be relatively fixed, and requires a set number of direct labor personnel on a continuing basis to operate production equipment and manually assemble products. Further, the production manager will realize much greater production efficiencies by holding on to an experienced production staff rather than letting them go as soon as production volumes make small incremental drops. Accordingly, it is better to budget based on reality, which is that direct labor personnel are usually retained, even if there are ongoing fluctuations in the level of production. Thus, direct labor should be shown in the budget as a fixed cost of production, within certain production volume parameters.

Also, this budget should describe staffing levels by type of direct labor position; this is driven by labor routings, which are documents that describe the exact type and quantity of staffing needed to produce a product. When multiplied by the unit volumes located in the production budget, this results in an expected level of staffing by direct labor position. This information is most useful for the human resources staff, which is responsible for staffing the positions.

The direct labor budget should also account for any contractually mandated changes in hourly rates that may be itemized in a union agreement. Such an agreement may also have restrictions on layoffs, which should be accounted for in the budget if this will keep labor levels from dropping in proportion with budgeted reductions in production levels. Such an agreement may also require that layoffs be conducted in order of seniority, which may force higher-paid employees into positions that would normally be budgeted for less expensive laborers. Thus, the presence of a union contract can result in a much more complex direct labor budget than would normally be the case.

The direct labor budget may also contain features related to changes in the efficiency of employees, and any resulting changes in pay. For example, one possible pay arrangement is to pay employees based on a piece rate, which directly ties their performance to the level of production achieved. If so, this will probably only apply to portions of the work force, so the direct labor budget may involve pay rates based on both piece rates and hourly pay. Another issue is that any drastic increases in the budgeted level of direct labor personnel will likely result in some initial declines in labor efficiency, as it takes time for new employees to learn their tasks. If this is the case, the budget should reflect a low level of initial efficiency, with a ramp-up over time to higher levels that will result in greater initial direct labor costs. Finally, efficiency improvements may be rewarded with staff bonuses from time to time; if so, these bonuses should be included in the budget.

Overhead budget

The overhead budget can be a simple one to create if there are no significant changes in production volume from the preceding year, because this involves a large quantity of static costs that will not vary much over time. Included in this category are machine maintenance; utilities; supervisory salaries, wages for the materials management, production scheduling, and quality assurance personnel; and facilities maintenance and depreciation expenses. Under the no-change scenario, the most likely budgetary alterations will be to machinery or facilities maintenance, which depend on the condition and level of usage of company property.

If there is a significant change in the expected level of production volume, or if new production lines are to be added, then one should examine this budget in great detail, for the underlying production volumes may cause a ripple effect that results in wholesale changes to many areas of the overhead budget. Of particular concern is the number of overhead-related personnel who must be either laid off or added when capacity levels reach certain critical points, such as the addition or subtraction of extra work shifts. Costs also tend to rise substantially when a facility is operating at very close to 100% capacity, as this tends to call for an inordinate amount of effort to maintain on an ongoing basis.

The purchasing, direct labor, and overhead budgets can then be summarized into a cost of goods sold budget. This budget should incorporate, as a single line item, the total amount of revenue so that all manufacturing costs can be deducted from it to yield a gross profit margin on the same document. This budget is referred to constantly during the budget creation process, because it tells management if its budgeting assumptions are yielding an acceptable gross margin result. As it is a summary-level budget for the production side of the budgeting process, this is also a good place to itemize any production-related statistics, such as the average hourly cost of direct labor, inventory turnover rates, and the amount of revenue dollars per production person.

Thus far, we have reviewed the series of budgets that descend in turn from the revenue budget and then through the production budget. However, there are other expenses that are unrelated to production. These are categories in a separate set of budgets. The first is the sales department budget. This includes the expenses that the sales staff must incur to achieve the revenue budget, such as travel and entertainment, as well as sales training. Of particular concern in this budget is the amount of budgeted headcount that is required to meet the sales target. It is essential that the actual sales per salesperson from the most recent completed year of operations be compared to the same calculation in the budget to ensure that there is a sufficiently large budget available for an adequate number of sales personnel. This is a common problem, for companies will make the false assumption that the existing sales staff can make heroic efforts to wildly exceed its previous-year sales efforts. Furthermore, the budget must account for a sufficient time period in which new sales personnel can be trained and form an adequate base of customer contacts to create a meaningful stream of revenue for the company. In some industries, this learning curve may be only a few days, but it can be the better part of a year if considerable technical knowledge is required to make a sale. If the latter situation is the case, it is likely that the procurement and retention of qualified sales staff is the key element of success for a company, which makes the sales department budget one of the most important elements of the entire budget.

The marketing budget is also closely tied to the revenue budget, for it contains all of the funding required to roll out new products, merchandise them properly, advertise for them, test new products, and so on. A key issue here is to ensure that the marketing budget is fully funded to support any increases in sales noted in the revenue budget. It may be necessary to increase this budget by a disproportionate amount if one is trying to create a new brand, issue a new product, or distribute an existing product in a new market. These costs can easily exceed any associated revenues for some time. A common budgeting problem is not to provide sufficient funding in these instances, leading to a significant drop in expected revenues.

Another nonproduction budget that is integral to the success of the corporation is the general and administrative budget. This contains the cost of the corporate management staff, plus all accounting, finance, and human resources personnel. Because this is a cost center, the general inclination is to reduce these costs to the bare minimum. However, to do so there must be a significant investment in technology to achieve reductions in the manual labor usually required to process transactions; thus, there must be some provision in the capital budget for this area.

There is a feedback loop between the staffing and direct labor budgets and the general and administrative budget, because the human resources department must staff itself based on the amount of hiring or layoffs that are anticipated elsewhere in the company. Similarly, a major change in the revenue volume will alter the budget for the accounting department, as many of the activities in this area are driven by the volume of sales transactions. Furthermore, a major increase in the capital budget, especially for items requiring prolonged construction activities, will require an investment in additional cost accounting personnel who will track these expenditures. Thus, the general and administrative budget generally requires a number of iterations in response to changes in many other parts of the budget.

Though salaries and wages should be listed in each of the departmental budgets, it is useful to list the total headcount for each position through all budget periods in a separate staffing budget. By doing so, the human resources staff can tell when specific positions must be filled so that they can time their recruiting efforts most appropriately. This budget also provides good information for the person responsible for the facilities budget; he or she can use it to determine the timing and amount of square footage requirements for office space. Rather than being a standalone budget, the staffing budget tends to be one whose formulas are closely intertwined with those of all other departmental budgets, so a change in headcount information on this budget will automatically translate into a change in the salaries expense on other budgets. It is also a good place to store the average pay rates, overtime percentages, and average benefit costs for all positions. By centralizing this cost information, the human resources staff can more easily update budget information. Salary-related costs tend to be the highest proportion of costs in a company (excluding materials costs), making this a heavily used budget.

The facilities budget is based on the level of activity that is estimated in many of the budgets just described. For this reason, it is one of the last budgets to be completed. This budget is closely linked to the capital budget, because expenditures for additional facilities will require more maintenance expenses in the facilities budget. This budget typically contains expense line items for building insurance, maintenance, repairs, janitorial services, utilities, and the salaries of the maintenance personnel employed in this function. It is crucial to estimate the need for any upcoming major repairs to facilities when constructing this budget, as these can greatly amplify the total budgeted expense.

Another budget that includes input from virtually all areas of a company is the capital budget. This should comprise either a summary listing of all main fixed asset categories for which purchases are anticipated, or else a detailed listing of the same information; the latter case is only recommended if there are comparatively few items to be purchased. The capital budget is of great importance to the calculation of corporate financing requirements because it can involve the expenditure of sums far beyond those that are normally encountered through daily cash flows. The contents of the capital budget should be carefully examined to determine whether it has an impact on a company's bottleneck operation. All too often expenditures are made that make other operations more efficient but do not increase the ability to produce more product by increasing the capacity of the bottleneck operation.[2] It is also necessary to ensure that capital items are scheduled for procurement far enough in advance of related projects that they will be fully installed and operational before the scheduled first activity date of the project. For example, a budget should not itemize revenue from a printing press for the same month in which the press is scheduled to be purchased, for it may take months to set up the press. A final item is that capital purchases may be tied to the pet projects of senior managers, rather than to the strategic or tactical goals of the company. Consequently, it may be useful to review all capital items in the budget to ensure that they are all needed to meet these goals.

[2]For more information about this topic, See Chapter 14, "Throughput Accounting," in Bragg, *Cost Accounting* (John Wiley & Sons, 2001).

The end result of all budgets just described is a set of financial statements that reflect the impact on the company of the upcoming budget. At a minimum, these statements should include the income statement and cash flow statement, which are the best evidence of fiscal health during the budget period. The balance sheet is less necessary because the key factors on which it reports are related to cash, and that information is already contained within the cash flow statement. These reports should be directly linked to all the other budgets so that any changes to the budgets will immediately appear in the financial statements. The management team will closely examine these statements and make numerous adjustments to the budgets to arrive at a satisfactory financial result.

The budget-linked financial statements are also a good place to store related operational and financial ratios so that the management team can review this information and revise the budgets to alter the ratios to match benchmarking or industry standards that may have been set as goals. Typical measurements in this area can include revenue and income per person, inventory turnover ratios, and gross margin percentages. This type of information is also useful for lenders, who may have required minimum financial performance results as part of loan agreements, such as a minimum current ratio or debt-to-equity ratio.

The cash forecast is of exceptional importance, for it tells company managers if the proposed budget model will be feasible. If cash projects result in major cash needs that cannot be met by any possible financing, then the model must be changed. The assumptions that go into the cash forecast should be based strictly on historical fact rather than on the wishes of managers. This stricture is particularly important in the case of cash receipts from accounts receivable. If the assumptions are changed in the model to reflect an advanced rate of cash receipts that exceeds anything the company has heretofore experienced, then it is very unlikely that it will be achieved during the budget period. Instead, it is better to use proven collection periods as assumptions and alter other parts of the budget to ensure that cash flows remain positive.

The cash forecast is a particularly good area in which to spot the impact of changes in credit policy. For example, if a company wishes to expand its share of the market by allowing easy credit to marginal customers, then it should lengthen the assumed collection period in the cash forecast to see if there is a significant downgrading of the resulting cash flows.

The other key factor in the cash forecast is the use of delays in budgeted accounts payable payments. It is common for managers to budget for extended payment terms to fund other cash flow needs, but there are several problems that can result from this policy. One is the possible loss of key suppliers who will not tolerate late payments. Another is the risk of being charged interest on late payments to suppliers. A third problem is that suppliers may relegate a company to a lower level on their lists of shipment priorities because they are being paid late. Finally, suppliers may simply raise their prices to absorb the cost of the late payments. Consequently, the late payment strategy must be followed with great care, only using it on those suppliers who do not appear to notice, and otherwise only doing it after prior negotiation with targeted suppliers to make the changed terms part of the standard buying agreement.

The last document in the system of budgets is the discussion of financing alternatives. This is not strictly a budget, though it will contain a single line item, derived from the cash forecast, which itemizes funding needs during each period itemized in the budget. In all other respects, it is simply a discussion of financing alternatives, which can be quite varied. This may involve a mix of debt, supplier financing, preferred stock, common stock, or some other, more innovative approach. The document should contain a discussion of the cost of each form of financing, the ability of the company to obtain it, and when it can be obtained. Managers may find that there are so few financing alternatives available, or that the cost of financing is so high, that the entire budget must be restructured to avoid the negative cash flow that calls for the financing. There may also be a need for feedback from this document back into the budgeted financial statements in order to account for the cost of obtaining the funding, as well as any related interest costs.

In the next section, we will review an example of the budgets that have just been described to see how they are formatted and link together in a cohesive set of budgets that can be used to conduct the future operations of a business.

7.3 SAMPLE BUDGET

In this section, we will review several variations on how a budget can be constructed, using a number of examples. The first budget covered is the revenue budget, which is shown in Exhibit 7.2. To conserve space, the exhibit uses quarterly revenue figures for a budget year rather than monthly. It contains revenue estimates for three different product lines that are designated as Alpha, Beta, and Charlie.

REVENUE BUDGET FOR THE FISCAL YEAR ENDED XX/XX/02

	Quarter 1	*Quarter 2*	*Quarter 3*	*Quarter 4*	*Totals*
Product Line Alpha					
Unit price	$15.00	$14.85	$14.80	$14.75	—
Unit volume	14,000	21,000	25,000	31,000	91,000
Revenue subtotal	$210,000	$311,850	$370,000	$457,250	$1,349,100
Product Line Beta					
Revenue subtotal	$1,048,000	$1,057,000	$1,061,000	$1,053,000	$4,219,000
Product Line Charlie					
Region 1	$123,000	$95,000	$82,000	$70,000	$370,000
Region 2	80,000	89,000	95,000	101,000	365,000
Region 3	95,000	95,000	65,000	16,000	271,000
Region 4	265,000	265,000	320,000	375,000	1,225,000
Revenue subtotal	$563,000	$544,000	$562,000	$562,000	$2,231,000
Revenue grand total	$1,821,000	$1,912,850	$1,993,000	$2,072,250	$7,799,100
Quarterly revenue proportion	23.3%	24.5%	25.6%	26.6%	100.0%
Statistics					
Product line proportion:					
Alpha	11.5%	16.3%	18.6%	22.1%	17.3%
Beta	57.6%	55.3%	53.2%	50.8%	54.1%
Charlie	30.9%	28.4%	28.2%	27.1%	28.6%
Product line total	100.0%	100.0%	100.0%	100.0%	100.0%

Exhibit 7.2. Revenue Budget

The Alpha product line uses a budgeting format that identifies the specific quantities that are expected to be sold in each quarter, as well as the average price per unit sold. This format is most useful when there are not so many products that such a detailed delineation would create an excessively lengthy budget. It is a very useful format, for the sales staff can go into the budget model and alter unit volumes and prices quite easily. An alternative format is only to reveal this level of detail for the most important products, and to lump the revenue from other products into a single line item, as is the case for the Beta product line.

The most common budgeting format is used for the Beta product line, where we avoid the use of detailed unit volumes and prices in favor of a single lump-sum revenue total for each reporting period. This format is used when there are multiple products within each product line, making it cumbersome to create a detailed list of individual products. However, this format is the least informative and gives no easy way to update the supporting information.

Yet another budgeting format is shown for the Charlie product line, where projected sales are grouped by region. This format is most useful when there are many sales personnel, each of whom has been assigned a specific territory in which to operate. This budget can then be used to judge the ongoing performance of each salesperson.

These revenue reporting formats can also be combined so that the product line detail for the Alpha product can be used as underlying detail for the sales regions used for the Charlie product line—though this will result in a very lengthy budget document.

There is also a statistics section at the bottom of the revenue budget that itemizes the proportion of total sales that occurs in each quarter, plus the proportion of product line sales within each quarter. Though it is not necessary to use these exact measurements, it is useful to include some type of measure that informs the reader of any variations in sales from period to period.

Both the production and inventory budgets are shown in Exhibit 7.3. The inventory budget is itemized at the top of the exhibit, where we itemize the amount of planned

PRODUCTION AND INVENTORY BUDGET FOR THE FISCAL YEAR ENDED XX/XX/02

	Quarter 1	*Quarter 2*	*Quarter 3*	*Quarter 4*	*Totals*
Inventory Turnover Goals					
Raw materials turnover	4.0	4.5	5.0	5.5	4.8
W-I-P turnover	12.0	15.0	18.0	21.0	16.5
Finished goods turnover	6.0	6.0	9.0	9.0	7.5
Product Line Alpha Production					
Beginning inventory units	15,000	21,000	20,000	15,000	—
Unit sales budget	14,000	21,000	25,000	31,000	91,000
Planned production	20,000	20,000	20,000	27,375	87,375
Ending inventory units	21,000	20,000	15,000	11,375	
Bottleneck unit capacity	20,000	20,000	20,000	40,000	
Bottleneck utilization	100%	100%	100%	68%	
Planned finished goods turnover	15,167	15,167	11,375	11,375	

Exhibit 7.3. Production and Inventory Budgets

inventory turnover in all three inventory categories. There is a considerable ramp-up in work-in-process inventory turnover, indicating the planned installation of a manufacturing planning system of some kind that will control the flow of materials through the facility.

The production budget for just the Alpha product line is shown directly below the inventory goals. This budget is not concerned with the cost of production, but rather with the number of units that will be produced. In this instance, we begin with an on-hand inventory of 15,000 units, and try to keep enough units on hand through the remainder of the budget year to meet both the finished goods inventory goal at the top of the exhibit and the number of required units to be sold, which is referenced from the revenue budget. The main problem is that the maximum capacity of the bottleneck operation is 20,000 units per quarter. To meet the revenue target, we must run that operation at full bore through the first three quarters, irrespective of the inventory turnover target. This is especially important because the budget indicates a jump in bottleneck capacity in the fourth quarter from 20,000 to 40,000 units—this will occur when the bottleneck operation is stopped for a short time while additional equipment is added to it. During this stoppage, there must be enough excess inventory on hand to cover any sales that will arise. Consequently, production is planned for 20,000 units per quarter for the first three quarters, followed by a more precisely derived figure in the fourth quarter that will result in inventory turns of 9.0 at the end of the year, exactly as planned.

The production budget can be enhanced with the incorporation of planned machine downtime for maintenance, as well as for the planned loss of production units to scrap. It is also useful to plan for the capacity needs of nonbottleneck work centers, as these areas will require varying levels of staffing depending on the number of production shifts needed.

The purchasing budget is shown in Exhibit 7.4. This contains several different formats for planning budgeted purchases for the Alpha product line. The first option summarizes the planned production for each quarter; this information is brought forward from the production budget. We then multiply this by the standard unit cost of materials to arrive at the total amount of purchases that must be made to adequately support sales. The second option identifies the specific cost of each component of the product so that management can see where cost increases are expected to occur. Though this version provides more information, it occupies a great deal of space on the budget if there are many components in each product or many products. A third option is shown at the bottom of the exhibit that summarizes all purchases by commodity type. This format is most useful for the company's buyers, who usually specialize in certain commodity types.

The purchasing budget can be enhanced by adding a scrap factor for budgeted production, which will result in slightly higher quantities to buy, thereby leaving less chance of running out of raw materials. Another upgrade to the exhibit would be to schedule purchases for planned production some time in advance of the actual manufacturing date so that the purchasing staff will be assured of having the parts on hand when manufacturing begins. A third enhancement is to round off the purchasing volumes for each item into the actual buying volumes that can be obtained on the open market. For example, it may only be possible to buy the required labels in volumes of 100,000 at a time, which would result in a planned purchase at the beginning of the year that would be large enough to cover all production needs through the end of the year.

PURCHASING BUDGET FOR THE FISCAL YEAR ENDED XX/XX/02

	Quarter 1	*Quarter 2*	*Quarter 3*	*Quarter 4*	*Totals*
Inventory Turnover Goals					
Raw materials turnover	4.0	4.5	5.0	5.5	4.8
Product Line Alpha Purchasing (Option 1)					
Planned production	20,000	20,000	20,000	27,375	
Standard material cost/Unit	$5.42	$5.42	$5.67	$5.67	
Total material cost	$108,400	$108,400	$113,400	$155,216	$485,416
Product Line Alpha Purchasing (Option 2)					
Planned production	20,000	20,000	20,000	27,375	
Molded part	$4.62	$4.62	$4.85	$4.85	
Labels	$0.42	$0.42	$0.42	$0.42	
Fittings and fasteners	$0.38	$0.38	$0.40	$0.40	
Total cost of components	$5.42	$5.42	$5.67	$5.67	
Product Line Alpha Purchasing (Option 2)					
Plastic Commodities					
Molded Part Units	20,000	20,000	20,000	27,375	
Molded Part Cost	$4.62	$4.62	$4.85	$4.85	
Adhesives Commodity					
Labels Units	20,000	20,000	20,000	27,375	
Labels Cost	$0.42	$0.42	$0.42	$0.42	
Fasteners Commodity					
Fasteners Units	20,000	20,000	20,000	27,375	
Fasteners Cost	$0.38	$0.38	$0.40	$0.40	
Statistics					
Materials as percent of revenue	36%	36%	38%	38%	

Exhibit 7.4. Purchasing Budget

The direct labor budget is shown in Exhibit 7.5. This budget assumes that only one labor category will vary directly with revenue volume. That category is the final assembly department, where a percentage in the far right column indicates that the cost in this area will be budgeted at a fixed 3.5% of total revenues. In all other cases, there are assumptions for a fixed number of personnel in each position within each production department. All of the wage figures for each department (except for final assembly) are derived from the planned hourly rates and headcount figures noted at the bottom of the page. This budget can be enhanced with the addition of separate line items for payroll tax percentages, benefits, shift differential payments, and overtime expenses. The cost of the final assembly department can also be adjusted to account for worker efficiency, which will be lower during production ramp-up periods when new, untrained employees are added to the work force.

DIRECT LABOR BUDGET FOR THE FISCAL YEAR ENDED XX/XX/02

	Quarter 1	Quarter 2	Quarter 3	Quarter 4	Totals	Notes
Machining Department						
Senior Machine Operator	$15,120	$15,372	$23,058	$23,058	$76,608	
Machining Apprentice	4,914	4,964	9,929	9,929	29,736	
Expense subtotal	$20,034	$20,336	$32,987	$32,987	$106,344	
Paint Department						
Senior Paint Shop Staff	$15,876	$16,128	$16,128	$16,128	$64,260	
Painter Apprentice	$5,065	$5,216	$5,216	$5,216	$20,714	
Expense subtotal	$20,941	$21,344	$21,344	$21,344	$84,974	
Polishing Department						
Senior Polishing Staff	$16,632	$11,844	$11,844	$11,844	$52,164	
Polishing Apprentice	4,360	4,511	4,511	4,511	17,892	
Expense subtotal	$20,992	$16,355	$16,355	$16,355	$70,056	
Final Assembly Department						
General Laborer	$63,735	$66,950	$69,755	$72,529	$272,969	3.5%
Expense subtotal	$63,735	$66,950	$69,755	$72,529	$272,969	
Expense grand total	$125,702	$124,985	$140,441	$143,215	$534,343	
Statistics						
Union Hourly Rates						
Senior Machine Operator	$15.00	$15.25	$15.25	$15.25		
Machining Apprentice	9.75	9.85	9.85	9.85		
Senior Paint Shop Staff	15.75	16.00	16.00	16.00		
Painter Apprentice	10.05	10.35	10.35	10.35		
Senior Polishing Staff	11.00	11.75	11.75	11.75		
Polishing Apprentice	8.65	8.95	8.95	8.95		
Headcount by Position						
Senior Machine Operator	2	2	3	3		
Machining Apprentice	1	1	2	2		
Senior Paint Shop Staff	2	2	2	2		
Painter Apprentice	1	1	1	1		
Senior Polishing Staff	3	2	2	2		
Polishing Apprentice	1	1	1	1		

Exhibit 7.5. Direct Labor Budget

A sample of the overhead budget is shown in Exhibit 7.6. In this exhibit, we see that the overhead budget is really made up of a number of subsidiary departments, such as maintenance, materials management, and quality assurance. If the budgets of any of these departments are large enough, it makes a great deal of sense to split them off into a separate budget so that the managers of those departments can see their budgeted expectations more clearly. Of particular interest in this exhibit is the valid capacity range noted on the far right side of the exhibit. This signifies the production activity level within which the budgeted overhead costs are accurate. If the actual capacity utilization

OVERHEAD BUDGET FOR THE FISCAL YEAR ENDED XX/XX/02

	Quarter 1	Quarter 2	Quarter 3	Quarter 4	Totals	Valid Capacity Range
Supervision						
Production Manager Salary	$16,250	$16,250	$16,250	$16,250	$65,000	—
Shift Manager Salaries	22,000	22,000	23,500	23,500	91,000	40%-70%
Expense subtotal	$38,250	$38,250	$39,750	$39,750	$156,000	
Maintenance Department						
Equipment Maintenance Staff	$54,000	$56,500	$58,000	$60,250	$228,750	40%-70%
Facilities Maintenance Staff	8,250	8,250	8,500	8,500	33,500	40%-70%
Equipment Repairs	225,000	225,000	275,000	225,000	950,000	40%-70%
Facility Repairs	78,000	29,000	12,000	54,000	173,000	40%-70%
Expense subtotal	$365,250	$318,750	$353,500	$347,750	$1,385,250	
Materials Management Department						
Manager Salary	$18,750	$18,750	$18,750	$18,750	$75,000	—
Purchasing Staff	28,125	18,750	18,750	18,750	84,375	40%-70%
Materials Management Staff	28,000	35,000	35,000	35,000	133,000	40%-70%
Production Control Staff	11,250	11,250	11,250	11,250	45,000	40%-70%
Expense subtotal	$86,125	$83,750	$83,750	$83,750	$337,375	
Quality Department						
Manager Salary	$13,750	$13,750	$13,750	$13,750	$55,000	—
Quality Staff	16,250	16,250	16,250	24,375	73,125	40%-70%
Lab Testing Supplies	5000	4,500	4,500	4,500	18,500	40%-70%
Expense subtotal	$35,000	$34,500	$34,500	$42,625	$146,625	
Other Expenses						
Depreciation	$14,000	$15,750	$15,750	$15,750	$61,250	—
Utilities	60,000	55,000	55,000	60,000	230,000	40%-70%
Boiler Insurance	3,200	3,200	3,200	3,200	12,800	—
Expense subtotal	$77,200	$73,950	$73,950	$78,950	$304,050	
Expense grand total	$601,825	$549,200	$585,450	$592,825	$2,329,300	

Exhibit 7.6. Overhead Budget

were to fall outside of this range, either high or low, a separate overhead budget should be constructed with costs that are expected to be incurred within those ranges.

A sample cost of goods sold budget is shown in Exhibit 7.7. This format splits out each of the product lines noted in the revenue budget for reporting purposes, and subtracts from each one the materials costs that are noted in the purchases budget. This results in a contribution margin for each product line that is the clearest representation of

COST OF GOODS SOLD BUDGET FOR THE FISCAL YEAR ENDED XX/XX/02

	Quarter 1	Quarter 2	Quarter 3	Quarter 4	Totals
Product Line Alpha					
Revenue	$210,000	$311,850	$370,000	$457,250	$1,349,100
Materials expense	108,400	108,400	113,400	155,216	485,416
Contribution Margin $$	$101,600	$203,450	$256,600	$302,034	$863,684
Contribution Margin %	48%	65%	69%	66%	64%
Product Line Beta					
Revenue	$1,048,000	$1,057,000	$1,061,000	$1,053,000	$4,219,000
Materials expense	12,000	14,000	15,000	13,250	54,250
Contribution Margin $$	$1,036,000	$1,043,000	$1,046,000	$1,039,750	$4,164,750
Contribution Margin %	99%	99%	99%	99%	99%
Revenue—Product Line Charlie					
Revenue	$563,000	$544,000	$562,000	$562,000	$2,231,000
Materials expense	$268,000	$200,000	$220,000	$230,000	$918,000
Contribution Margin $$	$295,000	$344,000	$342,000	$332,000	$1,313,000
Contribution Margin %	52%	63%	61%	59%	59%
Total Contribution Margin $$	$1,432,600	$1,590,450	$1,644,600	$1,673,784	$6,341,434
Total Contribution Margin %	79%	83%	83%	81%	81%
Direct Labor Expense	$125,702	$124,985	$140,441	$143,215	$534,343
Overhead Expense	$601,825	$549,200	$585,450	$592,825	$2,329,300
Total Gross Margin $$	$705,073	$916,265	$918,709	$937,744	$3,477,791
Total Gross Margin %	39%	48%	46%	45%	44%
Statistics:					
Number of Production Staff*	23	22	22	23	
Average Annual Revenue per Production Employee	$316,696	$347,791	$362,364	$360,391	

*Not including general assembly staff.

Exhibit 7.7. Cost of Goods Sold Budget

the impact of direct costs (i.e., material costs) on each one. We then summarize these individual contribution margins into a summary-level contribution margin, and then subtract the total direct labor and overhead costs (as referenced from the direct labor and overhead budgets) to arrive at a total gross margin. The statistics section also notes the number of production personnel budgeted for each quarterly reporting period, plus the average annual revenue per production employee—these statistics can be replaced with any operational information that management wants to see at a summary level for the production function, such as efficiency levels, capacity utilization, or inventory turnover.

The sales department budget is shown in Exhibit 7.8. This budget shows several different ways in which to organize the budget information. At the top of the budget is a block of line items that lists the expenses for those overhead costs within the department that cannot be specifically linked to a salesperson or region. In cases where the

SALES DEPARTMENT BUDGET FOR THE FISCAL YEAR ENDED XX/XX/02	Quarter 1	Quarter 2	Quarter 3	Quarter 4	Totals
Departmental Overhead					
Depreciation	$500	$500	$500	$500	$2,000
Office supplies	$750	$600	$650	$600	$2,600
Payroll taxes	$2,945	$5,240	$5,240	$8,186	$21,611
Salaries	$38,500	$68,500	$68,500	$107,000	$282,500
Travel and entertainment	$1,500	$1,500	$1,500	$2,000	$6,500
Expense subtotal	$44,195	$76,340	$76,390	$118,286	$315,211
Product Line Alpha	$32,000	$18,000	$0	$21,000	$71,000
Expenses by Salesperson					
Jones, Milbert	$14,000	$16,500	$17,000	$12,000	$59,500
Smidley, Jefferson	$1,000	$9,000	$8,000	$12,000	$30,000
Verity, Jonas	$7,000	$9,000	$14,000	$12,000	$42,000
Expense subtotal	$22,000	$34,500	$39,000	$36,000	$131,500
Expenses by Region					
East Coast	$52,000	$71,000	$15,000	$0	$138,000
Midwest	$8,000	$14,000	$6,000	$12,000	$40,000
West Coast	$11,000	$10,000	$12,000	$24,000	$57,000
Expense subtotal	$71,000	$95,000	$33,000	$36,000	$235,000
Expense grand total	$137,195	$205,840	$148,390	$190,286	$681,711
Statistics					
Revenue per salesperson	$607,000	$637,617	$664,333	$690,750	$2,599,700
T&E per salesperson	$500	$500	$500	$667	$2,167

Exhibit 7.8. Sales Department Budget

number of sales staff is quite small, *all* of the department's costs may be listed in this area.

Another alternative is shown in the second block of expense line items in the middle of the sales department budget, where all of the sales costs for an entire product line are lumped together into a single line item. If each person on the sales staff is exclusively assigned to a single product line, then it may make sense to break down the budget into separate budget pages for each product line, and list all of the expenses associated with each product line on a separate page.

A third alternative is shown next in Exhibit 7.8, where we list a summary of expenses for each salesperson. This format works well when combined with the departmental overhead expenses at the top of the budget, because this accounts for all of the departmental costs. However, this format brings up a confidentiality issue, because the compensation of each salesperson can be inferred from the report. Also, this format would include the commission expense paid to each salesperson; commissions are a variable cost that is directly associated with each incremental dollar of sales, so they should be itemized as a separate line item within the cost of goods sold.

A final option listed at the bottom of the example is to itemize expenses by sales region. This format works best when there are a number of sales personnel within the department who are clustered into a number of clearly identifiable regions. If there were no obvious regions or if there were only one salesperson per region, then the better format would be to list expenses by salesperson.

At the bottom of the budget is the usual statistics section. The sales department budget is only concerned with making sales, so it should be no surprise that revenue per salesperson is the first item listed. Also, as the primary sales cost associated with this department is usually travel costs, the other statistical item is the travel and entertainment cost per person.

Exhibit 7.9 shows a sample marketing budget. As was the case for the sales department, this one also itemizes departmental overhead costs at the top, which leaves space in the middle for the itemization of campaign-specific costs in the middle. The campaign-specific costs can be lumped together for individual product lines, as is the case for product lines Alpha and Beta in the exhibit, or with subsidiary line items, as is shown for product line Charlie. A third possible format, which is to itemize marketing costs by marketing tool (e.g., advertising, promotional tour, or coupon redemption) is generally not recommended if there is more than one product line, because there is no way for an analyst to determine the impact of individual marketing costs on specific product lines. The statistics at the bottom of the page attempt to compare marketing costs to sales; however, this should only be treated as an approximation; marketing efforts will usually not result in immediate sales, but rather will result in sales that build over time. Thus, there is a time lag after incurring a marketing cost that makes it difficult to determine the efficacy of marketing activities.

MARKETING BUDGET FOR THE FISCAL YEAR ENDED XX/XX/02

	Quarter 1	Quarter 2	Quarter 3	Quarter 4	Totals
Departmental Overhead					
Depreciation	650	750	850	1,000	3,250
Office supplies	200	200	200	200	800
Payroll taxes	4,265	4,265	4,265	4,265	17,060
Salaries	$55,750	$55,750	$55,750	$55,750	223,000
Travel and entertainment	5,000	6,500	7,250	7,250	26,000
Expense subtotal	65,865	67,465	68,315	68,465	270,110
Campaign-Specific Expenses					
Product Line Alpha	14,000	26,000	30,000	0	70,000
Product Line Beta	18,000	0	0	24,000	42,000
Product Line Charlie					0
Advertising	10,000	0	20,000	0	30,000
Promotional tour	5,000	25,000	2,000	0	32,000
Coupon redemption	2,000	4,000	4,500	1,200	11,700
Product samples	2,750	5,250	1,250	0	9,250
Expense subtotal	51,750	60,250	57,750	25,200	194,950
Expense grand total	117,615	127,715	126,065	93,665	465,060
Statistics					
Expense as percent of total sales	6.5%	6.7%	6.3%	4.5%	6.0%
Expense proportion by quarter	25.3%	27.5%	27.1%	20.1%	100.0%

Exhibit 7.9. Marketing Budget

A sample general and administrative budget is shown in Exhibit 7.10. This budget can be quite lengthy, including such additional line items as postage, copier leases, and office repair. Many of these extra expenses have been pruned from the exhibit to provide a compressed view of the general format to be used. The exhibit does not lump together the costs of the various departments that are typically included in this budget, but rather identifies each one in separate blocks; this format is most useful when there are separate managers for the accounting and human resources functions so that they will have a better understanding of their budgets. The statistics section at the bottom of the page itemizes a benchmark target of the total general and administrative cost as a proportion of revenue. This is a particularly useful statistic to track, because the general

GENERAL AND ADMINISTRATIVE BUDGET FOR THE FISCAL YEAR ENDED XX/XX/02

	Quarter 1	Quarter 2	Quarter 3	Quarter 4	Totals	Notes
Accounting Department						
Depreciation	4,000	4,000	4,250	4,250	16,500	
Office supplies	650	650	750	750	2,800	
Payroll taxes	4,973	4,973	4,973	4,973	19,890	
Salaries	$65,000	$65,000	$65,000	$65,000	260,000	
Training	500	2,500	7,500	0	10,500	
Travel and entertainment	0	750	4,500	500	5,750	
Expense subtotal	75,123	77,873	86,973	75,473	315,440	
Corporate Expenses						
Depreciation	450	500	550	600	2,100	
Office supplies	1,000	850	750	1,250	3,850	
Payroll taxes	6,598	6,598	6,598	6,598	26,393	
Salaries	$86,250	$86,250	$86,250	$86,250	345,000	
Insurance, business	4,500	4,500	4,500	4,500	18,000	
Training	5,000	0	0	0	5,000	
Travel and entertainment	2,000	500	500	0	3,000	
Expense subtotal	105,798	99,198	99,148	99,198	403,343	
Human Resources Department						
Benefits programs	7,284	7,651	7,972	8,289	31,196	**0.4%**
Depreciation	500	500	500	500	2,000	
Office supplies	450	8,000	450	450	9,350	
Payroll taxes	2,869	2,869	2,869	2,869	11,475	
Salaries	$37,500	$37,500	$37,500	$37,500	150,000	
Training	5,000	0	7,500	0	12,500	
Travel and entertainment	2,000	1,000	3,500	1,000	7,500	
Expense subtotal	55,603	57,520	60,291	50,608	224,021	
Expense grand total	236,523	234,591	246,411	225,278	942,804	
Statistics						
Expense as proportion of revenue	13.0%	12.3%	12.4%	10.9%	12.1%	
Benchmark comparison	11.5%	11.5%	11.5%	11.5%	11.5%	

Exhibit 7.10. General and Administrative Budget

and administrative function is a cost center and requires such a comparison to inform management that these costs are being held in check.

A staffing budget is shown in Exhibit 7.11. This itemizes the expected headcount in every department by major job category. It does not attempt to identify individual positions, which could lead to an excessively lengthy list. Also, because there may be multiple positions identified within each job category, the *average* salary for each cluster of jobs is identified. If a position is subject to overtime pay, its expected overtime percentage is identified on the right side of the budget. Many sections of the budget should have linkages to this page so that any changes in headcount here will be automatically reflected in the other sections. This budget may have to be

STAFFING BUDGET FOR THE FISCAL YEAR ENDED XX/XX/02

	Quarter 1	Quarter 2	Quarter 3	Quarter 4	Average Salary	Overtime Percent
Sales Department						
Regional Sales Manager	1	2	2	3	$120,000	0%
Salesperson	2	4	4	6	$65,000	0%
Sales Support Staff	1	1	1	2	$34,000	6%
Marketing Department						
Marketing Manager	1	1	1	1	$85,000	0%
Marketing Researcher	2	2	2	2	$52,000	0%
Secretary	1	1	1	1	$34,000	6%
General and Administrative						
President	1	1	1	1	$175,000	0%
Chief Operating Officer	1	1	1	1	$125,000	0%
Chief Financial Officer	1	1	1	1	$100,000	0%
Human Resources manager	1	1	1	1	$80,000	0%
Accounting Staff	4	4	4	4	$40,000	10%
Human Resources Staff	2	2	2	2	$35,000	8%
Executive Secretary	1	1	1	1	$45,000	6%
Research Department						
Chief Scientist	1	1	1	1	$100,000	0%
Senior Engineer Staff	3	3	3	4	$80,000	0%
Junior Engineer Staff	3	3	3	3	$60,000	0%
Overhead Budget						
Production Manager	1	1	1	1	$65,000	0%
Quality Manager	1	1	1	1	$55,000	0%
Materials Manager	1	1	1	1	$75,000	0%
Production Scheduler	1	1	1	1	$45,000	0%
Quality Assurance Staff	2	2	2	3	$32,500	8%
Purchasing Staff	3	2	2	2	$37,500	8%
Materials Management Staff	4	5	5	5	$28,000	8%
Total headcount	39	42	42	48		

Exhibit 7.11. Staffing Budget

restricted from general access, for it contains salary information that may be considered confidential.

The facilities budget tends to have the largest number of expense line items. A sample of this format is shown in Exhibit 7.12. These expenses may be offset by some rental or sublease revenues if a portion of the company facilities is rented out to other organizations. However, this revenue is only shown in this budget if the revenue amount is small; otherwise, it is more commonly found as an "other revenue" line item on the revenue budget. A statistics section is found at the bottom of this budget, which refers to the total amount of square feet occupied by the facility. A very effective statistic is the amount of unused square footage, which can be used to conduct an ongoing program of selling off, renting, or consolidating company facilities.

The research department's budget is shown in Exhibit 7.13. It is most common to segregate the department-specific overhead that cannot be attributed to a specific project at the top of the budget, and then cluster costs by project below that. By doing so, the management team can see precisely how much money is being allocated to each project. This may be of use in determining which projects must be cancelled or delayed as part of the budget review process. The statistics section at the bottom of the budget notes the proportion of planned expenses between the categories of overhead, research, and development. These proportions can be examined to see if the company is allocating funds to the right balance of projects that most effectively meets it product development goals.

FACILITIES BUDGET FOR THE FISCAL YEAR ENDED XX/XX/02

	Quarter 1	Quarter 2	Quarter 3	Quarter 4	Totals
Facilty Expenses					
Contracted services	$ 5,500	$ 5,400	$ 5,000	$ 4,500	$ 20,400
Depreciation	29,000	29,000	28,000	28,000	114,000
Electricity charges	4,500	3,500	3,500	4,500	16,000
Inspection fees	500	0	0	500	1,000
Insurance	8,000	0	0	0	8,000
Maintenance supplies	3,000	3,000	3,000	3,000	12,000
Payroll taxes	1,148	1,148	1,148	1,186	4,628
Property taxes	0	5,000	0	0	5,000
Repairs	15,000	0	29,000	0	44,000
Sewage charges	250	250	250	250	1,000
Trash disposal	3,000	3,000	3,000	3,000	12,000
Wages—Janitorial	5,000	5,000	5,000	5,500	20,500
Wages—Maintenance	10,000	10,000	10,000	10,000	40,000
Water charges	1,000	1,000	1,000	1,000	4,000
Expense grand total	$85,898	$66,298	$88,898	$61,436	$302,528
Statistics					
Total square feet	52,000	52,000	78,000	78,000	
Square feet/Employee	839	813	1,219	1,099	
Unused square footage	1,200	1,200	12,500	12,500	

Exhibit 7.12. Facilities Budget

RESEARCH DEPARTMENT FOR THE FISCAL YEAR ENDED XX/XX/02	Quarter 1	Quarter 2	Quarter 3	Quarter 4	Totals
Departmental Overhead					
Depreciation	$ 500	$ 500	$ 400	$ 400	1,800
Office supplies	750	2,000	1,500	1,250	5,500
Payroll taxes	9,945	9,945	9,945	11,475	41,310
Salaries	130,000	130,000	130,000	150,000	540,000
Travel and entertainment	0	0	0	0	0
Expense subtotal	$141,195	$142,445	$141,845	$163,125	$588,610
Research–Specific Expenses					
Gamma Project	$20,000	$43,500	$35,000	$12,500	$111,000
Omega Project	5,000	6,000	7,500	9,000	27,500
Pi Project	14,000	7,000	7,500	4,500	33,000
Upsilon Project	500	2,500	5,000	0	8,000
Expense subtotal	$39,500	$59,000	$55,000	$26,000	$179,500
Development–Specific Expenses					
Latin Project	$ 28,000	$ 29,000	$ 30,000	$ 15,000	$ 102,000
Greek Project	14,000	14,500	15,000	7,500	51,000
Mabinogian Project	20,000	25,000	15,000	10,000	70,000
Old English Project	6,250	12,500	25,000	50,000	93,750
Expense subtotal	$ 68,250	$ 81,000	$ 85,000	$ 82,500	$ 316,750
Expense grand total	$248,945	$282,445	$281,845	$271,625	$1,084,860
Statistics					
Budgeted number of patent applications filed	2	0	1	1	4
Proportion of expenses:					
Overhead	56.7%	50.4%	50.3%	60.1%	217.5%
Research	15.9%	20.9%	19.5%	9.6%	65.8%
Development	27.4%	28.7%	30.2%	30.4%	116.6%
Total Expenses	100.0%	100.0%	100.0%	100.0%	400.0%

Exhibit 7.13. Research Department Budget

The capital budget is shown in Exhibit 7.14. This format clusters capital expenditures by a number of categories. For example, the first category, entitled "budget-related expenditures," clearly focuses attention on those outgoing payments that will increase the company's key productive capacity. The payments in the third quarter under this heading are directly related to the increase in bottleneck capacity that was shown the production budget (Exhibit 7.3) for the fourth quarter. The budget also contains an automatic assumption of $7,000 in capital expenditures for any net increase in nondirect labor headcount, which encompasses the cost of computer equipment and office furniture for each person. If the company's capitalization limit is set too high to list these expenditures on the capital budget, then a similar line item should be inserted into the general and administrative budget so that the expense can be recognized under the office supplies or some similar account.

CAPITAL BUDGET FOR THE FISCAL YEAR ENDED XX/XX/02

	Quarter 1	Quarter 2	Quarter 3	Quarter 4	Totals
Bottleneck-Related Expeditures					
Stamping machine			$150,000		$150,000
Facility for Machine			$72,000		$72,000
Headcount-Related Expenditures					
Headcount change × $7,000 added staff	$0	$21,000	$0	$42,000	$63,000
Profit-Related Expenditures					
Blending machine		$50,000			$50,000
Polishing machine		$27,000			$27,000
Safety-Related Expenditures					
Machine shielding		$3,000	$3,000		$6,000
Handicapped walkways	$8,000	$5,000			$13,000
Required Expenditures					
Clean air scrubber			$42,000		$42,000
Other Expenditures					
Tool crib expansion				$18,500	$18,500
Total expenditures	$8,000	$106,000	$267,000	$60,500	$441,500

Exhibit 7.14. Capital Budget

The capital budget also includes a category for profit-related expenditures. Any projects listed in this category should be subject to an intensive expenditure review, using cash flow discounting techniques to ensure that they return a sufficient cash flow to make their acquisition profitable to the company. Other categories in the budget cover expenditures for safety or required items, which tend to be purchased with no cash flow discounting review. An alternative to this grouping system is to only list the sum total of all capital expenditures in each category, which is most frequently used when there are far too many separate purchases to list on the budget. Another variation is to only list the largest expenditures on separate budget lines, and cluster together all smaller ones. The level of capital purchasing activity will determine the type of format used.

All of the preceding budgets roll up into the budgeted income and cash flow statement, which is noted in Exhibit 7.15. This format lists the grand totals from each preceding pages of the budget to arrive at a profit or loss for each budget quarter. In the example, we see that a large initial loss in the first quarter is gradually offset by smaller gains in later quarters to arrive at a small profit for the year. However, the presentation continues with a cash flow statement that has less positive results. It begins with the net profit figure for each quarter, adds back the depreciation expense for all departments, and subtracts out all planned capital expenditures from the capital budget to arrive at cash flow needs for the year. This tells us that the company will experience a maximum cash shortfall in the third quarter. This format can be made more precise by adding in time lag factors for the payment of accounts payable and the collection of accounts receivable.

INCOME AND CASH FLOW STATEMENT FOR THE FISCAL YEAR ENDED XX/XX/02	Quarter 1	Quarter 2	Quarter 3	Quarter 4	Totals
Revenue	$1,821,000	$1,912,850	$1,993,000	$2,072,250	$7,799,100
Cost of Goods Sold					
Materials	$388,400	$322,400	$348,400	$398,466	$1,457,666
Direct Labor	125,702	124,985	140,441	143,215	534,343
Overhead					
Supervision	38,250	38,250	39,750	39,750	156,000
Maintenance Department	365,250	318,750	353,500	347,750	1,385,250
Materials Management	86,125	83,750	83,750	83,750	337,375
Quality Department	35,000	34,500	34,500	42,625	146,625
Other Expenses	77,200	73,950	73,950	78,950	304,050
Total Cost of Goods Sold	$1,115,927	$996,585	$1,074,291	$1,134,506	$4,321,309
Gross Margin	$705,073	$916,265	$918,709	$937,744	$3,477,791
Operating Expenses					
Sales Department	$137,195	$205,840	$148,390	$190,286	$681,711
General and Administrative Department					
Accounting	75,123	77,873	86,973	75,473	315,440
Corporate	105,798	99,198	99,148	99,198	403,343
Human Resources	55,603	57,520	60,291	50,608	224,021
Marketing Department	117,615	127,715	126,065	93,665	465,060
Facilities Department	85,898	66,298	88,898	61,436	302,528
Research Department	248,945	282,445	281,845	271,625	1,084,860
Total Operating Expenses	$826,176	$916,888	$891,609	$842,290	$3,476,963
Net Profit (Loss)	−$121,103	−$624	$27,100	$95,455	$828
	Quarter 1	Quarter 2	Quarter 3	Quarter 4	Totals
Cash Flow					
Beginning Cash	$100,000	$20,497	−$34,627	−$223,727	
Net Profit (Loss)	−$121,103	−$624	$27,100	$95,455	$828
Add Depreciation	$49,600	$51,500	$50,800	$51,000	$202,900
Minus Capital Purchases	−$8,000	−$106,000	−$267,000	−$60,500	−$441,500
Ending Cash	$20,497	−$34,627	−$223,727	−$137,772	

Exhibit 7.15. Budgeted Income and Cash Flow Statement

The final document in the budget is an itemization of the finances needed to ensure that the rest of the budget can be achieved. An example is shown in Exhibit 7.16, which carries forward the final cash position at the end of each quarter that was the product of the preceding cash flow statement. This line shows that there will be a maximum shortfall of $223,727 by the end of the third quarter. The next section of the budget outlines several possible options for obtaining the required funds (which are rounded up to $225,000)—debt, preferred stock, or common stock. The financing cost of each one is noted in the far right column, where we see that the interest cost on debt is 9.5%, the dividend on preferred stock is 8%, and the expected return by common stockholders is 18%.

The third section on the page lists the existing capital structure, its cost, and the net cost of capital. This is quite important, for anyone reviewing this document can see

FINANCING BUDGET FOR THE FISCAL YEAR ENDED XX/XX/02

	Quarter 1	Quarter 2	Quarter 3	Quarter 4	Financing Cost
Cash Position	$20,497	−$34,627	−$223,727	−$137,772	
Financing Option One					
Additional Debt		$225,000			9.5%
Financing Option Two					
Additional Preferred Stock	$225,000				8.0%
Financing Option Three					
Additional Common Stock	$225,000				18.0%
Existing Capital Structure					
Debt	$400,000				9.0%
Preferred Stock	$150,000				7.5%
Common Stock	$500,000				18.0%
Existing Cost of Capital	11.8%				
Revised Cost of Capital					
Financing Option One	10.7%				
Financing Option Two	11.2%				
Financing Option Three	12.9%				

Note: Tax rate equals 38%.

Exhibit 7.16. Financing Requirements

what impact the financing options will have on the capital structure if any of them are selected. For example, the management team may prefer the low cost of debt, but can also use the existing capital structure presentation to see that this will result in a very high proportion of debt to equity, which increases the risk that the company cannot afford to repay the debt to the lender.

The fourth and final part of the budget calculates any changes in the cost of capital that will arise if any of the three financing options are selected. A footnote points out the incremental corporate tax rate—this is of importance to the calculation of the cost of capital, because the interest cost of debt can be deducted as an expense, thereby reducing its net cost. In the exhibit, selecting additional debt as the preferred form of financing will result in a reduction in the cost of capital to 10.7%, whereas a selection of high-cost common stock will result in an increase in the cost of capital to 12.9%. These changes can have an impact on what types of capital projects are accepted in the future, for the cash flows associated with them must be discounted by the cost of capital in order to see if they result in positive cash flows. Accordingly, a reduction in the cost of capital will mean that projects with marginal cash flows will become more acceptable, while the reverse will be true for a higher cost of capital.

The budgeting examples shown here can be used as the format for a real-life corporate budget. However, it must be adjusted to include a company's chart of accounts and departmental structure so that it more accurately reflects actual operations. Also, it should include a detailed benefits and payroll tax calculation page, which will itemize the cost of social security taxes, Medicare, unemployment insurance, worker's compensation insurance, medical insurance, and so on. These costs are a substantial part of a company's budget, and yet are commonly lumped together into a simplistic budget model that does not accurately reflect their true cost.

Though the budget model presented here may seem excessively large, it is necessary to provide detailed coverage of all aspects of the corporation so that prospective changes to it can be accurately modeled through the budget. Thus, a detailed format is strongly recommended over a simple, summarized model.

7.4 FLEX BUDGET

One problem with the budget model shown in the last section is that many of the expenses listed in it are directly tied to the revenue level. If the actual revenue incurred is significantly different from the budgeted figure, then so many expenses will also shift in association with the revenue that the comparison of budgeted to actual expenses will not be valid. For example, if budgeted revenues are $1 million and budgeted material costs are $450,000, one would expect a corresponding drop in the actual cost of materials incurred if actual revenues drop to $800,000. A budget-to-actual comparison would then show a significant difference in the cost of materials, which would in turn cause a difference in the gross margin and net profit. This issue also arises for a number of other variable or semivariable expenses, such as salesperson commissions, production supplies, and maintenance costs. Also, if there are really large differences between actual and budgeted revenue levels, other costs that are more fixed in nature will also change, such as the salaries, office supplies, and even facilities maintenance (facilities may be sold off or added to, depending on which direction actual revenues have gone). These represent large step cost changes that will skew actual expenses so far away from the budget that it is difficult to conduct any meaningful comparison between the two.

A good way to resolve this problem is to create a flexible budget, or "flex" budget, that itemizes different expense levels depending on changes in the amount of actual revenue. In its simplest form, the flex budget will use percentages of revenue for certain expenses rather than the usual fixed numbers. This allows for an infinite series of changes in budgeted expenses that are directly tied to revenue volume. However, this approach ignores changes to other costs that do not change in accordance with small revenue variations. Consequently, a more sophisticated format will also incorporate changes to many additional expenses when certain larger revenue changes occur, thereby accounting for step costs. By making these changes to the budget, a company will have a tool for comparing actual to budgeted performance at many levels of activity.

Though the flex budget is a good tool, it can be difficult to formulate and administer. One problem with its formulation is that many costs are not fully variable, instead having a fixed cost component that must be included in the flex budget formula. Another issue is that a great deal of time can be spent developing step costs, which is more time than the typical accounting staff has available, especially when in the midst of creating the standard budget. Consequently, the flex budget tends to include only a small number of step costs, as well as variable costs whose fixed cost components are not fully recognized.

Implementation of the flex budget is also a problem, for very few accounting software packages incorporate any features that allow one to load in multiple versions of a budget that can be used at different revenue levels. Instead, some include the option to store a few additional budgets, which the user can then incorporate into the standard budget-to-actual comparison reports. This option does not yield the full benefits of a flex budget; it only allows for a few changes in expenses based on a small number of revenue changes, rather than a set of expenses that will automatically change in proportion to actual revenue levels incurred. Furthermore, the option to enter several different budgets means that someone must enter this additional information into the accounting software, which can be a considerable chore if the number of budget line items is large. For these reasons, it is more common to see a flex budget incorporated into an electronic spreadsheet, with actual results being manually posted to it from other accounting reports.

7.5 BUDGETING PROCESS

The budgeting process is usually rife with delays, which are caused by several factors. One is that information must be input to the budget model from all parts of the company—some of which may not put a high priority on the submission of budgeting information. Another reason is that the budgeting process is highly iterative, sometimes requiring dozens of budget recalculations and changes in assumptions before the desired results are achieved. The typical budgeting process is represented in Exhibit 7.17, where we see that there is a sequential process that requires the completion of the revenue plan before the production plan can be completed, which in turn must be finished before the departmental expense budgets can be finished, which then yields a financing plan. If the results do not meet expectations, then the process starts over again at the top of the exhibit. This process is so time consuming that the budget may not be completed before the budget period has already begun.

A number of best practices can be used to create a more streamlined budgeting process:

- *Reduce the number of accounts.* The number of accounts included in the budget should be reduced, thereby greatly reducing the amount of time needed to enter and update data in the budget model.
- *Reduce the number of reporting periods.* One can consolidate the 12 months shown in the typical budget into quarterly information, thereby eliminating two-thirds of the information in the budget. If the budget must later be reentered into the accounting system to provide budget-to-actual comparisons, then a simple formula can be used to divide the quarterly budget back into its monthly components—which is still much less work than maintaining 12 full months of budget information.
- *Use percentages for variable cost updates.* When key activities, such as revenues, are changed in the budget model, one must peruse the entire budget to determine what related expenses must change in concert with the key activities. A much easier approach is to use percentage-based calculations for variable costs in the budget model so that these expenses will be updated automatically. They should also be color-coded in the budget model so that they will not be mistaken for items that are manually changed.

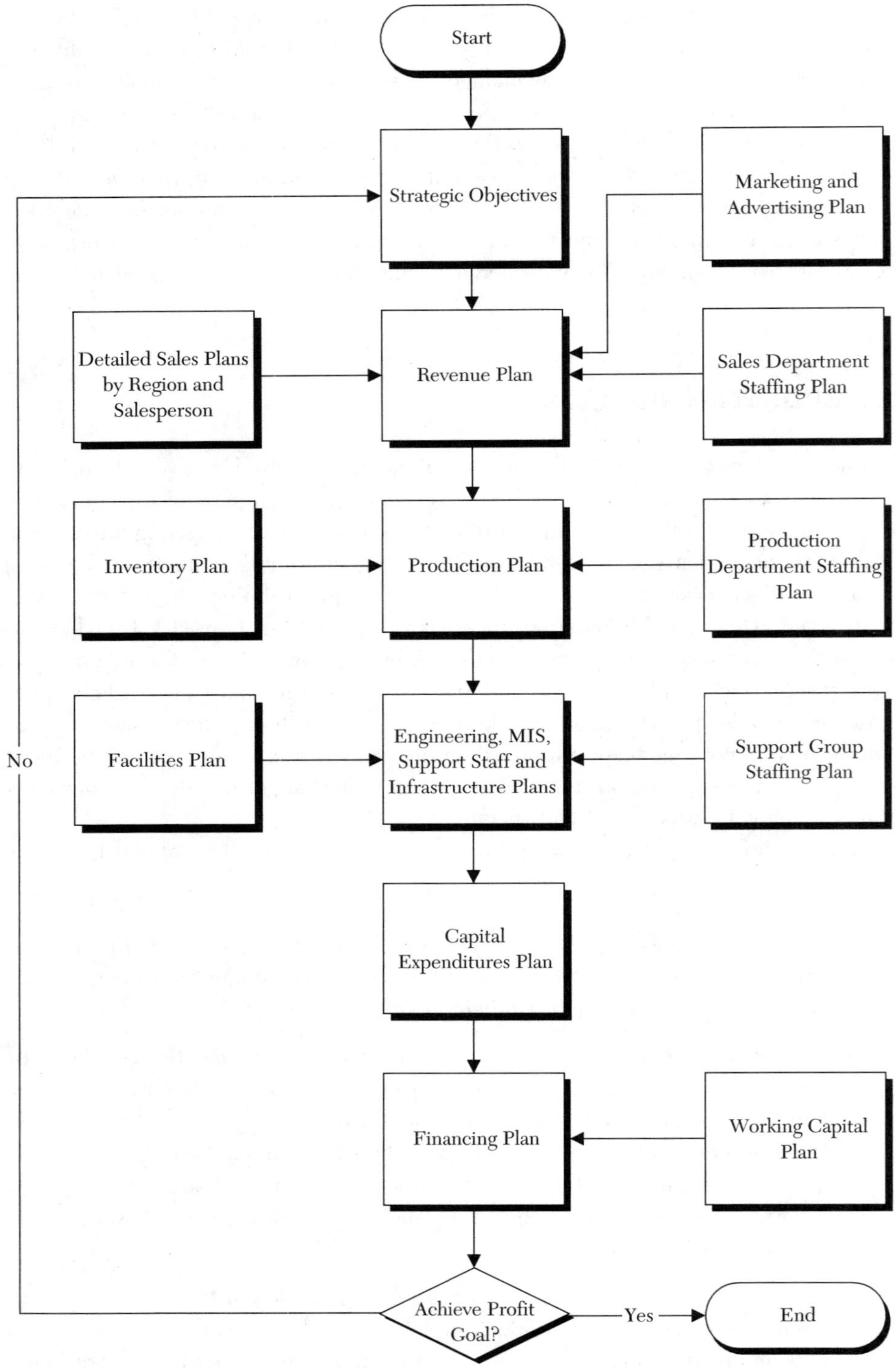

Exhibit 7.17. Traditional Budgeting Process

- *Report on variables in one place*. A number of key variables will impact the typical budget model, such as the assumed rate of inflation in wages or purchased parts, tax rates for income, payroll, and worker's compensation, and medical insurance rates. These variables are much easier to find if they are set up in a cluster within the budget so that one can easily reference and alter them. Under this arrangement, it is also useful to show key results (such as net profits) on the same page with the variables so that one can make alterations to the variables and immediately see their impact without having to search through the budget model to find the information.
- *Use a budget procedure and timetable*. The budget process is plagued by many iterations; the first results will nearly always yield profits or losses that do not meet a company's expectations. Furthermore, it requires input from all parts of a company, some of which may lag in sending in information in a timely manner. Accordingly, it is best to construct a budgeting procedure that specifically identifies what job positions must send budgeting information to the budget coordinator, what information is required of each person, and when that information is due. Furthermore, there should be a clear timetable of events that is carefully adhered to so that plenty of time is left at the end of the budgeting process for the calculation of multiple iterations of the budget.

In addition to these efficiency-improvement issues, the budgeting process can be modified in other ways so that it can be completed much more quickly:

- *Itemize the corporate strategy*. The strategy and related tactical goals that the company is trying to achieve should be listed at the beginning of the budget model. All too frequently, management loses sight of its predetermined strategy when going through the many iterations that are needed to develop a realistic budget. By itemizing the corporate strategy in the budget document, it is much less likely that the final budget model will deviate significantly from the company's strategic direction.
- *Identify step-costing change points*. The budget model should have notations incorporated into it that specify the capacity levels at which expenses are valid. For example, if the production level for Product A exceeds 100,000 per year, then a warning flag should be generated by the budget model that informs the budget manager of the need to add an extra shift to accommodate the increased production requirements. Another example is to have the model generate a warning flag when the average revenue per salesperson exceeds $1 million, because this may be the maximum expectation for sales productivity and will require the addition of more sales personnel to the budget. These flags can be clustered at the front of the budget model so that problems will be readily apparent to the reader.
- *Specify maximum amounts of available funding*. One of the warning flags just noted should include the maximum level of funding that the company can obtain. If an iteration of the budget model results in excessively high cash requirements, then the flag will immediately point out the problem. It may be useful

to note next to the warning flag the amount by which the maximum funding has been exceeded so that this information is readily available for the next budget iteration.

- *Base expense changes on cost drivers*. Many expenses in the budget will vary in accordance with changes in various activities within the firm. As noted earlier in this section, expenses can be listed in the budget model as formulas so that they vary in direct proportion to changes in budgeted revenue. This same concept can be taken a step farther by listing other types of activities that drive cost behavior, and linking still other expenses to them with formulas. For example, the amount of telephone expense is directly related to the number of employees, so it can be linked to the total number of employees on the staffing budget. Another example is the number of machine setup personnel, which will change based on the planned number of production batches to be run during the year. This level of automation requires a significant degree of knowledge of how selected expenses interact with various activities within the company.

- *Budget by groups of staff positions*. A budget can rapidly become unwieldy if every position in the company is individually identified, especially if the names of all employees are listed. This format requires constant updating as the budget progresses through multiple iterations. A better approach is to itemize by job title, which allows one to vastly reduce the number of job positions listed in the budget.

- *Rank projects*. A more complex budget model can incorporate a ranking of all capital projects so that any projects with a low ranking will be automatically eliminated by the model if the available amount of cash drops below the point where they could be funded. However, this variation requires that great attention be paid to the ranking of projects, because there may be some interrelationship between projects—if one is dropped but others are retained, the ones retained may not be functional without the missing project.

- *Issue a summary-level model for use by senior management*. The senior management team is primarily concerned with the summary results of each department, product line, or operating division, and does not have time to wade through the details of individual revenue and expense accounts. Further, they may require an increased level of explanation from the budgeting staff if they *do* choose to examine these details. Accordingly, the speed of the iteration process can be enhanced by producing a summary-level budget that is directly linked to the main budget so that all fields in it are updated automatically. The senior management team can more easily review this document, yielding faster updates to the model.

- *Link budget results to employee goal and reward system*. The budgeting process does not end with the final approval of the budget model. Instead, it then passes to the human resources department, which uses it as the foundation for an employee goal and reward system. The trouble is that, if budget approval is delayed, the human resources department will have very little time in which to create its goal and reward system. Accordingly, this add-on project should be incorporated directly into the budget model so that it is approved alongside the rest of the budget. For example, a goals and rewards statement added to the budget can specify a bonus payment to the manager of the production department if he or she can create the number of units of product specified in the production budget. Similarly, the sales manager can receive a bonus based on reaching the sales goals noted in the revenue budget. By inserting the bonus amounts in this page of the budget, the model can automatically link them to the final targets itemized in the plan, requiring minimal further adjustments by the human resources staff.

As a result of these improvements, the budgeting process will change to the format shown in Exhibit 7.18, where the emphasis changes away from many modeling iterations toward the incorporation of a considerable level of automation and streamlining into the structure of the budget model. By following this approach, the budget will require much less manual updating, allowing it to sail through the smaller number of required iterations with much greater speed.

7.6 BUDGETARY CONTROL SYSTEMS

A budget can be used to enhance a company's control systems in several ways so that objectives are met more easily and it is more difficult for costs to stray from approved levels.

One of the best methods for controlling costs is to link the budget for each expense within each department to the purchasing system. The computer system will automatically accumulate the total amount of purchase orders that have been issued thus far against a specific account, and will refuse any further purchase orders when the budgeted expense total has been reached. This approach can compare the monthly budget to monthly costs, or compare costs to annual budgeted totals. The later approach can cause difficulty for the inattentive manager, because actual expenses may be running well ahead of the budget for most of the year, but the system will not automatically flag the problem until the entire year's budget has been depleted. Alternatively, a comparison to monthly budgeted figures may result in so many warning flags on so many accounts that the purchasing staff is unable to purchase many items. One work around for this problem is to use a fixed overage percentage by which purchases are allowed to exceed the budget; another possibility is to only compare cumulative expenses to quarterly budget totals, which reduces the total number of system warning flags.

Another budgetary control system is to compare actual to budgeted results for the specific purpose of evaluating the performance of employees. For example, the warehouse manager may be judged based on actual inventory turnover of 12x, which compares unfavorably to a budgeted turnover rate of 15x. Similarly, the manager of a cost center may receive a favorable review if the total monthly cost of her cost center averages no more than $152,000. This also works for the sales staff, who can be assigned sales quotas that match the budgeted sales levels for their sales territories. In this manner, a large number of employees can have their compensation levels directly tied to the achievement of budgeted goals. This is a highly effective way to ensure that the budget becomes a fixture in the lives of employees.

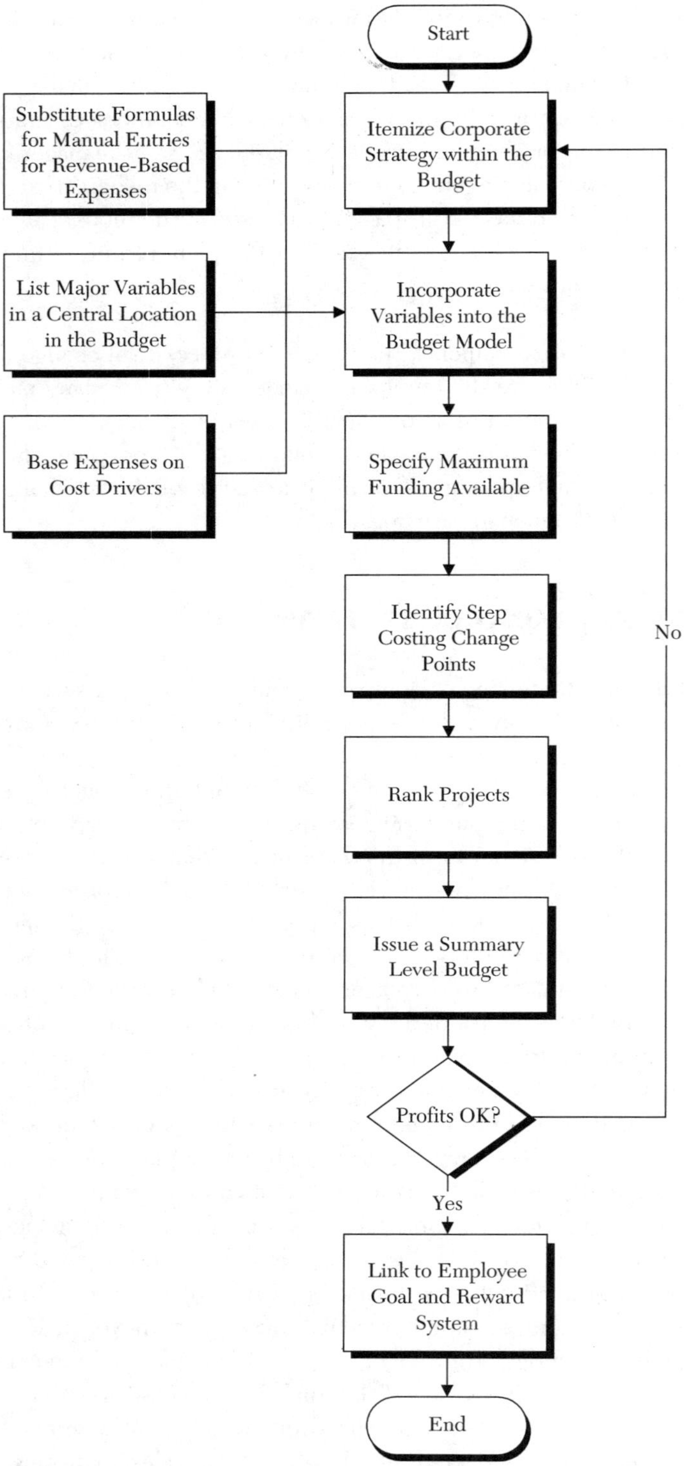

Exhibit 7.18. Streamlined Budgeting Process

Account No.	Description	Actual Results	Budgeted Results	Variance
4500-010	Arizona Revenue	$43,529	$51,000	−$7,471

Exhibit 7.19. Line Item Budget Reporting for Specific Employees

Yet another budgetary control system is to use it as a feedback loop to employees. This can be done by issuing a series of reports at the end of each reporting period that are specifically designed to match the responsibilities of each employee. For example, Exhibit 7.19 shows a single revenue line item that is reported to a salesperson for a single territory. The salesperson does not need to see any other detailed comparison to the budget, because he is not responsible for anything besides the specific line item that is reported to him. This reporting approach focuses the attention of many employees on just those segments of the budget that they have control over. Though this approach can result in the creation of dozens or even hundreds of reports by the accounting department, they can be automated on most packaged accounting software systems so that only the initial report creation will take up much accounting time.

An additional control use for the budget is to detect fraud. The budget is usually based upon several years of actual operating results, so unless there are major changes in activity levels, actual expense results should be fairly close to budgeted expectations. If not, variance analysis is frequently used to find out what happened. This process is an excellent means for discovering fraud, as the resulting variance analysis will detect a sudden surge in expense levels. The two instances in which this control will not work is when the fraud has been in existence for a long time (and so is incorporated into the budgeted expense numbers already) or the amount of fraud is so low that it will not create a variance large enough to warrant investigation.

Chapter 8

PROPERTY ACCOUNTING MANUAL

8.1 INTRODUCTION

The weakest documentation area in many organizations is the description of various types of property. Though this may not be considered a significant issue in some service organizations that are oriented toward human capital, many other types of entities have invested a large amount of capital in land, buildings, equipment, vehicles, and leasehold improvements. In the later case, it is extremely important to maintain a high level of record accuracy so that company management maintains proper control over its investment. Good record keeping in this area is also necessary for audit reviews, cost accounting allocations, insurance claims, and warranty tracking.

This chapter is oriented toward a large number of examples of property tracking forms, which include project cost sheets, land records, land improvement records, building records, equipment records, vehicle records, leasehold improvement records, and lease records. The formats shown can be expanded to included additional information required by individual organizations.

Property accounting should be assigned to a senior accountant who will be responsible for updating and maintaining the records. This person should have a descriptive title, such as Physical Property Manager, Fixed Asset Accounting Manager, or (as used herein) Property Accounting Manager.

The amount of record keeping recommended in this chapter may appear voluminous, but it is necessary to maintain sufficient information about the warranties, maintenance, vendor contact information, and other items about each asset. However, one can reduce the amount of record keeping by using a relatively high capitalization limit, below which assets are immediately charged to expense rather than being recorded as an asset.

Depreciation records used to be manually calculated for each of the records noted in this chapter, and stored with them. However, the advent of inexpensive computerized depreciation software has rendered this approach inefficient. Instead, one should record all depreciable asset information in a central database, from which depreciation calculations can be easily made.

8.2 PROJECT COST REPORT

If any capital assets are acquired or constructed that need additional work, one should use the Project Cost Sheet, noted later under retrieval number 2-520, to accumulate the changes. To complete the form for each asset, enter the descriptive heading information such as the name of the project or asset, assigned project number with a prefix letter to indicate the asset category (e.g., **L**and, **B**uilding, **F**actory, **E**quipment), the balance sheet account where the item will be recorded, and a brief description of the project. Additional information recorded on the form should include:

- Date project initiated
- Budget approval amount
- Asset serial number
- Materials used, including description, supplier, and cost
- Labor used, including date incurred and cost
- Contractors, including date incurred and cost
- Date of project completion
- Account number to which accumulated costs were transferred
- Summary totals for all cost categories

8.3 RECORD KEEPING FOR LAND PROJECTS

Maintain a record of the purchase price of land, including tax stamps, recording fees, surveys, title insurance, and any state fees. However, this should not include property taxes or the cost of land improvements (see the next section). Information about each land purchase should be maintained on a separate property accounting record, noted later under retrieval number 2-530, which should contain:

- General description of the land site
- Purchase cost
- Postal address of the location

- Township (if in a Western state) and county location
- Approximate size
- Legal description
- Zoning classification, such as residential single or multiple unit, commercial retail, or light or heavy industry
- Easements for electricity, water, sewers, or gas lines
- Use restrictions
- Year of valuation and assessed value

8.4 RECORD KEEPING FOR LAND IMPROVEMENT PROJECTS

Land improvements are depreciable. Examples of land improvements are fences and gates, parking lots, roads, sewage ponds, and signs. Information about each land improvement should be maintained on a separate property accounting record, noted later under retrieval number 2-540, which should contain:

- General description
- Purchase cost
- Date put into use
- Approximate size
- Construction materials used
- Useful life
- Assessed valuation

In the category of "Construction materials used," the description for fences and gates should note whether they are constructed of wood, brick, or chain link. For roads or parking lots, the description should note the use of gravel, asphalt, or concrete.

8.5 RECORD KEEPING FOR BUILDING PROJECTS

A record of each company-owned building should be maintained. Use a sufficiently high capitalization limit to ensure that small additions, such as a small wall or shed attachment, do not become part of the building asset. Each building should have a name or number for reference purposes.

Information about each building should be maintained on a separate property accounting record, noted later under retrieval number 2-550, which should contain:

- Building name or number
- General description

- Type of construction
- Intended use
- Cost, date put into use, and useful life
- Approximate size
- Assessed valuation

8.6 RECORD KEEPING FOR FACTORY EQUIPMENT PROJECTS

In a manufacturing environment, the factory equipment is the largest-dollar asset category and therefore requires special attention, especially in regard to asset warranty information that may be used.

Information about each piece of factory equipment should be maintained on a separate property accounting record, noted later under retrieval number 2-560, which should contain:

- General description
- Purpose of the equipment
- Fixed or portable equipment designation
- Location by building and room number
- Cost, date put into use, and useful life
- Model and serial number
- Vendor name and address
- Warranty provisions and the period covered
- Property tag number

8.7 RECORD KEEPING FOR OFFICE EQUIPMENT PROJECTS

The increasing uses of technology in the modern office mean that the volume of office equipment can make this the largest asset category, especially in service industries where the entire staff is equipped with computers. Examples of office equipment are personal computers, video presentation equipment, fax machines, and copiers.

Information about each piece of office equipment should be maintained on a separate property accounting record, noted later under retrieval number 2-570, which should contain:

- General description
- Purpose of the equipment
- Fixed or portable equipment designation

- Location by building and room number
- Cost, date put into use, and useful life
- Model and serial number
- Vendor name and address
- Warranty provisions and the period covered
- Property tag number

8.8 RECORD KEEPING FOR VEHICLES

Anything that is portable and can be ridden upon by a person is a vehicle. Cars, trucks, trailers, motorcycles, boats, airplanes, lift trucks, snowmobiles, riding lawnmowers, and construction equipment are all vehicles.

Information about each vehicle should be maintained on a separate property accounting record, noted later under retrieval number 2-580, which should contain:

- General description
- Serial or vehicle identification number
- Purpose of equipment
- Location where stored
- Cost
- Vendor name and address
- Warranty provisions and period covered
- Property tag number
- Person assigned to

8.9 RECORD KEEPING FOR LEASEHOLD IMPROVEMENTS

Leasehold improvements are additions to leased land and buildings. Examples are storage cabinets, shelves, counters, refrigeration units, drapes, air conditioning, parking lots, roads, signs, fences and gates, or anything else that will be abandoned when the lease contract expires. The amortization of these improvements is recorded over the time period of the lease agreement. If the lease term exceeds the useful life, only calculate depreciation through the useful life of the asset.

Information about each leasehold improvement should be maintained on a separate property accounting record, noted later under retrieval number 2-590, which should contain:

- General description
- Serial number (if available)

- Purpose of improvement
- Location where stored
- Cost, date put into use, and useful life
- Vendor name and address
- Warranty provisions and period covered
- Property tag number
- Lease record number

8.10 RECORD KEEPING FOR LEASES

Maintain a separate record for each lease entered into by the organization. All leasehold improvements recorded elsewhere are tied to these lease records by the item number of the lease. If the company is required to have annual financial statements prepared by a certified public accountant, the lease information is needed for a footnote disclosure in the financial statements, itemizing the future lease payments for each of the following five years.

Information about each lease should be maintained on a separate property accounting record, noted later under retrieval number 2-600, which should contain:

- Description of the leased property
- Serial number (if available)
- Location of property
- Name and address of lessor
- Beginning and ending dates of the lease
- Lease amount
- Required maintenance by the lessee
- Lease renewal provisions
- Termination provisions

8.11 SAMPLE PROPERTY ACCOUNTING MANUAL

The remaining pages of this chapter contain a sample property accounting policy and procedure manual.

PROPERTY ACCOUNTING
POLICY/PROCEDURE MANUAL
COMPANY NAME

Distribution: Chief Financial Officer
Controller
Facilities Manager
Tax Manager
Property Accounting Manager

PROPERTY ACCOUNTING
POLICY/PROCEDURE

Company Name

- RETRIEVAL NO. Index
-
- PAGE 1 of 1
-
- DATE July 1, 200X

SUBJECT: INDEX

Retrieval Number	Subject
1-010	General Policy and Procedures

PROPERTY ACCOUNTING
POLICY/PROCEDURE

Company Name

- RETRIEVAL NO. 1-010
-
- PAGE 1 of 1
-
- DATE July 1, 200X
-
- SUPERSEDES

SUBJECT: GENERAL POLICY AND PROCEDURES

Policy

The Company will maintain a detailed record of each fixed asset acquired. Current property categories are:

- Land
- Land Improvements
- Buildings
- Factory Equipment
- Office Equipment
- Vehicles
- Leasehold Improvements
- Leased Land, Buildings, and Equipment

The purpose of these records is to:

- Support the recorded cost of fixed assets on the balance sheet.
- Calculate annual depreciation and amortization on these assets.
- Assist the internal and external auditors in their audits.
- Determine if casualty insurance coverage is adequate in case of a catastrophe.
- Determine compliance with lease provisions.
- Compile information for the personal property tax return.
- Take equipment inventories at least annually.

Procedures

Data on all purchases recorded as physical asset properties will be reported to the Property Accounting Manager who will then prepare a record for each item costing over $500, the minimum capitalization amount. The Manager will prepare correcting journal entries if any items under $500 were misclassified. The Manager will review all entries to repair and maintenance accounts to determine that no assets over $500 were misclassified to expense.

The Manager will maintain the Project Cost Sheets for items under construction, modification, or installation.

The Manager will maintain copies of the active records in an off-premise location for insurance purposes in case of a catastrophe such as a fire, explosion, or acts of God.

FORMS MANUAL
PROPERTY ACCOUNTING
COMPANY NAME

Departmental Copy

Normal Distribution
Chief Financial Officer
Controller
Property Accounting Manager
Internal Auditor
External Auditor

FORMS MANUAL
PROPERTY ACCOUNTING

Company Name

- RETRIEVAL NO. Index
-
- PAGE 1 of 1
-
- DATE July 1, 200X

SUBJECT: INDEX

Retrieval Number		Form
2-520	PA—1	Project Cost Sheet
2-530	PA—2	Land Record
2-540	PA—3	Land Improvement Record
2-550	PA—4	Building Record
2-560	PA—5	Factory Equipment Record
2-570	PA—6	Office Equipment Record
2-580	PA—7	Vehicle Record
2-590	PA—8	Leasehold Improvement Record
2-600	PA—9	Lease Record

FORMS MANUAL

PROPERTY ACCOUNTING

Company Name

• RETRIEVAL NO. 2-520
•
• PAGE 1 OF 4
•
• DATE July 1, 200X
•
• SUPERSEDES

NAME OF FORM: Project Cost Sheet
FORM NUMBER: PA-1 DATE OF LAST REVISION:

PURPOSE: To maintain details of costs of land, land improvements, buildings, equipment, and leasehold improvements which require alterations, additions, or installation before being put into use.

COPY	COLOR	DESTINATION OR DISTRIBUTION OF COPIES
1.	White	Prepared and maintained by Property Accounting Manager
2.		
3.		
4.		

IS THE FORM PRENUMBERED? _ YES X NO

DEPARTMENT SUPPLYING FORM: Property Accounting

PRINTING SOURCE: C:\WPDATA\PROPERTY\PROJECT.1

DISTRIBUTION OF THIS RELEASE: Normal

Retrieval No. 2-520
Page 2 of 4

INSTRUCTIONS FOR COMPLETING THE "PROJECT COST SHEET"

Front of Form PA-1, enter:

1. Project no.: Enter consecutive project number.
2. Name of project: Describe project such as Building x, Factory Equipment milling machine, and so on.
3. B/S a/c: Enter balance sheet account where this project will be entered.
4. Description of project: Describe what is to be done to complete project.
5. Date initiated: Enter date project began.
6. Budget approval amount: Enter amount budgeted for project, if required.
7. Serial no.: Enter, if available for this item.
8. Materials: For purchased items, enter date received, vendor invoice number, vendor name, description of item, and amount paid, including freight and sales tax, if any.
9. Direct labor: If company labor is used, enter date of payroll, payroll ending date or number, type of work done such as electrical, installation, and so forth, and gross amount of labor on that payroll for this project.
10. Contractors: If any outside contractors are used, for example to install or modify machine, enter date of service, contractor invoice number, description of service, and amount paid.
11. Date project completed: Enter date completed and put into use.
12. Transferred to balance sheet a/c: Enter account number.
13. Summary: Enter the listed totals for materials, direct labor, and contractor services.

Back of Form PA-1:

Same as 8, 9, and 10 above.

When completed, the form is held by Property Accounting.

Retrieval No. 2-520
Page 3 of 4

Front of Form PA-1

PROJECT COST SHEET Project No.__________

Name of Project______________ ___________________B/S a/c_____________

Description of Project____

Date Initiated______________Budget approval amount__________Serial No.__________

Item	Date	Inv. #	Vendor or Payroll	Item or Service	Amount	
Materials						
Direct Labor						
Contractors						

Date Project completed______________________ Transferred to Balance Sheet a/c_____________	Total Materials Total Direct Labor Total Contractors		
	Total Project		

Retrieval No. 2-520
Page 4 of 4

Back of Form PA-1

PROJECT COST SHEET Project No.__________

Item	Date	Inv. #	Vendor or Payroll	Item or Service	Amount	
Materials						
Direct Labor						
Contractors						

FORMS MANUAL

PROPERTY ACCOUNTING

Company Name

• RETRIEVAL NO. 2-530
•
• PAGE 1 OF 4
•
• DATE July 1, 200X
•
• SUPERSEDES

NAME OF FORM: Land Record
FORM NUMBER: PA-2

DATE OF LAST REVISION:

PURPOSE: To record details of land acquisitions.

COPY	COLOR	DESTINATION OR DISTRIBUTION OF COPIES
1	White	Prepared and held by Property Accounting Manager
2.		
3.		
4.		

IS THE FORM PRENUMBERED? _ YES X NO

DEPARTMENT SUPPLYING FORM: Property Accounting

PRINTING SOURCE C:\WPDATA\PROPERTY\PA2LAND.1

DISTRIBUTION OF THIS RELEASE: Normal

Retrieval No. 2-530
Page 2 of 4

INSTRUCTIONS FOR COMPLETING THE "LAND RECORD"

Front of Form PA-2, enter:

Consecutive property number.

1. General description such as factory site, retail stores, and so on
2. Purchase cost which may be allocated portion of purchase price, and date purchased
3. Postal address of this location
4. City, state, and zip code of this address
5. Township and county where this property is located
6. Approximate size of land area
7. Legal description of property as shown by deed or tax bills
8. Zoning classification which may be single residence, multiple residence, commercial retail, light industry, and so on
9. List any easements such as "south 6 feet for utility lines."
10. List any restriction on use such as height of buildings permitted, protected wetlands, type of fence permitted, and so forth.

Back of Form PA-2:

1. Enter year of valuation and assessed valuation for property tax purposes.
2. Enter brief descriptions of land improvements on this property.
3. Enter brief description of buildings on this property.

When completed, the form is held by Property Accounting.

Retrieval No. 2-530
Page 3 of 4

Front of Form PA-2

PROPERTY ACCOUNTING – LAND RECORD

Property No: L__________

1. General Description:

2. Cost: **Date Purchased:**

3. Address:

4. City, State, Zip Code:

5. Township: **County:**

6. Approximate Size:

7. Legal Description:

8. Zoning Classification:

9. Easements:

10. Restrictions on use:

11. Assessed valuation for property taxes:

Form PA-2

Retrieval No. 2-530
Page 4 of 4

Back of Form PA-2

PROPERTY ACCOUNTING – LAND RECORD

Property No: L__________

1. Assessed Valuation: Year_______Amount____________________
   Year_______Amount____________________
   Year_______Amount____________________

2. Land Improvements:

3. Buildings:

Form PA-2

FORMS MANUAL

PROPERTY ACCOUNTING

Company Name

- RETRIEVAL NO. 2-540
-
- PAGE 1 OF 3
-
- DATE July 1, 200X
-
- SUPERSEDES

NAME OF FORM: Land Improvement Record
FORM NUMBER: PA-3

DATE OF LAST REVISION:

PURPOSE: To maintain a detailed record of each land improvement such as fences and gates, parking lots, roadways, signs, and other such improvements to the land. Buildings are not recorded as land improvements

COPY	COLOR	DESTINATION OR DISTRIBUTION OF COPIES
1.	White	Prepared and maintained by Property Accounting Manager
2.		
3.		
4.		

IS THE FORM PRENUMBERED? _ YES X NO

DEPARTMENT SUPPLYING FORM: Property Accounting

PRINTING SOURCEC:\WPDATA\PROPERTY\LANDIMP.1

DISTRIBUTION OF THIS RELEASE: Normal

Retrieval No. 2-540
Page 2 of 3

COMPLETING THE "LAND IMPROVEMENT RECORD"

Front of Form PA-3, enter:
Consecutive property number.

1. General description such as factory site, retail stores, and so on
2. Purchase cost which may be allocated portion of purchase price or completed project cost
3. Date put in use is date purchased or project completed date
4. Approximate size:

   Fences, height and length

   Roadways, width and length or square feet

   Parking lot, width and length or square feet

   Sign, width and height
5. Construction materials: Describe general materials such as chain link, concrete, wood, asphalt, steel, and so on

When completed, the form is held by Property Accounting.

Retrieval No. 2-540
Page 3 of 3

Form PA-3

PROPERTY ACCOUNTING – LAND IMPROVEMENT RECORD

Property No: LI__________

1. General Description:
2. Cost:
3. Date Put in Use:
4. Approximate Size:
5. Construction Materials:
6. Useful Life:
7. Assessed valuation increase, if applicable (See Land):

Form PA-3

FORMS MANUAL

PROPERTY ACCOUNTING

Company Name

- RETRIEVAL NO. 2-550
-
- PAGE 1 OF 3
-
- DATE July 1, 200X
-
- SUPERSEDES

NAME OF FORM: Building Record
FORM NUMBER: PA-4

DATE OF LAST REVISION:

PURPOSE: To maintain a detailed record of each building.

COPY	COLOR	DESTINATION OR DISTRIBUTION OF COPIES
1.	White	Prepared and maintained by Property Accounting Manager
2.		
3.		
4.		

IS THE FORM PRENUMBERED? _ YES X NO

DEPARTMENT SUPPLYING FORM: Property Accounting

PRINTING SOURCE C:\WPDATA\PROPERTY\BUILDING.1

DISTRIBUTION OF THIS RELEASE: Normal

Retrieval No. 2-550
Page 2 of 3

COMPLETING THE "BUILDING RECORD"

Front of Form PA-4, enter:
Consecutive property number.

1. Building name and/or number as appropriate
2. General description: Purpose, general style of architecture
3. Type of construction: Brick, concrete block, wood, steel, and so on
4. General use of building: Retail stores, factory, office, storage, and so forth
5. Cost: Total cost, excluding land

   Date put in use: Date first occupied or used

   Useful life: Estimated useful life for depreciation purposes
6. Approximate size:

   Length and width of main floor

   No. of floors

   Approximate square feet of useable floor space
7. Assessed valuation: Enter date and property taxing authority valuation each time it changes

When completed, the form is held by Property Accounting.

Retrieval No. 2-550
Page 3 of 3

Form PA-4

PROPERTY ACCOUNTING – BUILDING RECORD

Property No: B__________

1. Building Name and/or Number:
2. General Description:
3. Type of Construction:
4. General Use of Building:
5. Cost: Date Put in Use: Useful Life:
6. Approximate Size: Length: Width:
   No. of Floors:
   Approximate Square Feet of Floor Space:
7. Assessed Valuation:

Year	Valuation
_____	______________
_____	______________
_____	______________
_____	______________

Form PA-4

FORMS MANUAL

PROPERTY ACCOUNTING

Company Name

• RETRIEVAL NO. 2-560
•
• PAGE 1 OF 3
•
• DATE July 1, 200X
•
• SUPERSEDES

NAME OF FORM: Factory Equipment Record
FORM NUMBER: PA-5

DATE OF LAST REVISION:

PURPOSE: To maintain a detailed record of each unit of factory equipment, whether permanently installed or portable.

COPY	COLOR	DESTINATION OR DISTRIBUTION OF COPIES
1.	White	Prepared and maintained by Property Accounting Manager
2.		
3.		
4.		

IS THE FORM PRENUMBERED? _ YES X NO

DEPARTMENT SUPPLYING FORM: Property Accounting

PRINTING SOURCE C:\WPDATA\PROPERTY\FACTORY.1

DISTRIBUTION OF THIS RELEASE: Normal

Retrieval No. 2-560
Page 2 of 3

COMPLETING THE "FACTORY EQUIPMENT RECORD"

Front of Form PA-5, enter:
Consecutive property number.

1. General description: Size of machine or equipment
2. Purpose of equipment: Describe general use of equipment
3. Fixed or portable: enter as appropriate
4. Location, building and room: Enter building name or number, and room number or use
5. Cost: Total cost, including installation

    Date put in use: Date first installed or put into use

    Useful life: Estimated useful life for depreciation purposes

6. Model and serial number, if any: Enter appropriate data
7. Vendor name and address: Enter name of company from whom purchased
8. Warranty provisions and period covered: Period of guaranty and any exclusions and inclusions
9. Property tag no.: Enter metal or plastic tag placed on equipment by Property Accounting.

When completed, the form is held by Property Accounting.

Retrieval No. 2-560
Page 3 of 3

Form PA-5

PROPERTY ACCOUNTING – FACTORY EQUIPMENT RECORD

Property No: FE__________

1. General Description:
2. Purpose of Equipment:
3. Fixed or Portable:
4. Location, Building and Room:
5. Cost: Date Put in Use: Useful Life:
6. Model and Serial Number:
7. Vendor Name and Address:
8. Warranty provisions and period covered:
9. Property Tag No.

Form PA-5

FORMS MANUAL	• RETRIEVAL NO. 2-570
	•
PROPERTY ACCOUNTING	• PAGE 1 OF 3
	•
	• DATE July 1, 200X
Company Name	•
	• SUPERSEDES

NAME OF FORM: Office Equipment Record
FORM NUMBER: PA-6 DATE OF LAST REVISION:

PURPOSE: To maintain a detailed record of each piece of office equipment, whether permanently installed or portable.

COPY	COLOR	DESTINATION OR DISTRIBUTION OF COPIES
1.	White.	Prepared and maintained by Property Accounting Manager
2.		
3.		
4.		

IS THE FORM PRENUMBERED? _ YES X NO

DEPARTMENT SUPPLYING FORM: Property Accounting

PRINTING SOURCE: PC C:\WPDATA\PROPERTY\OFFICE.1

DISTRIBUTION OF THIS RELEASE: Normal

Retrieval No. 2-570
Page 2 of 3

COMPLETING THE "OFFICE EQUIPMENT RECORD"

Front of Form PA-6, enter:
Consecutive property number.

1. General description: Size of machine or equipment
2. Purpose of equipment: Describe general use of equipment.
3. Fixed or Portable: Enter as appropriate.
4. Location, building and room: Enter building name or number, and room number or use.
5. Cost: Total cost, including installation

   Date put in use: Date first installed or put into use

   Useful life: Estimated useful life for depreciation purposes
6. Model and serial number, if any: Enter appropriate data
7. Vendor name and address: Enter name of company from whom purchased.
8. Warranty provisions and period covered: Period of guaranty and any exclusions and inclusions
9. Property tag no.: Enter metal or plastic tag placed on equipment by Property Accounting.

When completed, the form is held by Property Accounting.

Retrieval No. 2-570
Page 3 of 3

Form PA-6

PROPERTY ACCOUNTING – OFFICE EQUIPMENT RECORD

Property No: OE__________

1. General Description:
2. Purpose of Equipment:
3. Fixed or Portable:
4. Location, Building and Room:
5. Cost: Date Put in Use: Useful Life:
6. Model and Serial Number:
7. Vendor Name and Address:
8. Warranty provisions and period covered:
9. Property Tag No.

Form PA-6

FORMS MANUAL

PROPERTY ACCOUNTING

Company Name

- RETRIEVAL NO. 2-580
-
- PAGE 1 OF 3
-
- DATE July 1, 200X
-
- SUPERSEDES

NAME OF FORM: Vehicle Record
FORM NUMBER: PA-7

DATE OF LAST REVISION:

PURPOSE: To maintain a detailed record of each Vehicle, including anything that a person rides upon except permanent installations such as hoists.

COPY	COLOR	DESTINATION OR DISTRIBUTION OF COPIES
1.	White	Prepared and maintained by Property Accounting Manager
2.		
3.		
4.		

IS THE FORM PRENUMBERED? _ YES X NO

DEPARTMENT SUPPLYING FORM: Property Accounting

PRINTING SOURCE C:\WPDATA\PROPERTY\VEHICLE.1

DISTRIBUTION OF THIS RELEASE: Normal

Retrieval No. 2-580
Page 2 of 3

COMPLETING THE "VEHICLE RECORD"

Front of Form PA-7, enter:
Consecutive property number.

1. General description: Make: Enter make such as Ford, Toro, and so on.

   Model: Enter 4-dr or other model description.

   Color: Enter predominant color.
2. Serial or vehicle identification no.: Enter as appropriate.
3. Purpose of equipment: Describe general use of equipment such as delivery or snow removal, and so forth.
4. Location where stored: Building name or number and room number, if applicable.
5. Cost: Total cost, including special equipment added

   Date put in use: Date purchased or put into use

   Useful life: Estimated useful life for depreciation purposes
6. Vendor name and address: Enter name of company from whom purchased.
7. Warranty provisions and period covered: Period of guaranty and any exclusions and inclusions
8. Property tag no.: Enter metal or plastic tag placed on equipment by Property Accounting.
9. Person assigned to: Enter name.

When completed, the form is held by Property Accounting.

Retrieval No. 2-580
Page 3 of 3

Form PA-7

PROPERTY ACCOUNTING – VEHICLE RECORD

Property No: V__________

1. **General Description:**
   - **Make:**
   - **Model:**
   - **Color:**
2. **Serial or Vehicle Identification No. (VIN):**
3. **Purpose of Equipment:**
4. **Location where stored or parked:**
5. **Cost:** **Date Put in Use:** **Useful Life:**
6. **Vendor Name and Address:**
7. **Warranty provisions and period covered:**
8. **Property Tag No.:**
9. **Person assigned to, if appropriate:**

Form PA-7

FORMS MANUAL

PROPERTY ACCOUNTING

Company Name

• RETRIEVAL NO. 2-590
•
• PAGE 1 of 3
•
• DATE July 1, 200X
• SUPERSEDES

NAME OF FORM: Leasehold Improvement Record
FORM NUMBER: PA-8

DATE OF LAST REVISION:

PURPOSE: To maintain a detailed record of each Leasehold Improvement which has a shorter lease life than the useful life.

COPY	COLOR	DESTINATION OR DISTRIBUTION OF COPIES
1.	White	Prepared and maintained by Property Accounting Manager
2.		
3.		
4.		

IS THE FORM PRENUMBERED? _ YES X NO

DEPARTMENT SUPPLYING FORM: Property Accounting

PRINTING SOURCE: C:\WPDATA\PROPERTY\LEASEIMP.1

DISTRIBUTION OF THIS RELEASE: Normal

Retrieval No. 2-590
Page 2 of 3

COMPLETING THE "LEASEHOLD IMPROVEMENT RECORD"

Front of Form PA-8, enter:
Consecutive property number.

1. General description: Brief description of improvement
2. Serial no.: Enter if appropriate.
3. Purpose of improvement: Describe general use of improvement such as air conditioning, drapes, and so forth.
4. Location where stored: Building name or number and room number, if applicable
5. Cost: Including special equipment added

   Date put in use: Date purchased or put into use

   Useful life: Estimated useful life for depreciation purposes
6. Vendor name and address: Enter name of company from whom purchased.
7. Warranty provisions and period covered: Period of guaranty and any exclusions and inclusions
8. Property tag no.: Enter metal or plastic tag placed on equipment by Property Accounting.
9. Lease record no.: Enter lease number to which this improvement is attached.

When completed, the form is held by Property Accounting.

Retrieval No. 2-590
Page 3 of 3

Form PA-8

PROPERTY ACCOUNTING – LEASEHOLD IMPROVEMENT RECORD

Property No: LSI__________

1. General Description: Make:
   Model:
2. Serial No, if applicable:
3. Purpose of Improvement:
4. Location where installed, Building and Room:
5. Cost: Date Put in Use: Leasehold Life:
6. Vendor Name and Address:
7. Warranty provisions and period covered:
8. Property Tag No.:
9. Lease Record No.:

Form PA-8

FORMS MANUAL

PROPERTY ACCOUNTING

Company Name

- RETRIEVAL NO. 2-600
- PAGE 1 OF 4
- DATE July 1, 200X
- SUPERSEDES

NAME OF FORM: Lease Record
FORM NUMBER: PA-9

DATE OF LAST REVISION:

PURPOSE: To maintain a record of all leased land and buildings, equipment, and vehicles. This information is used to audit rent payments and the future lease calculations for the footnote to the financial statements. Leasehold Improvements are related to these records by the LE number shown on the Lease Record.

COPY	COLOR	DESTINATION OR DISTRIBUTION OF COPIES
1.	White	Held by Property Accounting Manager
2.		
3.		
4.		

IS THE FORM PRENUMBERED? _ YES X NO

DEPARTMENT SUPPLYING FORM: Property Accounting Manager

PRINTING SOURCE: C:\WPDATA\PROPERTY\LEASE.1

DISTRIBUTION OF THIS RELEASE: Normal

Retrieval No. 2-600
Page 2 of 4

COMPLETING THE "LEASE RECORD"

Front of Form PA-9, enter:
Consecutive property number:

1. Description of property rented: Brief description of land and building, equipment, or vehicle
2. Serial no.: Enter if appropriate.
3. Location of property: Address if land and building, building and room number or area if equipment
4. Name and address of lessor: Enter for communication purposes.
5. Date of lease: Beginning and ending date of lease period
6. Rental amount: Monthly rent and annual rental if different
7. Maintenance by lessee, type and frequency: Any periodic maintenance required by our company should be described
8. Lease renewal or extension provisions: Enter as appropriate.
9. Provision for termination by lessor or lessee: Enter all pertinent provisions.

Back of Form PA-9, enter:

1. Year paid
2. Amount of rent paid for that year

Retrieval No. 2-600
Page 3 of 4

Front of Form PA-9

PROPERTY ACCOUNTING – LEASE RECORD

No: LE__________

1. Description of property rented:

2. Serial Number, if any:
3. Location of Property:

4. Name and Address of Lessor:

5. Dates of Lease: Begin Date End Date

6. Rental Amount: Monthly Rental Annual Rental
7. Maintenance by Lessee, type and frequency:

8. Lease Renewal or Extension provisions:

9. Provision for termination by lessor or lessee:

PA-9

Retrieval No. 2-600
Page 4 of 4

Back of Form PA-9

ANNUAL RENTAL					
Year	Total Rent	Comments	Year	Total Rent	Comments

Chapter 9

FORMS MANUAL

9.1 INTRODUCTION

The forms manual is the easiest documentation module to prepare. However, given the absence of a forms specialist, this documentation is rarely completed, and it typically includes forms that reduce the efficiency with which accounting transactions are completed. In this chapter, we will cover the identification of needed forms, review the rules for constructing forms, and describe how to create the forms manual. There is also a brief discussion of ways to eradicate the use of superseded forms from an organization.

9.2 IDENTIFY NEEDED FORMS

The first step in the creation of a forms manual is to complete a forms survey. In a small accounting operation, the controller could probably describe adequately all the forms used in the operation without a forms survey, but a larger organization will contain so many forms that the survey method is mandatory. The survey can be handled by various employees who are familiar with specific forms, or may be done on a consulting basis by one or two experienced people discussing the form with the person most familiar with its use. If a large number of forms are to be surveyed, the consultant method is more efficient.

Exhibit 9.1 shows a form survey worksheet that simplifies the information-gathering process. The survey is generally limited to forms initiated or processed by the accounting department, such as purchase orders, remittance vouchers, and forms for time

FORM SURVEY   Survey No. ________

Name of Form ______________________________________

Form No. ________________ Date of Last Revision ________________

Copies and destination or use. Number of parts ________

Copy No.	Color	Destination or Use
1	________	______________________________
2	________	______________________________
3	________	______________________________
4	________	______________________________
5	________	______________________________

Is the form prenumbered? ____ Yes ____ No

Source of supply:

____ Purchased. Name of printer, if known ________________

____ Own Print Shop

____ From another department? Which? ________________

____ Other. Describe ________________

If retained in Accounting, how is form filed? ________________

Estimated quantity used per month ________________

Originating Department ________________

How is Form completed:
____ Handwritten
____ Typewriter
____ Computer output (Invoice, check, etc.)
____ Terminal device or Personal Computer
____ Other ________________

Remarks: ______________________________________

____

____

Prepared by ________________ Date ____________ Information Provided by ____________

Attach original or copy of Form

Exhibit 9.1. Form Survey Worksheet

reporting, payroll deduction authorizations, travel expense reimbursements, inventory moves, sales, and petty cash transactions.

In either case, the requested information is entered on the form survey and an actual form or a copy of it is attached. If possible, a copy of a completed form should be attached to show what information is entered by users. The survey forms should be numbered so they can be located later when writing the forms manual. The survey form is completed as follows:

1. If making a general survey of existing forms, enter a generated survey number, such as "Payroll 1" or "Accounts Payable 3."
2. Enter the form's name, identifying number, and last revision date.
3. Enter the number of copies, their identifying colors, and the use of each one.
4. Indicate if the form is prenumbered.
5. Indicate the supplying vendor.
6. If a copy is retained in the accounting department, note the method of filing, such as alphabetically, numerically, or by date.
7. Estimate the quantity of forms used per year.
8. Note the department that first enters information on the form.
9. Indicate the normal method of preparation, such as handwriting, typing, stamping, or bar coding.
10. Enter the name of the person preparing the survey form and the date on which it is prepared.

9.3 RULES FOR FORM CREATION

As a result of the forms survey, the controller may find that several forms must be rewritten or new forms created. If so, several rules for creating forms can contribute to lower costs, more efficient use, and easier user comprehension:

- *Purpose of the form.* Determine which function within the accounting department will be the primary user, because the data needed by that function will generally determine the form's minimum content. Next, determine whether the form relates to the updating of a master file—such as an employee payroll file, price file, or supplier master file—or whether it is a dollar or quantity accounting transaction form. If the form updates a master file, its layout can be somewhat informal, because the preparer is probably an accountant familiar with the information and how it is used. A transaction form initiated by an outside department typically needs to be more explicit in its content and preparation, due to the user's reduced level of accounting training.
- *Usage of the form.* Determine which department initiates the form and how the data are developed and entered. The answer determines where the working supply of forms will be stored. Follow the form through its various processing steps and indicate by number or letter which person or function enters information in each space. For example, assign a letter to each person or function

entering data on the form. The foreman could be "A," the production supervisor "B," the cost accountant "C," and so on. An "A" would then be placed in each space on the form completed by the foreman. Continue this process until every blank space requiring information has been filled.

- *Number of copies and distribution.* Forms are expensive, especially if multipart forms are printed. Retention of a copy implies permanent storage and future reference, both expensive operations. Thus, there must be a strong reason given when a department wants to retain a copy. If information is to be entered manually on a form, the maximum number of copies that may be used is usually four, including the original. Any form of more than four copies must be typewritten or computer printed in order to obtain readable copies.
- *Permanent or interim document.* If the form is to be retained permanently, how will it be filed and how will it be accessed after filing? The answers determine the type and quantity of future storage and the quality of paper and printing used. For example, some photocopies do not retain images well, and will not be legible after a few years.
- *Forms numbering.* Prenumbering a form with consecutive numbers is only done to establish control over them. Printing forms with consecutive numbers is very expensive and should be avoided unless required for reference and control purposes. Be certain of the need for numbering before adding this feature to a form.
- *Form size.* Unless required by the volume of data needed, an accounting form should match the standard paper size of 8½ by 11 inches. To avoid extra printing charges, forms smaller than a full-size page should be designed to be cut from regular paper stock sizes. Oversize pages are difficult to file and require more expensive storage cabinets. Very small forms, if retained, may also require special storage trays. Small forms that are attached to other documents tend to become separated in the filing process.
- *Manual or typewritten entry.* If entries are to be typed on the form, all spacing from top to bottom should be in multiples of one-sixth of an inch, which is standard vertical typewriter spacing. If entries are to be handwritten, vertical spacing should be one-quarter to one-third of an inch or multiples thereof. Because most typing is done with elite print of 12 characters to the inch, a grid chart with both horizontal and vertical lines spaced at intervals of one-sixth of an inch is very useful in designing a rough draft of a form for subsequent printing.
- *Data entry form layout.* Entering data from a form to other media is usually done manually via a data entry terminal, though some fields may include a preprinted bar code that can be scanned directly into the terminal. In all cases, the forms should be designed so the needed items are selected in a logical sequence. If the reader's eyes have to jump all over the form to pick up the information for transcription or data entry operations, the form itself is causing significant inefficiency in the transcription of data. This problem leads to fatigue, transcription errors, and even the loss of data. Exhibit 9.2 shows an accounting input document that is difficult to use due to the location of required data fields. If a document is relatively simple, one can add a section that summarizes the information in the proper sequence for the data entry operation. For instance, Exhibit 9.3

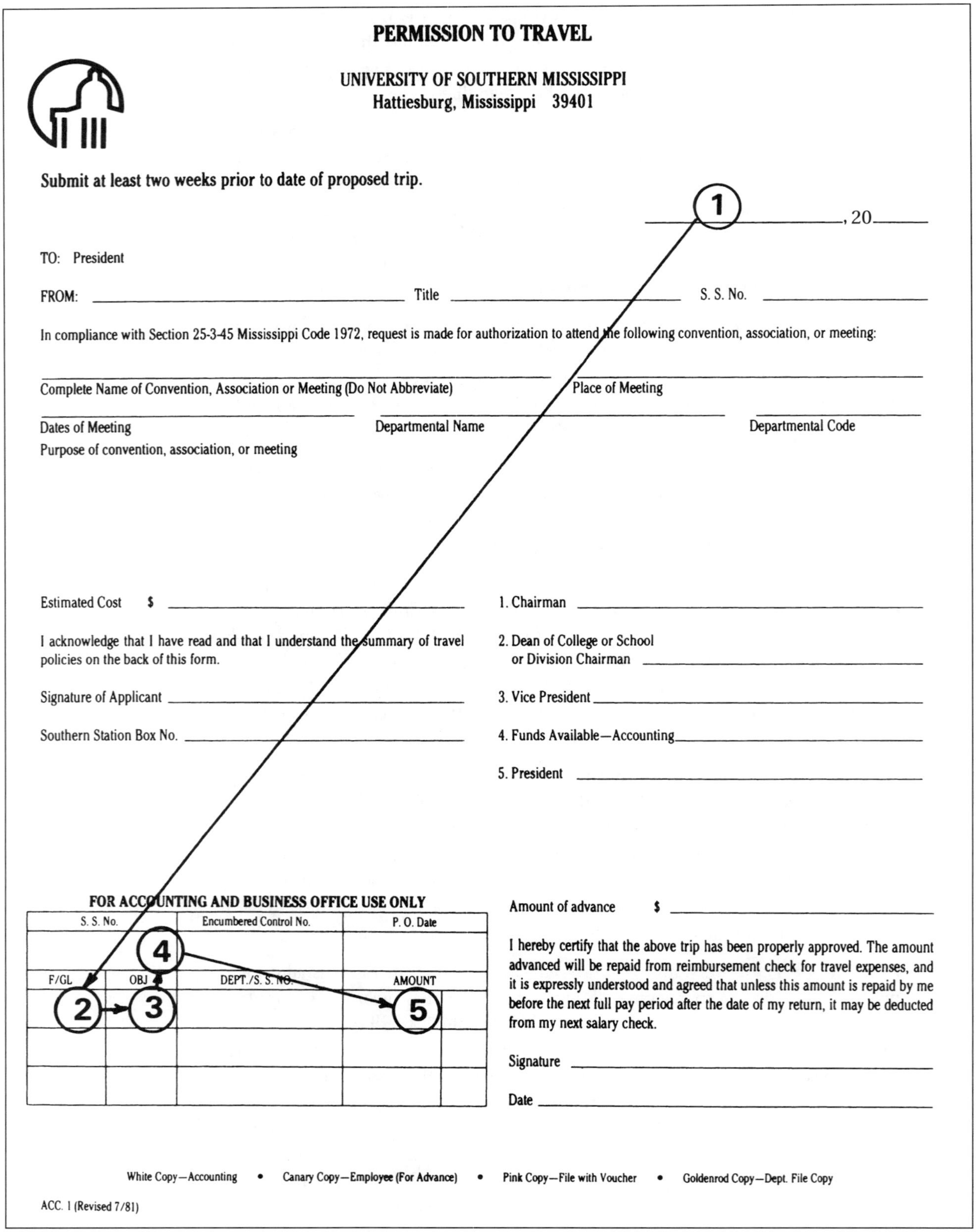

PERMISSION TO TRAVEL

UNIVERSITY OF SOUTHERN MISSISSIPPI
Hattiesburg, Mississippi 39401

Submit at least two weeks prior to date of proposed trip.

(1) ____________________, 20____

TO: President

FROM: ____________________ Title ____________________ S. S. No. ____________________

In compliance with Section 25-3-45 Mississippi Code 1972, request is made for authorization to attend the following convention, association, or meeting:

Complete Name of Convention, Association or Meeting (Do Not Abbreviate) ____________________ Place of Meeting ____________________

Dates of Meeting ____________________ Departmental Name ____________________ Departmental Code ____________________

Purpose of convention, association, or meeting

Estimated Cost $ ____________________

I acknowledge that I have read and that I understand the summary of travel policies on the back of this form.

Signature of Applicant ____________________

Southern Station Box No. ____________________

1. Chairman ____________________
2. Dean of College or School or Division Chairman ____________________
3. Vice President ____________________
4. Funds Available—Accounting ____________________
5. President ____________________

FOR ACCOUNTING AND BUSINESS OFFICE USE ONLY

S. S. No.		Encumbered Control No.	P. O. Date	
	(4)			
F/GL	OBJ	DEPT./S. S. NO.	AMOUNT	
(2) →	(3)		(5)	

Amount of advance $ ____________________

I hereby certify that the above trip has been properly approved. The amount advanced will be repaid from reimbursement check for travel expenses, and it is expressly understood and agreed that unless this amount is repaid by me before the next full pay period after the date of my return, it may be deducted from my next salary check.

Signature ____________________

Date ____________________

White Copy—Accounting • Canary Copy—Employee (For Advance) • Pink Copy—File with Voucher • Goldenrod Copy—Dept. File Copy

ACC. 1 (Revised 7/81)

Exhibit 9.2. Poorly Designed Input Document

PERMISSION TO TRAVEL

Submit at least two weeks prior to date of proposed trip (90 days prior to foreign travel).

THE UNIVERSITY OF SOUTHERN MISSISSIPPI

______________________, 20____

Name: ______________ Title ______________ S.S. No. ______________

In compliance with Section 25-3-45 Mississippi Code 1972, request is made for authorization to attend the following convention, association, or meeting:

______________________________ ______________

Complete Name of Convention, Association or Meeting (Do Not Abbreviate) Place of Meeting

______________ ______________ ______________

Dates of Meeting Department Name Department Code

Purpose of convention, association, or meeting (If an advance is needed, but cost of trip will be reimbursed by an outside organization, please explain).

Estimated Cost $ __________

I acknowledge that I have read and that I understand the summary of travel policies on the back of this form.

____

Signature of Applicant

Southern Station Box No. __________

Domestic Travel

1. Chairman ______________
2. Dean or Division Chairman ______________
3. Funds Available—Accounting (5143) ______________

Foreign, Hawaii, Alaska Travel

4. Vice President ______________
5. President ______________

FOR ACCOUNTING AND BUSINESS OFFICE USE ONLY

ADVANCE (Cannot exceed estimated cost above)

Amount of advance $ __________ Signature ______________________ Date __________

I hereby certify that the above trip has been properly approved. The amount advanced will be repaid from reimbursement check for travel expenses, and it is expressly understood and agreed that unless this amount is repaid by me before the next full pay period after the date of my return, it may be deducted from my next salary check.

ACCOUNT RECEIVABLE

Date MMDDYY	F/GL	OBJ	SOCIAL SEC. NO.	AMOUNT	DR
(1) →	(2) → 1014	1169 (3) →	(4) →	(5)	4

ENCUMBRANCE

P.O. CONTROL	F/GL	OBJ.	DEPARTMENT	SOCIAL SEC. NO.	AMOUNT	DATE MMDDY

White Copy—Accounting • Canary Copy—Employee (For Advance) • Pink Copy—File with Voucher • Goldenrod Copy—Dept. File Copy

ACC 1 (Revised 7/84)

Exhibit 9.3. Input Document Designed for Efficient Data Entry shows the same information as Exhibit 9.2, but with the addition of a data entry block. In this real data entry situation, the data entry error rate dropped from 5% to almost zero.

9.4 CREATING THE FORMS MANUAL

Having learned how to collect information about available forms and how to create them, we can now assemble the forms manual. It contains sections that describe the physical characteristics of each form, examples of the forms, and exactly what information should be entered in each field. Also shown are the position titles or department names that are responsible for completing each part of the form. Most forms require three pages in the manual to impart this information. An example of the contents of a three-page description is as follows:

Page 1. *Physical description of the form* (Exhibit 9.4). This contains the following information:

- Name of the form being described.
- The identifying number of the form.
- Its last revision date.
- The number of parts, the color of each one, and its destination or use.
- A prenumbering identifier.
- The name of the department that stores blank copies of the form (which is the chief internal source of this document).
- The name of the supplier that prints the form.
- The form's purpose, such as to "request payment of items not requiring a supplier invoice, such as payments for dues, subscriptions, and periodic tax payments."
- The names of the employees, departments, or outside entities to whom the copies are sent. This can include notes on how the forms are delivered, such as by certified mail or an overnight delivery service.

An example of a completed form description is shown in Exhibit 9.5.

Page 2. *Copy of the form with sequential numbers/letters added*. The reference numbers or letters should be in bold print so they are not confused with the form itself. A simple approach is to draw quarter-inch circles in the center of each form field, and then type the identifying numbers or letters within these circles. An example is shown in Exhibit 9.6. It is useful to have the form completion and form pages on facing pages of the manual so that the reader can more readily reference back and forth between a picture of the form and a description of how the form is filled out.

FORM DESCRIPTION

NAME OF FORM ____

FORM NO. ____________________ DATE OF LAST REVISION ______________________

COPY NO.	COLOR	DESTINATION OR USE
1	________	______________________________
2	________	______________________________
3	________	______________________________
4	________	______________________________
5	________	______________________________

IS THE FORM PRENUMBERED? ____ YES ____ NO

DEPARTMENT SUPPLYING FORM:

PRINTING SOURCE:

PURPOSE:

DISTRIBUTION OF THE COPIES:

Exhibit 9.4. Form Description Page in the Forms Manual

FORM DESCRIPTION

NAME OF FORM Multiple-Invoice Voucher

FORM NO. ACC 11 DATE OF LAST REVISION 1-01

COPY NO.	COLOR	DESTINATION OR USE
1	White	Accounting
2	Canary	Vendor
3	Pink	Department
4		
5		

IS THE FORM PRENUMBERED? ____ YES X NO

DEPARTMENT SUPPLYING FORM: Accounting

PRINTING SOURCE: Printing Center

PURPOSE:

Used by those departments who handle their own large-volume purchasing such as the Bookstore, Library and Food Services. It is also used by the Athletic Department for required medical examination fees and by Accounting Services to process partial payments or payments on standing purchase orders for the Physical Plant operations.

The form is identical to the Remittance Voucher form ACC 14 except for the description area.

Supporting documents are to be attached to the accounting copy of the form.

DISTRIBUTION OF THE COPIES:

Accounting - Permanent accounts payable file.

Vendor - Mailed with check.

Department - Retains and compares to next monthly Budget Report.

Exhibit 9.5. Completed Form Description Page in the Forms Manual

THE UNIVERSITY OF SOUTHERN MISSISSIPPI

MULTIPLE-INVOICE VOUCHER
UNIVERSITY OF SOUTHERN MISSISSIPPI
HATTIESBURG, MISSISSIPPI 39406-5143

DEPT NAME	**A**
ACCT NO	**B**
TEL NO	**C**

VENDOR **D**

VENDOR CODE **L**

PURCHASE ORDER NUMBER	INVOICE NUMBER	INVOICE DATE	RECEIVING REPORT NUMBER	INVOICE PRICE	LESS DISCOUNT	NET PRICE
E1	**E2**	**E3**	**E4**	**E5**	**E6**	**F**

REQUESTED BY	DATE	APPROVED BY	DATE	TOTAL	
H		**I**			**G**

ACCOUNTING USE	GL	OBJECT	DEPARTMENT	LIQUIDATION	EXPENDITURE
VOUCHER NUMBER **M**		**J**		**T**	**K**
VOUCHER DATE **N**					
PURCHASE ORDER NUMBER **O**					
PROCESSED BY DATE **P**					

VERIFIED BY:	SPECIAL CHECK NO.	ACCOUNTING USE
Q	**R**	**S**

ACC. 11 (REV. 1-83) WHITE—ACCOUNTING CANARY—VENDOR PINK—DEPARTMENT

Exhibit 9.6. Form with Sequential Numbering Added

Page 3. *Completing the form.* To complete the description, one must enter sequential numbers or letters in each area of the form requiring data, in the order in which the data is entered. This sequence is vital as it permits separating the entries into groups of sequential users. With this numbering in place, once can then create a sequential description of how to fill out the form. An example is shown in

COMPLETING THE MULTIPLE-INVOICE VOUCHER

Department enters:

A. Department name.
B. Account number.
C. Telephone number of preparer.
D. Name and address of vendor.
E. Description of each invoice to be paid.

   1. Purchase order number assigned to the purchase.
   2. Vendor invoice number.
   3. Invoice date.
   4. Receiving report number.
   5. Total dollar amount of the invoice.
   6. Dollar amount of cash discount permitted by vendor.

F. Amount to be paid. Attach supporting document, if any.
G. Total to be paid on this voucher.
H. Signature of person requesting payment and date signed.
I. Approval signature and date. Payments to individuals require two approval signatures if an invoice is not available.
J. General Ledger Code, Object Code and Department to be charged. If Department is not entered, the charge will be made to the account shown at the top of the form.
K. Amount to be charged to this account. Form provides distribution for up to eight accounts.

Financial Affairs enters:

L. Vendor code number.
M. Voucher number.
N. Voucher date.
O. Purchase Order Number, if any.
P. Name of person processing the voucher and date processed.
Q. Name of person reviewing or verifying information.
R. Preprinted number of special check used to pay voucher.
S. Special handling required or enclosure to be mailed with check.
T. Amount of encumbrance to be liquidated, if any.

Exhibit 9.7. Form Completion Page

Exhibit 9.7, where there is a complete description of the fields previously shown in Exhibit 9.6.

If a form is two-sided, use the same approach, except that two pages are added to show the back page and instructions on how to complete it. The form documentation would consist of the following five pages:

1. Physical description of the form
2. Front of the actual form
3. Instructions for completing the front of the form
4. Back of the actual form
5. Instructions for completing the back of the form

9.5 ELECTRONIC FORMS

A common difficulty for companies of any size is that too many versions of the same form are being used. This can be a major problem if people are using an old form that does not require certain information that is now necessary to complete a transaction. As a result, the recipient of the form must track down the person who completed the old form and have him or her add the extra information. Not only is this a waste of time for the form recipient, but it also increases the time before the transaction represented by the form is completed. Further, the new form may exclude information that was required on the old form, resulting in extra labor by anyone using the old form, because they are adding unnecessary information. In the days before computer systems, it was nearly impossible to eradicate old forms from a company, because each employee kept a "stash" of forms for use whenever needed, which might last for months or years after the forms were superseded.

However, one can use electronic forms to completely eliminate old form versions. This can be done in two ways. One is to program forms right into the computer system so one can enter information directly into the computer database, with no need for any paperwork at all. This is the best approach from the standpoint of avoiding old form versions, but requires the most programming time to accomplish. A simpler, though less effective approach is to store the files for all forms in the computer system, in a location where the majority of employees can access them. Employees then print out the forms, complete them, and submit them in the usual manner. This approach allows any company with a computer network to eliminate any paper files of forms. However, once a form file is printed, an employee may be tempted to retain a paper-based copy rather than go back to the computer network for a new version each time the form is needed; this can still result in caches of old forms scattered throughout an organization. Thus, though it is a simple and easily implemented approach, it is not as effective as the complete elimination of paper forms that can be achieved through the first approach.

No matter which variation is used, a company can achieve a significant improvement in its ability to store and disseminate forms to its employees by using electronic forms.

Chapter 10

USER MANUAL

10.1 INTRODUCTION

The user manual is a conglomeration of documentation that relates to the wide array of transactions with which employees will deal in a typical work week. Some of these transactions are closely linked to the accounting department, while others involve only a slight interaction with this area. The user manual is designed to address the broad range of employee activities, rather than have a narrow focus on accounting activities. Examples of activities that may be addressed are:

- Complete the annual budget form for operations.
- Approve hiring an applicant for employment.
- Terminate an employee for cause.
- Requisition a commodity or service through the purchasing operation.
- Request service or supplies from another department.
- Prepare or approve employee time reports.
- Count inventory for the accounting system.
- Complete material receiving reports.
- Complete travel expense reports for reimbursement.

There are certainly other transactions too, but these are enough for starters. Every one of the actions listed results in one or more pieces of paper being received in accounting as a transaction input document. These documents usually are reports providing information or forms requiring some action to be taken and recorded. The problem is that many of these reports and forms are designed or prepared by accountants but are used by people who are not accountants—hence the need for a user manual. It is a training manual for new line and staff supervisors and for the employees who are using the reports and forms. It is a reference manual when a rare or unusual event occurs. It is an information manual to inform the users about company policies and the procedures for completing accounting forms.

10.2 STARTING THE MANUAL

If you have a policy/procedure statement system in place, start by reviewing each statement and ask if officers, department managers, or individual employees are involved in the receiving of data, forms, or reports from accounting. If yes, then mark that statement for possible inclusion in the user manual. Then review each accounting form and ask if information is initiated or processed by an outside user before the form reaches accounting. If so, that form should be selected for the manual.

If the policy/procedure system and forms manual are not in place, then review the list of actions at the beginning of this chapter and list those in use at your operation. Continue beyond these lists and identify other forms or actions with which the non-accounting employee may be involved. Either way, you now have a list of potential accounting policies, procedures, or forms that may be included in the user manual.

One other approach for formulating the contents of a user manual is tracking the number of recurring input document errors or the number of inquiries received daily or weekly from employees initiating the addition of information to the accounting forms at their respective locations. Steadily recurring errors on input documents is a positive sign that a user manual is needed.

Before going further, make a rough list of the potential distribution of such a manual. Is it every senior officer and department manager? Is it just selected departments? Could it be all employees above a certain classification level? Is it all professionals in a professional service organization? Or will just one copy go to each branch office? This list could range from a few dozen locations or persons to hundreds.

If the list is extremely diverse, you may elect to issue different manuals to different users. For example, there could be a factory user manual that includes only policies and procedures that affect those operations. The factory manual may cover only hourly payroll procedures and forms, while the travel policies and cash and accounts receivable sections may be deleted. A special section on inventory control forms may be included in this manual.

Likewise, the manual for branch operations may be expanded to cover special problems such as procedures for shipping goods from the home office and receiving them at the branch. There may also be special provisions for transmitting data and for the automatic deposit of payroll checks of branch employees. The procedure for handling and reporting branch deposits of cash would be included here.

Another user manual may be the administrative department accounting manual. This manual may cover special reports prepared by the sales department, forms for reporting customer credit ratings, or special reports covering research and development located only at the company's primary office.

10.3 OUTLINING AND UPDATING THE USER MANUAL

The next step is to outline the manual, generally by accounting function such as payroll, accounts payable, cashier, accounts receivable, receiving, and so on. A sentence outline should provide enough information to select the various policy and procedure documents and to write explanations or rewrite existing form instructions or other information.

Putting the user manual together is now a matter of selecting the available documentation, adding or deleting information where needed, preparing an index, and printing and publishing the manual. Unlike a book, the index or contents should be on the cover where it is immediately available. Each topic, instruction sheet, and form should be indexed by name and page number. The user manual is usually between 20 and 100 pages long; any longer manual tends not to be used.

Study the materials brought together for the user manual. Some policies or procedures may be quite long, with extensive introductions as well as copies of laws and regulations. If the materials are adequate as originally printed, use them as is. If not, prepare a condensed version for the user manual, stripping out material of little interest to the departmental user.

The manual may be printed on both sides of the paper, but printing on only one side is recommended. Printing on one side leaves the back of the preceding page available for user notes, additions, deletions, and changes until a new manual is published. Use standard white paper and provide an index and date of issue on the cover. After collating, the manual should be held together with a single staple in the upper left corner unless it is placed in a three-ring binder.

If the manual is to be issued to department supervisors, provide a second copy of the manual marked "Office Copy," for most accounting documents prepared at remote locations will be done by the departmental secretary under the direction of the supervisor. It will be the secretary who will be calling the accounting department for assistance with a problem.

Distribute the manual to the selected recipients through the normal delivery system used in the company. The first time the user manual is distributed, a cover letter explaining its purpose and use would be helpful.

Periodically updating parts of the user manual by issuing corrected insert sheets is not generally recommended. Users tend not to delete superceded pages or add new pages to a previously published manual. One way of notifying such users of changes is through interoffice correspondence to the original holders of the manuals. The *From* section of the correspondence would be the accounting department, and the *Subject* section would indicate the specific page and item to be changed. The first paragraph could explain the addition or change in detail; the second paragraph notes the exact location of the change in the user manual. In most cases, the user can reference this correspondence while updating the manual in writing.

The user manual should be fully updated and published annually, especially if the document continues to receive a large number of changes on an ongoing basis.

10.4 SAMPLE USER MANUAL

There are many types of user manuals that can be made specific to certain functions within a company, such as one that is tailored to the needs of the receiving staff, detailing how to inspect incoming materials, write up return documentation, and match receipts to authorizing purchase orders. Rather than provide a sample of a user manual that is specific to a single function, this section contains a more general user manual containing information that is most likely to be used by the majority of a company's employees, containing information about travel policies, filling out expense reimbursement forms, and so on. This information can be used as the core of a general user manual, and can be substantially modified to create user manuals for more specific functions. The example is shown in Exhibits 10.1 through 10.10.

General User Manual Brasto Publishing **Subject: Contents**	Retrieval No.: Page: Issue Date: Supercedes:	GUSE-01 1 of 1 10/28/0X N/A

GENERAL USER MANUAL

CONTENTS

1. Listing of key employees by function and phone number
2. Company holidays
3. Time reporting
4. Travel policies
5. Expense reporting
6. Accounting codes for expense reports
7. Benefit contact information
8. Requisitioning supplies
9. Recording petty cash transactions

Exhibit 10.1. Sample User Manual, Contents

General User Manual	Retrieval No.:	GUSE-02
Brasto Publishing	Page:	1 of 1
	Issue Date:	10/28/0X
Subject: Key Employees	Supercedes:	N/A

Type of Problem	Go To—Primary	Go To—Secondary
401(k)	Mitch Bothward	Anne Boardman
Computer Problem	James Teacher	Peter Vanders
Copier Problem	Caitlin Ward	
Customer Service	Sally Dunne	Jim Evans
Dental Insurance	Mitch Bothward	Anne Boardman
Expense Reports	Anne Boardman	
Fax Problem	Caitlin Ward	
Harassment	Mitch Bothward	Anne Boardman
Marketing	Alexandra Wright	
Medical Insurance	Mitch Bothward	Anne Boardman
Network Problem	James Teacher	
Office Supplies	Caitlin Ward	
Paycheck	Anne Boardman	
Phone List	Caitlin Ward	
Phones	Caitlin Ward	
Quality Assurance	Carrie Archer	
Sales	Mark Chowdry	Tim Mannesman
Time-keeping System	Peter Vanders	Anne Boardman

Exhibit 10.2. Sample User Manual, Key Employees

General User Manual Brasto Publishing **Subject: Company Holidays**	Retrieval No.: Page: Issue Date: Supercedes:	GUSE-03 1 of 1 10/01/0X N/A

The following holidays are recognized by the company for the year 200X. These holidays match those required by the federal government, which the company follows as part of its obligations as a federal contractor.

Holiday	2002 Date of Observance
New Year's Day	January 1, Monday
Martin Luther King Day	January 21, Monday
Washington's Birthday	February 18, Monday
Memorial Day	May 27, Monday
Independence Day	July 4, Thursday
Labor Day	September 2, Monday
Columbus Day	October 14, Monday
Veterans Day	November 11, Monday
Thanksgiving Day	November 28, Thursday
Friday after Thanksgiving	November 29, Friday
Christmas Eve (1/2 Day)	December 24, Tuesday
Christmas	December 25, Wednesday

Exhibit 10.3. Sample User Manual, Company Holidays

General User Manual

Brasto Publishing

Subject: Time Reporting

Retrieval No.:	GUSE-04
Page:	1 of 1
Issue Date:	10/28/0X
Supercedes:	N/A

Policies: Each employee is responsible for recording his or her time in the time-keeping system. No one may record hours worked on another's time record. Tampering with another's time record is cause for disciplinary action, including possible dismissal, of both employees.

If an employee does not record his or her time in the time-keeping system, then the company has no way of tracking vacation time taken. If this happens, the company will assume that an employee has taken all of his or her vacation time, rendering that person unable to carry forward any vacation hours to the next year; nor will an employee be paid any accrued vacation hours at such time as he or she leaves the company.

Submission Notes, Specific: The following items relate to the blocked identifying letters listed on the sample expense report form shown on the next page:

A. Enter the name of the employee whose time is recorded on the form.
B. Enter the employee number (located on the bottom of the employee badge) of the employee whose time is recorded on the form.
C. Enter the date on which time was worked.
D. Enter the start time of the activity.
E. Enter the time at which the activity stopped.
F. Enter the difference between the start and stop time for the activity. Be sure to include a grand total at the bottom of this column after all line item entries have been made.
G. Enter the job or project code against which time is to be charged.
H. Enter the earnings code, located in the table at the bottom of the form, that corresponds to the hours worked.
I. Have the employee's immediate supervisor sign and date the form.

Exhibit 10.4. Sample User Manual, Time Reporting

Brasto Publishing

Time and Attendance Report

Employee Name: ______ A ______ Employee ID Number: ______ B __

Date	Start Time	Stop Time	Net Time	Job Code	Earnings Code
C	D	E	F	G	H

Total Time Worked ______

I hereby certify that the time reported above is a true statement of hours worked: ______________ ______________

Name Date

Earnings Codes:

REG	Regular Hours	JUR	Jury Duty
OT	Overtime	SIC	Sick Leave
HOL	Holiday	VAC	Vacation Leave

Exhibit 10.4. Sample User Manual, Time Reporting Form (Continued)

General User Manual	Retrieval No.:	GUSE-05
Brasto Publishing	Page:	1 of 2
	Issue Date:	10/28/0X
Subject: Travel Policies	Supercedes:	N/A

Policy: Employees are reimbursed for reasonable and necessary expenses incurred during approved travel.

Authorization: Travel requires approval of the department manager. The Permission to Travel form is required for conferences, conventions, and professional meetings, and must be submitted at least two weeks in advance of the departure date. Requests for foreign travel of the same type must be submitted at least four weeks in advance. The form is not required for business travel.

Change or Cancellation of Travel Request: An amended Permission to Travel form must be submitted to change the place or date of a meeting, or to cancel it.

Advance Payment of Conference Registration Fees: To pay registration fees in advance of a conference, the request should be made at least 20 days in advance of the conference date on an expense report. Literature concerning the conference and fee amount and a copy of the Permission to Travel form must be attached to the voucher.

Reimbursement of Travel Expense: Immediately upon returning from a trip, an employee should submit an expense report for reimbursement. All expense reports require an approval signature from an employee's immediate supervisor. Expense reports will be reimbursed within five business days.

Lodging: If more than one person is indicated on the lodging bill, the single room rate should be shown; otherwise, reimbursement will be made at 50% of the room charge. Lodging reimbursement will be made for the final evening of the trip if the traveler is not able to return home by 9 PM.

Meals: Reimbursement for meals is on a per diem basis, and is tied directly to the federal government's Federal Travel Regulation rates, which should be consulted regularly to view updates.

Mileage: Mileage for the use of a personal vehicle on company business matches the standard Internal Revenue Service rate. Employees will be notified once a year of changes in this rate. Private vehicle mileage reimbursement cannot exceed the cost of round-trip air coach fare to the named destination.

Public Carrier: Airline tickets must be purchased through the corporate travel office. Certification that coach fare was not available is necessary when tickets are purchased for first-class travel. Business-class seats are allowable for flights exceeding six hours in duration. A ticket coupon is required to document the cost of a flight.

Registration Fees: Fees are reimbursed on an expense report when supported by a paid receipt.

Exhibit 10.5. Sample User Manual, Travel Policies

General User Manual Brasto Publishing **Subject: Travel Policies**	Retrieval No.: Page: Issue Date: Supercedes:	GUSE-05 2 of 2 10/28/0X N/A

Tips: Tips for meals, taxis, and other services should be noted on the expense report. Tips can include baggage-handling tips when arriving or departing a hotel or airport, and should not exceed $1 per bag.

Taxi and Limousine: Actual charges, including tip, are reimbursable. The cost of a private limousine should not exceed the cost of similar taxi service.

Parking and Tolls: Actual parking charges and road and bridge tolls are reimbursable if using a personal vehicle or rental car on company business, but not if the charges are incurred during a daily commute to the office.

Car Rental: The actual cost of a car rental is reimbursable if a receipt is attached to the expense report. The company will only reimburse for the cost of a mid-sized car, with the incremental cost of any upgrades to larger vehicles being charged back to employees. Do not accept optional insurance coverage when renting a car on company business, because this is covered by a company insurance policy. Car rental should be made through the corporate travel office to take advantage of corporate volume discounts.

Exhibit 10.5. Sample User Manual, Travel Policies (Continued)

General User Manual	Retrieval No.:	GUSE-06
Brasto Publishing	Page:	1 of 1
	Issue Date:	10/28/0X
Subject: Expense Reporting	Supercedes:	N/A

Purpose: To reimburse employees for approved travel and other expenditures.

Submission Notes, General: To be reimbursed for all authorized expenses, you must submit an expense report accompanied by receipts for all expenses incurred, and with an approval signature by your manager. Please submit your expense report promptly after incurring an expense. Expense reports with errors or missing documentation will be returned to employees for correction.

Submission Notes, Specific: The following items relate to the blocked identifying letters listed on the sample expense report form shown on the next page:

A. Enter your name, social security number, and department.
B. Enter your employee number, official job title, and the name of your immediate supervisor.
C. Enter the pay periods during which the expenses reported on this form were incurred.
D. Enter the date on which an expense was incurred. This should be the date listed on the receipt.
E. Enter the account number to which the expense should be charged. The most commonly used charge codes are listed later in this manual under the heading "Accounting Codes." Accounting codes used should only be those for your department. If any expenses are to be charged to a different department, then the supervisor of that department must also sign off on the form.
F. Briefly describe the incurred expense. If the expense was a meal, list the name of the people attending and the purpose of the meal.
G. Seven categories of commonly used expenses are listed. Please enter the amount of the expense in the category that most closely indicates the purpose of the expense. If none of the categories match the expense, then list it in the "Other" category. Once entered, the total expense will automatically appear in the "Total" column.
H. Enter the amount of any offsetting advances already issued to you, and against which no expenses have yet been charged.
I. Have your immediate supervisor sign in this block.

Prior to submitting your expense report, please make a copy for your records.

Exhibit 10.6. Sample User Manual, Expense Reporting

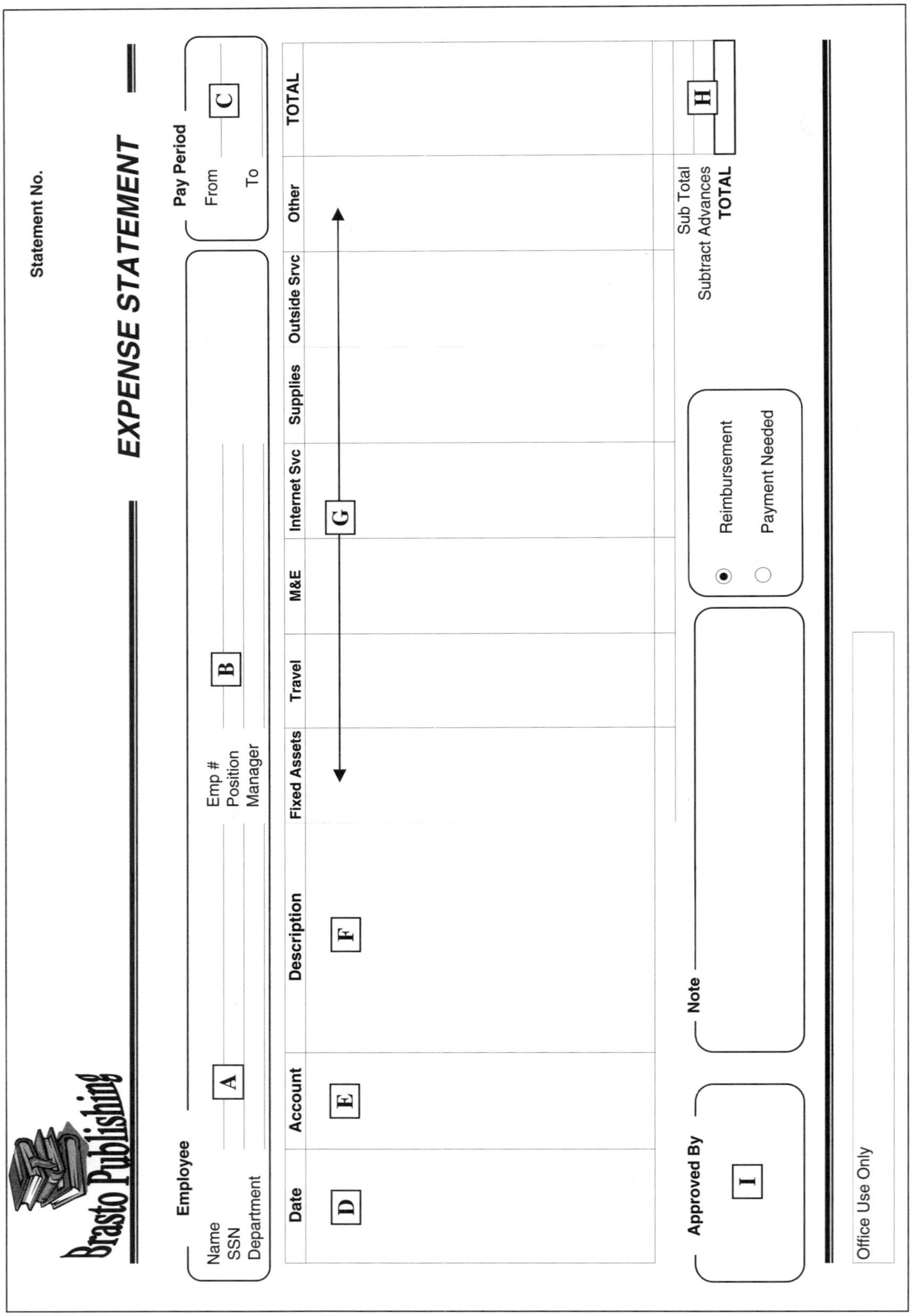

Exhibit 10.6. Sample User Manual, Expense Report Form (Continued)

General User Manual		
Brasto Publishing	Retrieval No.:	GUSE-07
	Page:	1 of 2
	Issue Date:	10/28/0X
Subject: Accounting Codes	Supercedes:	N/A

Use the following account codes when filling out your expense report:

Account Number	Account Description
60500-01	Dues and Publications—G&A
60500-02	Dues and Publications—Development
60500-03	Dues and Publications—Consulting
60500-04	Dues and Publications—Marketing
60500-05	Dues and Publications—Production
60500-06	Dues and Publications—Sales
60950-01	Licenses and Fees—G&A
60950-02	Licenses and Fees—Development
60950-03	Licenses and Fees—Consulting
60950-04	Licenses and Fees—Marketing
61050-01	Meals—G&A
61050-02	Meals—Development
61050-03	Meals—Consulting
61050-04	Meals—Marketing
61050-05	Meals—Production
61050-06	Meals—Sales
61150-01	Postage—G&A
61150-02	Postage—Development
61150-03	Postage—Consulting
61150-04	Postage—Marketing
61150-06	Postage—Sales
62200-01	Supplies—G&A
62200-02	Supplies—Development
62200-03	Supplies—Consulting
62200-04	Supplies—Marketing
62200-05	Supplies—Production
62200-06	Supplies—Sales
62300-01	Telephone—G&A
62300-02	Telephone—Development
62300-03	Telephone—Consulting
62300-04	Telephone—Marketing
62300-05	Telephone—Production
62300-06	Telephone—Sales
62350-04	Trade Shows
62400-01	Training—G&A
62400-02	Training—Development
62400-03	Training—Consulting
62400-04	Training—Marketing

Exhibit 10.7. Sample User Manual, Accounting Codes

General User Manual Brasto Publishing **Subject: Accounting Codes**	Retrieval No.: Page: Issue Date: Supercedes:	GUSE-07 2 of 2 10/28/0X N/A

Account Number	Account Description
62400-05	Training—Production
62400-06	Training—Sales
62450-01	Travel—G&A
62450-02	Travel—Development
62450-03	Travel—Consulting
62450-04	Travel—Marketing
62450-05	Travel—Production
62450-06	Travel—Sales

Exhibit 10.7. Sample User Manual, Accounting Codes (Continued)

General User Manual Brasto Publishing **Subject: Benefits Contact Information**	Retrieval No.: Page: Issue Date: Supercedes:	GUSE-08 1 of 1 10/28/0X N/A

The staff of the human resources department should be able to answer most of your questions regarding benefits. However, if you are more comfortable contacting the benefit provider directly, or if your question arises after hours, please use the following contact information:

401(k) Plan Customer Service	800-621-8912
Cafeteria Plan Customer Service	800-702-3597
COBRA Payments	800-593-0421
Dental Reimbursement	800-555-8543
Life Insurance Customer Service	800-391-8371
Medical Account Representative (Susan Allen)	800-423-8010
Medical Customer Service	800-341-9020
Medical Reimbursement	800-877-9777

Exhibit 10.8. Sample User Manual, Benefits Contact Information

General User Manual Brasto Publishing **Subject: Requisitioning Supplies**	Retrieval No.: Page: Issue Date: Supercedes:	GUSE-09 1 of 1 10/28/0X N/A

Purpose: When supplies or equipment are needed, one should complete a requisition form. The original copy is sent to the purchasing department and the canary copy is retained by the requisitioning department for later comparison to the purchase order. When the purchase order is prepared by the purchasing department, one copy is sent to the requisitioning department.

Submission Notes, Specific: The following items relate to the blocked identifying letters listed on the sample expense report form shown on the next page:

A. Enter the date on which the requisition was filled out.
B. The purchasing department will fill in the purchase order number, unless the requisitioning employee has obtained the number in advance.
C. Enter the account code or name to which the requisition will be charged.
D. Enter the date by which the service or product must be received.
E. Enter the name of the person to whom delivery should be made.
F. Enter the reason why the service or product is being ordered. If available, enter the project name or number for which it is being used.
G. Enter the contact information for any suggested suppliers.
H. Enter the quantity, description, and estimated price of each item being requested. The actual price and total extended price will be entered by the purchasing department.
I. If the amount being requested is under $5,000 then only the signatures of the requesting person and budgetary authority (the person against whose budget this expense will be charged) are needed. If the amount exceeds $5,000 but is less than $50,000, then the signature of the chief financial officer must be added. If the requisition exceeds $50,000, then the signature of the president must be added.

Exhibit 10.9. Sample User Manual, Requisitioning Supplies

REQUISITION

Date: ___ **A** ___ Purchase Order No. ___ **B** ___

Account to Charge: ___ **C** ___ Required Delivery Date: ___ **D** ___

Deliver to: ___ **E** ___ To be used for: ___ **F** ___

Name and Address of Suggested Suppliers:

1 ___ **G** ___ 2 ___

3 ___ 4 ___

Quantity	Description	Estimated Price	Actual Price	Total
	H			

Authorization:

Requested By: ___ **I** ___ Name ___ Date

Budgetary Authority: ___ Name ___ Date

Chief Financial Officer: ___ Name ___ Date

President: ___ Name ___ Date

Exhibit 10.9. Sample User Manual, Requisitioning Supplies (Continued)

General User Manual	Retrieval No.:	GUSE-10
Brasto Publishing	Page:	1 of 1
	Issue Date:	10/28/0X
Subject: Petty Cash Transactions	Supercedes:	N/A

Purpose: To obtain cash for emergency purchases under $50.

Discussion: If a department has a petty cash fund, disbursements are accumulated until the fund is nearly depleted. The receipts and one copy of the petty cash voucher form are brought to the finance department. The cashier will issue cash to replace the amount of expenses itemized on the petty cash voucher.

If a department has no petty cash fund, a receipt under $50 can be brought to the finance department and exchanged for cash or a company check.

Distribution of Completed Form: The completed petty cash voucher form is filed with the accounts payable vouchers.

Exhibit 10.10. Sample User Manual, Recording Petty Cash Transactions

PREPARING A PETTY CASH VOUCHER

Complete the form according to the following instructions.

A. Department - Enter the complete account title.

B. Date - Enter the date the voucher is prepared.

C. Date - Enter date of each transaction.

D. Vendor - List the name of the vendor on each transaction.

E. G.L. - Enter general ledger code of each transaction.

F. Object Code - Enter object code of each transaction.

G. Department - Enter the department account number for each transaction.

H. Amount - Enter the total of each transaction.

I. Total - Enter total to be reimbursed.

J. Summarize information in E, F, G, H.

K. Submitted By - Name of individual to receive the reimbursement.

L. Approved By - The signature of the budgetary authority as listed in the Chart of Accounts.

M. Verified By - For accounting use only.

N. Approved By - Approved signature by accounting department.

O. Date - Enter the date the voucher is approved by the Accounting Department.

P. Petty Cash Authorization No. - Accounting enters the number of the authorization.

(Continues)

Exhibit 10.10. Continued

Petty Cash Voucher

DEPARTMENT **A** DATE **B**

DATE	VENDOR	G.L.	OBJECT	DEPARTMENT	AMOUNT	
C	**D**	**E**	**F**	**G**	**H**	
			TOTAL		**I**	

DEPARTMENT

SUBMITTED BY **K**

APPROVED BY **L**

FINANCIAL AFFAIRS

VERIFIED BY **M**

APPROVED BY **N**

DATE **O**

P.C. AUTHORIZATION NO. **P**

G.L.	OBJECT	DEPARTMENT	AMOUNT	
J	**J**	**J**	**J**	
		TOTAL	**I**	

Exhibit 10.10. Sample User Manual, Recording Petty Cash Transactions (Continued)

Chapter 11

INFORMATION TECHNOLOGY MANUAL

11.1 INTRODUCTION

The controller or CFO frequently has management responsibility over the information technology (IT) department, so this chapter is included to address a variety of documentation issues related to this function. A key task that can be better controlled through a properly documented process is the system development process, which is covered in the next section. A key part of the system development process for many activities is a complete or partial survey of existing systems, which can be conducted using the series of forms presented in Section 11.3, "System Survey Forms" section. We also present a number of IT policies and procedures, which can be modified to form the core of an IT policies and procedures manual. The chapter concludes with several discussions that are centered on outputs from the IT department—reports documentation, database table documentation for use with report writers, and a computer reports questionnaire that can be used to prune the number of reports currently in use. There is also a short discussion of the contents of a disaster recovery manual.

11.2 SYSTEM DEVELOPMENT PROCESS

The systems development process can be an extremely time-consuming process, and is subject to a high rate of failure. To increase the odds of success, one should use the six-step system development process that is outlined in this section. It allows for a relatively rigid, sequential process that forces the development team to complete a series of steps that will allow it to complete a project in an orderly manner. An overview of the system development process, using all six steps, is noted in Exhibit 11.1. Each step is followed by a decision to redo the work, terminate it, or proceed to the next step.

In sequential order, the six steps in the development process are as follows:

1. *Project initiation step*. This step is shown in Exhibit 11.2, and starts when someone in the organization presents a request for new or changed data processing services to the Data Processing Steering Committee (which approves or drops projects, and also prioritizes those that are approved). The request should be written so that the problem or purpose of the new information is clearly communicated, which enables the IT department to determine whether it can fill the need. The IT department responds to the request and makes recommendations for further action, after which the steering com-

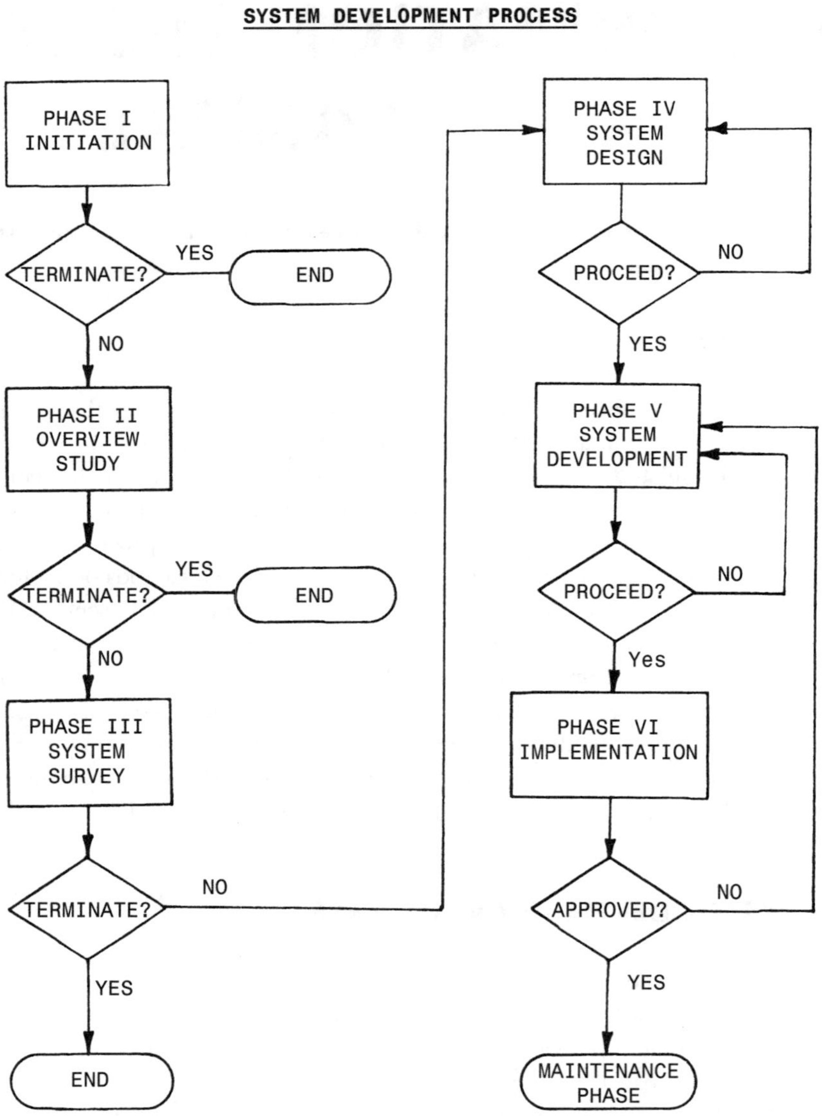

Exhibit 11.1. Six Phases of the System Development Process

mittee makes a decision to proceed or terminate the request, based on the costs and benefits of the proposal.

2. *Overview study step*. As shown in Exhibit 11.3, the study extends the review of the initial proposal to the entire subject area to see if a more comprehensive solution may be in order. The steering committee then makes a decision to proceed or terminate the request, as was the case in the first step.

3. *System survey step*. This step is shown in Exhibit 11.4, and involves the appointment of a project team that is composed of both IT and user department personnel. The team's task is to conduct a system survey, which requires the gathering of all key information about the existing system, the system to be designed, and the development of a tentative design. The survey involves research, interviews, and other types of data-gathering activities. The result is a proposal containing a tentative system design, budget, requirements for personnel and equipment, benefits and limitations, and a plan for development, implementation, and future operations. The steering committee receives the team report, and makes the usual "go" or "no go" decision.

4. *System design step*. This step is shown in Exhibit 11.5, and requires the development of a highly detailed system design. The output is a detailed set of system specifications, which includes a system summary, file specifications (file identifications, formats, and data descriptions), input specifications (input identifications, output formats, and pro forma report layouts), processing specifications (functions to be performed, rules of logic to be followed, tables, formulas, and so on), and the system test plan (test objectives, validity criteria, and a test outline). The package should be reviewed by users and IT managers, and adjustments made. The steering committee does not normally review this work product.

5. *System development step*. As shown in Exhibit 11.6, development involves assigning work to personnel, monitoring their progress against the plan, and testing the results. If the program chosen is a standalone package from an outside supplier, then the package is installed and tested. Someone should also write user instructions, which may be in the form of a user manual. When completed, the user manual is used to conduct orientation sessions with anyone intending to use the resulting system. Once the programs are ready, the users trained, the data conversion methods are completed, and the system test can be conducted. If the system test is satisfactory, it may be desirable to conduct a pilot test of actual data used in the replaced system to see whether it can be handled by the new system. After this test, an evaluation report is prepared to compare the objectives in the system proposal with the actual results obtained with the new system. The evaluation report is reviewed by the users and IT management to determine whether they can accept the results and are ready to implement the system.

6. *Implementation step*. Implementation, as shown in Exhibit 11.7, involves the conversion of data to the new system, the completion of any remaining procedures and manuals, plus an evaluation of system results. The project team evaluates the results to determine whether the system is performing according to approved specifications. The evaluation report comments on any areas needing management attention. After a final review by the steering committee, the system enters a maintenance phase for ongoing operations.

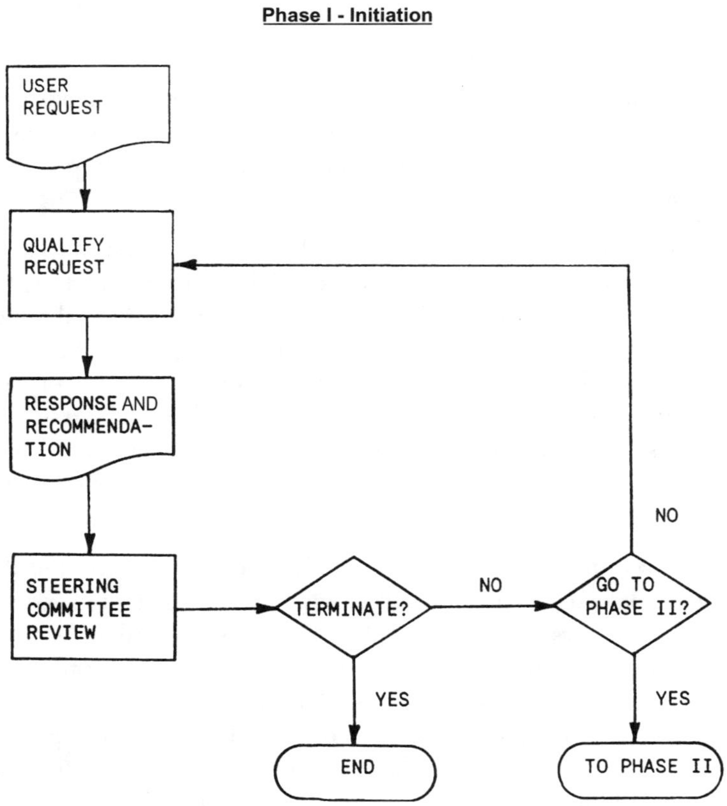

Exhibit 11.2. Project Initiation

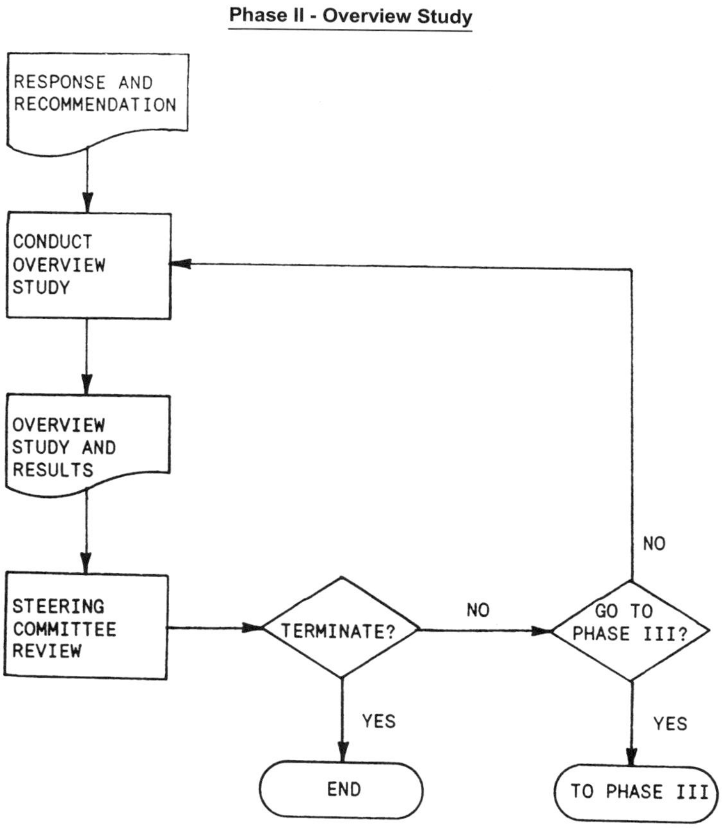

Exhibit 11.3. Overview Study

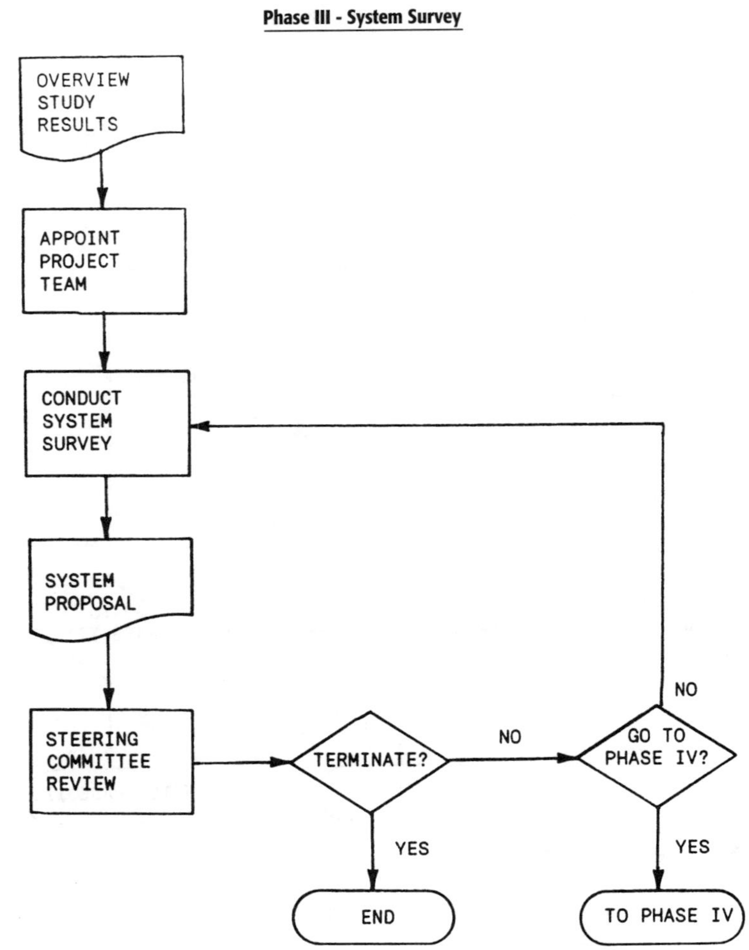

Exhibit 11.4. System Survey

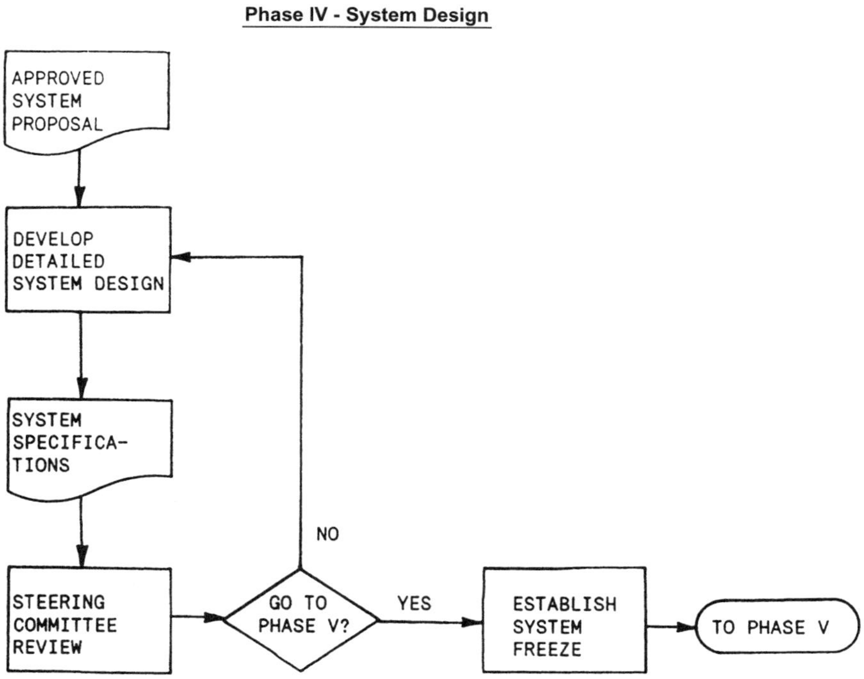

Exhibit 11.5. System Design

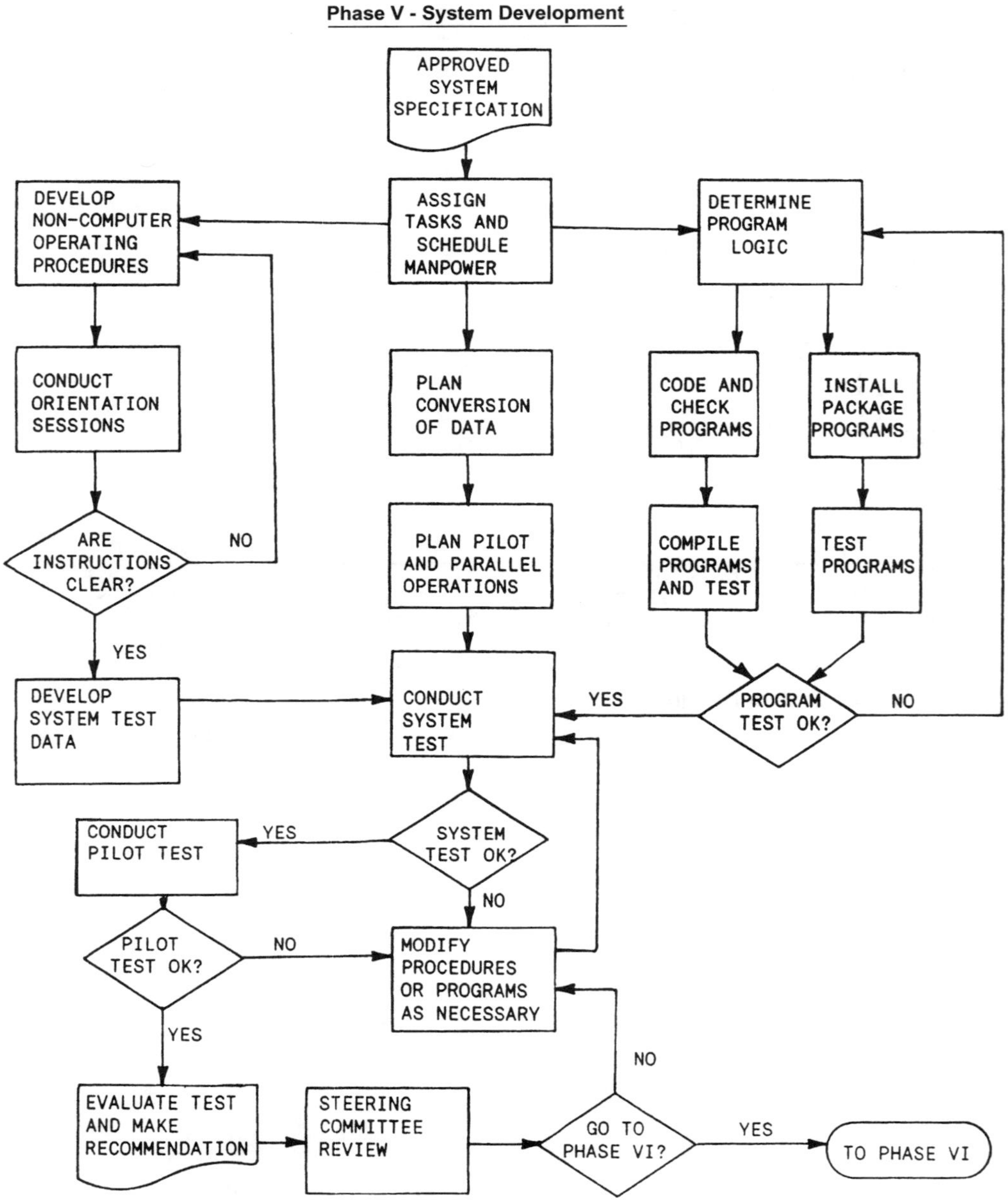

Exhibit 11.6. System Development

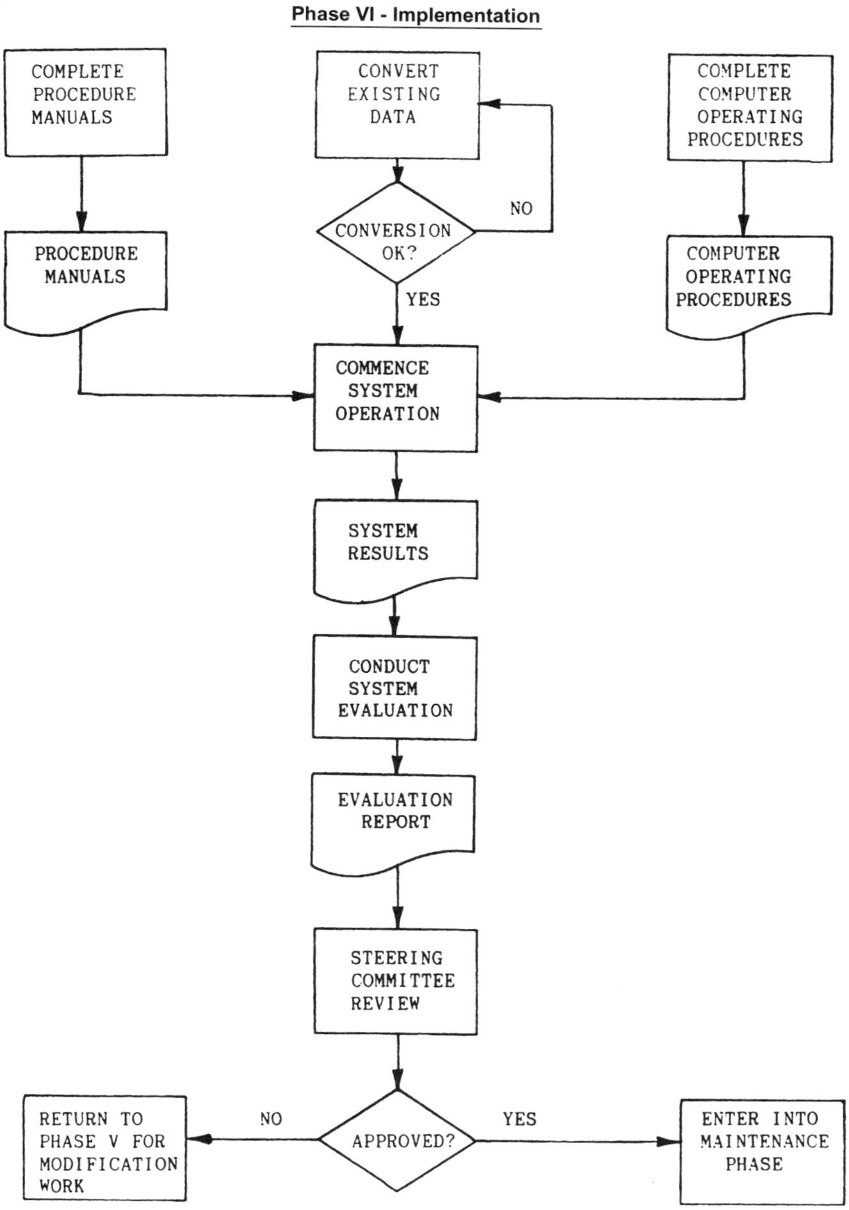

Exhibit 11.7. Implementation

An example procedure that encompasses all six steps of the system development process is noted in Exhibit 11.8. This procedure assumes that the majority of all systems will be purchased from suppliers, rather than developed internally.

Policy/Procedure Statement	Retrieval No.:	DEV-01
Brasto Publishing	Page:	1 of 3
	Issue Date:	10/28/03
Subject: System Development Procedure	Supercedes:	N/A

PROJECT INITIATION

1. Determine the need for the replacement of various software and hardware systems based on the age of systems, system problems, maintenance requirements, and any scheduled stoppages in supplier maintenance.
2. Issue "bullet point" list of recommended changes the Steering Committee.

OVERVIEW STUDY

1. Determine which systems are linked to those systems targeted for changes, and see if those systems will require replacement or upgrading as part of the initial planned replacement or upgrade.
2. Issue a summary list of recommended system replacements or upgrades to the Steering Committee.

SYSTEM SURVEY

1. Determine organization priorities based on long-range planning.
2. Identify key employees of the various functional areas to participate on the information systems project team. Distribute the information system planning materials to help educate team members on the system planning process.
3. Prepare a summary of all currently used software:
   - Operating system
   - Application software
   - Utility software
4. Prepare a summary of all hardware, including:
   - CPUs
   - Terminals
   - Printers
   - Storage devices
   - Communication devices
5. Gather and condense all information from previous system planning sessions and distribute to team members.
6. Distribute and analyze a questionnaire to key system users to obtain their assessment and comments on the current system strengths and weaknesses.
7. Issue report to the Steering Committee for review and approval.

Exhibit 11.8. System Development Procedure

Policy/Procedure Statement Brasto Publishing **Subject: System Development Procedure**	Retrieval No.: Page: Issue Date: Supercedes:	DEV-01 2 of 3 10/28/03 N/A

SYSTEM DESIGN

1. Analyze the various software options and determine which ones make sense. Options include:
   - Custom designed programs
   - Integrated package programs
   - Non-integrated package programs
   - Modified package programs
2. Analyze the various hardware options, including cable and communications needs, and determine which will be included in the investigation.
3. Analyze systems trends in the industry, both administrative and operational.

SYSTEM DEVELOPMENT

1. Identify those application areas where automation will be considered.
2. Prepare general hardware technical specifications, including:
   - Communications qualifications
   - Storage requirements
   - Cabling requirements
   - Current and projected number of users to be supported
   - Networking requirements
   - System administration requirements
   - Required access times and processing speed
3. Prepare general software technical specifications, including:
   - Ease of use
   - Look and feel concerns
   - Accessibility of data
   - Audit trail
   - System security
   - Integration
   - Training and support
4. Prepare application software specifications for each application area.
   - Transaction volume
   - File sizes, both master and transaction
   - Data elements to be maintained
   - Required outputs
   - Functional capabilities required
5. Identify potential system suppliers.
6. Based on the developed system specifications, prepare a request for proposal and send it to each prospective supplier.

Exhibit 11.8. Continued

Policy/Procedure Statement	Retrieval No.:	DEV-01
Brasto Publishing	Page:	3 of 3
	Issue Date:	10/28/03
	Supercedes:	N/A
Subject: System Development Procedure		

7. Complete the supplier evaluation, narrowing the prospective list to 3–5 suppliers. Those selected will be analyzed in detail using the following process:
   - Quantitative analysis
     - Supplier capabilities
     - Software capabilities
     - Cost comparison
     - Delivery time
   - Qualitative analysis
     - System demonstration
     - Supplier reference checks
8. Project team recommendation.
9. Notify selected supplier.

IMPLEMENTATION

1. Working with the system supplier, develop a system implementation plan. Considerations should include:
   - System priorities established during the system survey.
   - Logical ordering required due to the database and file structures of the software.
2. Begin system implementation.

Exhibit 11.8. System Development Procedure (Continued)

11.3 SYSTEM SURVEY FORMS

A significant part of many development projects is the survey of current data processing installations and practices. Depending on the type of information required, the following forms can be used, either in total or individually, to develop a complete picture of a company's computer systems. This information can then be used as background material for the replacement, updating, or consolidation of a company's computer systems. The required forms are:

- *Installation physical layout*. This form is used to sketch the computer room, file storage area, and data entry room. The form shows the adequacy of the rooms used for computer operations.
- *Data processing equipment inventory*. This form is used to indicate the level of sophistication of the current operations and equipment.
- *Other equipment inventory*. This form is used to itemize all other types of equipment used in IT operations.
- *Personnel skill inventory*. This form is used to determine the skill level of all IT personnel.
- *Inquiries*. This form provides some indication of the types of reports used to answer queries, and what types of information were needed and obtained by inquiries from other departments. It also gives an idea of the level of sophistication of communications.
- *Summary of applications*. This form is used to provide a numbered index of the applications found during the survey.
- *Individual application details*. This form is used to provide an overview of the input forms, files, and general processing methods used in each application. It also gives some indication of the general processing requirements of an application. Use one form for each application surveyed.
- *Form survey worksheet*. This form is used to describe each form used by the IT operation. Use one form for each form surveyed.
- *Narrative memorandum of job*. This form is used to describe what each application does.

The forms are illustrated in Exhibits 11.9 through 11.17.

Completing form DP1 - Physical Layout

1. Heading:
   Name of company, agency, or institution.
   Name of data processing department.
   Location of data processing such as building, floor, room number.
   Name of data processing manager or director.
   Name of person preparing the layout form.
   Date the form is completed.

2. Scale. For small areas, one square indicates two square feet; in large areas, four square feet. As a guide for distances, suspended ceiling tiles are usually one square foot, two feet squares, or two by four feet rectangles.

3. Grid: Draw a sketch of the area using the following symbols.

   Wall is solid line.

   Window. W

   Door with direction of opening.

   Support post.

   Electrical outlet. E

   Show data entry areas by outlining such areas with dotted lines. Show areas not used for data processing but in the same room by blocking out such areas.

4. General information.

   Ceiling height. Estimated height in feet.
   Air Conditioning. Indicate yes or no.
   False flooring. Indicate yes or no.
   Supply room adjacent (to computer room). Indicate yes or no.
     If not adjacent, indicate where supply room is located. Enter building, floor, or room number.
   File Storage location. Enter building, floor, room number.
   Special wiring. Indicate yes or no.
   Backup power supply. Indicate yes or no.

5. Area sizes. Enter the approximate square feet of each of the following data processing areas.
   Processing area.
   Data Entry area.
   Supply Room area.
   File Storage area.
   Total square feet of all areas.

6. Provide any other information that may be useful.

Exhibit 11.9. Completing the Physical Layout Form

DP1 **DATA PROCESSING INSTALLATION PHYSICAL LAYOUT** Sketch of area including adjacent storage. SCALE □=______FT. SQ. Include built-in cabinets.	COMPANY DP DEPT. LOCATION NAME OF DP MANAGER PREPARED: BY DATE

CEILING HEIGHT__________________FT.

AIR CONDITIONING YES___ NO___

FALSE FLOORING YES___ NO___

SUPPLY ROOM ADJACENT YES___ NO___

IF NOT, WHERE LOCATED______________

____

FILE STORAGE LOCATION______________

SPECIAL WIRING YES___ NO___

BACKUP POWER SUPPLY YES___ NO___

PROCESSING AREA _____SQ. fT.

DATA ENTRY AREA _____SQ. FT.

SUPPLY ROOM AREA _____SQ. FT.

FILE STORAGE AREA _____SQ. FT.

TOTAL _____SQ. FT.

OTHER PERTINENT INFORMATION

____

____

____

____

Exhibit 11.9. Continued

Completing Form DP2 - Data Processing Equipment Inventory

1. Heading:
   Name of company, agency, or institution.
   Name of data processing department.
   Location of data processing such as building, floor, room number.
   Name of data processing manager or director.
   Name of person preparing the Equipment Inventory form.
   Date the form is completed.

2. Name of Item. Enter name of item such as CPU, tape drives, disk drives, printers, other input or output devices. Also list terminals, PCs, modems, and so on connected to the mainframe by cable, even if in other departments or locations. Do not include fax machines, special file cabinets, work tables, copy machines, or nonprocessing equipment which will be listed on Form DP3, Other Equipment Inventory.

3. Model No. Enter exact model number of each piece of equipment, including letter prefix or suffix.

4. Annual Rent. Complete for each piece of equipment, even if estimated. If purchased outright, indicate this.

5. Special Features and Attachments. Indicate core size, special read features such as optical character recognition (OCR), external switches, special printer carriage widths, and so on.

Exhibit 11.10. Data Processing Equipment Inventory Form

DP2 DATA PROCESSING EQUIPMENT INVENTORY	COMPANY
	DP DEPT.
	LOCATION
	NAME OF DP MANAGER
	PREPARED: BY DATE

NAME OF ITEM	MODEL NO.	ANNUAL RENT	SPECIAL FEATURES AND ATTACHMENTS

Exhibit 11.10. Continued

Completing Form DP3 - Other Equipment Inventory

1. Heading:
   Name of company, agency, or institution.
   Name of data processing department.
   Location of data processing such as building, floor, room number.
   Name of data processing manager or director.
   Name of person preparing the Other Equipment Inventory Form.
   Date the form is completed.

2. Name of Equipment Item. List copy machines, fax machines, typewriters, modems, chairs, tables, cabinets, files, bursters, decollators, and so forth. List the number of telephones, main line and extension.

3. Quantity. Enter quantity of each listed item.

4. Descriptive Data. Enter any special features, model numbers, size, manufacturer, and so forth. List carriage width of typewriters.

Exhibit 11.11. Other Equipment Inventory Form

DP3 DATA PROCESSING OTHER EQUIPMENT INVENTORY	COMPANY DP DEPT. LOCATION NAME OF DP MANAGER PREPARED: BY DATE

NAME OF EQUIPMENT ITEM (Decollators, bursters, copy machines, modems, etc.)	QUANTITY	DESCRIPTIVE DATA (MFR., MODEL NO., SIZE)

Exhibit 11.11. Continued

Completing Form DP4 - Personnel Skill Inventory

1. Heading:
   Name of company, agency, or institution.
   Name of data processing department.
   Location of data processing such as building, floor, room number.
   Name of data processing manager or director.
   Name of person preparing the Personnel Skill Inventory form.
   Date the form is completed.

2. Name of Employee. Enter full name. Also list unfilled established positions.

3. Title (Level). Enter employee title used by personnel or in budget. For government units, list civil service level.

4. Funct. Indicate percent of performance in each of the following job functions:

   OP - Operating
   PR - Programming
   SU - Supervision
   DE - Data Entry
   CL - Clerical
   ST - Staff

   (Example: DE 70%)
   CL 30%)

5. Type. Enter type of position as follows:

   F - Full-time employee
   T - Temporary employee (indicate termination date))
   P - Part-time employee (indicate weekly hours)

6. Sex. Male or female.

7. Yrs. DP. Enter years of experience in data processing. Supervisor may have to estimate in some cases.

8. Highest DP Skill. List the highest data processing skill for each person such as Programmer, Operator, Data Entry, Supervision, System Analyst, and so on. Important secondary skills may be listed.

Note: In some surveys, additional important information may be included, such as budgeted overtime for this department, salaries for all employees and total salaries for the department, including unfilled positions. If substantial changes have been approved but not implemented, this fact should be noted.

Exhibit 11.12. Personnel Skill Inventory Form

DP4

DATA PROCESSING INSTALLATION

PERSONNEL SKILL INVENTORY

COMPANY	
DP DEPT.	
LOCATION	
NAME OF DP MANAGER	
PREPARED: BY	DATE

NAME OF EMPLOYEE	TITLE (LEVEL)	FUNCT.	TYPE	SEX	YRS. DP	HIGHEST DP SKILL

COMMENTS:

Exhibit 11.12. Continued

Completing Form DP5 - Inquiries—Incoming

The purpose of this form is to determine the need for additional telephones, terminals, file clerks, or letter writers, or if the data must be kept at a special location in data processing to answer such inquiries. A high volume would indicate that an online inquiry capability may be desirable.

1. Heading:
   Name of company, agency, or institution.
   Name of user department (may be data processing department).
   Location of data processing such as building, floor, room number.
   Name of department manager or director.
   Name of person preparing the DP5 form.
   Date the form is completed.

2. Requested By: Name of department, division, customer, vendor, or individual making the inquiry. This information is a summary of such inquiries over a period of time (at least a week, preferably one full month) by everyone in the department who answers a telephone or handles mail.

3. Mode. Indicate method of inquiring as follows:

   TEL - telephone inquiry
   MAIL - mail inquiry
   TERM - terminal inquiry
   PER - in-person request (in department or over-the-counter).
   IDC - intra-department correspondence
   FAX - fax machine

4. No. Per Day. Average number per day based on information obtained in item 2 above.

5. File Used for Reply. Indicate as follows:

   Paper file (correspondence file or similar paper form file)
   Computer report
   Terminal (inquiry to computer)
   Microfilm

6. Data Required and How Quickly Answer Is Required. Use one or two words to describe data, such as Customer Number, Vendor Address, Employee Information, Part Number or Description, Telephone Number, Dollar Amount in Account, and so on.

   Time required can be instantly (online?), one hour, same day, within 24 hours, or by outgoing mail.

Exhibit 11.13. Inquiries Form

DP5 DATA PROCESSING INQUIRIES – INCOMING	
	COMPANY
	USER DEPT.
	LOCATION
	NAME OF DEPT. MANAGER
	PREPARED: BY DATE

REQUESTED BY	MODE OF COMMUNICATION	NO. PER DAY	FILE USED FOR REPLY	DATA REQUIRED AND HOW QUICKLY ANSWER IS REQUIRED

Exhibit 11.13. Continued

Completing Form DP5A - Inquiries—Outgoing

The purpose of this form is to determine whether this department needs a master report of some kind (alphabetic customer list with account numbers, account balances, and so on) to replace the need for inquiries to others. A high volume would indicate that an online inquiry capability may be needed.

1. Heading:
   Name of company, agency, or institution.
   Name of user department (may be data processing department).
   Location of data processing such as building, floor, room number.
   Name of department manager or director.
   Name of person preparing the DP5A form.
   Date the form is completed.

2. Request Sent To: Name of department, division, customer, vendor, or individual making the inquiry. This information is a summary of such inquiries over a period of time (at least a week, preferably one full month) by everyone in the department who makes inquiries to outsiders.

3. Mode. Indicate method of inquiring as follows:

   TEL - telephone inquiry
   MAIL - mail inquiry
   TERM - terminal inquiry
   PER - in-person request (to department or over-the-counter).
   IDC - intra-department correspondence
   FAX - fax machine

4. No. Per Day. Average number per day based on information obtained in item 2 above.

5. Data Required and How Quickly Answer Is Required. Use one or two words to describe data, such as Customer Number, Vendor Address, Employee Information, Part Number or Description, Telephone Number, Dollar Amount in Account, and so on.

   Time required can be instantly (online?), one hour, same day, within 24 hours, or by incoming mail.

Exhibit 11.13. Inquiries Form (Continued)

DP5A	COMPANY
DATA PROCESSING	USER DEPT.
	LOCATION
INQUIRIES – OUTGOING	NAME OF DEPT. MANAGER
	PREPARED: BY DATE

REQUEST SENT TO	MODE OF COMMUNICATION	NO. PER DAY	DATA REQUIRED AND HOW QUICKLY ANSWER IS REQUIRED

Exhibit 11.13. Continued

Completing Form DP6 - Summary of Applications

1. Heading:
   Name of company, agency, or institution.
   Name of data processing department.
   Location of data processing such as building, floor, room number.
   Name of department manager or director.
   Name of person preparing the DP6 form.
   Date the form is completed.

2. Summary Reference Number. A consecutive number beginning with "1" assigned to each application reviewed and documented with forms DP7 and DP8.

3. Individual Application Title. A meaningful term describing the application being reviewed. Such terms as "Updating customer files" or "Printing vendor checks" is adequate. It may be helpful to add the department's program number and working name.

Exhibit 11.14. Summary of Applications Form

DP6 DATE PROCESSING INSTALLATION SUMMARY OF APPLICATIONS	COMPANY
	DP DEPT.
	LOCATION
	NAME OF DP MANAGER
	PREPARED: BY DATE

SUMMARY REFERENCE NUMBER	INDIVIDUAL APPLICATION TITLE

COMMENTS:

Exhibit 11.14. Continued

Completing Form DP7 - Individual Application Details

Note: This form can be printed on a 9 by 12 clasp envelope and the Survey Forms placed therein.

1. Heading:
   Summary Reference No. Assign number so that application can be traced from form DP6-Summary of Applications.
   Frequency. Enter average frequency that this job is run, such as daily, weekly, monthly, annually, and so forth.
   Name of data processing manager or director.
   Name of person preparing the DP7 form.
   Date the form is completed.

2. Input:
   A. Survey Form No. One line for each form listed and placed in the envelope with Form DP8-Form Survey Worksheet.
   B. Name of Form. Actual title of form if known, or a simple description such as check, deposit slip, remittance advice, purchase order, and so on.
   C. Method of Input. Enter type of input such as paper, direct terminal entry, floppy disk, magnetic tape, hard disk file, and so forth.
   D. Dept. Form No. Enter, if known.
   E. Average Input Quantity. Approximate number of entries each time this job is run.
   F. Characters per Entry. Average number of characters of the input form used in the processing.
   G. Other. Any other information concerning the input that may be useful.

3. Output:
   A. Survey Form No. One line for each form listed and placed in the envelope with Form DP8-Form Survey Worksheet.
   B. Name of Form or Other Output. Actual title of form, if known, or name of printed report, or name of machine-generated file.
   C. Type of Form. Indicate whether output is paper, printed report, disk file, tape file, or other.
   D. Dept. Form No. If output is a form used by another department, enter the form number such as "AR8-Accounts Receivable Statement."
   E. Average Output Quantity. Approximate number of forms, printed report lines, or transaction records on tape or disk.
   F. Other Information.

4. Files Maintained:
   A. Name of File. Briefly describe each file kept on a current basis.
   B. Type of File. Enter disk, floppy disk, magnetic tape, paper forms, and so on.
   C. Size of File. Emter number of forms, number of transaction records, number of master file records, and so forth.
   D. Basis for Retention or Purging. Estimate the retention or purging time such as "until employee leaves," "until next update," "monthly when summary report is printed," and so forth.

5. Short Job Description:
   Provide a simple general flow chart showing input and output with Survey form numbers. Form DP9 provides a narrative description.

Exhibit 11.15. Individual Application Details Form

DP7 DATA PROCESSING INSTALLATION INDIVIDUAL APPLICATION DETAILS	SUMMARY REFERENCE NO. FREQUENCY
	JOB TITLE
	NAME OF DP MANAGER
	PREPARED: BY DATE

INPUT

SURVEY FORM NO.	NAME OF FORM	METHOD OF INPUT	DEPT. FORM NO.	AVERAGE INPUT QN.	CHAR.PER ENTRY	OTHER
1						
2						
3						
4						
5						

OUTPUT

SURVEY FORM NO.	NAME OF FORM OR OTHER OUTPUT	TYPE OF FORM	DEPT. FORM NO.	AVERAGE OUTPUT QN	OTHER INFORMATION
6					
7					
8					
9					
10					

FILES MAINTAINED

NAME OF FILE	TYPE OF FILE	SIZE OF FILE	BASIS FOR RETENTION (OR PURGING)

SHORT JOB DESCRIPTION:

Exhibit 11.15. Continued

Completing Form DP8 - Form Survey worksheet

An original or a copy of the form being described should be attached to each Form DP8.

1. Heading:
   Enter the Summary Reference Number assigned on Form DP7.
   Enter the Input No. or Output No. assigned on Form DP7.
   Enter name of person providing information about this form. This person may be in data processing or user department.
   Name of person preparing the DP8 form.
   Date the form is completed.

2. Name of Form. Enter the official name of the form or descriptive heading on form.

3. Form No. Enter form number, if known, and date of last revision, if known.

4. Copies and Destination or Use. For each copy of the form (original is copy 1), enter the color of the form and the final destination of that copy or the use of the copy. An example might be an invoice form, as follows:

1	White	To customer
2	Yellow	To Accounts Receivable Department
3	Pink	To Shipping as authorization to ship

5. Is the Form Prenumbered? Check yes or no.

6. Source of Supply. Can be purchased, printed in own print shop, supplied by another department or agency, photocopied in originating department, and so on.

7. Estimated Quantity Used Per Month. Enter quantity determined. Check if this is about the same as the input entries to the data processing application.

8. How is Form Completed. Check method such as handwritten based on personal contact with individual, typewriter, computer output (i.e., turnaround remittance advice), on a terminal or personal computer, or other ways.

9. Remarks. Enter any other information which may be of interest in understanding the application.

Exhibit 11.16. Form Survey Worksheet

DP8 FORM SURVEY WORKSHEET	SUMMARY REFERENCE NO. INPUT NO. ______ OUTPUT NO. ______
	INFORMATION PROVIDED BY:
	PREPARED: BY DATE

NAME OF FORM____

FORM NO.______________DATE OF LAST REVISION, IF KNOWN______________

COPIES AND DESTINATION OR USE:

COPY	COLOR	DESTINATION OR USE
1	____________	______________________________
2	____________	______________________________
3	____________	______________________________
4	____________	______________________________
5	____________	______________________________

IS THE FORM PRENUMBERED? YES___ NO___

SOURCE OF SUPPLY: _____ PURCHASED. NAME OF PRINTER, IF KNOWN______________

_____ OWN PRINT SHOP

_____ FROM ANOTHER DEPARTMENT. WHICH______________

_____ OTHER. DESCRIBE______________

ESTIMATED QUANTITY USED PER MONTH ____________

ORIGINATING DEPARTMENT______________________________

HOW IS FORM COMPLETED:
___ HANDWRITTEN
___ TYPEWRITER
___ COMPUTER OUTPUT
___ TERMINAL OR PERSONAL COMPUTER
___ OTHER ______________________________

REMARKS:____

____

ATTACH ORIGINAL OR COPY OF FORM

Exhibit 11.16. Continued

DP9 NARRATIVE MEMORANDUM OF JOB	SUMMARY REFERENCE NO.
	JOB : DESCRIPTION:
	PREPARED BY: DATE:

The surveyor should indicate in brief, narrative form, what the job consists of and whether there are any requirements that would be difficult to fulfill if application is moved. Also whether, in his or her opinion, the job is suitable for processing at another location, and, if not, why not?

Exhibit 11.17. Narrative Memorandum of Job Form

11.4 INFORMATION TECHNOLOGY POLICIES

Many IT departments do not have any policies that control the manner in which their development projects are managed, which can lead to considerable inefficiencies in their completion, if they are completed at all. This section contains policies for the establishment of a project charter, the establishment of work plans, job responsibilities, and so on that are the foundation of a properly managed development system. These policies can be used as the core set of policy statements for the IT development function.

Policy/Procedure Statement	Retrieval No.:	ITPOL-01
Brasto Publishing	Page:	1 of 1
	Issue Date:	10/28/0X
Subject: Project Charter Standards	Supercedes:	N/A

Policy: A project charter will be created and approved for all approved IT projects.

Objectives/Benefits: The development of a project charter will:

- Document the project's description for a variety of perspectives and thus facilitate more effective project planning.
- Define a baseline project scope and thus facilitate project scope management and control.
- Gain up-front approval of the project by the project sponsor and thus facilitate improved expectation setting.

Development of Initial Charter:

- The IT Project Charter Template is used to initiate development of a project-specific charter. This template includes basic project charter elements but can be expanded on as deemed necessary to more fully describe/define a project.
- The project manager is responsible for project charter development.

Approval of Initial Project Charter:

- At a minimum, the project charter is to be approved, via signature, by the IT director, project sponsor, and project manager.

Maintenance of Project Charter:

- The project manager is responsible for maintaining the project charter. It should be modified during the course of the project to reflect any materially significant changes to the project (i.e., reference to approved project scope change requests).
- Any approved project scope change requests become a de facto part of the project charter.

Project Charter Standards

Policy/Procedure Statement Brasto Publishing **Subject: Work Plan Standards**	Retrieval No.: Page: Issue Date: Supercedes:	ITPOL-02 1 of 1 10/28/0X N/A

Policy: A work plan will be developed and maintained for all approved IT projects using the defined standards.

Standard Work Plan Tool: Microsoft Project

Initial Work Plan Development:

- The project manager is responsible for initial work plan development.
- An initial work plan is developed in conjunction with project charter development.
- The IT Project Work Plan Template is used to initiate development of a project-specific work plan. This template includes basic project management-related work plan elements (e.g., project start-up activities, ongoing project management activities, and concluding project activities) that should be part of every project plan. The template has also been used to establish standards for work plan formats such as the timescale format.
- Work plans are to be created using a multitiered work breakdown structure (e.g., phases, activities, tasks) to facilitate work effort organization and planning.
- Where appropriate, dependencies should be created between work structure elements.
- The lowest level of work breakdown structure should never have a duration of more than five days—tasks that exceed this parameter should be further broken down.
- There must be at least one milestone associated with each hierarchical set of tasks.
- Work plans are to be stored in the project's electronic knowledge repository.

Baselining a Work Plan: A project's baseline represents the initial view of the project that can then be tracked against its actual ongoing course. The actual dates can be compared to the baseline dates to see where a project varied from its original plan.

- All work plans are to be baselined.
- A baseline should be created after a plan has been initially built, but before any execution of the plan begins.

Maintenance of the Work Plan:

- The project manager is responsible for work plan maintenance.
- Project work plans, at a minimum, should be updated weekly to support project status reporting needs. Specifically, the following maintenance should be completed:
    - Update the percent complete data.
    - Adjust the start date/duration of tasks to accurately reflect actual and planned work effort.
    - Update task resources to reflect any planned resource-related changes.

Work Plan Standards

Policy/Procedure Statement	Retrieval No.:	ITPOL-03
Brasto Publishing	Page:	1 of 1
	Issue Date:	10/28/0X
	Supercedes:	N/A
Subject: Project Team Roles and Responsibilities		

Business/Systems

- Assesses current systems

Analyst

- Develops and maintains models of business requirements
- Participates in evaluation of software solutions
- Participates in development of implementation strategies and plans
- Participates in execution of implementation strategies and plans

Key User

- Provides source information to the team
- Provides expert business understanding of the organization
- Represents the user area in identifying current or future requirements
- Represents the user area in evaluating potential solutions
- Represents the user area in developing implementation strategies and plans

Project Manager

- Overall project management responsibility
- Review and approve intermediate work products
- Develops and maintains project charter and project plans
- Updates IT director and project sponsor on project progress
- Tracks and disposes of issues
- Helps resolve issues and change requests
- Tracks action items and budgets

Project Sponsor

- Controls the business aspects of the project
- Assists in developing the project charter and project plans
- Executes formal reviews and management reviews
- Disposes of issues and change requests
- Makes user resources available
- Approves work products
- Responsible for functional quality of the solution

Technical Specialist

- Acts as a specialist in one or more particular technologies (e.g., operating system, database technology, communications technology, programming language)
- Provides expertise in applying leading edge technologies in process innovation/reengineering projects.

Project Team Roles and Responsibilities

Policy/Procedure Statement Brasto Publishing **Subject: Risk Management Standards**	Retrieval No.: Page: Issue Date: Supercedes:	ITPOL-04 1 of 1 10/28/0X N/A

Policy: All approved IT projects will follow the defined risk management process.

Definition of a Project Risk: A characteristic or circumstance of the project, or a feature of its environment that is recognized to have a potentially adverse effect on the project or the quality of its deliverables. When determining the material significance of a specific risk, both the risk probability (estimated likelihood that it will occur) and the risk severity (if risk occurs, estimated extent of its negative impact on the project) should be taken into consideration.

Definition of Risk Management: A means of minimizing the likelihood and impact of a known project risk. Risk management actions should be preventive and proactive. Every project has an inherent amount of risk. Risk management is the process of identifying the materially significant risks; implementing strategies to mitigate/manage them; and designing contingency plans to supplement those strategies should the risk actually begin to affect project success. Risk management is all about increasing the probability of project success.

Risk Management Process:

- The project manager is responsible for the risk management process.
- The Project Risk Assessment Template should be used as a starting point to conduct the initial and subsequent periodic risk assessments—the assessment template should be appropriately enhanced to reflect the types of risks a specific project may be facing.
- Identified key project risks and their corresponding mitigation/management should be included as part of the project charter.

Policy/Procedure Statement Brasto Publishing **Subject: Project Status Reporting Standards**	Retrieval No.: Page: Issue Date: Supercedes:	ITPOL-05 1 of 1 10/28/0X N/A

Policy: Weekly status reporting is required on all approved IT projects via the IT Project Scorecard. The weekly status period will be defined as Monday through Friday. Scorecards are to be developed for each status period by no later than two workdays following the end of the period.

Development of Project Status Reports:

- The project manager is responsible for project status reporting.
- The IT Project Scorecard template is used to initiate development of project-specific status reports. The template is composed of the following sections:
  - *Header Information*—This section is used to title the scorecard:
    - Project Name
    - Week Ending Date
    - Project Sponsor
    - Project Manager
  - *Project Health at a Glance*—This section is used to provide a high-level assessment of a project's "health" from the following perspectives:
    - Budget: Is the project's budget at risk of being exceeded? (Yes/No)
    - Schedule: Is the project's current schedule at risk of not being met? (Yes/No)
    - Quality: Is the quality of any project deliverable at risk? (Yes/No)
    - Team: Is the project team at risk for any reason? (Yes/No)

  If a "Yes" is reported for any project health element, a corresponding issue must be reported (see next).
  - *Issues/Risks, Mitigation of*—This section is used to document any key issues and/or risks facing the project (i.e., those that have put the project's budget, schedule, quality, and/or team at risk) and what mitigation strategy is being used to address the issue/risk.
  - *Milestone Progress*—This section is used to document the key milestone-related accomplishments of the reporting period and upcoming planned accomplishments.
  - *Project Metrics*—This section is used to display any key project-related metrics and/or the project's milestones; the type of project will determine what is appropriate to include in this section. Some potential elements include:
    - *Milestone View of Work Plan*—presents the milestone view of the project work plan for a date range appropriate to the reporting period.
    - *Budget Planned versus Actual Information*—graphical depiction of the current status of a project's budget.
    - *Achieved*—graphical depiction of project-specific achievement (current and planned).
  - *Project Dates*—This section shows the project's start date and its currently defined end date.

Project Status Reporting Standards

Policy/Procedure Statement Brasto Publishing **Subject: Issue Management Standards**	Retrieval No.: Page: Issue Date: Supercedes:	ITPOL-06 1 of 1 10/28/0X N/A

Policy: All approved IT projects will follow the defined issue management process.

Definition of Issue: An issue is any formally defined matter that may impede the project's progress and about which no agreement/resolution has yet been reached.

Benefits of Issue Management: Effective issue management allows for:

- A visible decision-making process
- A means of reaching consensus on questions concerning the project
- A project audit trail

Issue Management Process:

- The project manager is responsible for the issue management process.
- The Issues Log Template is used to document all issues and their resolutions, including identification of "key" decision makers.
- If issues evolve into scope change requests, the appropriate scope change management standards should be followed.

Issue Management Standards

Policy/Procedure Statement	Retrieval No.:	ITPOL-07
Brasto Publishing	Page:	1 of 1
	Issue Date:	10/28/0X
	Supercedes:	N/A
Subject: Project Completion Debriefing Standards		

Policy: All approved IT projects will follow the defined project completion debriefing process at their conclusion.

Purpose/Benefits of the Completion Debriefing Process: The basic purpose of the project completion debriefing process is to document what worked well and what could have been improved on and why in order to:

- Gain customer feedback to facilitate enhanced future customer service.
- Document lessons learned so they can be shared and applied to both ongoing and future IT projects.
- Support the performance management/evaluation process of IT personnel.

Project Completion Debriefing Process:

- The project manager is responsible for the project completion debriefing process.
- The Project Debriefing Template is used as a starting point for the debriefing process. It should be enhanced to address any additional project-specific elements.
- A project completion debriefing session is the primary vehicle for completion of the debriefing process. Key employees who should be in attendance are:
    - Project Sponsor
    - Project Manager
    - IT Director
    - Key Project Team Members

  The purpose of this session is to identify constructive lessons learned—what went well and what could have gone better and why. All session participants should be provided the project-specific debriefing template before the session so they come prepared to contribute.

- The project completion debriefing documentation becomes part of the project's knowledge repository.

Project Completion Debriefing Standards

11.5 INFORMATION TECHNOLOGY PROCEDURES

The controller or CFO should include a number of procedures in the accounting manual for dealing with the most common information technology issues. This section includes three flowcharts for the most common clusters of computer-related activities: the processing of daily computer maintenance transactions, the completion of the programming cycle, and the setup of new employees with computers. It is very useful to first create process flows for all major work flows so that one can ensure that all possible procedures have been described. These flowcharts are noted in Exhibits 11.18 through 11.20.

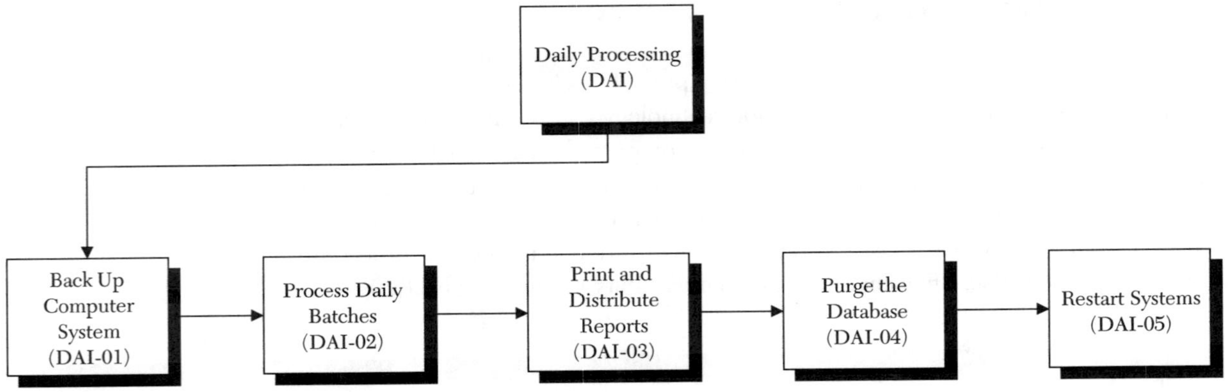

Exhibit 11.18. Process Flow for Daily Computer Maintenance Transactions

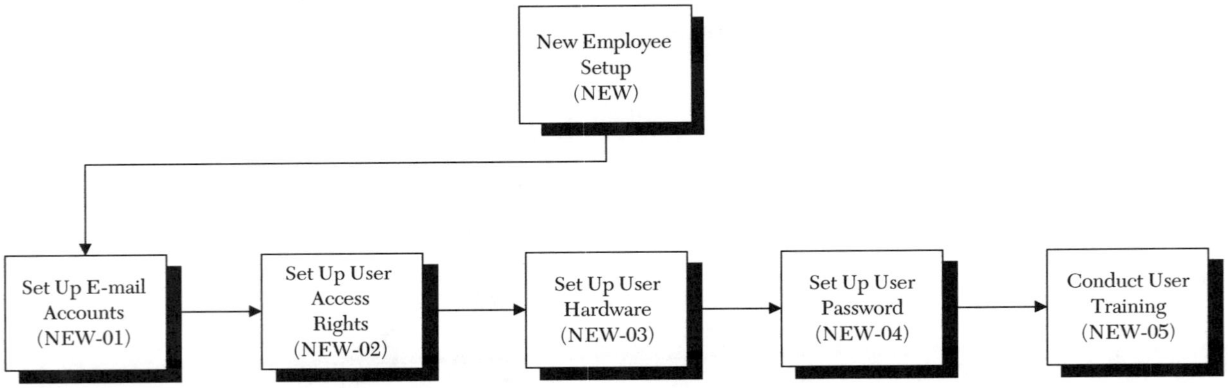

Exhibit 11.19. Process Flow for the Setup of New Employees with Computers

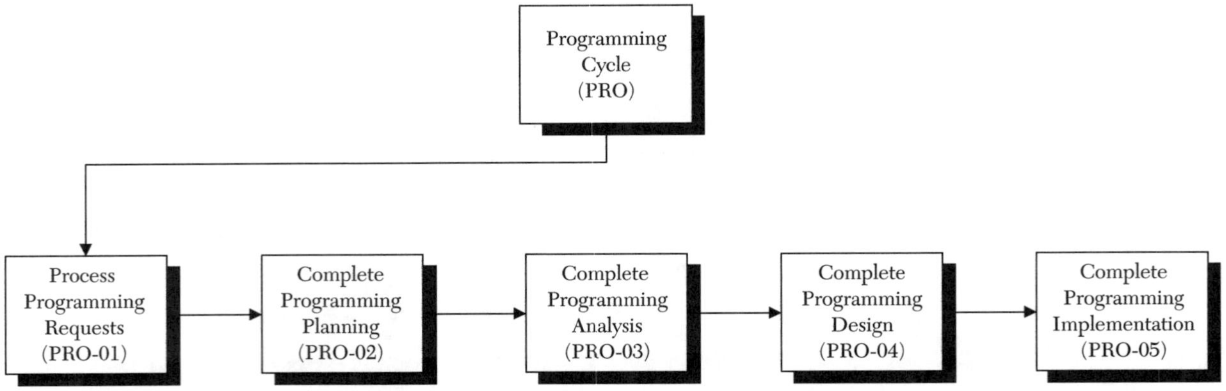

Exhibit 11.20. Process Flow for the Completion of the Programming Cycle

The next step is to create the procedures referenced in the process flowcharts. They are itemized through the remainder of this chapter. The retrieval number listed in the bottom of each square in the process flowcharts corresponds to the procedure number listed in the top right corner of the header block in each procedure; this makes it easy for the reader to find a procedure in the flowcharts and quickly reference the detail based on the procedure numbers. The complete list of detailed procedures listed in this section is:

1. **Daily computer maintenance transactions (DAI)**
   - Backup computer system (DAI-01)
   - Process daily batches (DAI-02)
   - Print and distribute reports (DAI-03)
   - Purge the database (DAI-04)
   - Restart systems (DAI-05)
2. **New employee setup (NEW)**
   - Set up e-mail account (NEW-01)
   - Set up user access rights (NEW-02)
   - Set up user hardware (NEW-03)
   - Set up user password (NEW-04)
   - Conduct user training (NEW-05)
3. **Programming cycle (PRO)**
   - Process programming requests (PRO-01)
   - Complete programming planning (PRO-02)
   - Complete programming analysis (PRO-03)
   - Complete programming design (PRO-04)
   - Complete programming implementation (PRO-05)
4. **Unrelated procedures (UNR)**
   - Conduct basic e-mail operations (UNR-01)
   - Maintain computer system security (UNR-02)
   - Restore backups to the computer system (UNR-03)

These procedures are simplified versions of actual procedures, and so will require some enhancement in most cases. However, they can be used as the basic operational template for a set of more detailed computer system procedures for most companies, if information is added regarding specific file and screen names that fit one's specific applications.

Policy/Procedure Statement	Procedure No.:	DAI-01
Brasto Publishing	Page:	1 of 1
	Issue Date:	10/28/0X
Subject: Back Up Computer System	Supercedes:	N/A

1. PURPOSE AND SCOPE

This procedure is used by the computer systems coordinator to administer daily backups of the computer system.

2. RESPONSIBILITIES

MIS COORD **MIS Coordinator**

3. PROCEDURES

3.1 MIS COORD

Remove and Store Backup Tapes

1. Go to the tape backup box, located next to the mini-computer. Remove the tape from the backup box and insert it back into the protective plastic sleeve located next to the box.
2. Take this tape home for storage. The tape already being stored at home is now from the previous day's backup. Take this older tape back to the office and store it in the company safe.
3. There will already be an older tape in the company safe, which is from the backup that occurred two days ago. Take this tape out of the safe and move it to the tape storage file, which is located in the computer room.

3.2 MIS COORD

Identify a New Tape for the Next Backup

There are tape backups in the tape storage box for two weeks of backups. The backups are used in sequence. To identify the next tape to be used for backup, look at the day and week marked on the tape that was just used, and select the next tape in sequence from that one. No backups are conducted for the weekend, so there are no tapes in the storage box for those days.

3.3 MIS COORD

Start Next Backup

Put the new tape into the backup box and close the lid. Wait for the device to interrogate the new tape. If the READY light on the box flashes green, the tape is usable. If it flashes red, then remove the tape and dispose of it; obtain a new tape and insert it into the backup box.

3.4 MIS COORD

Changes to the Backup Program

It may sometimes be necessary to alter the time at which the backup software runs. To make this change, go to the BACKUP subdirectory and click on the "Backup" command. Click on the "Time Change" icon and type in the new time at which you want the backup to run. To keep the software from running at all, click on the "Activate" box in the same screen so that the checkmark in that box no longer appears.

Policy/Procedure Statement Brasto Publishing **Subject: Process Daily Batches**	Retrieval No.: Page: Issue Date: Supercedes:	DAI-02 1 of 2 10/28/0X N/A

1. PURPOSE AND SCOPE

This procedure is used by the MIS coordinator to run the daily batch processing jobs that are part of the normal operations of the computer services center.

2. RESPONSIBILITIES

MIS COORD — **MIS Coordinator**

3. PROCEDURES

3.1 MIS COORD — **Identify Batches to Run**

Go to the BATCHES.XLS file that is updated by the programming staff each day, and print out the listing of batches that must be run. Verify any program flags that must be set for each batch, and note the order in which they must be run. Print the report.

3.2 MIS COORD — **Notify Users of Downtime**

Send an e-mail to all computer users, informing them of the time of day when the system will be taken down for batch processing. The message should also include the time when the system is expected to come back up for use, as well as which portions of the software will be inaccessible while the batch processing is occurring.

3.3 MIS COORD — **Schedule Batch Processing**

Note the processing time on the BATCHES.XLS report and issue it to the night processing staff. Leave an extra e-mail for the processing staff to describe any special processing requirements.

3.4 MIS COORD — **Run Batch Processing**

The night processing staff runs the batch processes identified by the programming staff, using the recommended start time. If previous processing runs longer than expected, the processing staff must send an e-mail to all logged-in users, informing them of a delay in the batch processing.

Process Daily Batches (1 of 2)

Policy/Procedure Statement Brasto Publishing **Subject: Process Daily Batches**	Retrieval No.: Page: Issue Date: Supercedes:	DAI-02 2 of 2 10/28/0X N/A

3.5 MIS COORD

Verify Completion of Batch Processes

The night processing staff prints all error logs after the batches have completed their processing. Keep only those reports showing errors.

3.6 MIS COORD

Notify Programming Staff of Batch Problems

The night processing staff forwards all error log printouts containing errors to the programming staff. The night processing staff also keeps a copy of all errors in a separate file, in case the original error log is lost by or is in transit to the programming staff.

Process Daily Batches (2 of 2)

Policy/Procedure Statement	Retrieval No.:	DAI-03
Brasto Publishing	Page:	1 of 1
	Issue Date:	10/28/0X
	Supercedes:	N/A
Subject: Print and Distribute Reports		

1. PURPOSE AND SCOPE

This procedure is used by the computer systems coordinator to determine which reports to print each day, as well as how to do so and to whom the reports must then be distributed.

2. RESPONSIBILITIES

MIS COORD — **MIS Coordinator**

3. PROCEDURES

3.1 MIS COORD — **Review Report Calendar**

1. Access the reports calendar, which lists all reports to be printed by day of the month.
2. Print out the report calendar for the following day's reports and highlight the report identification numbers for all the reports to be printed in the evening report printing batch.

3.2 MIS COORD — **Adjust Print Job for Scheduled Reports**

Access the PRINT.BAT file in the computer system and enter the report identification numbers highlighted on the report calendar in the previous step. Review it for errors and then save the file.

3.3 MIS COORD — **Print Scheduled Reports**

1. Go to the BATCH menu in the software and access the REPORTS option. Set the scheduled print start date for today, and the start time to 11:00 PM.
2. The evening computer system operator takes the reports from the printer and compares them to the reports listed on the report calendar to ensure that all reports have been completed. If not, readjust the PRINT.BAT file for the reports that must be reprinted and rerun the print batch file.

3.4 MIS COORD — **Distribute Scheduled Reports**

Using the distribution list on the reports calendar, issue all scheduled reports to employees.

Print and Distribute Reports

Policy/Procedure Statement	Retrieval No.:	DAI-04
Brasto Publishing	Page:	1 of 1
	Issue Date:	10/28/0X
	Supercedes:	N/A
Subject: Purge the Database		

1. PURPOSE AND SCOPE

This procedure is used by the MIS coordinator to purge old or unneeded data from the computer system.

2. RESPONSIBILITIES

MIS COORD **MIS Coordinator**

3. PROCEDURES

3.1 MIS COORD **Review List of Files to Purge**

Review the list of files to be purged, as was noted the last time a purge was conducted. Include the database administrator in this review to see if there are any inordinately large files that should be added to the list.

3.2 MIS COORD **Determine Purge Date**

Work with the database administrator and computer systems staff to determine the best date on which to conduct a database purge, based on the needs of other employees who are using the system.

3.3 MIS COORD **Determine Archiving Method**

Review the current archiving method with the database administrator. Determine if this is an appropriate method to continue using, based on the archiving time required, cost of the archiving method, and ability to retrieve information from the archived information. If a new method is decided on, test the new archiving system before making it part of the standard archiving process.

3.4 MIS COORD **Notify Users of Purge**

Notify users of the files to be purged, the date range to be deleted, and the time when the purge will take place. Give them a name or e-mail address to contact in case they have an objection to any of the proposed file deletions.

3.5 MIS COORD **Conduct System Purge**

Archive the files to be deleted and verify that the files have been successfully recorded on the storage media. Do a sample restore of a selection of files to verify that the archiving was a success. Then delete the files from the main database. Verify that the files have been deleted.

Purge the Database

Policy/Procedure Statement Brasto Publishing **Subject: Restart Systems**	Retrieval No.: Page: Issue Date: Supercedes:	DAI-05 1 of 1 10/28/0X N/A

1. PURPOSE AND SCOPE

This procedure is used by the computer systems coordinator to restart the computer systems for user access, once the evening batch processing has been completed.

2. RESPONSIBILITIES

MIS COORD **MIS Coordinator**

3. PROCEDURES

3.1 MIS COORD **Review Batch Processing Checklist**

1. Print out the batch processing list, which is located in N:\FILES\ BATCH.DOC.
2. Access the LOG.BAT file in the N:\LOG subdirectory and verify that all batches processed match those listed in the batch processing list.
3. Itemize any differences between the two lists, and e-mail this information to the system administrator.

3.2 MIS COORD **Restart Systems**

1. Access the RESTART screen, which is located under the SYSTEM OPERATIONS menu.
2. Enter the restart date as NOW and the restart time as NOW.
3. Press ENTER.
4. Once the restart is complete, verify that all systems are operational. If not, page the system administrator.

3.3 MIS COORD **Issue User Alert Regarding Restart**

Once the restart has been confirmed, go to e-mail and send a universal message to all users, notifying them that the system is now available for use.

Policy/Procedure Statement Brasto Publishing **Subject: Set Up E-Mail Accounts**	Retrieval No.: Page: Issue Date: Supercedes:	NEW-01 1 of 1 10/28/0X N/A

1. PURPOSE AND SCOPE

This procedure is used by the computer systems coordinator to set up new e-mail accounts.

2. RESPONSIBILITIES

MIS COORD **MIS Coordinator**

3. PROCEDURES

3.1 MIS COORD **Create an E-Mail Account**

1. Right-click on the Start button. Then press the Open, Programs, Applications commands.
2. Access the File, New, Shortcut, Browser commands.
3. Go to Windows Explorer and access the EMAIL.EXE file. Rename it "email".
4. Right-click on the new file, copy it, and paste it into the STARTUP menu.
5. Go to the user's AUTOEXEC.BAT file and add "SET MEAS = YES" to the file.
6. Go to the e-mail menu and access NEW USER. Enter the user identification.
7. Enter the user's full name.
8. Inform the system administrator that the person should be given access rights.
9. Write a memo to the new e-mail user, telling this person his or her user ID and describing how to access and use the e-mail system.

Policy/Procedure Statement Brasto Publishing **Subject: Set Up User Access Rights**	Retrieval No.: Page: Issue Date: Supercedes:	NEW-02 1 of 1 10/28/0X N/A

1. PURPOSE AND SCOPE

This procedure is used by the computer systems coordinator to determine the correct set of access privileges for each user, as well as the steps required to create those privileges in the computer system.

2. RESPONSIBILITIES

MIS COORD — **MIS Coordinator**

3. PROCEDURES

3.1 MIS COORD — **Determine Access Rights by Position**

Go to the Network Access Rights section in the Security Manual and find the network access rights for the position level of the person for whom computer access is being granted. Copy the access rights. Also go to the Application Software Access Rights section of the Security Manual and extract the same data from there, except that this is for application software access.

3.2 MIS COORD — **Create Network Access Rights**

1. Go to the network OPERATIONAL APPLICATIONS screen and set up the user's identification code with the same group access code used for everyone else with the same job description.
2. If this is a new job description for which no group access code has previously been constructed, go to the CONSTRUCT GROUP CODE screen and create the access restrictions for the new position. Then return to the first step to complete the network access entry.

3.3 MIS COORD — **Create Application Software Access Rights**

Go to the application software SECURITY screen and set up the user's identification code with the specific screen and field access privileges noted in the Security Manual. Be sure to verify that each screen has the correct "read/write" or "read only" access privileges.

3.4 MIS COORD — **Notify User of Access Rights**

Send a copy of the access privileges from the Security Manual to the user by interoffice mail.

Set Up User Access Rights

Policy/Procedure Statement	Retrieval No.:	NEW-03
Brasto Publishing	Page:	1 of 1
	Issue Date:	10/28/0X
Subject: Set Up User Hardware	Supercedes:	N/A

1. PURPOSE AND SCOPE

This procedure is used by the computer systems coordinator to determine the appropriate types of computer hardware required for each user, based on the type of position occupied, as well as where to obtain the hardware.

2. RESPONSIBILITIES

MIS COORD **MIS Coordinator**

3. PROCEDURES

3.1 MIS COORD **Define Hardware Requirements**

1. Go to the Hardware Requirements Manual and look up the standard hardware configuration for the user's job title.
2. If there is no standard configuration, then e-mail the company's minimum configuration to the user's supervisor to see if this is acceptable.
3. Enter the supervisor's recommended configuration in the electronic version of the Hardware Requirements Manual.

3.2 MIS COORD **Compare Requirements to Available Hardware**

Itemize the list of hardware from the preceding step and compare it to the inventory of hardware currently on hand. If some parts are missing, note them on a purchase requisition form, including part numbers and the name of the supplier.

3.3 MIS COORD **Order Hardware**

1. Turn the requisition form in to the purchasing department. Obtain from this department the approximate dates when all parts are expected to be received, as well as the cost of the parts.
2. Manually summarize the cost of all hardware and subtract this from the computer services department's computer hardware budget.
3. If there is no funding left in the budget, notify the controller of the problem, as well as the supervisor of the department where the hardware is to be used.

3.4 MIS COORD **Notify User of Installation Date**

1. E-mail the user who is to receive the computer hardware and notify this person of the expected date when the hardware will be installed, as well as the latest possible installation date.
2. If the user needs hardware sooner, review the situation with the supervisor of the user's department to see if a partial set of equipment can be delivered sooner.

3.5 MIS COORD **Install Hardware**

1. Once the hardware arrives, compare the packing slips for the newly received equipment to the items listed on the requisition form to ensure that the same equipment that was ordered was actually shipped.
2. Assemble all computer equipment and test it to ensure that all components are functional.
3. Load and test any needed application software, using the site license for each application.
4. Move the equipment to the user's location, assemble it, and test it to ensure that the entire system works correctly.

Set Up User Hardware

Policy/Procedure Statement Brasto Publishing **Subject: Set Up User Password**	Retrieval No.: Page: Issue Date: Supercedes:	NEW-04 1 of 1 10/28/0X N/A

1. PURPOSE AND SCOPE

This procedure describes how to set up a password in the computer system for a user.

2. RESPONSIBILITIES

MIS COORD **MIS Coordinator**

3. PROCEDURES

3.1 MIS COORD **Obtain Desired Password from User**

Ask the user for a password that is of the required system length of no less than five characters. Write down the password.

3.2 MIS COORD **Set Up Password in Computer System**

Access the computer software and the PASS screen. Enter the user's identification code. This is the person's first initial and first four letters of his or her last name. If there is already a person with this identification code in the system, replace the last digit with a number. Then enter the password and verify it by entering it again in the next field. Set the automatic password replacement requirement to one month so the user is forced to change the password at regular intervals.

3.3 MIS COORD **Inform the User**

Go to Word and access the SECURITY.DOC menu. Enter the user's identification code and password in the memo. Print the memo, put it in a sealed envelope, and have it delivered to the user through interoffice mail.

Set Up User Password

Policy/Procedure Statement	Retrieval No.:	NEW-05
Brasto Publishing	Page:	1 of 1
	Issue Date:	10/28/0X
Subject: Conduct User Training	Supercedes:	N/A

1. PURPOSE AND SCOPE

This procedure is used by the computer systems coordinator to determine the correct types of training to give users, as well as where to obtain training materials.

2. RESPONSIBILITIES

MIS COORD **MIS Coordinator**

3. PROCEDURES

3.1 MIS COORD **Determine User Training Requirements**

1. Go to the Training Summary Manual and extract the list of training classes needed for the user, based on that person's job description.
2. Look up the class training dates for the required classes.
3. If classes will not be offered, block out training dates for one-on-one training.

3.2 MIS COORD **Notify User of Training Dates**

1. E-mail the user the list of training classes and their dates, as well as any secondary dates for which classes are offered.
2. If classes will not be offered, also e-mail on-site training dates and times.
3. Verify that the user has scheduled the training dates.

3.3 MIS COORD **Obtain Training Materials**

1. Go to the training department's intranet site that contains electronic copies of all required training materials. Download this information.
2. Print the downloaded files and also forward it to the user, either by e-mail or interoffice mail.
3. Review the materials for recommended trainer study information and review this before conducting training.

3.4 MIS COORD **Train User**

1. Conduct training with the user.
2. Evaluate the user's grasp of the information and notify the user's supervisor of comprehension issues requiring additional training.

3.5 MIS COORD **Record Completed Training in Training Log**

Enter the user's completion data in the company training log, which is located at N:\TRAINING\LOG.

Policy/Procedure Statement		
Brasto Publishing	Retrieval No.:	PRO-01
	Page:	1 of 1
	Issue Date:	10/28/0X
	Supercedes:	N/A
Subject: Process Programming Requests		

1. PURPOSE AND SCOPE

This procedure is used by the computer systems coordinator to sort through and prioritize any programming requests submitted by employees.

2. RESPONSIBILITIES

MIS COORD **MIS Coordinator**

3. PROCEDURES

3.1 MIS COORD **Log In All Programming Requests**

When a user submits a request for programming, have the person fill out a "Programming Request" form and review it with the user to ensure that all information is complete. Give a copy of the form to the programming staff for a determination of costs and duration.

3.2 MIS COORD **Summarize All Programming Requests**

Enter a brief description of the proposed programming request into the PROGRAMS.XLS spreadsheet. File the original request form for later use.

3.3 MIS COORD **Determine Costs and Durations for Requests**

Obtain the programming staff's estimate of the project's cost and time duration, and enter this information into the summary spreadsheet. Issue this spreadsheet to all members of the management committee at least two days in advance of the next scheduled meeting.

3.4 MIS COORD **Submit Programming Requests for Prioritization**

Go to the management committee and answer any questions the committee members may have regarding each of the requested projects. Strike off any projects the committee rejects and assign the committee's priorities to the remaining ones.

3.5 MIS COORD **Insert New Priorities into Department Priorities List**

Insert the added programming tasks into the existing set of department projects. Notify the accounting department of any likely cost changes for which budget requests will be submitted. Also, notify the personnel department of any upcoming personnel hires that will be requested as a result of the new programming projects.

3.6 MIS COORD **Notify the Requestor of Management Approval**

Notify the project requestor that the programming request has been approved. Include the most likely time of completion and the cost the requestor will be charged for the programming work.

Process Programming Requests

Policy/Procedure Statement Brasto Publishing **Subject: Complete Programming Planning**	Retrieval No.: Page: Issue Date: Supercedes:	PRO-02 1 of 2 10/28/0X N/A

1. PURPOSE AND SCOPE

This procedure is used by the computer systems coordinator to integrate the overall computer systems strategy into a review of current capabilities and operations for use in constructing plans for programming development.

2. RESPONSIBILITIES

MIS COORD **MIS Coordinator**

3. PROCEDURES

3.1 MIS COORD **Prepare for Project**

1. Determine the scope of the project by obtaining a summary-level requirements listing from the user and determining the number of functional areas that will be impacted by the change.
2. Based on the project scope, make a rough estimate of the man-hours and cost required to complete the project, as well as an estimated completion date.

3.2 MIS COORD **Determine Project Requirements and Issues**

1. Gather additional information about the project, both from one-on-one interviews and group sessions with the most knowledgeable users.
2. Based on this additional input, specify the project's goals, as well as all problems that have been identified through this first limited round of data gathering.

3.3 MIS COORD **Assess Current Information Systems**

1. Identify the flow of data in the current systems that will be impacted by the new project.
2. Identify the geographic locations that will be impacted by the new project.
3. Identify those parts of the organizational structure that will be impacted by the new project.
4. Summarize this information.

3.4 MIS COORD **Gather and Analyze Operations Information**

Interview users regarding the current flow of operations in the areas impacted by the new project. This involves all information flows, including those not necessarily using the current computer system. Be sure to include all paper flows.

Complete Programming Planning (1 of 2)

Policy/Procedure Statement Brasto Publishing **Subject: Complete Programming Planning**	Retrieval No.: Page: Issue Date: Supercedes:	PRO-02 2 of 2 10/28/0X N/A

3.5 MIS COORD

Develop Cost/Benefit Analysis

1. Based on the additional information collected, determine the approximate cost of the analysis, design, and programming work required to complete the project.
2. Based on the changes in functionality so far uncovered through additional analysis, determine the cost savings that will result from completing and using the new system.
3. Calculate the payback period and net present value of the project based on the stream of estimated cash inflows and outflows.

3.6 MIS COORD

Complete Project Plan

1. Combine the cost/benefit analysis, system requirements, and issues into a planning report.
2. Gain signed approval from the project sponsor.

Complete Programming Planning (2 of 2)

Policy/Procedure Statement	Retrieval No.:	PRO-03
Brasto Publishing	Page:	1 of 1
	Issue Date:	10/28/0X
	Supercedes:	N/A
Subject: Complete Programming Analysis		

1. PURPOSE AND SCOPE

This procedure is used by the computer systems coordinator to determine the requirements needed for a programming project, as well as to explore the possibility of acquiring a software package that fulfills the requested needs.

2. RESPONSIBILITIES

MIS COORD — MIS Coordinator

3. PROCEDURES

3.1 MIS COORD — **Estimate the Analysis Phase Workload**

Based on the additional information collected from previous procedures, determine the remaining cost of the analysis, programming, and implementation phases of the project.

3.2 MIS COORD — **Complete Data Flow and Entity Relationship Diagrams**

1. Form a project team that includes process experts, experienced users, and systems analysts.
2. Create data flow diagrams based on the required new processes.
3. Create entity relationship diagrams based on the data listed in the data flow diagrams.

3.3 MIS COORD — **Select Software Package**

1. If a software package is part of the solution, then create a requirements package of features needed.
2. Create a list of qualified software package suppliers.
3. Send the requirements package to the supplier list, with a request for responses by a specified due date.
4. Develop a rating system for scoring supplier responses.
5. Evaluate supplier responses and rank the software packages.

3.4 MIS COORD — **Negotiate Contract with Supplier**

1. Itemize contractual issues.
2. Negotiate changes with the supplier.
3. Finalize and sign the contract.

3.5 MIS COORD — **Complete Screen and Report Designs**

1. Create prototype screens with user input.
2. Gain screen design approval from the user group.
3. Create prototype reports with user input.
4. Gain report design approval from the user group.

3.6 MIS COORD — **Estimate Programming Costs and Lead Times**

Estimate remaining costs and lead times for design and implementation based on the updated information completed in this procedure.

Complete Programming Analysis

Policy/Procedure Statement Brasto Publishing **Subject: Complete Programming Design**	Retrieval No.: Page: Issue Date: Supercedes:	PRO-04 1 of 1 10/28/0X N/A

1. PURPOSE AND SCOPE

This procedure is used by the computer systems coordinator as a guideline for the design, writing, data conversion, testing, and implementation of a programming project.

2. RESPONSIBILITIES

MIS COORD **MIS Coordinator**

3. PROCEDURES

3.1 MIS COORD **Estimate the Programming Phase Workload**

Based on the additional information collected from previous procedures, determine the remaining cost of the design and implementation phases of the project.

3.2 MIS COORD **Install and Test Software Package**

1. If there is a software package, install it in a test subdirectory.
2. Test the functionality of the software.

3.3 MIS COORD **Design and Prototype Database**

1. Create the logical database design for the new application.
2. Gain approval of the design from the database administrator.
3. Create a prototype of the database design.
4. Test the prototype and adjust as necessary.

3.4 MIS COORD **Design Information Systems for New System**

1. Determine the hardware and supporting system requirements for the new system, based on the previous analyses.
2. Determine the cost of the additional information systems.
3. Gain approval from the project sponsor for any cost overruns for additional information systems.

3.5 MIS COORD **Design a Data Conversion Plan**

1. Create a batch file design for converting data from the original format in the current system to the format to be used for the new system.
2. Create designs for all data conversion screens, reports, and interfaces.

3.6 MIS COORD **Estimate Implementation Costs and Lead Times**

Estimate remaining costs and lead times for implementation based on the updated information completed in this procedure.

Policy/Procedure Statement		
Brasto Publishing	Retrieval No.:	PRO-05
	Page:	1 of 2
	Issue Date:	10/28/0X
	Supercedes:	N/A
Subject: Complete Programming Implementation		

1. PURPOSE AND SCOPE

This procedure is used by the computer systems coordinator as a guide for creating the procedures, final tests, training, and switchover associated with a programming project.

2. RESPONSIBILITIES

MIS COORD **MIS Coordinator**

3. PROCEDURES

3.1 MIS COORD **Estimate the Programming Phase Workload**

Based on the additional information collected from previous procedures, determine the remaining cost of the implementation phases of the project.

3.2 MIS COORD **Create Programming Code**

Based on previous designs, create the code for the database to be used for the new application, as well as all application programming, screen formats, report layouts, and data conversion programs.

3.3 MIS COORD **Create Documentation**

Create documentation for all the programs, reports, and screens created in the preceding step. These should include field definitions, descriptions of all required entries, and "quick start" descriptions for rapidly using them.

3.4 MIS COORD **Test the New System**

1. Test the system for acceptability by users.
2. Test the system based on its ability to handle large transaction volumes.
3. Revise the system based on test results.
4. If necessary, change system documentation based on the results of testing revisions.

3.5 MIS COORD **Train Users**

1. Create training documentation that incorporates system documentation.
2. Create a list of users and determine which ones require training in various parts of the new system.
3. Schedule users for training.
4. Conduct an error-check of training materials.
5. Conduct training.
6. Obtain post-training reviews from users, and modify training materials based on the reviews.

Complete Programming Implementation (1 of 2)

Policy/Procedure Statement Brasto Publishing **Subject: Complete Programming Implementation**	Retrieval No.: Page: Issue Date: Supercedes:	PRO-05 2 of 2 10/28/0X N/A

3.6 MIS COORD

Convert Data

1. Install the data conversion system.
2. Test the conversion system for accuracy and speed of conversion.
3. Train the conversion staff in the use of the conversion software.
4. Conduct a conversion test with a sample database.
5. Correct any problems found during the test.
6. Convert the old database to the new database.

3.7 MIS COORD

Switch Over to the New System

1. Shift the new system from the test directory to the active directory.
2. Reroute all users to the new system.
3. Archive the old application files and database.
4. Create feedback loop from the help desk staff to the programming staff to ensure that user problems are dealt with as rapidly as possible.
5. Conduct a postimplementation review of the project.

Complete Programming Implementation (2 of 2)

Policy/Procedure Statement	Retrieval No.:	UNR-01
Brasto Publishing	Page:	1 of 2
	Issue Date:	10/28/0X
	Supercedes:	N/A
Subject: Conduct Basic E-Mail Operations		

1. PURPOSE AND SCOPE

This procedure helps employees access and use their e-mail accounts.

2. RESPONSIBILITIES

MIS COORD **MIS Coordinator**

3. PROCEDURES

3.1 MIS COORD **Start E-Mail**

Select your name from the e-mail login list at startup. The list is alphabetical by first name; scroll down the list to find your name, click on it, then press the OK button at the bottom of the screen.

3.2 MIS COORD **Access E-Mail**

A message button will appear in the center of the screen to tell you that you have received an e-mail message. Click on the button at the bottom of this message, and your mail message will appear.

3.3 MIS COORD **Archive a Message**

Click on the "Archive Message" button at the bottom of the e-mail screen.

3.4 MIS COORD **Delete a Message**

Click on the "Delete Message" button at the bottom of the screen.

3.5 MIS COORD **Send a Message**

Click on the "Send a Message" button at the bottom of the screen. To send the message to a single recipient, click on the "Recipient" button. To send to many recipients, first click on the "To Distribution" button. In either case, click on one or more people from the employee list that will appear on the screen. Then type a header and message, and press the "Send" button. To distribute to a previously saved list of recipients, click on the "Saved Lists" button and select the saved list you wish to use.

3.6 MIS COORD **Create a Distribution List**

Click on the "To Distribution" button. Then select the names on the pop-up list to be on the distribution list. Then press the "Save" or "Save As" buttons to save the new list. If you pressed "Save As," enter the name of the new distribution list.

Conduct Basic E-Mail Operations (1 of 2)

Policy/Procedure Statement Brasto Publishing **Subject: Conduct Basic E-Mail Operations**	Retrieval No.: Page: Issue Date: Supercedes:	UNR-01 2 of 2 10/28/0X N/A

3.7	MIS COORD	**Send an Attached File** Click on the "Attached Files" button in the upper right corner of the screen. Then enter the rest of the message, as usual, and press the "Send" button. The "Attach File" window will open. Select the file to be sent from that menu, and press the "Attach File" button.
3.8	MIS COORD	**View Messages** The most recent message will appear on your screen. You may press the "Delete" button to eliminate this message, or "Reply to Message" to write the message back to the sender. To view saved messages, go to the View option in the menu and select the "Messages Received" option.
3.9	MIS COORD	**View an Attached File** Click on the attachment logo within the e-mail message. You will have the choice of opening the file or saving it.
3.10	MIS COORD	**Forward a Message** When in the message you want to forward, go to the FILE option in the menu, select the person from the list to whom you want to forward the message, and click on the OK button.
3.11	MIS COORD	**Print a Message** When in the message you want to print, go to the FILE option in the menu and select the PRINT MESSAGE option.

Conduct Basic E-Mail Operations (2 of 2)

Policy/Procedure Statement	Retrieval No.:	UNR-02
Brasto Publishing	Page:	1 of 1
	Issue Date:	10/28/0X
	Supercedes:	N/A
Subject: Maintain Computer System Security		

1. PURPOSE AND SCOPE

This procedure establishes a security access plan that allows users access to the screens and fields they need in the accounting software.

2. RESPONSIBILITIES

MIS COORD **MIS Coordinator**

3. PROCEDURES

3.1 MIS COORD **Determine User's Security Level**

Obtain the job description of a new employee from the human resources department. Go over this position with the new employee's supervisor to determine the most appropriate level of computer system access.

3.2 MIS COORD **Refer to Security Matrix**

Go to the matrix of security codes, which is located in the SECURITY.XLS file. Determine the mix of security codes required for the employee that will give access to only those screens that were agreed on in the previous step.

3.3 MIS COORD **Install Correct Security Level**

Go to the SECURE screen in the accounting software package and enter the security codes noted in the security matrix for the user.

3.4 MIS COORD **Inform the User**

Issue a memo to the new employee that itemizes all the screens and fields to which that person has been allowed access.

Policy/Procedure Statement	Retrieval No.:	UNR-03
Brasto Publishing	Page:	1 of 1
	Issue Date:	10/28/0X
	Supercedes:	N/A
Subject: Restore Backups to the Computer System		

1. PURPOSE AND SCOPE

This procedure is used by the MIS coordinator to restore data to the computer system from backup tapes.

2. RESPONSIBILITIES

MIS COORD **MIS Coordinator**

3. PROCEDURES

3.1 MIS COORD **Retrieve Correct Backup Tape**

If a user has erroneously deleted a file, work with that person to determine when the deletion occurred, and select the correct backup tape based on that information. For example, if the deletion was two days ago, the most recent backup that will still include the information is from three days ago. If the entire system must be restored, use the most recent tape.

3.2 MIS COORD **Select File to Retrieve**

If a user needs to have a specific file restored, access the recovery software and scroll through the file directory for the tape to find the correct file for the user. If the entire system must be restored, flag all files on the tape for restoration.

3.3 MIS COORD **Move Files from Backup Tape to Main Drive**

Go to the RESTORE screen in the restore software and verify that you want to restore the file or files from the tape. Wait for the transfer to be completed.

3.4 MIS COORD **Verify Transferred Files**

If you are restoring only a few files, be sure to access all of them after the restoration is complete, to verify that the correct information was transferred and that the date of the transferred information is correct. If all files are being transferred, verify this information for just a selection of files. Return the backup tape to its protective box and put it back in storage.

Restore Backups to the Computer System

11.6 OUTPUT REPORTS

Comprehensive accounting systems purchased as a total package from an independent software company are usually documented quite well, particularly in the output reports. However, systems developed internally by internal programmers are more inclined to emphasize input systems and controls. Also, new reports added to the system after installation tend not to be very well defined or explained. The solution is to develop a standard method for defining a single report that will inform the reader of the purpose of the report, its frequency and distribution, the order in which the data elements are stored, its retention, and the description of each repetitive data item in the report. Most computer-generated reports can be completely defined and documented with three pages: (1) report description, (2) report contents, and (3) copy of the report with each data item numbered for reference.

The report description form has been developed solely to describe in detail the general attributes of a single computer report. An example of a blank form is shown in Exhibit 11.21. The form includes the following fields:

- *Report title*. Enter the exact name of the report as printed in its heading.
- *Number*. Enter the report's unique identifying number, if any.
- *Type*. Enter the general class or type of report, such as edit, table maintenance, control and audit, controller's report, informational and reference, or cash.
- *Frequency*. Enter the frequency of the report, such as daily, weekly, monthly, quarterly, annually, on demand, or whenever changes are made to the underlying data.
- *Sequence*. Enter the sequence of the report's line items. Typical sequences are alphabetical, by social security number, transaction type, purchase order or invoice number, or date.
- *Report produced by program*. Enter the program number that generated this report, which is usually shown on the report itself in most data processing systems.
- *Number of copies and distribution*. Enter the name of the department to which each copy of the report is sent.
- *Retention and disposition*. Describe the retention of the report and its final disposition. Typical retention cycles may be until a new report is produced, until the next accounting period is begun, until the year-end audit has been completed, or permanent.
- *Purpose*. Note the specific use to which the report is put. If several purposes are served, they can be listed in descending order of importance. Usual purposes of accounting reports are to provide an audit listing of changes, provide control over data entry accuracy and editing, provide a reference list, and so on. Almost anything can be written in this section to provide more assistance to the user of the report.
- *Procedure*. Briefly describe the procedure accomplished by this report. Make reference here to unusual input forms and procedures used to initiate or complete the report.

FINANCIAL ACCOUNTING SYSTEM
REPORT DESCRIPTION

REPORT TITLE ______________________ NUMBER __________

TYPE ______________________

FREQUENCY ______________________

SEQUENCE ______________________

NUMBER OF COPIES AND DISTRIBUTION - REPORT PRODUCED BY PROGRAM __________

1.

2.

3.

4.

5.

6.

RETENTION AND DISPOSITION:

PURPOSE:

PROCEDURE:

Exhibit 11.21. Report Description Form

The report contents form is tied directly to a copy of the actual report, and is used to describe each item on the report itself. The individual sections or items on the report are numbered consecutively and these numbers are used as line numbers on the report contents form (which is shown in Exhibit 11.22). The form includes the following fields:

- *Report title*. Enter the exact name shown as a heading on the computer report and on the report description form that precedes this page in the output report section of the data processing manual.
- *Report Number*. Enter the report number printed on the computer output report.
- *Reference*. This is a preprinted list of consecutive numbers used to reference the definitions in the related report. Second sheets are numbered 21 to 40. Very few computer-generated reports contain more than 40 separate data fields or items.
- *Characters*. Enter the maximum number of characters capable of being printed in this data field.
- *Field definition*. This is a free-form description of each data field on the report from the heading to the final control total or ending indicator. The meaning of the field or the method of calculation may be described if meaningful to the report user.

The preceding two exhibits only contained blank forms. For complete examples of the concept, Exhibits 11.23 and 11.24 each contain three-page examples of the report description form, report contents form, and a sample report. Exhibit 11.23 addresses a table maintenance editing application, and Exhibit 11.24 addresses a batch editing application.

An index of all reports is needed to facilitate looking up a specific report description, contents, and layout. Most reports are numbered for reference purposes by the programmer. The report numbers should form a logical sequence. However, if some reports are not numbered, the programmers should be asked to number them. If the report titles are quite descriptive and if there are not many reports, a unique report number may not be needed.

FINANCIAL ACCOUNTING SYSTEM

REPORT CONTENTS

REPORT TITLE ______ REPORT NO.

REF.	CHARS.	FIELD DEFINITION
1		
2		
3		
4		
5		
6		
7		
8		
9		
10		
11		
12		
13		
14		
15		
16		
17		
18		
19		
20		

Exhibit 11.22. Report Contents Form

FINANCIAL ACCOUNTING SYSTEM
REPORT DESCRIPTION

REPORT TITLE Reference Table Maintenance Listing NUMBER GL-E01

TYPE Table Maintenance Edit

FREQUENCY When additions, deletions or changes are entered

SEQUENCE Table, Reference Number Within Table

NUMBER OF COPIES AND DISTRIBUTION - REPORT PRODUCED BY PROGRAM GL1965

1. Accounting Control
2. Data Processing
3.
4.
5.
6.

RETENTION AND DISPOSITION: Filed until a new reference table is produced. Table can be produced on request.

PURPOSE:

1. Provides audit listing of changes for manual review.
2. Provides control over changes to reference table items.
3. Provides additional reference in conjunction with the reference table listing.

PROCEDURE: Table additions, deletions, and changes are entered on table maintenance forms, processed and printed on the reference table maintenance listing for verification. Deleted entries remain in table until end of fiscal year.

Exhibit 11.23. Report Descriptions, Contents, and Sample Forms (First Example)

FINANCIAL ACCOUNTING SYSTEM

REPORT CONTENTS

REPORT TITLE Reference Table Maintenance Listing REPORT NO. GL-E01

REF.	CHARS.	FIELD DEFINITION
1	6	Report number
2	-	Title of report and date processed
3	-	Consecutive page number of report
4	3	Transaction type or table code
5	4	Transaction type or table name
6	-	Letters indicate beginning of each field and 80-column record
7	80	Contents of record before change (old) and after change (new)
8	3	Error message number (see message table for definition)
9	1	Severity of message defined in message table
10	20	Short error message
11	2	Number of transactions listed (new records)
12	2	Number of transactions listed (new records) with errors
13		
14		
15		
16		
17		
18		
19		
20		

Exhibit 11.23. Continued

```
GL-E01 (1)                                                                              (3) PAGE 1
                                        (2) REFERENCE TABLE MAINTENANCE LISTING
              (4)                                PROCESS DATE 09/13/03

TRANS TYPE  TA2                    (6)
          (5) TRANSACTION TABLES-FIELD INPUT EDIT & EXPLODE.
                                                                                       E R R O R
                                  RECORD IMAGE BEFORE AND AFTER                  MSG # SEVERITY MESSAGE
                                                                                  (8)        (9)
BEFORE    TA2CD21601DT03504                     107104M             OBJECT CODE
AFTER  (7)TA2CD21601DT03504             AAA041032107104M
BEFORE    TA2CD31801DT03504                     107104M307104M      OBJECT CODE                  (10)
AFTER     TA2CD31801DT03504             AAA014032107104M307104M
      (11)NUMBER OF TRANSACTIONS-      2
          NUMBER OF TRANSACTIONS WITH ERRORS-      0 (12)
```

Exhibit 11.23. Report Descriptions, Contents, and Sample Forms (First Example) (Continued)

FINANCIAL ACCOUNTING SYSTEM
REPORT DESCRIPTION

REPORT TITLE Batch Error Report NUMBER GL-E02

TYPE Transaction Edit

FREQUENCY Daily or when transaction batches are entered for processing.

SEQUENCE Same as transaction entries. Only records with errors printed.

NUMBER OF COPIES AND DISTRIBUTION - REPORT PRODUCED BY PROGRAM ________

1. Accounting control
2.
3.
4.
5.
6.

RETENTION AND DISPOSITION: Held until batch appears on Batch Transaction List GL-E03.

PURPOSE:

1. Provides link between input transaction batch and batch transaction list of accepted batches.
2. Provides information to correct transaction errors determined by edit and validation routines.
3. Error messages are defined in message tables.

PROCEDURE: Editing and validating routines are performed against each transaction and errors are identified for correction. Batch total is compared to generated batch totals for differences. When errors are corrected, the batch details will be printed on the Batch Transaction List GL-E03.

Exhibit 11.24. Report Descriptions, Contents, and Sample Forms (Second Example)

FINANCIAL ACCOUNTING SYSTEM

REPORT CONTENTS

REPORT TITLE Batch Error Report REPORT NO. GL-EO2

REF.	CHARS.	FIELD DEFINITION
1	6	Report number
2		Title of Report and date processed
3		Consecutive page number of report
4		Batch number
5		Type of transactions in batch
6	80	Batch header card information (?)
7	4	Generated consecutive number
8	80	Transaction input image without editing
9	3	Error message number (see message table for definition)
10	1	Severity of message (define 1, 2, 3, 4, etc.)
11	20	Short error message
12		Number of transactions in batch card
13		Number of transactions read
14	9	Dollar amount in batch card
15	9	Dollar amount of transactions read
16	?	Number of transactions with errors (not number of errors)
17		End of report balance total message
18		
19		
20		

Exhibit 11.24. Report Descriptions, Contents, and Sample Forms (Second Example) (Continued)

```
GL-E02 (1)                                                                                         (3) PAGE 1

                                        (2) BATCH ERROR REPORT
                                            PROCESS DATE 03/03/03

BATCH NO:  ABCDE02 (4)                      (5) CASH DISB

    1234567890123456789012345678901234567890123456789012345678901234567890123456789 0
(6) CASH DISBURSEMENT                                                                00000580

MIS                              TRANSACTION                                         E R R O R
REF                              INPUT IMAGE                                MSG #  SEVERITY  MESSAGE

0001  CDO               (8)       C01000000200005              ABCDE0200000900   (9)     (10)       (11)
0002  CD11234567890123456781234     00000040001V02  810303CAPS  ABCDE0200000950
0003  CD11234567890123456781234     00000040001V02  810303CAPS  ABCDE0200000950  103      2      INVALID LEDGER CODE
 (7)                                                                             101      2      INVALID ACTIVITY
                                                                                 102      2      INVALID FUND CODE
                                                                                 103      2      INVALID LEDGER CODE

0004  CD11234567890123456781234     00000040001V02  810303CAPS  ABCDE0200000950  103      2      INVALID LEDGER CODE
                                                                                 101      2      INVALID ACTIVITY
                                                                                 102      2      INVALID FUND CODE
                                                                                 103      2      INVALID LEDGER CODE

0005  CD11234567890123456781234     00000040001V02  810303CAPS  ABCDE0200000950  102      2      INVALID FUND CODE
                                                                                 103      2      INVALID LEDGER CODE

0006  CD11234567890123456781234     00000040001V02  810303CAPS  ABCDE0200000950  104      2      INVALID OBJECT CODE
                                                                                 101      2      INVALID ACTIVITY

                           NO. OF TRANS          AMOUNT (14)
BATCH TOTAL                    (12) 5           2,000.05
COMPUTER TOTAL                      5 (13)      2,000.05 (15)

NUMBER OF TRANSACTIONS WITH ERRORS:     4 (16)        (17)
```

Exhibit 11.24. Continued

11.7 DATABASE TABLES

It is common for the accounting department to purchase a software package that contains a reasonable number of standard reports, and to also buy a third-party report-writing package that will give it the ability to create a large array of additional customized reports. When using a third-party reporting package, it is useful to have some knowledge of the variety of tables that comprise the accounting database so that one can devise appropriate linkages between the tables to create reports. The tables are usually listed either in the documentation that accompanies the software package or in its onscreen help documentation. However, any in-house systems generally do not include this documentation. If the later situation is the case, work with the programming staff to itemize the following information about each table:

- The identifying table name
- A list of all field names within the table
- A description of each field within the table
- The length of each field within the table
- The fields that are used as an index

With this information in hand, one can more easily fashion a report with a report writer that contains the correct information and is appropriately linked between different tables within the database.

11.8 COMPUTER REPORTS QUESTIONNAIRE

Reports may have only been ordered from the IT department for a single use, but they may have been incorporated into its regular processing routine and therefore been issued for much longer than needed. This can cause a waste of time, processing power, and paper. To mitigate the problem, a computer reports questionnaire, such as the one shown in Exhibit 11.25, can be attached to output reports at predetermined intervals. The recipient of each copy of a report is asked to complete and return the questionnaire. Its basic purpose is to determine whether the report is serving a useful purpose and is actually being employed to assist users.

The answers to the first 10 questions will suggest several possible future actions concerning a particular report. If a recipient's answer to Question 1 is "No," the report can be eliminated as far as this user is concerned. If the answer to Question 2 is "Read for information only," there may be a better way to provide the information, such as in a summary report. If the answer is "Read and use for compiling other report," perhaps these other reports can be computerized or their information added to this report.

If Question 4 indicates that the reader never uses the information in the report, perhaps it should be discontinued. In Question 5, if the report is ranked at the bottom third of the reports received, a study should be made to see whether it can be made more meaningful or should be discontinued.

Question 6 points out that a change in frequency of reporting should be studied. A "No" answer to Question 7 should alert the IT staff that the system should be examined

INSTRUCTIONS: Please detach. Indicate your opinions by placing an "X" in the appropriate square. Add your comments where necessary and return this form to data processing.

COMPUTER REPORTS QUESTIONNAIRE

Report Title ______________________________

Report Number ______________________________

Frequency of Issue
❐ On Request ❐ Daily ❐ Weekly ❐ Monthly ❐ Quarterly ❐ Semi-annually
❐ Annually ❐ Other ______________________________

1. Do you wish to continue to receive this report?
   ❐ Yes-----Answer all remaining questions.
   ❐ No------Do not answer remaining questions.

2. What do you do with this report after you receive it?
   ❐ Read and use to make decisions.
   ❐ Read for information only.
   ❐ Read and use for compiling other reports.
   ❐ Other (explain) ______________________________

3. Do you pass this report on to others?
   ❐ Yes → If yes, ❐ For their information.
   ❐ No ❐ For them to take action.

4. How often do you use the information in this report?
   ❐ Daily ❐ Weekly ❐ Monthly ❐ Quarterly ❐ Never

5. How do you rank this report as to relative information in comparison to other reports you receive?
   ❐ Top one-third ❐ Middle one-third ❐ Bottom one-third

6. In view of the above ranking, should this report be issued:
   ❐ More frequently? ❐ Less frequently? ❐ At same frequency?
   If change is indicated what frequency of issue do you suggest? ______________

7. Does this report reach you soon enough? ❐ Yes ❐ No

8. Would control of your operation or planning your responsibilities be materially impaired without this report? ❐ Yes ❐ No

9. Is this report suitable in its present form? ❐ Yes ❐ No
   Or should additional data be provided such as
   ❐ Percentages? ❐ Ratios? ❐ Prior period figures? ❐ Year-to-date figures?

10. If others who receive copies of this report agree to its discontinuance, would you still want it for your use only?
    ❐ Yes ❐ No

11. Any other comments or suggestions as to form, scope, method of preparation, etc.?
    ____
    ____
    ____

Signed ______________ Department ______________ Date ______________

Exhibit 11.25. Computer Reports Questionnaire

for ways to speed up the reporting process. Question 8 relates to the value of the reported information; a "No" answer suggests that either changes should be made in the information or the report should be discontinued. Question 9 allows the user of the report to enter his or her input into the reporting process; a "No" answer indicates that the contents of the report should be analyzed a determination made as to whether additional information should be added to the report.

Question 10 provides a last chance to eliminate the report to this user. Although a user may answer the other questions in a way that shows the report is useful, a "No" answer here is a strong indication that the user feels the report is no longer necessary to the particular operation.

11.9 DISASTER RECOVERY MANUAL

One of the primary procedures that must be completed for the IT department is one dealing with disaster recovery. This is needed when the primary computer systems are shut down or destroyed, perhaps by a natural disaster. A system startup must begin as quickly as possible with backup information, possibly in a different location. Without a good plan for taking these steps, a company can be faced with a complete shutdown of its operations.

To create the procedure, it is first necessary to break down the recovery process into its key components so that it is easier to complete the documentation of each one in turn. The primary components are:

- *Timeline*. The management team must define the maximum time interval it will allow before the computer systems must be fully operational. For example, an airline will probably find even one minute of downtime by its reservation systems to be intolerable. Also, other components of the computer system may be allowed different recovery times. For example, some personal computers may not have to be recovered for several weeks, while some communications linkages may have to be turned on again within a few minutes.
- *Key activities*. Once the timelines have been determined, one should define the key activities to include in the procedure. There should be a listing of what steps to complete, which employee positions are responsible for completing them, and how each task will be completed. This is a very detailed step requiring significant testing to ensure that it will work in the event of a disaster.
- *Recovery schedule*. This should include all key activities and specify exactly when each one will be completed. This schedule is useful not only for running training exercises with the recovery team, but also for providing time estimates to the rest of the company regarding when certain components of the recovery plan will be completed.

These three steps are crucial to the proper documentation of a reliable disaster recovery plan. If they are not used as a foundation, it is likely that key steps will be omitted or that actual recovery efforts may focus on the restoration of less necessary computer subsystems, which will unfavorably impact company operations.

The next activity is to compile the resulting information into a disaster recovery manual. The manual should contain the following six components:

1. *Executive summary*. Place a short summary of the purpose and scope of the manual at its front. It should do a creditable job of describing the manual's contents, as it will most likely be perused by senior management people who are responsible for funding the project.

2. *Emergency activities*. This section should include, in sequence, those steps to follow to shut down the computer systems, which includes the suppression of fires, gas leaks, and water leaks; evacuation of the computer facility; and notification of the rapid response team that is responsible for recovering the computer systems.

3. *Action schedule*. The emergency response team needs an action schedule that delineates a series of steps for assessing the level of damage, notifying company employees of system downtime, and beginning the recovery process.

4. *Recovery procedures*. The emergency response team needs a series of procedures for shifting activities to a computer hot site, activating systems, verifying computer linkages to company terminals, calling up stored data, testing the data, and verifying that company locations are brought up on the new system in a timely manner. These procedures may go on to describe the complete restoration of all computer systems, including the purchase of new hardware and software, the conversion of data, and system testing.

5. *System tests*. The manual should also describe a series of continuing tests that the emergency response team should practice on a regular basis, not only to ensure that the procedures are still valid, but also to keep the team in practice to ensure a thorough, effective, and rapid response in the event of a real emergency.

6. *Additional information*. Depending on the level of expertise of members of the emergency response team, it may be necessary to include a glossary for special terms used in the procedure. If not, there should still be an updated set of insurance policies describing insurance coverage on all computer systems, as well as an inventory of major hardware and software systems, descriptions of supplier support agreements, and descriptions of where stored data is kept offsite.

It is not sufficient to file away the disaster recovery manual once it has been completed. Instead, periodic testing is needed to ensure that all components of the manual are still valid and accurately describe action steps in the correct order. Consequently, one should schedule periodic tests using the manual, followed by a review with the team that tested the manual. This process is also an excellent way to ensure that the team doing the testing is kept in practice in case a real disaster requires immediate use of the manual. Only by occasional testing of this key procedure can a company be assured of having a quality plan that can be used to restore its computer systems from a major disaster.

Chapter 12

HUMAN RESOURCES MANUAL

12.1 INTRODUCTION

The human resources department has always been closely related to the accounting payroll function. Initial payroll information is provided by the human resources staff, as are data about salary changes, employee transfers, deductions from pay, and terminations. The human resources and payroll departments are jointly involved whenever a major change in either department's systems is planned and installed. For these reasons, the controller or chief financial officer frequently has control over the human resources function, which leads us to include this chapter alongside the other accounting-related chapters in this book.

This chapter contains a large number of policies and procedures for the human resources department—so many that they could be used as the foundation for a complete manual for this department.

12.2 HUMAN RESOURCES POLICIES

Policy statements tend to have a longer shelf life than procedures, but still require regular updating. Statements that are no longer effective should be terminated, and those that require changes should be superseded and replaced with updated versions of the information contained therein. If manuals are lost, they should be replaced at once.

This section contains 28 policies, which are itemized in the following policy index. The policies are subdivided into employment policies, payroll and budget policies, fringe benefits, grievances, and other policies. A complete policy statement for each policy then follows the index. Each one uses a consistent header statement, which includes a policy-specific retrieval number, a page count indicator, the issue date, and a notation stating what document is being superseded (none in these examples). Nothing is superseded by an initial document release, so there is no need for a superseded retrieval number. When a subsequent statement carries a superseded retrieval number, pages with the number shown are to be removed and replaced with the new statement.

Policy/Procedure Statement Brasto Publishing Subject: Index	Retrieval No.: Page: Issue Date: Supercedes:	Index 1 of 2 10/28/0X N/A

Retrieval Number	Subject
Employment Policies	
HR-1010	Equal Employment Opportunity
HR-1020	Preemployment
HR-1030	Terms and Conditions of Employment
HR-1040	Types of Employment Status
HR-1050	Work Schedules and Rest Periods
HR-1060	Changes in Employment Status
HR-1070	Personnel Records
HR-1080	Termination Policy and Requirements
HR-1090	Reduction In Force Policy
HR-1100	Nepotism
HR-1110	Discipline Policy
Payroll and Budget	
HR-2010	Deductions
HR-2020	Fair Labor Standards Act
Fringe Benefits	
HR-3010	Personal Leave
HR-3020	Family and Medical Leave
HR-3030	Leave of Absence without Pay
HR-3040	Holiday Leave
HR-3050	Military Leave
HR-3060	Health Insurance
HR-3070	Consolidated Omnibus Budget Reconciliation Act
HR-3080	Salary Continuation Insurance Plans
HR-3090	Additional Group Policies Available
HR-3100	Workers' Compensation

Index (1 of 2)

Policy/Procedure Statement Brasto Publishing **Subject: Index**	Retrieval No.: Page: Issue Date: Supercedes:	Index 2 of 2 10/28/0X N/A

Grievance Policy

HR-4010	Grievance Policy
HR-4020	Sexual Harassment Policy

Other Policies

HR-5010	Drug-Free Workplace Policy
HR-5020	The Americans with Disabilities Act
HR-5030	Jury Duty and Elections

Index (2 of 2)

Policy/Procedure Statement	Retrieval No.:	HR-1010
Brasto Publishing	Page:	1 of 1
	Issue Date:	10/28/0X
	Supercedes:	N/A
Subject: Equal Employment Opportunity		

The company provides equal employment opportunities without regard to age, race, color, religion, sex, national origin, veteran status, or physical and/or mental disability. The company is also pledged to develop and support an environment of affirmative action toward this policy, including active recruitment of minority groups, women, and the physically and/or mentally disabled for positions at all levels. The policy applies to all employees and applicants for employment, regardless of position or source of funds.

It is the responsibility of all persons making employment decisions to support this policy as established in the company's affirmative action compliance program.

To Comply with the Corporate Affirmative Action Program

All department heads recruiting for staff positions should follow these procedures:

1. The department notifies the Department of Human Resources, via a Termination/ Leave Form, that an employee will terminate.
2. The position that will become vacant is then posted in the Department of Human Resources, on the corporate e-mail system, and on designated bulletin boards for a period of five working days so that all staff will have an opportunity to apply for the vacancy.
3. All candidates must formally apply for the employment through the Department of Human Resources. For those positions requiring typing, the Department of Human Resources will test all applicants prior to their applying for the vacancy. A minimum score of 40 words per minutes is generally required for all clerical staff openings.
4. Once the budget authority has made a selection, a completed Employment Form on the selected applicant and a completed Interview/Selection Report are forwarded to the Department of Human Resources.
5. All offers of employment must be approved by the Department of Human Resources before actual commitment can be made to the applicant selected. Approval is indicated by the completed and approved Employment Form. Certain selections may require a vice president's or the president's approval.
6. The Department of Human Resources will offer employment for all staff positions after all necessary administrative approvals and signatures have been obtained.
7. All offers of employment for staff positions will be made by the department head after receipt of education or work history from the selected applicant, and after all necessary administrative approvals and signatures have been obtained.

These affirmative action employment procedures will be followed for all administrative and staff positions, regardless of the source of funding.

Equal Employment Opportunity

Policy/Procedure Statement		
Brasto Publishing	Retrieval No.:	HR-1020
	Page:	1 of 1
	Issue Date:	10/28/0X
Subject: Preemployment	Supercedes:	N/A

Recruitment

The company is committed to a program of recruitment and retention of excellent employees. Recruiting the best candidate for a position vacancy is accomplished by:

1. *On-premises posting*. The position vacancy must be posted for a period of five working days. If a holiday falls within the posting period, it will not be considered within the minimum posting period. A department head may extend a posting period past the minimum five-day period by requesting the extension from the Department of Human Resources.
2. *Public advertisements*. If the on-premises posting has not yielded a candidate suitable for the vacancy, a public advertisement will be approved by the Department of Human Resources. The recruiting department should follow these steps:
   a. Write the Employment Advertisement using the information listed in the on- premises posting. More specific information may be required for the public advertisement.
   b. Submit the advertisement to the Department of Human Resources so that EEOC language can be approved.
   c. Request that grammar and structure be given separate review and approval.
   d. Follow corporate purchasing procedures for paid advertisements.

Selection

All staff position selections are the final responsibility of the recruiting budget authority.

Employment Eligibility Verification

An Immigration and Naturalization Service form, INS Form I-9, entitled "Employment Eligibility Verification," must be completed by each employee before he or she is placed on the payroll. At least two forms of identification will be required before employment. The INS I-9 form must be completed within three business days of hire or the employment contract will be void.

Preemployment

Policy/Procedure Statement	Retrieval No.:	HR-1030
Brasto Publishing	Page:	1 of 2
	Issue Date:	10/28/0X
	Supercedes:	N/A
Subject: Terms and Conditions of Employment		

The company is an equal opportunity employer and selects the best matched individual for the position based on job-related qualifications, regardless of race, color, creed, sex, national origin, age, veteran status, or physical and/or mental disability.

Employees will understand and agree that:

1. Any material misrepresentation or deliberate omission of a fact in the employment application may be justified for refusal of or, if employed, termination from employment.
2. The company will make a thorough investigation of the applicant's entire work history and may verify all data given in the application for employment, related papers, or oral interviews. Employees will authorize such investigation and the giving and receiving of any information requested by the company and shall release from liability any person giving or receiving any such information. Falsification of data so given or other dero-gatory information discovered as a result of this information may prevent employment or, if employed, may subject the employee to immediate dismissal.
3. Employment may be terminated by the company at any time without liability for wages or salary except such as may have been earned at the date of such termination.
4. Although management makes every effort to accommodate individual preferences, business needs may at times make the following conditions mandatory: overtime, shift work, a rotating work schedule, or a work schedule other than Monday through Friday. Employees must understand and accept these as conditions of employment.

Employment Conditions

The following conditions of employment apply to all staff positions:

- All full-time employees are given the option of participating in the corporate 401(k) retirement plan.
- All full-time employees receive group health insurance free of cost. An employee must sign a waiver if this coverage is not desired, and the waiver must be approved by the Department of Human Resources before coverage can be revoked.

Briefing a New Employee

All new employees are required to attend an orientation session conducted by the Department of Human Resources. These sessions are held each Monday from 8:30 AM to 10:30 AM. The Department of Human Resources will notify the employees to ensure their attendance. At this time, employees will be assisted in completing the necessary payroll forms. Also, company policies, procedures, and fringe benefits will be explained. Department heads are requested to emphasize to new employees the importance of attending this session.

Terms and Conditions of Employment (1 of 2)

Policy/Procedure Statement	Retrieval No.:	HR-1030
Brasto Publishing	Page:	2 of 2
	Issue Date:	10/28/0X
	Supercedes:	N/A
Subject: Terms and Conditions of Employment		

The supervisor is responsible for introducing a new employee to his or her fellow workers. A good introduction requires an extended period of gradual orientation and should answer questions on matters such as the following:

- Specific duties and responsibilities of the job
- Work standards and progress expected in the job
- Hours of work
- Operation of equipment required to do the job
- Reporting absences to the supervisor
- Permission to leave the work area
- Immediate safety precautions
- Security measures
- Attendance rules
- Supplies and requisition procedures
- Policy for overtime and/or compensatory time
- Leave time policy and completion of the Attendance and Leave Form
- Break time

This list is not comprehensive; each supervisor should use it as the foundation for a more comprehensive listing that is tailored to each area's specific needs.

Probationary Period

The probationary period shall be used by the department head for observing closely the employee's work and for securing the most effective adjustment of the employee to the position and to the persons with whom the employee must interact. It serves as a means of rejecting an employee whose performance does not meet required standards. All staff employees are required to serve on a probationary basis, which consists of 90 days of employment. Supervisors are responsible for initiating termination if a staff member's performance is not acceptable. The employee will be given a written notice from the supervisor if probationary termination is necessary.

A probationary period of 90 days will be resumed for an employee who transfers on a lateral move from one position to another or who is promoted to a higher classified level position or who is placed in a lower classification level.

The Director of Human Resources is authorized to extend the 90-day probationary period up to 180 days upon the recommendation of a department manager.

Terms and Conditions of Employment (2 of 2)

Policy/Procedure Statement		
Brasto Publishing	Retrieval No.:	HR-1040
	Page:	1 of 1
	Issue Date:	10/28/0X
Subject: Types of Employment Status	Supercedes:	N/A

Regular Employment

A full-time employee is employed in a regular, full-time (40 hours per week) position. This full-time status entitles the employee to all company benefits programs. Full-time employees are employed, promoted, and given raises in accordance with the company's classification system.

A part-time employee working less than 20 hours per week is not entitled to any company benefits. One who works at least 20 hours, but less than 40 hours per week is entitled to all company benefit programs on a prorated basis. This part-time status entitles the employee to holiday, sick, and annual leave prorated proportionately according to the number of hours worked.

Temporary Employment

A temporary employee is defined as one whose employment agreement is for an established work schedule for a period not to exceed 4½ months in one calendar year, or whose services are on an hourly basis with no established basic work schedule as to hours each day, or days each week, for a period not to exceed 4½ months per calendar year.

Exempt and Nonexempt

Employees subject to the provisions of the Fair Labor Standards Act are referred to as "nonexempt," and employees not subject to the provisions of the Act are referred to as "exempt" employees. The Fair Labor Standards Act requires that nonexempt employees be paid time and one-half of their regular rate for hours worked in excess of 40 hours per work week.

Types of Employment Status

Policy/Procedure Statement	Retrieval No.:	HR-1050
Brasto Publishing	Page:	1 of 1
	Issue Date:	10/28/0X
Subject: Work Schedules and Rest Periods	Supercedes:	N/A

Work Schedules

The established regular hours of work comprising full-time employment for staff employees shall be 40 hours per week. All offices shall be open during the hours 8 AM to 5 PM, Monday through Friday, except for official company holidays.

Rest Periods

Rest periods or coffee breaks may be offered at midmorning and midafternoon and will not exceed 15 minutes per break. Time not used for rest periods cannot be substituted for time off at the end of the work week nor added to the lunch period or to the beginning or end of a vacation or sick-leave period.

Flex-Time Work Schedule

The company's normal operating hours are 8 AM to 5 PM. However, some departments may want to use a flexible work schedule to ensure that their work is conducted before or after the normal operating period. When such an adjustment is desired, the total number of hours worked by the employee will be eight hours per day. In no case should a salaried employee work less than eight hours and be compensated for eight hours' work.

Work Schedules and Rest Periods

Policy/Procedure Statement Brasto Publishing **Subject: Changes in Employment Status**	Retrieval No.: Page: Issue Date: Supercedes:	HR-1060 1 of 2 10/28/0X N/A

Promotions
Opportunities for promotion at the company occur when a higher-level position becomes vacant. Employees are encouraged to prepare for possible promotion by taking advantage of growth and educational opportunities available to them and by performing current duties with excellence. When a vacancy occurs and is posted, employees are encouraged to investigate it and, if qualified, apply for it.

Classification levels are based on the level of difficulty of a position, not on the merit, education, longevity, experience, efficiency, or personality of the incumbent. Pay rates initially are based on the minimum for the established level. After initial employment, increases are based on the merit of the incumbent and usually on imposed budget constraints.

Promotions are not automatic. When a vacancy occurs, it must be posted for five days. During that period, anyone qualified for the vacancy can apply. The hiring authority is mandated to select the best candidate available. If the best candidate has applied from an on-premises position at a lower level, then a promotion can occur. If, however, a better candidate applies, the manager must select that person. No job or promotion is guaranteed at the company; each vacancy is considered an opening and is available to applicants who are interested and who qualify.

The company encourages supervisors and hiring authorities to consider company employees first for promotional opportunities. If an employee cannot be found who will qualify for the position, either in the immediate department or elsewhere on the premises, then the manager can consider outside applicants.

Applications for a promotional opportunity are managed the same way as any opening or vacancy is handled. Interested employees must complete an application and submit it to the Department of Human Resources. This serves as official notification of interest in the vacancy. No candidate will be considered for any staff position unless an application has been filed in the human resources department.

Transfers
A staff employee is eligible for consideration for a lateral transfer or reassignment to another company position after serving in a staff position for a period of six months, provided the request can be justified. However, it is possible to be reassigned earlier than six months if the transfer is made for the convenience of the company. Early transfers must have the approval of the vice president of human resources.

Every effort will be made to assign an employee to an activity that will be commensuratewith his or her background, training, and experience. Employees interested in transferring to another area should first inform their supervisor and then the Department of Human Resources.

Transfers within departments or between departments must proceed according to affirmative action hiring guidelines. A vacancy cannot be filled automatically within a department or between departments.

Changes in Employment Status (1 of 2)

Policy/Procedure Statement Brasto Publishing **Subject: Changes in Employment Status**	Retrieval No.: Page: Issue Date: Supercedes:	HR-1060 2 of 2 10/28/0X N/A

Dates of transfer shall be arranged for a time mutually agreeable to both the receiving and releasing departments, but should not be less than two weeks nor more than four weeks from the date of acceptance by the staff member.

Lateral transfers (moving from one position to another with the same job level) may not carry a pay increase. Transfers to positions at a lower classification level may carry a lower rate of pay. However, the transferring employee shall not be paid less than the minimum of the new pay level.

Changes in Employment Status (2 of 2)

Policy/Procedure Statement	Retrieval No.:	HR-1070
Brasto Publishing	Page:	1 of 1
	Issue Date:	10/28/0X
	Supercedes:	N/A
Subject: Personnel Records		

The Department of Human Resources keeps an individual record of personal and payroll data for each employee. Pertinent information is also maintained in the data processing center, for reports and statistical analysis. Because this information is frequently used for various reports, it is important that it be accurate.

Individual employees and their supervisors should keep the Department of Human Resources informed of any changes in personal status. Changes such as births or deaths in an employee's immediate family, or a change in marital status may affect such things as income tax withholding, retirement, or the type of hospital insurance coverage in effect. In emergency situations, it is important that current information relating to the name, address, or telephone number of the employee be available. All changes should be reported immediately to the Department of Human Resources.

An employee's personal information will not be disclosed by the Department of Human Resources to any unauthorized person or agency. Authorized agencies, such as a court of law, are supplied required information upon presentation of a proper request. Supervisors are obligated to adhere strictly to this policy, and it is generally advisable to refer such requests to the Department of Human Resources. An employee may have access to his or her personnel file by sending a written request to the Department of Human Resources and receiving approval from the vice president for human resources.

Personnel Records

Policy/Procedure Statement Brasto Publishing **Subject: Termination Policy and Requirements**	Retrieval No.: Page: Issue Date: Supercedes:	HR-1080 1 of 1 10/28/0X N/A

Termination

A termination interview is required for all exiting staff employees and will be conducted by the Department of Human Resources. All discharges of staff employees must have prior clearance through the Department of Human Resources by completing the Termination/ Leave form. When termination is the result of a discharge for cause, no advance notice need be given by the company, nor will the employee be considered for reemployment by the company.

Arrests

Employees charged with a felony or misdemeanor offense may be placed on a leave of absence. However, if the employee's actions or the nature of the crime is determined to affect the image or operation of the company, additional steps may be taken to prevent the employee from returning to the workplace. The vice president of human resources will determine the employment status of each person arrested and not convicted of a crime.

Notice Requirements

Notice of 10 working days is requested from all nonexempt staff employees who wish to terminate their employment with the company. The resignation notice should be addressed to the employee's supervisor. Notice of 15 working days is requested from all exempt staff employees prior to termination.

Clearance Requirements

Staff employees must complete and file with the Department of Human Resources a Termination Clearance before the last payroll check will be released. This form is available in the Department of Human Resources, and must accompany or be preceded by the Termination/ Leave Form and the final month's payroll sheet. It is the responsibility of the department to ensure that the terminating employee reports to the Department of Human Resources for a terminal interview on, or prior to, his or her last day of work. The Department of Human Resources will discuss any questions the employee has concerning his or her termination, including retirement refunds, continuation of insurance coverage, forwarding addresses, and so on.

Final paychecks will be processed on the next following scheduled payroll date for the employee. Payroll schedules prevent the payment of the employee's final paycheck on the day of departure unless that day coincides with the scheduled payroll date. An employee who is discharged for cause may receive payment on the day of departure through an advance payment request. In these situations, a minimum of 24 hours' notice is required from the department head.

Termination Policy and Requirements

Policy/Procedure Statement	Retrieval No.:	HR-1090
Brasto Publishing	Page:	1 of 2
	Issue Date:	10/28/0X
	Supercedes:	N/A
Subject: Reduction In-Force Policy		

Policy

A reduction in force may be required in the event of reorganization of a department or unit, changes in departmental organization or services; or elimination or reduction in funding. When a reduction in force is necessary, the following policy is used.

Procedure

Step one. The president shall determine those departments whose budgets must be reduced. This determination will be based on a systematic allocation of budget reductions and shall be rationally related to the corporation's mission statement.
Step two. If a reduction in personnel is necessary to meet the budget reductions for each department, the budget director will analyze and evaluate the necessity of each position within the department in consideration of its mission, the mandated budget reduction, and other positions within the department. The budget director will determine which positions will be recommended for elimination.
Step three. The budget director will consider the employees holding these positions within the department and shall determine which employees will be recommended for layoff. The following criteria will be considered when making recommendations to lay off personnel:

- The overall personnel needs of the department
- The possible consolidation of job responsibilities
- Employee skill levels
- Previous performance
- Protected employment status due to active military service
- Corporate affirmative action policies

If, after considering all of these criteria, two or more employees are rated the same or nearly so, the department manager will consider retaining the employee with the longest period of continuing service to the company.

Step four. The vice presidents will forward their termination recommendations to the company's affirmative action officer for review in relation to its affirmative action policies.
Step five. Written notification of layoff, including the reason for the layoff, shall be prepared by the Department of Human Resources. Such notification shall include a copy of this policy and shall be delivered by the department manager making the original recommendation for layoff.

Reduction In-Force Policy (1 of 2)

Policy/Procedure Statement Brasto Publishing **Subject: Reduction In-Force Policy**	Retrieval No.: Page: Issue Date: Supercedes:	HR-1090 2 of 2 10/28/0X N/A

Rights of Laid-Off Employees

Each department manager shall prepare a skills description for each laid-off employee. These descriptions shall be referred to the vice president of human resources for possible reassignment to other company departments. Any employee laid off under this reduction in force policy will be considered for reemployment for any position for which the employee is qualified that becomes available during the one-year period following layoff. To qualify for such consideration, each laid-off employee shall:

- Maintain with the Department of Human Resources a current address and telephone number at which he or she can be located.
- Indicate in writing to the vice president of human resources within five days of receipt of notification of a job opening, his or her intent to accept an offer of reemployment.
- Report to work no later than 15 calendar days from receipt of an offer of reemployment.

Failure to comply with these requirements shall constitute a waiver of consideration for reemployment.

Reduction In-Force Policy (2 of 2)

Policy/Procedure Statement Brasto Publishing **Subject: Nepotism**	Retrieval No.: Page: Issue Date: Supercedes:	HR-1100 1 of 1 10/28/0X N/A

A department may not employ any person in any capacity if such a person is related by blood or marriage within the third degree to any other employee in the same department if either one of the two related employees will have supervision of the other. A relation within the third degree is defined as a person related by blood or marriage, which would include parents, children, brothers, sisters, aunts, uncles, nieces, nephews, grandchildren, grandparents, great-grandparents, and step relatives.

This policy also applies to employees paid through contracts.

Nepotism

Policy/Procedure Statement	Procedure No.:	HR-1110
Brasto Publishing	Page:	1 of 1
	Issue Date:	10/28/0X
	Revision Date:	N/A
Subject: Discipline Policy		

The purpose of the disciplinary action policy is to correct improper employee behavior. In instances where employees exhibit no interest in improving their behavior, those employees may be terminated at will. Regardless of the existence of a disciplinary policy, there is no intent to negate the employment-at-will policy.

If disciplinary measures are imposed, it is essential that:

- Each problem be investigated to determine the facts of the situation.
- Any action taken must be primarily corrective rather than punitive and must be appropriate for the offense.
- The dignity of the employee is respected.

The following acts may result in dismissal or disciplinary suspension, pending investigation:

- Fraud in securing employment
- Incompetency
- Neglect of duty
- Insubordination
- Dishonesty
- Drunkenness on duty
- Use of narcotics while on duty
- Noncompliance with company safety rules
- Absence without leave
- Conviction of a felony or misdemeanor involving moral turpitude
- Poor work performance
- Gambling on company property
- Willful disobedience
- Misuse of company property
- Unprofessional conduct
- Sleeping on duty
- Willful property damage
- Physical fights
- Tardiness
- Unauthorized possession of firearms or explosives on company property
- Threats or pressure or physical action against other employees
- Dishonesty, theft, or the commission of any crime on company property
- Falsifying timekeeping records
- Refusal to accept instructions, including failure to perform assigned work
- Careless performance of duties
- Failure to report to work at the beginning of the work period and leaving work prior to the end of the work period
- Failure of absent employees to notify their supervisor during an absence
- Using company phones or Internet connections excessively for personal calls

Discipline Policy

Policy/Procedure Statement	Retrieval No.:	HR-2010
Brasto Publishing	Page:	1 of 1
	Issue Date:	10/28/0X
	Supercedes:	N/A
Subject: Deductions		

New employees of the company are required to report to the Department of Human Resources to complete initial paperwork. The date and time of this meeting will be scheduled by the Department of Human Resources. The employee will complete and sign personnel and payroll forms necessary to begin the pay schedule and will be advised regarding fringe benefits and insurance packages available through the company. Federal and state laws require the following payroll deductions by the company:

- Federal withholding tax
- State withholding tax
- Social security tax
- Retirement contributions

Some of the other deductions that may be made at the election of the employee include:

- 401(k) plan deductions
- Group medical insurance for dependent coverage
- Life insurance
- Group accident insurance
- Credit union dues
- Disability insurance
- United Way contributions

Premiums will be deducted from the employee payroll checks. Insurance premiums for the group health insurance coverage are deducted in advance: premiums paid in the current month pay for coverage in the next month.

All deductions are shown on the payroll check stub. Employees who have questions or who need assistance in understanding the deductions shown on the check should bring the check stub to the Department of Human Resources and request assistance.

Employees desiring to change deductions or premium payments should come to the Department of Human Resources. All tax changes and insurance benefit changes require completion of new forms and the employee's signature. Except for changes in family status, these changes can only be made during open enrollment each year.

Policy/Procedure Statement	Retrieval No.:	HR-2020
Brasto Publishing	Page:	1 of 1
	Issue Date:	10/28/0X
	Supercedes:	N/A
Subject: Fair Labor Standards Act		

The Fair Labor Standards Act (FSLA) is a federal law that sets minimum wage, overtime pay, equal pay, and child labor standards for employment subject to its provisions. The company complies with the provisions of the FLSA. For more information concerning this law, please contact the human resources department.

Overtime

In order to comply with this Act, determination must first be made as to any employee's exempt or nonexempt status. If an employee is categorized as nonexempt, then overtime pay is due for any hours worked in excess of 40 within a given pay week.

Overtime rates are paid at one and one-half the employee's regular hourly rate of pay. It is the responsibility of the department manager to keep accurate records of time worked in excess of 40 hours. The FLSA requires that both the regular wage and any overtime pay due an employee be computed on the basis of the hours worked in each workweek by an employee and that the compensation earned by an employee in a particular workweek be paid on the regular payday for the pay period in which the workweek ends.

Compensatory Time

If a nonexempt employee of the company works more than 40 hours in a given workweek, that employee may receive compensatory time off at a rate of not less than one and one-half hours for each hour of overtime worked. The use of compensatory time must be in accordance with an agreement reached between the company and the employee prior to the performance of the work. Compensatory time received by an employee in lieu of cash must be at the rate of not less than one and one-half hours of compensatory time for each hour of overtime work, just as the monetary rate for overtime is calculated at the rate of not less than one and one-half times the regular rate of pay.

Fair Labor Standards Act

Policy/Procedure Statement	Retrieval No.:	HR-3010
Brasto Publishing	Page:	1 of 2
	Issue Date:	10/28/0X
Subject: Personal Leave	Supercedes:	N/A

Regular Staff Employees
Regular staff employees are entitled to personal leave benefits beginning on their first effective date of employment with the company. Part-time employees accrue on a pro rata basis, depending on the number of hours worked. Accrual rates for full-time employees are:

Personal Leave Accrual

Service Time	Hours per Month	Days per Year
1 month to 3 years	12	18
37 months to 8 years	14	21
97 months to 15 years	16	24
Over 15 years	18	27

Personal leave can only be taken with approval of the employee's supervisor and may be denied if such leave causes a major problem in the workload distribution within the department.

Terminal Leave Policies
To avoid major disruptions in the work environment, employees may be granted a maximum of 30 days personal leave within the six-month period immediately preceding termination. This leave can be taken only with approval of the employee's supervisor and may be denied if such leave causes a major problem in the workload distribution within the department.

Vacations
Vacations shall be scheduled by departments in recognition of the needs of the company but with consideration of an employee's continuous service credit and amount of personal leave accrued and unused. Within the requirement to maintain work schedules, each department will do everything possible to accommodate the employee's personal leave preferences.

Illnesses
The first eight hours of absence due to illness will be charged to personal leave. Absence due to the same illness in excess of eight hours will be charged to major medical leave.

Death
Should an employee die having accumulated personal leave credit, the wages or salary for the total unused personal leave time shall be paid to the person designated by the employee for this purpose or, in the absence of such designation, to the beneficiary of such employee.

Personal Leave (1 of 2)

Policy/Procedure Statement	Retrieval No.:	HR-3010
Brasto Publishing	Page:	2 of 2
	Issue Date:	10/28/0X
Subject: Personal Leave	Supercedes:	N/A

Reemployment

When an employee is reemployed by the company after a break in service of more than 30 days, personal and major medical leave time will be earned as a new employee. An employee rehired within 30 days of termination is not entitled to 240 hours of termination leave pay. If the individual has received this payment and returns to work within the 30 day period, the payment should be refunded to the company in order to continue earning leave at the prior accrual rates.

Payment of Leave

An employee terminating from service and requesting lump-sum payment for unused personal leave will receive payment for up to a maximum of 240 hours for the leave time at the next scheduled pay period following his or her date of termination.

Personal Leave (2 of 2)

Policy/Procedure Statement	Retrieval No.:	HR-3020
Brasto Publishing	Page:	1 of 2
	Issue Date:	10/28/0X
	Supercedes:	N/A
Subject: Family and Medical Leave		

The Family and Medical Leave Act of 1993 was passed by Congress to balance the demands of the workplace with the needs of families, to promote the stability and economic security of families, and to promote national interests in preserving family integrity. It minimizes the potential for employment discrimination on the basis of sex by ensuring generally that leave is available for eligible medical reasons and for compelling family reasons.

Eligible Employees

An employee who has been employed with the company for at least one year and who has worked at least 1,250 hours during the past 12 months is entitled to a total of 12 workweeks, paid or unpaid, of leave during any 12-month period for one or more of the reasons listed below:

- For the birth of a child and to care for the child after birth, provided the leave is taken within 12 months of the birth.
- For the employee to care for a child placed with the employee for adoption, provided the leave is taken within a 12-month period following adoption.
- For the employee to care for the employee's child, spouse, or parent, where that child, spouse, or parent has a serious health condition.
- Because the employee has a serious health condition that makes the employee unable to perform the functions of the employee's position.

This policy does not cover temporary employees because the maximum length of a temporary appointment is 4½ months. If a husband and wife are employed by the company, the aggregate number of workweeks of leave is limited to 12 workweeks during any 12-month period.

Intermittent Leave or Reduced Work Schedule Leave

Pursuant to this policy, the employee may not take leave intermittently or on a reduced work schedule for childbirth and birth-related child care or for adoption, unless the employee and the company agree otherwise. The employee may take leave intermittently or on a reduced schedule to care for the employee's child, spouse, or parent who has a serious health condition, or because the employee has a serious health condition. If such leave is foreseeable and based on planned medical treatment, the company may require the employee to transfer temporarily to an available alternative position for which the employee is qualified and that has equivalent pay and benefits and better accommodates recurring periods of leave.

Family and Medical Leave (1 of 2)

Policy/Procedure Statement	Retrieval No.:	HR-3020
Brasto Publishing	Page:	2 of 2
	Issue Date:	10/28/0X
Subject: Family and Medical Leave	Supercedes:	N/A

Employee Responsibility

The employee shall apply in writing to the supervisor for leave requested under this policy as follows:

1. *Birth or adoption*. The employee shall give the company no less than 30 days' notice, in writing, of the intention to take leave, subject to the actual date of the birth or adoption. If the date of the birth or adoption requires less than 30 days, the employee shall provide such notice as is practicable.
2. *Planned medical treatment*. When leave is necessary to care for the employee's child, spouse, or parent or because the employee has a serious health condition, the employee must make a reasonable effort to schedule the treatment so as not to unduly disrupt operations, subject to the approval of the employee's health care provider. The employee should also give 30 days' notice of the intention to take leave, subject to the actual date of the treatment.

After the period of leave pursuant to this policy, if the employee will not return to work, the company should be notified immediately. Failure to report at the expiration of the leave, unless an extension has been requested, may be considered as a resignation.

Employment and Benefit Protection

- *Reinstatement*. The employee shall be reinstated to the same position held when the leave began or one of like pay, grade, benefits, or other conditions of employment. The company may require the employee to report at reasonable intervals on the employee's status and intention to return to work. The company shall also require that the employee receive certification that the employee is able to return to work.
- *Benefits*. The employee shall be instated without loss of benefits accrued when the leave began. All benefits accrue during any period of paid leave; however, no benefits will be accrued during any period of leave without pay.
- *Health benefits*. The company shall maintain coverage for the employee under the company's group health plan, at no cost to the employee, only for the duration of the leave. The company may recover the premiums if the employee fails to return after the period of leave to which the employee is entitled has expired, for a reason other than the continuation, recurrence, or onset of a serious health condition or other circumstances beyond the employee's control.

Family and Medical Leave (2 of 2)

Policy/Procedure Statement	Retrieval No.:	HR-3030
Brasto Publishing	Page:	1 of 1
	Issue Date:	10/28/0X
	Supercedes:	N/A
Subject: Leave of Absence Without Pay		

In no instance are leaves of absence granted automatically. All leaves of absence require a written request from the employee, approval and support of the employee's supervisor, and the final approval of the vice president for human resources.

Leaves of absence without pay may be granted to staff employees for the following reasons:

- Necessary absences due to illness or for emergency reasons when such absences extend beyond available personal and major medical leave accruals.
- Approved professional development in the areas of education, research, and advanced training. This reason must be justified as being in the best interest of the company.

Reinstatement
Leaves of absence will be granted with the assurance of reinstatement to the same or a comparable position within the company unless circumstances make it clearly impractical. Personal and major medical leave time will not accrue during leaves of absence without pay; however, earned leave credit may be carried forward.

Employee Benefits
When on leave of absence without pay, an employee may continue to participate in certain employee benefit programs, such as the group health insurance plan. The total cost of participation while on leave without pay must be paid by the employee. The employee is responsible for making arrangements with both the Department of Human Resources and the Department of Business and Finance so that benefits can continue during his or her absence.

Employment Requirements
Leaves of absence without pay will not be granted to any employee with less than one year's previous service with the company. A Termination/Leave form, prepared by the appropriate supervisor, will be required on all employees returning from leave of absence without pay status. This form will reactivate the employee and place him or her back on active pay status.

Leave of Absence Without Pay

Policy/Procedure Statement	Retrieval No.:	HR-3040
Brasto Publishing	Page:	1 of 1
	Issue Date:	10/28/0X
Subject: Holiday Leave	Supercedes:	N/A

This policy establishes a uniform number of holidays and defines payment of holidays for all company staff employees. The company recognizes the following days as holidays:

- New Year's Day
- Martin Luther King Jr. Day
- Memorial Day
- Independence Day
- Labor Day
- Veterans Day
- Thanksgiving Day
- Friday after Thanksgiving Day
- Christmas Day

All holidays are subject to change if there is a conflict with the work schedule, and those changes will be at the discretion of the president.

Eligibility

All full-time or part-time employees on the active payroll will be eligible for holiday pay on the days listed above, in accordance with the following provisions:

- Employees must work their normally scheduled work hours on the day immediately preceding and following the holiday. With the approval of the supervisor, the employee may elect to take personal leave days immediately prior to or following a holiday period. If the employee has an excused absence on both such days, holiday pay will be authorized.
- Holiday pay will be at the employee's current rate of pay.
- Part-time employees will not be paid holiday pay.
- If any official holiday falls within a period of an employee's approval personal or major medical leave, it shall be considered holiday leave and shall not be deducted from the employee's accrued personal leave.
- An employee must work on his or her last official day of employment. Holidays falling within the terminal leave period for a terminating employee are charged to accumulated personal leave.

Religious Holiday

Full-time or part-time employees who desire to observe an "official" religious holiday, in accordance with their religious preference, may do so with their supervisor's approval. The time and attendance record should reflect the time taken as personal leave.

Holiday Leave

Policy/Procedure Statement	Retrieval No.:	HR-3050
Brasto Publishing	Page:	1 of 1
	Issue Date:	10/28/0X
Subject: Military Leave	Supercedes:	N/A

Employees of the company who are called to active military service on short notice as a result of a national emergency may be granted military leave of absence without pay beginning on the date of the call to military service.

Maximum Leave Time

A leave of absence with pay, not to exceed 15 working days annually, may be granted to regular employees, who, as members of the National Guard or members of any of the reserve components of the Armed Forces, are ordered to active duty.

When a company employee, who is a member of the National Guard or Reserve, is ordered to active duty for a period in excess of 15 days, the employee is entitled to a leave of absence, continuation of insurance benefits, and use of accrued personal leave. The employee may not use accrued major medical leave during this absence.

Approval for any military leave must be secured in advance from the Department of Human Resources. A copy of the military orders shall be filed with the Department of Human Resources.

Policy/Procedure Statement	Retrieval No.:	HR-3060
Brasto Publishing	Page:	1 of 1
	Issue Date:	10/28/0X
	Supercedes:	N/A
Subject: Health Insurance		

The company pays the employee-only portion of premiums for health insurance coverage. Dependent coverage is available; premiums will be at the employee's expense. Dependent coverage is offered only to those employees who are covered by the plan. Application must be made within 31 days of acquiring an eligible dependent.

Employees will enroll or waive coverage on the first day of employment. A group insurance booklet will be provided to the employee upon enrollment. This booklet will answer questions regarding claim procedures and payments, eligibility, special plan features, and so on. Should an employee have questions that the booklet does not answer, the plan administrator should be contacted. Employees should contact the fringe benefits manager in the Department of Human Resources if their booklets have been lost, if assistance is needed in filing a claim, or if a change occurs in dependent coverage, beneficiaries, or a covered employee's address.

Dependent Coverage

If an employee chooses not to enroll dependents at the initial employee enrollment, then dependents can only be added during open enrollment in December with an effective date of January 1.

Open Enrollment

The group health plan allows for an open enrollment to occur one time during the calendar year, which the company conducts in December. At that time, employees may:

- Add or drop dependent coverages.
- Add or drop any company-offered insurance benefit.
- Elect to keep insurance benefits as they presently exist.
- Elect to participate in dependent care reimbursement or medical reimbursement plans.

Employees are cautioned that open enrollment occurs once a year and this is the only time when changes can be made to insurance programs, unless a change in family status occurs. This change in status is defined as marriage, divorce, death of a spouse or dependent child, birth or adoption of a child, and termination or employment of a spouse.

Policy/Procedure Statement Brasto Publishing Subject: COBRA	Retrieval No.: Page: Issue Date: Supercedes:	HR-3070 1 of 1 10/28/0X N/A

The federal law known as Consolidated Omnibus Budget Reconciliation Act (COBRA) went into effect in 1987. Under this law, all employees and employee family members who are covered under the group health plan are entitled to continuation coverage. This coverage will be made available to covered persons in the event of employee termination, divorce, separation, or death, and in certain other instances.

Under the provisions of COBRA, employees have 60 days in which to accept continuation coverage of the company's medical insurance following their termination from employment. If they accept this coverage, then they will pay the insurer-designated premium for a period not to exceed 18 months following the date of termination. If they do not accept this coverage within the 60-day acceptance period, then they lose the right to accept it at a later date.

Upon acceptance of COBRA coverage by a former employee, the company will notify the insurance carrier of the change in status, at which point the insurer will bill the employee directly for the cost of continuing monthly coverage.

Policy/Procedure Statement	Retrieval No.:	HR-3080
Brasto Publishing	Page:	1 of 1
	Issue Date:	10/28/0X
	Supercedes:	N/A
Subject: Salary Continuation Insurance Plans		

Long-Term Disability

This plan is designed to guarantee an employee a monthly income if the employee should become disabled from sickness or injury and can no longer work for a living. It pays 60 percent of the employee's base pay, subject to a maximum benefit limit, less any amount payable under workers' compensation, social security, and any disability, retirement, or other benefits provided by or through the company. The minimum benefit is $100 per month. The benefit becomes available after a 90-day waiting period.

All full-time staff members under 65 years of age are eligible to enroll in this insurance plan during the first 30 days of employment. Enrollment after the initial period will be subject to acceptance by the insurance company and will require evidence of insurability.

Short-Term Disability

This program is designed to provide income while (1) totally disabled and unable to work due to an accident, beginning on the first day of disability, and (2) totally disabled and unable to work resulting from a covered sickness beginning on the eighth day of disability.

All full-time employees under the age of 65 working at least 30 hours per week will be eligible to enroll during their initial employment payroll period. An employee who applies after the enrollment period has expired will be required to supply evidence of insurability and will be subject to acceptance by the insurance company.

Policy/Procedure Statement	Retrieval No.:	HR-3090
Brasto Publishing	Page:	1 of 2
	Issue Date:	10/28/0X
	Supercedes:	N/A
Subject: Additional Group Policies Available		

If employees choose not to enroll themselves or their dependents in the optional group policies at the initial employment enrollment, they can only be added during open enrollment in December, with an effective date of January 1.

Group Life Insurance

Eligibility is determined by the same criteria as the comprehensive health plan. The amount of insurance will be an amount equal to the employee's annualized rate of pay, rounded up to the nearest $1,000. There is a maximum benefit of $100,000. Retired employees may purchase coverage under this plan in increments of $1,000, up to a maximum benefit of $50,000.

Employees interested in obtaining coverage will be enrolled on their first day of employment and provided with a booklet outlining policy coverages and provisions. The company will pay 50 percent of the premium, with the employee paying the remainder through payroll deductions.

Accidental Death and Dismemberment Insurance

Accidental death and dismemberment coverage on a 24-hour basis is available at group rates to all active full-time employees under the age of 70. Dependent coverage is also available; however, dependents may only be covered if the employee is also enrolled.

Medical Reimbursement Plan

This plan is designed to allow an employee to set aside pretax dollars to cover out-of-pocket medical expenses, not paid by group health insurance benefits, that occur during the plan year. The Internal Revenue Service has established strict guidelines for moneys not used by the end of the plan year. If one contributes dollars to a medical reimbursement account and does not use all of the moneys contributed, he or she will lose any remaining balance in the account at the end of the plan year.

Group Dental Coverage

Group rates are available for employee and dependent dental care. Coverage is available for preventive and diagnostic treatment: basic benefits for fillings and extractions, major benefits to include oral surgery, and orthodontic programs for children under age 19. The employee is responsible for total premium payments under this program.

Additional Group Policies Available (1 of 2)

Policy/Procedure Statement	Retrieval No.:	HR-3090
Brasto Publishing	Page:	2 of 2
	Issue Date:	10/28/0X
	Supercedes:	N/A
Subject: Additional Group Policies Available		

401(k) Retirement Plan

Employees may enroll in the company's 401(k) plan at any time following their first 90 days of employment. They may contribute up to 15% of their payroll dollars to this plan, and designate any mix of investment plans offered to which the money shall be contributed, up to a federally designated maximum amount per year. Employees can change the mix of investment plans and the amount of their contributions at any time. The plan also provides for a loan program, with loans offsetting the amount of any contributions already made to the plan. The details of this plan are available at the Department of Human Resources.

Additional Group Policies Available (2 of 2)

Policy/Procedure Statement	Retrieval No.:	HR-3100
Brasto Publishing	Page:	1 of 1
	Issue Date:	10/28/0X
Subject: Workers' Compensation	Supercedes:	N/A

The company provides standard workers' compensation coverage under a self-insurance program in accordance with state laws which prescribe the amounts of indemnity payable for the degrees of disability and for death if the injury or disability occurs on the job. These laws also provide for medical care, hospitalization, and weekly compensation for the period of disability. All on-the-job injuries should be reported immediately to the employee's supervisor. A claim form must be completed for all injuries, and the Safety Department must be notified of the incident.

Policy/Procedure Statement		
Brasto Publishing	Retrieval No.:	HR-4010
	Page:	1 of 1
	Issue Date:	10/28/0X
	Supercedes:	N/A
Subject: Grievance Policy		

It is the company's policy to provide an immediate and fair method by which to settle disputes that may arise between the company and its employees.

Grievance Procedures

The number of required steps in this procedure may vary, depending on the department involved and the number of supervisors above the employee. Employees may use the following steps to seek redress of a grievance:

1. *An informal attempt to resolve the grievance through a meeting with the employee's immediate supervisor.* This first step must be made within 10 working days of the incident, and the employee must state to his or her immediate supervisor that a grievance is being initiated. The written grievance should state the nature of the complaint and the action requested to resolve the grievance. The immediate supervisor must render a response to the written grievance within five working days of the initial complaint.
2. *A formal written statement of the grievance, submitted through administrative channels, stating the nature of the complaint and the desired adjustment.* The employee assumes responsibility for advancing the complaint to the next higher level within one week of an answer that is unsatisfactory to him or her.
3. *The use of "chain of command" supervision to resolve the complaint.* If an answer from the responding supervisor is unsatisfactory to resolve the complaint, the employee may, within 10 working days of receipt of the answer, submit to the appropriate vice president of his or her area a written request to review all materials related to the complaint. The vice president will evaluate all facts presented and conduct a meeting with the employee to attempt to resolve the grievance. The vice president will, within five working days of the meeting, render a decision regarding the complaint.
4. *The convening of a grievance committee to hear the case and make a recommendation to the president.* The employee may submit to the Equal Employment Opportunity/Affirmative Action officer a written request to conduct a hearing. The company grievance committee will then be convened to hear the grievance.
5. *A review and final decision by the president.* Copies of the final decision will be transmitted to the employee, the department manager, the vice president of the area in which the employee is employed, the company's affirmative action officer, and the vice president for human resources.

At the outset of this process, the employee is invited to the human resources office for procedural guidance. Every effort should be made to settle the grievance by mutual consent at the lowest administrative level possible.

Grievance Policy

Policy/Procedure Statement Brasto Publishing **Subject: Sexual Harassment Policy**	Retrieval No.: Page: Issue Date: Supercedes:	HR-4020 1 of 2 10/28/0X N/A

Subject: Sexual Harassment Policy
The company, in its efforts to foster an environment of respect for the dignity and worth of all members of the company community, is committed to maintaining a work environment free of sexual harassment. It is the policy of the company that no member of its community shall sexually harass another. An employee who violates this policy is subject to disciplinary action.

Sexual harassment is illegal under both state and federal law. Vice presidents and other supervisory personnel are directed to take appropriate steps to disseminate this policy statement to inform employees of procedures for lodging complaints.

The following procedures are intended to provide alternatives for resolving complaints of sexual harassment. However, the company shall fully retain all rights to discipline or discharge an employee who engages in misconduct or other behavior that is prohibited by law or other company policy, notwithstanding the remedies and procedures offered in this policy.

Definition of Sexual Harassment
Unwelcome sexual advances, requests for sexual favors, and other verbal or physical conduct of a sexual nature constitute sexual harassment when:

- Submission to such conduct is made either explicitly or implicitly a term or condition of an individual's employment.
- Submission to or rejection of such conduct by an individual is used as the basis for employment decisions affecting that individual.
- Such conduct has the purpose or effect of substantially interfering with an individual professional performance or creating an intimidating, hostile, or offensive employment environment.

Procedures for prompt, appropriate corrective action are an essential part of the company's effort to deal with sexual harassment. Action on harassment complaints will be taken immediately and appropriately through administrative channels. At all stages of the presentation and processing of a complaint, the employee and the alleged offender will be free from restraint, interference, coercion, discrimination, or reprisal.

Sexual Harassment Policy (1 of 2)

Policy/Procedure Statement	Retrieval No.:	HR-4020
Brasto Publishing	Page:	2 of 2
	Issue Date:	10/28/0X
Subject: Sexual Harassment Policy	Supercedes:	N/A

Confidentiality

Because of the sensitivity of the information involved, any documents pertaining to sexual harassment cases and any resulting disciplinary action will be transferred to and maintained in confidential files under the supervision of the Equal Employment Opportunity/Affirmative Action officer.

Investigation Procedures

Any supervisor, department head, or administrator to whom a complaint of sexual harassment is brought, is to proceed as follows:

1. Hold separate preliminary discussions with the employee and the accused.
2. Facilitate a swift and confidential investigation of the allegation.
3. Inform the employee and the accused of existing company support programs, such as the counseling program, health center, and employee assistance program.
4. Follow through to see that the appropriate administrator has resolved the complaint and taken prompt and appropriate corrective action when necessary.
5. Advise the employee and the accused of procedures to follow if there is an unresolved complaint (see the grievance policy).

Every effort is made through these procedures to resolve, with promptness and confidentiality, a sexual harassment complaint and to take appropriate corrective action when necessary.

Sexual Harassment Policy (2 of 2)

Policy/Procedure Statement	Retrieval No.:	HR-5010
Brasto Publishing	Page:	1 of 1
	Issue Date:	10/28/0X
	Supercedes:	N/A
Subject: Drug-Free Workplace Policy		

The company prohibits the unlawful possession, use, or distribution of illicit drugs and alcohol by employees on the company's property or as part of any of its activities. The company will maintain a drug-free workplace. The unlawful manufacture, distribution, dispensation, possession, or use of a controlled substance is prohibited on company property. Employees who violate these laws are subject to appropriate personnel sanctions, including possible termination of employment, as well as any penalties imposed by a court of law.

The company makes available to its employees an employee assistance program that includes drug counseling and rehabilitation. The services are provided in a confidential manner. Employees having substance abuse problems:

- Are encouraged to seek assistance voluntarily on a confidential basis by contacting their immediate supervisor or the company's employee assistance program.
- Have a right to accept or refuse help as they choose; however, individual work performance must always meet acceptable standards or be subject to existing personnel procedures for below-standard performance.

The company's group health insurance may cover part of the cost of certain drug-related treatment programs. Employees are advised to contact the human resources department for more information concerning benefits. Treatment costs not covered by the company's group health plan must be paid for by the employee.

It is the responsibility of company officers and staff to abide by the terms and provisions of the drug-free workplace policy, and to notify the company of any criminal drug conviction for a violation occurring in the workplace no later than five days after such conviction.

The company has the responsibility to impose sanctions or require satisfactory participation in an approved drug abuse assistance or rehabilitation program by any employee who is convicted of a drug-related violation in the workplace, and to conduct periodic training and counseling for employees concerning the hazards of drugs in the workplace.

Drug-Free Workplace Policy

Policy/Procedure Statement	Procedure No.:	HR-5020
	Page:	1 of 1
	Issue Date:	10/28/0X
	Revision Date:	N/A
Subject: The Americans with Disabilities Act		

The Americans with Disabilities Act (ADA) makes it unlawful to discriminate against an applicant or employee, whether disabled or not, because of the individual's family, business, social, or other relationship or association with an individual with a disability. Under the ADA, a person has a disability if he or she has a physical or mental impairment that substantially limits a major life activity. A substantial impairment is one that significantly limits a major life activity such as hearing, seeing, speaking, breathing, performing manual tasks, walking, caring for oneself, or working.

To be protected by the ADA, an individual with a disability must also be qualified to perform the essential functions of the job with or without reasonable accommodations. This means that the applicant or employee must satisfy job requirements for education background, employee experience, skills, licenses, and any other qualification standards that are job-related, and be able to perform those tasks that are essential to the job, with or without reasonable accommodation.

Essential Functions

Factors to consider in determining whether a function is essential include:

- Whether the reason the position exists is to perform the function.
- The number of other employees available to perform the function or among whom the performance of the function can be distributed.
- The degree of expertise or skill required to perform the function.

Reasonable Accommodation

Reasonable accommodation is any change or adjustment to a job or work environment that does not promote an undue hardship on the employer and that permits a qualified applicant or employee with a disability to participate in the job application process, to perform the essential functions of a job, or to enjoy benefits and privileges of employment equal to those enjoyed by employees without disabilities. For example, reasonable accommodation may include:

- Acquiring or modifying equipment or devices
- Job restructuring
- Part-time or modified work schedules
- Reassignment to a vacant position
- Adjusting or modifying examinations, training materials, or policies
- Providing readers and interpreters
- Making the workplace readily accessible to and usable by people with disabilities

It is a violation of the ADA to fail to provide reasonable accommodation to the known physical or mental limitations of a qualified individual with a disability, unless to do so would impose an undue hardship on the operation of the business. Undue hardship means that the accommodation would require significant difficulty or expense.

The Americans with Disabilities Act

Policy/Procedure Statement	Retrieval No.:	HR-5030
Brasto Publishing	Page:	1 of 1
	Issue Date:	10/28/0X
	Supercedes:	N/A
Subject: Jury Duty and Elections		

Jury Duty

Jury duty is recognized as a civic responsibility. A regular employee who is called for jury duty or summoned to appear as a witness on behalf of any town, city, county, state, or federal government shall be granted special leave with pay. The payment granted to an employee for serving on a jury may be retained by the employee. When an employee has been granted special leave for court attendance, he or she shall report immediately to his or her official place of duty whenever he or she is excused by the court.

Special leave with pay shall not be granted for court attendance when the employee is the defendant or is engaged in personal litigation. Personal leave shall be used for this purpose.

Elections

Most employees live or work close enough to the election polls to vote before or after working hours. Should this not be possible, the employee may have time off to vote in county, state, or federal elections with the prior approval of his or her immediate supervisor.

Jury Duty and Elections

12.3 HUMAN RESOURCES PROCEDURES

Human resources procedures are organized in accordance with the process flowchart shown in Exhibit 12.1. These process flows show the standard flow of transactions for most human resources activities. Using this approach forces one to review an entire process and identify all possible procedures, which results in a more complete set of documentation. By using the index number at the bottom of each square in the flow charts, one can refer to the procedure numbers in this chapter to find the appropriate underlying procedure.

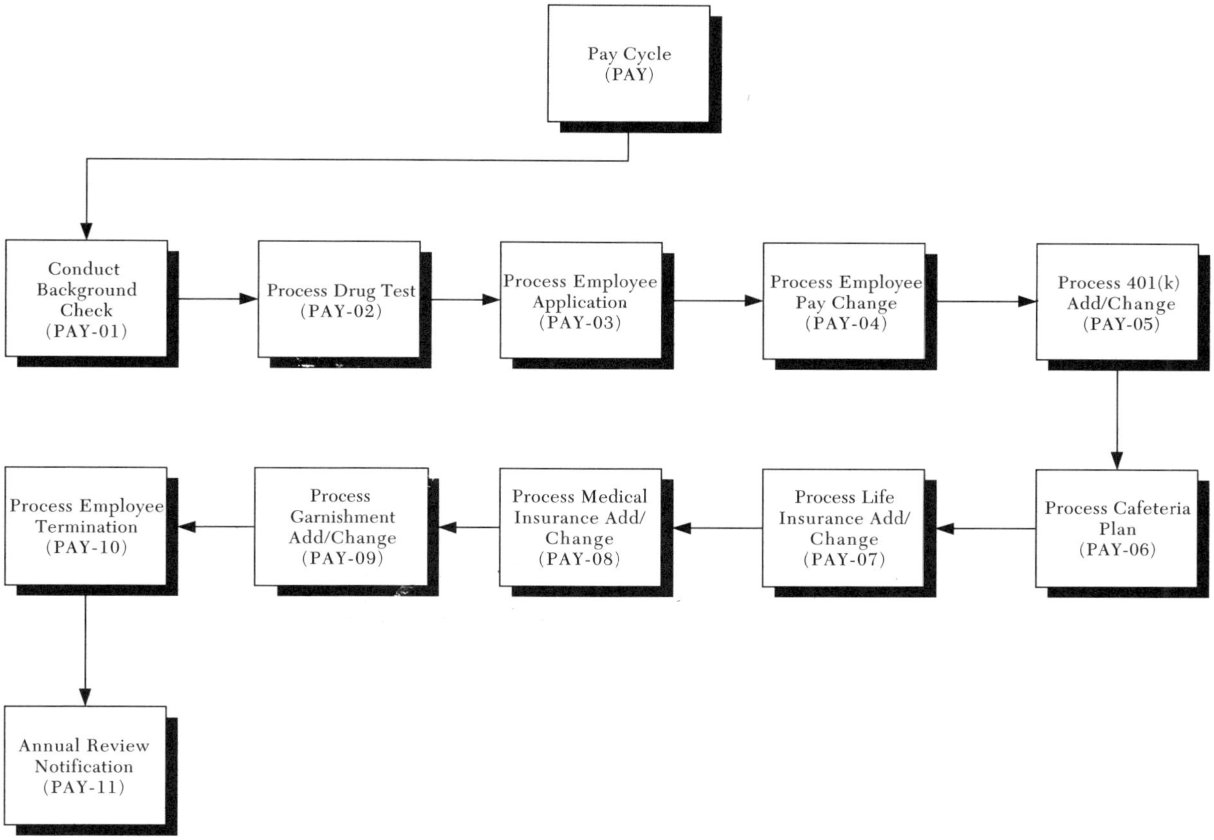

Exhibit 12.1. Process Flow for the Pay Cycle

The complete list of detailed procedures listed in this chapter are:

1. Pay Cycle (PAY)

   - Conduct Background Check (PAY-01)
   - Process Drug Test (PAY-02)
   - Process Employee Application (PAY-03)
   - Process Employee Pay Change (PAY-04)
   - Process 401(k) Add/Change (PAY-05)
   - Process Cafeteria Plan Add/Change (PAY-06)
   - Process Life Insurance Add/Change (PAY-07)
   - Process Medical Insurance Add/Change (PAY-08)
   - Process Garnishment Add/Change (PAY-09)
   - Process Employee Termination (PAY-10)
   - Annual Review Notification (PAY-11)

These procedures are simplified versions of actual procedures, so they will require some enhancement in most cases. However, they can be used as the basic operational template for a set of more detailed computer system procedures for most companies, if information is added regarding specific file and screen names that fit a company's specific applications.

Policy/Procedure Statement	Retrieval No.:	PAY-01
Brasto Publishing	Page:	1 of 2
	Issue Date:	10/28/0X
Subject: Conduct Background Check	Supercedes:	N/A

1. PURPOSE AND SCOPE

This procedure is used by the human resources coordinator to review the references, credit history, and legal history of all new job applicants.

2. RESPONSIBILITIES

HR COORD **Human Resources Coordinator**

3. PROCEDURES

3.1 HR COORD **Have Applicant Fill Out Permission Forms**

1. Have applicant sign permission forms for school transcripts, personal references, and business and credit references.
2. Compare the person's signature on the forms to his or her signature on driver's license.

3.2 HR COORD **Send Transcript Request Forms to Applicant's School**

1. Send transcript request forms to all colleges and high schools listed on the applicant's job application.
2. Send a follow-up form if the original request is not responded to within two weeks.

3.3 HR COORD **Send Reference Forms to Applicant References**

1. Send personal reference forms to all references listed on the applicant's job application.
2. Call the reference if a written response has not been received within two weeks.

3.4 HR COORD **Send Reference Forms to Former Employers**

1. Send employer reference forms to all employers listed on the job application for the last 10 years.
2. Call the employers if a written response has not been received within two weeks.

3.5 HR COORD **Conduct Credit and Legal Investigations**

1. Purchase credit reference information from a credit history recording firm.
2. Purchase legal history from legal history recording firm, covering all states and local jurisdictions.

Conduct Background Check (1 of 2)

Policy/Procedure Statement Brasto Publishing Subject: Conduct Background Check	Retrieval No.: Page: Issue Date: Supercedes:	PAY-01 2 of 2 10/28/0X N/A

3.6 HR COORD

Assemble Materials and Follow Up on Discrepancies

1. Compare all received information to the job application, and follow up on any missing documentation.
2. Verify that all time periods in the applicant's 10-year history are covered by employer references.
3. Contact the applicant for additional information if there are discrepancies between the job application and the reference materials.

3.7 HR COORD

Issue Recommendation to Hiring Supervisor

1. Based on the received materials, record all job history discrepancies and credit and legal problems.
2. Discuss these issues with the human resources manager, and issue a hiring recommendation to the hiring supervisor.

Conduct Background Check (2 of 2)

Policy/Procedure Statement	Retrieval No.:	PAY-02
Brasto Publishing	Page:	1 of 1
	Issue Date:	10/28/0X
Subject: Process Drug Test	Supercedes:	N/A

1. PURPOSE AND SCOPE

This procedure is used by the human resources coordinator to have job applicants tested, as well as to act upon the results of those tests in extending job offers to applicants.

2. RESPONSIBILITIES

HR COORD **Human Resources Coordinator**

3. PROCEDURES

3.1 HR COORD **Send Applicant to Medical Facility**

Give applicant directions to the medical facility that conducts drug tests for the company, with instructions regarding the type of test to be taken.

3.2 HR COORD **Evaluate Drug Test Findings**

1. Once the medical facility has sent back the results of its drug test, compare the results to the company's acceptable drug levels in various drug categories.
2. Summarize the drug results and forward them to the human resources manager.

3.3 HR COORD **Issue Recommendation to Hiring Supervisor**

Discuss any drug issues with the human resources manager, and issue a hiring recommendation to the hiring supervisor.

Process Drug Test

Policy/Procedure Statement Brasto Publishing **Subject: Process Employee Application**	Retrieval No.: Page: Issue Date: Supercedes:	PAY-03 1 of 1 10/28/0X N/A

1. PURPOSE AND SCOPE

This procedure is used by the human resources coordinator, primarily as a checklist, to ensure that all legal and internal paperwork associated with an employee application has been completed.

2. RESPONSIBILITIES

HR COORD **Human Resources Coordinator**

3. PROCEDURES

3.1 HR COORD **Assemble All Forms for Completion**

1. Go to the forms cabinet and use the checklist on the door to extract all needed forms. These should include the I-9, W-4, job application, cafeteria plan, and 401(k) forms.
2. If there are few forms remaining in any category, relay this problem to the human resources secretary.

3.2 HR COORD **Review All Forms with Applicant**

1. Review all forms with the applicant. Be sure to verify applicant identification for the I-9 form.
2. Once the applicant has completed all the forms, review them again in the presence of the applicant to ensure that all fields are filled out.

3.3 HR COORD **Copy and Distribute Forms**

Copy the W-4 form and the signed pay level authorization, and send the copies to the payroll department via interoffice mail. Be sure to keep all originals.

3.4 HR COORD **File Forms**

1. Create a file folder for the new employee and store all completed forms in it.
2. File the folder in the employee record storage area. Be sure to lock the storage area when finished.

Policy/Procedure Statement	Retrieval No.:	PAY-04
Brasto Publishing	Page:	1 of 1
	Issue Date:	10/28/0X
Subject: Process Employee Pay Change	Supercedes:	N/A

1. PURPOSE AND SCOPE

This procedure helps managers to complete pay raises and perform reviews in a timely fashion.

2. RESPONSIBILITIES

HR COORD — **Human Resources Coordinator**

3. PROCEDURES

3.1 HR COORD

Notification of Anniversary

Give to managers a monthly "Notification of Anniversary" report that lists the employees who are due for annual reviews and pay increases. Anniversary dates are located in the payroll system and can be printed with the "Anniversary Report" command.

3.2 HR COORD

Personal Action Form

Give each manager a Personal Action Form for each employee to whom the manager wants to give an annual pay raise. When this is returned, set up all pay raises as of the first day of the following pay period.

3.3 HR COORD

Annual Review Form

Give each manager an Annual Review Form for each employee to whom the manager wants to give an annual performance review. When this is returned, file it in the employee's personnel folder.

Process Employee Pay Change

Policy/Procedure Statement	Retrieval No.:	PAY-05
Brasto Publishing	Page:	1 of 1
	Issue Date:	10/28/0X
	Supercedes:	N/A
Subject: Process 401(k) Add/Change		

1. PURPOSE AND SCOPE

This procedure is used by the human resources coordinator to process employee changes in their 401(k) plan investments.

2. RESPONSIBILITIES

HR COORD **Human Resources Coordinator**

3. PROCEDURES

3.1 HR COORD **Issue Change Form to Employee**

Issue either the Change of Investments, Withdrawal of Funds, or Change of Beneficiary Form to an employee requesting a change in his or her plan. For the Withdrawal of Funds and the Change of Beneficiary forms, the employee must obtain the signature of a spouse, if the person is married. In any case, explain to each employee how to fill out the forms, and have them returned when completed.

3.2 HR COORD **Notarize the Change Form**

Notarize the change form and give a copy to the employee. Put another copy in the employee's personnel file.

3.3 HR COORD **Submit Form to 401(k) Administration Company**

Fax the completed form to the 401(k) administration company for processing, and also mail the original of the form to it.

3.4 HR COORD **File Form**

Wait until the 401(k) change has been completed and notification of the change has been received. Then send a copy of the notification to the employee. Staple the original of the notification to the copy of the change form that was put in the employee's personnel folder, and return the two documents to that folder.

Process 401(k) Add/Change

Policy/Procedure Statement	Retrieval No.:	PAY-06
Brasto Publishing	Page:	1 of 1
	Issue Date:	10/28/0X
	Supercedes:	N/A
Subject: Process Cafeteria Plan Add/Change		

1. PURPOSE AND SCOPE

This procedure is used by the human resources coordinator as a guideline for changing the cafeteria plan benefits of employees.

2. RESPONSIBILITIES

HR COORD — **Human Resources Coordinator**

3. PROCEDURES

3.1 HR COORD — **Issue Change Form to Employee**

Go to the cafeteria plan forms folder in the forms storage cabinet and extract a copy of the Cafeteria Plan Change Form. Give it to the employee, along with the associated instruction sheet.

3.2 HR COORD — **Explain Changes to Employee**

Describe to the employee the impact and risk of changes to the cafeteria plan, including the benefits of putting some funds into the plan and the tax benefits of doing so, versus the risk of losing unused funds that are deposited there. Update this information as new tax rules are brought into force.

3.3 HR COORD — **Notarize Completed Form**

After the employee fills out and signs the form, notarize it and give the employee a copy.

3.4 HR COORD — **Revise Employee Deductions in Payroll System**

Alter the deduction amount in the payroll system that was authorized by the employee in the change form. Print the deduction report prior to running payroll to verify that the change was stored in the payroll database.

3.5 HR COORD — **File Change Form**

File the change form in the employee's personnel folder.

Process Cafeteria Plan Add/Change

Policy/Procedure Statement	Retrieval No.:	PAY-07
Brasto Publishing	Page:	1 of 1
	Issue Date:	10/28/0X
	Supercedes:	N/A
Subject: Process Life Insurance Add/Change		

1. PURPOSE AND SCOPE

This procedure is used by the human resources coordinator as a guideline for changing the life insurance benefits of employees.

2. RESPONSIBILITIES

HR COORD **Human Resources Coordinator**

3. PROCEDURES

3.1 HR COORD **Issue Life Insurance Form to Employee**

Go to the life insurance forms folder in the forms storage cabinet and extract a copy of the Life Insurance Change Form. Give it to the employee, along with the instruction sheet.

3.2 HR COORD **Explain Change Options to Employee**

Go over the form with the employee, noting the changes in deductions, resulting changes in life insurance coverage, and activation dates of any changes. Also describe the list of all possible beneficiaries.

3.3 HR COORD **Notarize Completed Form**

Once the employee has completed and signed the form, notarize it and give the employee a copy.

3.4 HR COORD **Forward Copy of Form to Insurance Company**

Both mail and fax a copy of the Life Insurance Change Form to the insurance company.

3.5 HR COORD **Change Deduction Amount in Payroll System**

Access the DEDUCTIONS screen in the payroll system and enter the changes to the deduction level that correspond to the life insurance amount desired by the employee. Print the deductions report to verify that the payroll system has accepted the change.

3.6 HR COORD **File Form**

File the change form in the employee's personnel folder.

3.7 HR COORD **Verify that Insurer Changed the Coverage**

When the monthly billing statement comes in from the insurance company, cross-check the reported life insurance levels on the billing and verify that the insurer has altered the employee's insurance level as requested.

Policy/Procedure Statement	Retrieval No.:	PAY-08
Brasto Publishing	Page:	1 of 1
	Issue Date:	10/28/0X
	Supercedes:	N/A
Subject: Process Medical Insurance Add/Change		

1. PURPOSE AND SCOPE

This procedure is used by the human resources coordinator as a guideline for changing the medical insurance of employees.

2. RESPONSIBILITIES

HR COORD **Human Resources Coordinator**

3. PROCEDURES

3.1 HR COORD **Issue Life Insurance Form to Employee**

Go to the medical insurance forms folder in the forms storage cabinet and extract a copy of the Medical Insurance Change Form. Give it to the employee, along with the instruction sheet.

3.2 HR COORD **Explain Possible Changes to Employee**

Go over all fields in the form that the employee can change, such as changes in the deduction level, switching doctors, switching plans, or shifting between single and family plans. Be sure to explain all changes in costs to the employee that will result from these changes. Also note the time period before any changes will go into effect.

3.3 HR COORD **Notarize Completed Form**

Once the employee completes the form, notarize it and give the employee a copy.

3.4 HR COORD **Forward a Copy to the Insurance Company**

Both fax and mail a copy of the completed form to the insurance company. If the change is on a rush basis, it may be necessary to call the insurance company to verify that the information has been received and is being processed.

3.5 HR COORD **Alter Payroll Deductions**

Access the DEDUCTIONS screen in the payroll system and enter the changes to the deduction level that correspond to the medical insurance amount desired by the employee. If the changes do not take effect for one month, then the deduction change should not be recorded until that time. Print the deductions report to verify that the payroll system has accepted the change.

3.6 HR COORD **File Form**

File the form in the employee's personnel folder.

3.7 HR COORD **Verify that Insurer Changed the Policy**

When the monthly billing statement arrives, cross-check thereported medical insurance levels on the billing and verify that the insurer has altered the employee's insurance coverage as requested. This review will only note changes to the type of coverage; the billing will not describe any changes in doctors or specific family members covered.

Process Medical Insurance Add/Change

Policy/Procedure Statement	Retrieval No.:	PAY-09
Brasto Publishing	Page:	1 of 1
	Issue Date:	10/28/0X
	Supercedes:	N/A
Subject: Process Garnishment Add/Change		

1. PURPOSE AND SCOPE

This procedure is used by the human resources coordinator to log in garnishment orders, as well as track them through to final payment.

2. RESPONSIBILITIES

HR COORD **Human Resources Coordinator**

3. PROCEDURES

3.1 HR COORD **Log in Received Garnishment Order**

1. Upon receipt of garnishment materials from the mail room, enter the name of the garnishee, the amount to be deducted, the monthly deduction frequency, the court address, and
the start and stop dates for the garnishment in the garnishment log.
2. Copy the garnishment order and send a copy to the affected employee.
3. File the original garnishment order in the garnishments file.

3.2 HR COORD **Calculate Payroll Deduction**

Recalculate the court's garnishment amount, based on the payroll frequency per month. For example, if the garnishment is for $100 per month and there are two payrolls per month, then the garnishment deduction per payroll will be $50.

3.3 HR COORD **Send Garnishment Notification to Payroll Staff**

1. Fill out the garnishment deduction form (Form #215) with the periodic deduction amounts, employee name and number, and start and stop dates.
2. Copy the form and keep one copy in the garnishments file. Forward the other copy to the payroll and accounts payable departments (so that the first department can process the deduction, and the later can process the payment to the court).

3.4 HR COORD **Track Garnishment Termination Date**

Once a month, review the garnishment log to see which garnishments can be terminated. Remind the payroll department when garnishment orders are about to be completed.

Policy/Procedure Statement	Retrieval No.:	PAY-10
Brasto Publishing	Page:	1 of 1
	Issue Date:	10/28/0X
Subject: Process Employee Termination	Supercedes:	N/A

1. PURPOSE AND SCOPE

This procedure is used by the human resources coordinator to ensure that all steps are followed, from a legal and final payment perspective, when an employee departs.

2. RESPONSIBILITIES

HR COORD **Human Resources Coordinator**

3. PROCEDURES

3.1 HR COORD

Assemble All Forms for Completion

Go to the forms cabinet and use the checklist on the door to extract all needed forms. These should include the equipment turn-in list, 401(k) rollover form, and the exit interview form.

3.2 HR COORD

Review All Forms with Employee

1. Review all fields on the forms with the employee. Make sure that he or she signs all legal documents, such as the 401(k) rollover form.
2. Ensure that the employee has reviewed the calculations for payment of remaining vacation and sick time, and agrees with the calculated payment total.

3.3 HR COORD

Copy and Distribute Forms

Copy the exit interview form and forward the copy to the departing employee's supervisor, as well as the general manager. Record the reason for departure in the department summary report.

3.4 HR COORD

File Forms

Add all completed forms to the employee's personnel folder and store this in the employee record storage area. Be sure to lock the storage area when finished.

Process Employee Termination

Policy/Procedure Statement		
Brasto Publishing	Retrieval No.:	PAY-11
	Page:	1 of 1
	Issue Date:	10/28/0X
Subject: Annual Review Notification	Supercedes:	N/A

1. PURPOSE AND SCOPE

This procedure helps the human resources coordinator to issue notices to managers listing employees who are overdue for their annual pay and performance reviews.

2. RESPONSIBILITIES

HR COORD **Human Resources Coordinator**

3. PROCEDURES

3.1 HR COORD **Extract Data from the Payroll Software**

Go to the DATA EXTRACT screen in the payroll module of the accounting software and run an extract on employee review dates for all current employees.

3.2 HR COORD **Create Report**

Access Excel and go to the payroll subdirectory. Locate the PAYSUMMARY.XLS file and open it. This lists all employees and the dates on which they had their most recent reviews and pay increases, as well as their current pay levels. Delete all employees for whom there is a review date within the past 11 months, and sort the report by department.

3.3 HR COORD **Issue Report to Managers**

Print the report for each department subcategory and issue it to the managers of each department. This will tell the managers which of their employees are due for a review in the upcoming month.

3.4 HR COORD **File Report**

File the report in the human resources storage area in the pay notification folder. It is only necessary to keep this information for one month.

Index